OBAKU ZEN

OBAKU ZEN

THE EMERGENCE OF THE THIRD SECT
OF ZEN IN TOKUGAWA JAPAN

Helen J. Baroni

University of Hawai'i Press
Honolulu

00 01 02 03 04 05   5 4 3 2 1

Library of Congress Cataloging-in-Publication Data
Baroni, Helen Josephine.
Obaku Zen : the emergence of the third sect of Zen
in Tokugawa Japan / Helen J. Baroni.
p.   cm.
Includes bibliographical references and index.
ISBN 0–8248–2195–5 (cloth : alk. paper).—
ISBN 0–8248–2243–9 (pbk. : alk. paper)
1. Ōbaku (Sect)—History.
BQ9312.B36   2000
294.3'927'0952—dc21   99–35525
                                          CIP

University of Hawai'i Press books are printed on acid-free
paper and meet the guidelines for permanence and
durability of the Council on Library Resources.

Designed by Kenneth Miyamoto
Printed by Edwards Brothers, Inc.

In memory of my father
George B. Baroni
1911–1998

Contents

Acknowledgments

Over the years I was preparing this manuscript, I received assistance and support from numerous individuals and organizations whom I wish to thank. I am grateful for all the help and guidance I received from faculty and fellow students at Columbia University, especially Philip Yampolsky, Ryuichi Abé, Paul Watt, Henry Smith, and Sarah Thal. The initial research for my dissertation was generously funded by a grant from the Japan Foundation, and the first write-up was funded by a grant from the Weatherhead Foundation. During my initial period of research in Kyoto, I received hours of assistance from members of the staff at the International Research Institute for Zen Buddhism at Hanazono University and other faculty and staff at Hanazono, including Yanagida Seizan, Urs App, Nishio Kenryū, Maeda Naomi, and Murakami Takashi. At Mampuku-ji, Otsuki Mikio, Tanaka Chisei, and other scholar-monks from the monastery library were generous in providing me access to the collection and their insights into the practice of Obaku Zen.

The second phase of the research and the preparation of the present manuscript were made possible by a research grant from the Center for Japanese Studies at the University of Hawai'i at Mānoa. I am also grateful to my colleagues and graduate assistants in the Department of Religion at the University of Hawai'i, who supported the process. In particular I must mention George Tanabe, who read and commented on an early version of the manuscript. Patricia Crosby at the University of Hawai'i Press guided me through the review process. Without her encouragement and support, this project would never have been completed.

Finally, I wish to thank my family, especially my husband, Rod Low, who support my work and make the effort worthwhile.

OBAKU ZEN

ONE

Introduction

To understand how and why Obaku took shape as an independent sect of Zen in Japan, it is not sufficient to look at it and its near relative Rinzai as they appear today. The differences between the two in the present alone will not tell the full story. Nor does it suffice simply to look back some 350 years through the lens of modern historical accounts to the founding of Obaku in Japan. As participants in the modern process of self-definition, Obaku and Rinzai have partially re-created their own histories, a process that has deeply influenced Obaku's presentation in secondary literature. In fact, if one were to rely on modern secondary accounts alone, one would see Obaku, in effect, through a series of distorting lenses. Which of Obaku's own versions should we accept: Obaku of the postwar period, which portrays itself as true Rinzai; Obaku of the war years, casting itself as a loyalist, imperially favored sect; Obaku of the Meiji period, struggling to survive and to throw off the taint of bakufu support? Or perhaps we should favor a Rinzai lens: Obaku as a catalyst for Rinzai reform; Obaku as a false form of the Dharma; Obaku as an example of Ming period Zen, tainted by the accretions of other forms of Buddhist practice and therefore rejected by Rinzai reformers in favor of a purer form.

To gain a more accurate view of Obaku as it would have appeared in the seventeenth century, we must rely on accounts contemporary with its early development. The Tokugawa sources, however, pose similar problems related to perspective. Once again one finds a series of conceptualizations of Obaku, often contradictory. Anti-Obaku sources cast images of Obaku as Other, images against which Rinzai reformers could formulate their own understanding of what Rinzai should be. In less negative portraits drawn by its early Japanese sup-

1

porters, Obaku nevertheless appears as strange, a glimpse for the Japanese of exotic China. Obaku leadership fostered the group's Chinese look, which served both to strengthen its internal cohesion as a self-defined entity and as a basis for appeal outside the group. Obaku masters sometimes capitalized on the group's exotic qualities, occasionally even an aspect of spectacle, to promote interest and support at different levels of Japanese society.

Armed with an awareness of the issues shaping modern and Tokugawa accounts, one can use them to paint a multifaceted picture of Obaku as it was viewed in the seventeenth and eighteenth centuries and as it is viewed today. Rather than attempting naively to remove the distortions of perspective to disclose an unmediated view of Obaku, this study will explore various perspectives and the purposes they serve. While some perspectives upon careful evaluation will be judged more historically accurate than others, even the most distorted rendering of Obaku can prove useful in understanding how and why various individuals and groups responded to this form of Zen as they did. For the purpose of understanding Obaku from various perspectives, the study draws primarily upon three frames of reference from the Tokugawa period: Obaku's self-understanding, Obaku within the context of Tokugawa Buddhism, and Obaku in relation to the secular authorities. In addition, attention will be given to modern perspectives as portrayed in the secondary literature.

Questions related to Obaku's establishment and growth as an independent sect of Zen fall into two categories. First, why did a group that made claims to a Rinzai lineage attain an independent institutional identity distinct from the existing Rinzai sect? Second, how did Obaku, as a new Buddhist school without any institutional base in Japan, succeed in spreading in the constrained landscape of Tokugawa Buddhism? Answering the first question requires an exploration of those teachings and practices distinctive to Obaku, not shared with Rinzai, and a close examination of relations between the nascent sect and the existing Rinzai community. In order to answer the second question, one must describe the strategies employed in spreading the new sect within the legal confines of the Tokugawa codes for Buddhist temples and clergy, the work performed by the early generations of Chinese and Japanese Obaku monks who laid the groundwork for a successful movement, and Obaku's relations with the secular authorities.

The broader significance of the development of the Obaku sect lies in its implications for our current understanding of Buddhism in the early Tokugawa period. The common view that the Buddhism of the day, especially Zen, was degenerate, ossified, and in desperate need of restoration suits well the tendency to glorify such later figures as Hakuin as early modern saviors of a troubled tradition. The rapid growth of the Obaku movement throughout its first century, as well as the initial interest that its Chinese founders inspired in the Japanese Buddhist community, however, suggests that this accepted portrait of seventeenth- and early eighteenth-century Japanese Buddhism may need to be reconsidered. The perspective of the Buddhist world provided by its newest sect indicates a vital, sometimes contentious, intellectual environment.

Obaku in Zen Scholarship

Since its earliest history, Obaku has been portrayed in a number of ways in the early primary sources as well as in the modern secondary literature, with each portrayal being dependent upon the perspective of the viewer. There are two basic axes along which I see these positions arrayed: insider/outside to the Zen Buddhist tradition, and pro-/anti-Obaku. By insider, I mean individuals who have some level of commitment to Zen Buddhism and whose commitment informs, either explicitly or implicitly, their writing in reference to Obaku. Through their scholarship, insiders actively participate in the religious debate about the nature of Zen. I refer to any scholarship that takes an insider perspective as sectarian, whether the writer is Rinzai, Obaku, or Sōtō in orientation. Outsiders, whatever their personal commitments, avoid participation in the more obvious religious debates. They are, at least in their approach, nonsectarian in orientation. As for the pro- and anti-Obaku axis, the full range can be seen among both insiders and outsiders, although insiders are typically more obvious in their sentiments.

Neither the sectarian nor the nonsectarian approaches as they have been applied to Obaku thus far have provided an adequate explanation for Obaku Zen's entrenchment and growth in Japan. While their conclusions all have some basis in historical fact, their answers remain too limited, and often too biased, to describe the complex process by which the Obaku line took hold in Japan and became an independent sect of Zen. What is needed is a balanced portrait of Obaku, one that explains the qualities that set it apart from its larger relative, Rinzai, and tries to clarify its position in the world of Tokugawa Buddhism and the larger social and cultural framework of the Tokugawa period.

Toward this end, I not only focus my work on the primary and secondary sources produced within the Obaku sect but make use of sources external, and sometimes hostile, to the sect, as a means to balance the portrait. Not only do such anti-Obaku texts as Mujaku Dōchū's Ōbaku geki (An outside account of Obaku) and the anonymous Zenrin shūhei shū (A compilation of evil habit of the Zen School) provide alternative and decidedly less saintly views of Obaku masters, they also provide a wealth of information about the Rinzai response to Obaku at the time of its establishment. Although scholars have made reference to and perhaps quoted these materials, none have analyzed them in order to gain an understanding of the response of the Japanaese Zen community toward Obaku.

In attempting to draw a balanced portrait of Obaku, I shall draw upon concepts and themes developed in the study of new religious movements (NRMs) in the contemporary West. There are compelling similarities between the sort of questions I wish to answer about Obaku and the questions raised in studies of NRMs: how NRMs recruit and retain members; how they establish a financial basis; how their beliefs and practices compare with those of established groups; how they fare with the secular authorities; how they move themselves from the tenuous status of new movement into accepted traditions within a given culture. Some aspects of the theoretical discussion within the field of NRMs center on the relationship between religious movements and issues of modernity and contemporary social problems. Nevertheless, the general approach to new movements and their relations with existing religious traditions provides an alternative perspective from which to view Obaku, one that has certain advantages. The basic strength of this perspective is that it can accommodate both the newness and the foreignness of Obaku in early Tokugawa Japan as well as its familiarity as a form of Zen.

When scholars present a history of Japanese Zen or describe its beliefs and practices, they generally focus their attention on the two larger schools, namely Rinzai and Sōtō. There has been almost no mention of Obaku in the scholarly literature of the West, even in the less limited range of Japanese literature. Nor has Obaku inspired much interest beyond the reaches of its own sectarian historians. It is often completely ignored in the large, general surveys of Japanese Buddhism and is frequently excluded even from texts dedicated specifically to Zen in Japan.[1] Some reasons for this exclusion have little to do with

Obaku per se but reflect biases implicit in the literature. Scholars have shown a marked preference for exploring earlier periods of Zen development in Japan or for the work of a few later reformers, especially Hakuin. The operative assumption underlying these preferences seems to be that, during these times, Zen was purer in form and more vibrant in its practice, and therefore more worthy of study. In this regard, Obaku simply falls outside the purview of those periods deemed important or instructive for understanding Zen in Japan.

Until very recently, scholarly material addressing Obaku's teachings and its emergence as an independent sect of Zen in Japan was predominantly sectarian in nature. Rinzai scholars have generally dismissed Obaku as an aberrant or even heretical form of Rinzai practice, the study of which adds nothing significant to an understanding of Rinzai teaching or history. Rinzai scholars have employed a short and simple explanation, a *teisetsu*, to set Obaku in its proper place vis-à-vis Rinzai, and few scholars seek to broaden the scope beyond this circumscribed description. In its most simplistic form, the accepted explanation for Obaku's emergence as an independent sect of Zen is based on its identification as a form of "Nembutsu Zen," sometimes alternatively referred to as Ming-style Zen.

The term "Nembutsu Zen" may be applied to any style of Zen practice that seeks to incorporate Pure Land practices and beliefs, especially the practice of the *nembutsu*, chanting the name of Amida Buddha. The term, however, is not value-neutral. It is almost invariably used as a derogatory label designed to place rival groups or styles of practice outside the pale of legitimate or orthodox Zen Buddhism. Obaku Zen did include Pure Land elements in both its monastic and lay practice, as was the norm in Ming China, and this is generally presented as the basic cause for the schism between the Obaku and Rinzai sects. By referring to Obaku as Ming-style Zen, scholars replace the more overtly offensive terminology of Nembutsu Zen with a euphemism. Despite the more polite tone, the language may nevertheless prove to be equally dismissive. Implicit in references to Ming-style Zen may be the critical assumption that the Zen practiced during the Ming period represents a corruption and deterioration of the "purer" Sung style preserved by Japanese Rinzai Zen.[2] Despite its dubious status as a "true" form of Zen, Rinzai scholars sometimes acknowledge that Obaku served as a catalyst to revitalize the Japanese Zen community of early Tokugawa Japan, which all seem to agree was in dire need of reform.[3]

From the early pioneers of this century, such as Washio Junkei, through contemporary writers like Hayashi Bunshō and Nakao Fumio, scholars sympathetic to Obaku typically retain a defensive tone in their works, responding to explicit and implicit criticism from the dominant Rinzai community.[4] Obaku continues to defend itself against "slanderous accusations" that it believes have been directed against it since the early years of the founder's work in Japan. They are eager to present Obaku in ways that reject such stereotypes as "Nembutsu Zen"; they strive to project on the sect's history and doctrine a positive interpretation. What form exactly each positive interpretation takes is, of course, shaped according to the concerns of the individual scholar and his times.[5] Even when Obaku scholars are not obviously on the defensive, they generally tend to accentuate positive qualities in their early leaders and to gloss over or completely omit any negative qualities or actions. This may be seen as a natural tendency in any religious group's presentation of its own sacred history, especially one that perceives of itself as misunderstood.

In the recent past, scholars have attempted to describe the development of Obaku from perspectives that are less apologetic and nonsectarian.[6] In seeking a less value-laden, more detached point of view, however, they have tended to reformat the argument, turning their attention away from the religious issues dividing Obaku from Rinzai, and recasting the schism in terms of social and political pressures. Some maintain that the separation of Rinzai lineages into distinct sects resulted from cultural exclusivism: the Japanese rejected the foreignness (Chinese-ness) of Obaku while at the same time the Chinese masters were haughty toward their Japanese hosts.[7] Others stress competition within the Buddhist world for the limited resources available at the time; in this case, Obaku is seen as a drain on the material and human resources of Rinzai, which led to infighting and ultimately irreconcilable differences.[8] While appreciating the effort to avoid sectarian biases, I shall argue that no picture of Obaku within the context of Japanese Buddhism would be complete without directly addressing the religious issues that contributed to its emergence as an independent sect.

The Emergence of Obaku as an Independent Sect

In seeking a new approach that carries the project beyond the limitations inherent in earlier works, it is useful to consider Carl Bielefeldt's reflections on Zen scholarship in his study of Dōgen, *Dōgen's Manu-*

als of Zen Meditation. Although Bielefeldt was investigating the Sōtō school during a different period in the history of Chinese and Japanese Zen, he also addressed issues that led to intrasectarian disputes. In discussing the scholarly interpretations of Zen debates on meditation, for example, Bielefeldt observes:

> Where traditional treatments preserved the model of the *shōbō genzō* by explaining the discontinuities of Ch'an and Zen history apparent in its various factional disputes as the ongoing struggle between the true *dharma* and its heretical interpreters, some modern treatments have tended in effect to explain away these disputes as mere theological decoration on what was "really" political and social competition. My own approach here tries to avoid both these forms of reductionism and seeks rather to view the discontinuities in terms of the recapitulations, under various historical circumstances, of certain continuing tensions inherent in the Ch'an teachings themselves—tensions, for example, between exclusive and inclusive visions of the school's religious mission, between esoteric and exoteric styles of discourse, and especially between theoretical and practical approaches to its meditation instruction.[9]

Bielefeldt's observation that the traditional (sectarian) and the more strictly academic modern approaches are both forms of reductionism can be applied equally to the existing treatments of Obaku. Sectarian presentations of Obaku often seem to depict an underlying struggle between the true Dharma and heretical practice, however that may be understood by the particular author. This is especially clear in the work of the twentieth-century Obaku scholar Akamatsu Shinmyō, who defended the sect's teachings as a true form of Zen.[10] Scholars seeking a more neutral position are preoccupied with other, less religious factors that lead to the schism.[11] Bielefeldt's proposal that the tensions within Zen teaching itself could contribute to internal disputes suggests another direction for rethinking Obaku's history that might prove fruitful.

First, combining the valid aspects of the sectarian and the nonsectarian approaches, that is, recognizing that significant philosophical differences as well as political and social competition contributed to the emergence of Obaku as an independent sect, produces a much more nuanced portrait than limiting the focus to one side or the other. It takes into account the nature of living religions, which are not only concerned with preserving and transmitting beliefs and practices but must also function within the sociopolitical realities of a particular historical context. Suggesting that either philosophical dissention or sociopolitical competition exhausts the field of contributing factors to the exclusion of the other is to oversimplify the picture. Next, the realization that disputes may arise within Zen schools from tensions inherent in the teachings themselves, not only from corruption or heretical interpretations of the teachings, may provide an alternative basis for evaluating the reasons Obaku split from Rinzai, one that allows for a discussion of philosophical differences without the assumption that one or the other sect has a superior claim to the true Dharma.

For purposes of analysis, the reasons for Obaku's schism from Japanese Rinzai, its emergence as a third sect of Zen, and its success in taking root and spreading throughout the country can be classified into four basic spheres: (1) the internal matters of belief and practice; (2) the political and social factors of the period; (3) the cultural tensions between the Chinese and Japanese principals; and (4) the successful strategies employed by the Chinese founders and their first generation of Japanese disciples. The issues involved in each of these areas are tightly interrelated, but for the present it is useful to set them out separately in broader strokes.

1. The internal matters of belief and practice at issue between Obaku and Rinzai were of such basic importance for Zen practice that it would be a mistake to dismiss the disputes as mere camouflage for political and social competition. As Bielefeldt has noted, when arguments over doctrine have occurred within the Zen school, the issue has almost always revolved around a matter of practice, usually meditation.[12] Most of the internal tension between Obaku and Japanese Rinzai arose in relation to their divergent understanding of Zen practice in the broad sense rather than the practice of meditation per se. The differences go far beyond the most obvious distinction: that Obaku incorporated certain Pure Land practices while Rinzai did not. The conflicts that arose between Obaku and Rinzai in the seventeenth and eighteenth centuries encompass such major issues as the proper interpretation of the monastic precepts and discipline, the role of study and interpretation of the Buddhist scriptures and the Zen corpus, and the role and usage of kōan, as well as a host of minor concerns.

Scholars have often maintained that the root of these problems is to be found in the differences between the Sung style of Zen from which Japanese Zen developed and the later, Ming-style that Obaku represents. Nonetheless, this recognition often assumes that Ming Zen was corrupted by influences from other Buddhist schools and became an impure form. On the other hand, it is possible to see the Obaku or Ming style of practice as a different but still valid configuration of Zen practice. In the mid-seventeenth century, Ming masters and their Japanese Rinzai counterparts found themselves on opposing sides of the spectrum on a number of issues arising from tensions inherent in the Zen teachings. In this sense, tension between Obaku and Japanese Rinzai can be seen as internal competition within the Rinzai school between factions proposing alternative ways of understanding Zen practice and the best methods for revitalizing the school.

2. When one considers the political and social realities that prevailed in Tokugawa Japan during the first decades of the seventeenth century, however, it becomes immediately apparent that external forces contributed to the shaping of Obaku history. The first and most obvious obstacle Obaku had to surmount was the newly completed government policy that legally forbade Chinese nationals, including Buddhist masters, from emigrating to Japan outside the confines of the port city of Nagasaki.[13] Some level of government cooperation was therefore necessary for Obaku masters to settle permanently in Japan. Once this initial hurdle was surmounted, Obaku monks and temples faced the same array of political strictures the government had placed on all Buddhist sects, but without the advantages of an established network of temples and an extensive system of elite patronage or popular support.

During the first half of the seventeenth century, Japanese Buddhism fell under increasing government control as the Tokugawa bakufu consolidated its power over all segments of society. For example, the government set strict limits on the freedom to construct new temples and compelled all existing temples to be incorporated into a fixed hierarchy. While many established Buddhist sects enjoyed a comfortable level of economic security as a result of other bakufu policies, notably the mandatory family registration at local temples, a new group such as Obaku would have found little opportunity to build a financial base or to increase its number of temples without encroaching on the resources of existing groups. Moreover, the intense personal interest generated by Obaku in large numbers of Japanese monks threatened other groups with potential losses of human talent. Obaku, therefore, did compete on several levels with other Buddhist groups during its first formative decades in Japan. Undeniably, the sect most affected by this competition was Japanese Rinzai, from the ranks of which Obaku drew the highest percentage of converts. Modern scholars have rightly interpreted Rinzai's negative reaction to Obaku as, in part, a defensive response to the drain on their human and financial resources.

3. Cultural differences further widened the sharp divisions between Obaku and Japanese Rinzai. Judging from the descriptions of early encounters, both the Chinese and the Japanese felt a certain superiority over one another. Once they had seen and evaluated the state of Ming Zen as exemplified by the Obaku monks, many Japanese Rinzai monks came to believe that the Japanese had actually surpassed their former masters, the Chinese. They felt that their own lineages had managed far better to preserve the original style of Zen that had been transmitted from China centuries earlier. In some cases, they found the Chinese practices and styles abhorrent, apparently for their very foreignness.

For their part, the Chinese masters maintained aspects of life known to them in China that an outside observer might tend to classify as culturally rather than religiously significant, including the language used in ritual, the design of monastic robes and shoes, clerical hairstyles, and the like. Obaku monks seemed committed to preserving their cultural identity as Chinese in the face of the dominant Japanese culture surrounding them. As native speakers of Chinese, they also expressed some skepticism about the ability of the Japanese to fully understand and utilize the large corpus of Zen literature written in Chinese.

4. Naturally, both the Chinese and the Japanese benefited from the cultural exchanges in some respects. Many individual Japanese were initially drawn to Obaku because they found its Chinese quality to be both exotic and appealing. Some Japanese monks viewed interaction with Chinese masters on Japanese soil as an acceptable substitute for study in China, an option that was not, in any case, available to them. In addition, many Japanese artists and classical scholars considered the Chinese masters invaluable resources of Chinese culture and language. For this reason, many of them actively sought out contact with Chinese monks and fostered relationships that would provide them a direct link to the more secular aspects of Chinese culture. From the Obaku perspective, the Chinese masters could only succeed in spreading their Zen style to a wider Japanese audience through the successful translation of their words, ideas, and symbols into meaningful Japanese formulations by their Japanese disciples. The early years of growth represent the effective collaboration of Chinese and Japanese masters.

The founding generation of Chinese masters, especially Yin-yüan and his Dharma heirs Mu-an Hsing-t'ao (1611–1684; J. Mokuan Shōtō) and Chi-fei Ju-i (1616–1671; J. Sokuhi Nyoitsu), attracted a remarkable group of Japanese converts whom I refer to as the first generation of Japanese disciples. Ryōkei Shōsen (1602–1670), Tetsugen Dōkō (1630–1682), Tetsugyū Dōki (1628–1700), and Chōon Dōkai (1628–1695) are among the best known of this group of highly gifted and motivated individuals who worked to spread Obaku throughout Japan. It was these Japanese converts who facilitated early relations with the Tokugawa bakufu, laid the groundwork for imperial support, and then worked within the Buddhist monastic community and among the common people to establish Obaku's teachings on the popular level. While the Chinese masters were largely responsible for determining the character and monastic style of the main temple, Mampuku-ji, where future generations of monks were trained, the first generation of Japanese disciples founded a large percentage of the Obaku branch temples that constituted the broader framework of the sect.

Previous studies of Obaku have tended to favor either the first or the second category of issues, those related to teachings and to sociopolitical conditions, as the crucial determining factors. This study argues first that any adequate explanation for Obaku's emergence as an independent sect of Japanese Zen must address all of the four areas of concern. No single set of factors alone can suffice to explain the complex process of formation and development of a religious movement. Moreover, it will argue that the third and fourth categories, those related to cultural differences and the early leadership, which have thus far been largely overlooked in studies of Obaku, may have been the dominant factors operative during the early stages of Obaku's history in Japan. In particular, Japanese responses to the cultural distinctiveness of Obaku monasteries and practices, whether positive or negative, tipped the scale in Obaku emerging as an independent institution and shaped its overall success and failure at surviving in and influencing the world of Japanese Buddhism.

The chapters that follow will elaborate on the themes briefly raised here. Chapter 2 will explore some definitional issues: first, the ambiguities and problems inherent in the traditional language used to identify Obaku and other religious groups in Japan; and, second, new perspectives suggested by applying typologies from the study of NRMs. Chapters 3 and 4 provide a historical sketch of the early history of the Obaku movement, from its roots in Ming China to the foundation of the main monastery in Japan. Chapter 5 provides a portrait of the Chinese founders who brought Obaku from China; and Chapter 6 continues the discussion of Obaku leadership with a discussion of the first generation of Japanese converts who made Obaku a viable tradition in Japan. Chapters 7 and 8 examine the characteristic beliefs and practices that set Obaku apart from Japanese Rinzai; Chapter 7 focuses on material related to the Obaku monastic code; and Chapter 8 explores influences from Pure Land Buddhism and other religious systems. Chapter 9 describes relations between Obaku and other schools of Buddhism in Japan, particularly the Rinzai school. Chapter 10 explores Obaku's place within the political and social arena of Tokugawa Japan, concentrating on its relationships with the two secular powers, the Tokugawa bakufu and the imperial family.

A note about the transliteration, I decided to dispense with the macron over the "O" in Obaku in an effort to make this lesser-known third sect of Zen more accessible to broad audience.

TWO

School, Sect, or Lineage?

Understanding Obaku's place in the world of Japanese Buddhism is complicated by ambiguities in the terminology and concepts related to sectarian divisions within it. In passages related to Obaku and in discussions with contemporary Zen scholars, for example, Obaku may be identified variously as an independent denomination, school, or sect (Obaku-shū) of Japanese Zen Buddhism; as one sectarian branch (Obaku-ha) within the Rinzai school; or as a valid Rinzai lineage (Rinzai-shōshū). In any given text, more than one of these understandings may be operative simultaneously, so that an author may appear to be making contradictory claims to the effect that Obaku both is and is not Rinzai. Some of the confusion regarding Obaku's identity arises from factors unique to its history, and some from factors that apply more universally to Zen and East Asian Buddhism. The ambiguities can be divided into three basic configurations: (1) the application of Western religious categories such as school, denomination, sect, and cult to the Japanese context; (2) multivalent understandings of the term *shū* as a religious and historical concept, often conflated in any given context; and (3) changes in governmental systems that control and officially define Buddhist groups in Japan.

The Application of Western Categories

Applying English terminology related to religious institutions to Asian traditions obviously involves a generalization of concepts that were originally formulated with Western, predominantly Christian, models in mind. Even in a strictly Western context, scholars have not agreed universally on a single standard for the usage of terms such as school, sect, cult, new religious movement, and denomination. It is perhaps best, therefore, to set out explicitly how the terms will be used in this book. I understand the term "school" to apply to a religious group that shares a common teaching and practice but does not necessarily have a distinct institutional structure. In contrast, "sect" refers to a religious group that has established an independent institutional structure and has typically developed with some element of dissent or mutual rejection from other related religious groups. One may speak, for example, of a school of Pure Land Buddhism developing in Heian period Japan generations before distinctive sectarian institutions emerged during the Kamakura period.

I commonly use the term "sect" to describe Buddhist groups in Japan, where distinct institutional divisions have characterized the Buddhist world from an early period. The term "sect" then functions in this context in much the same manner as the term "denomination," which is employed in Western contexts to distinguish the various independent divisions falling under the general appellation of Christian. For the Chinese context, where institutional structures were less discrete, I generally use the term "school." It is also possible, however, to refer to the Zen school in Japan when speaking about all groups that share the teachings and practice of Zen despite their institutional division into distinct sects. At the present time, using these definitions, Obaku may be regarded as a Zen sect with its own institutional structure, distinctive beliefs, and so on, which, along with the Rinzai and Sōtō sects, comprises the broader notion of the Zen school in Japan.

Shū: School, Sect, and Lineage

In recent years, Buddhist scholars have become sensitive to historical changes and developments in the classical Chinese understanding of the term *tsung* and have sought ways to avoid inaccurate and anachronistic renderings of the notion. A debate has developed concerning the various usages of the term in classical Chinese Buddhist texts, centering around the issue of where it can rightly be understood to connote a religious school of thought or institution rather than a doctrine or the underlying theme of a given text.[1] A correlative discussion focuses on how best to render the former concept of *tsung* as religious institution into English.[2] Understanding the use of the correlate Japanese term *shū*, especially in texts composed in the early modern and modern periods, would seem to be far simpler. One may assume, after all, that it refers to a religious school or sect rather than to any other classical Chinese referent. Nevertheless, even in modern Japanese usage ambiguity remains.

The most common English translations for the Japanese term *shū* as it appears in early modern and modern Japanese Buddhist contexts are "school," "sect," or "lineage." Each of these English options conveys slightly different nuances of meaning for a Western audience while still remaining true to possibilities inherent in the original Japanese concept. The Japanese term "Obaku-shū" may then be accurately rendered as Obaku school, Obaku sect, or Obaku lineage, and in some cases a Japanese text may imply all three possibilities at once. Depending on the context, however, the process of translation into English, which necessarily requires a single choice, may serve to obscure multivalent meanings operative in the original word *shū*.

In a discussion about the contemporary Japanese understanding of the broader concept of *zenshū*, Foulk points out some of the lingering ambiguities.

> In Japan today the term *zenshū* refers, in the first place, to a school of Buddhism (comprising three main denominations: the Sōtō, Rinzai, and Obaku) that has an independent institutional structure, as well as a distinctive set of beliefs, sacred texts, and religious practices. Within the contemporary Zen school, the religious belief in a lineage of Dharma transmission stemming from the first patriarch Bodhidharma is still very much alive, and this too is called *zenshū*.[3]

Foulk distinguishes here two divergent modern referents of the term *zenshū*, the former being a historical entity that falls within the grasp of historical enquiry and the latter being a religious concept, better suited as a subject for theological rather than historical discussion. Foulk argues that scholars need to draw this distinction explicitly in order to avoid imposing anachronistic assumptions about the existence of an independent Zen school onto classical texts derived from early periods of Chinese Buddhist history. While anachronistic assumptions of the sort that concern Foulk do not arise in discussions of Obaku Zen, an analogous conflation of the modern referents of *zenshū* does complicate scholarly determinations of Obaku's relationship with Rinzai Zen.

Foulk's basic distinction between *shū* understood as a religious institution[4] and *shū* understood as an authentic Dharma lineage may help to clarify some of the problems inherent in discussions concerning Obaku's identity vis-à-vis Rinzai. Regardless of whether the term *shū* is translated as school, sect, or lineage, references to Obaku as (a part of) Rinzai-shū may relate either to the historical development of religious institutions or, alternatively, to religious claims of valid Dharma transmission. As shall be discussed below, in certain stages of Obaku history, it is technically accurate to describe Obaku as a part of the larger Rinzai institution. Despite the fact that Obaku has not enjoyed the same level of officially or legally defined institutional independence throughout its history, I would argue that one can nevertheless speak meaningfully of an Obaku sect, distinct from Rinzai, since the founding of its main monastery, Mampuku-ji. On the other hand, like the Rinzai sect, Obaku traces its Dharma lineage back to Lin-chi, laying claim to an identity as a valid Rinzai lineage understood in the theological sense. For this reason, Obaku's official institutional independence is not the only significant factor in assessing its relationship to the Rinzai sect. In some contexts, discussions of Obaku as a part of the Rinzai-shū have more to do with the religious claims of authentic Dharma transmission than with historical issues of institutional independence.

Both Obaku and Rinzai have a historical relationship with that segment of the Ch'an school which claimed to preserve the teaching style of the T'ang dynasty patriarch Lin-chi. If one traces the lines of inheritance back through generations of masters and disciples in much the same way that one might construct a family tree, both the Obaku sect and the Rinzai sect may be seen as two distinct branches emerging from a common trunk originating with Lin-chi and his immediate disciples. It bears repeating, however, that within the Zen school the concept of *zenshū* as lineage does not merely serve as a neutral means for tracing the historical roots of individual Zen masters or entire branches in an all-inclusive Zen school. Since lineage may explicitly or implicitly refer to religious claims that the Dharma is authentically preserved and transmitted within the ranks of the Zen school, lineage is often proffered as a polemical device to promote one's own group while undercutting and excluding the religious claims of other groups. In other words, to identify Obaku definitively as a Rinzai lineage or not, to say that it is or is not Rinzai-shū, may in some cases be tantamount to staking a religious claim rather than observing a historical fact.

At times, modern scholars interweave issues of Obaku's institutional history with implicit arguments about its validity as an authentic Rinzai Dharma lineage in discussions of Obaku's history and relationship to the Rinzai sect. A writer sympathetic to Obaku may argue that, despite its institutional independence from the historical Rinzai sect in Japan, Obaku is indeed a part of the Rinzai lineage. In many cases, the religious claim or belief that the Obaku institution has successfully preserved and transmitted the Dharma operates as an implicit assumption in this use of lineage terminology. Scholars unsympathetic to Obaku teachings may explicitly reject Obaku as an inauthentic lineage; that is, they may deny that Obaku faithfully transmits the Dharma, because of differences in its belief and practice. Others may imply their rejection by simply excluding Obaku from discussions of Japanese Zen.

Since I do not regard determining the authenticity of Dharma transmission part of my role as a historian, evaluating the validity of Obaku's claim will not be a topic for discussion in these chapters. Scholars writing from a position within the normative tradition, however, sometimes do make such determinations, and this may inform their understanding of Obaku's relationship to Rinzai. I have nevertheless adopted the terminology of lineage in discussions of Obaku as it relates to other parts of the Zen school and for its internal development. Without positing a simple correspondence between the religious concept of the Rinzai lineage and the historical Rinzai and Obaku institutions, I employ the term "lineage" to recognize the common historical connections claimed by both of these sects. In addition, it should be noted that issues of lineage are so intrinsic to any Zen self-definition that it would be misleading to expunge the language from the present discussion.

Legal Conceptualizations of Shū

As alluded to earlier, Obaku's identity as an officially recognized sect under the Japanese government's religious policies has undergone change over its history. In some cases, government definitions blur the distinctions between Obaku and Rinzai, compounding confusion over how to understand their relationship. The Tokugawa government required all Buddhist temples to be incorporated into clearly delineated hierarchical structures under main monasteries. While the main purpose of this policy was to facilitate governmental control over Buddhist groups, it also served to codify sectarian divisions. When the government recognized Mampuku-ji as the main monastery for Obaku temples, it implicitly granted the sect the same level of institutional independence as other Buddhist sects. The Meiji government carried the process of solidifying sectarian divisions a step further by defining them into law.

After the Meiji Restoration, the new government took a direct role in reconfiguring the Buddhist world, officially defining and delimiting the number and makeup of the various sects. In its early policy decisions, the Meiji government sought to rationalize and centralize control of Buddhist organizations by recognizing only seven sects (shū) of Buddhism: Tendai, Shingon, Jōdo, Zen, Shin, Nichiren, and Ji. Subdivisions within these sects, the number of which was likewise subject to governmental control, were to be known as branches, *ha*. The government thus established modern legal definitions of these terms, effectively ending the vagaries of earlier usage. In a decree from June 1872, the government determined that each of the seven sects would have only one administrative head (kanchō), who would answer to the government for the whole.[5] Under the initial policy, Rinzai, Sōtō, and Obaku were treated as a unified Zen sect and thus forced to select a single administrative head. Theoretically, the position as head of the unified Zen sect was to rotate on a yearly basis to candidates selected from the Gozan temples, Eihei-ji, Daitoku-ji, Myōshin-ji, Sōji-ji, Tenryū-ji, and Mampuku-ji. The first individual to hold the position was Yuri Tekisui from Tenryū-ji, who served one year.[6]

The government gradually relaxed its policy, later allowing the three Zen sects that it had artificially combined to emerge as independent entities. First, in February 1874, a government decree formally recognized Rinzai and Sōtō as independent sects but explicitly defined Obaku as a *ha* within the Rinzai sect. Neither Rinzai nor Obaku officials found this arrangement acceptable, and they continued to petition the government to rectify the situation. Finally, in February 1876, the government reversed its previous decision, legally defining Obaku as an independent sect in its own right. From that time on, there were three legally recognized sects of Zen, Sōtō-shū, Rinzai-shū, and Obaku-shū.

In the postwar period, the Japanese government no longer asserts its control over Buddhist groups, since the constitution guarantees separation of religion and the state. It has established laws enabling religious groups, including the various Buddhist denominations, to incorporate as religious juridical persons (shūkyōhōjin) if they so choose,[7] but these groups are otherwise self-defined. Today, Obaku-shū is one among twenty-three registered Zen organizations, including fifteen separate Rinzai-shū branches *(ha)* and Sōtō-shū.[8]

Obaku: A New Religious Movement

I would like to introduce one final set of considerations for under-standing Obaku's relationship with Rinzai and Japanese Buddhism, considerations which draw upon concepts developed for the study of new religious movements (hereafter NRM). The term "new religious movement" was coined in an attempt to avoid the negative connota-tions popularly associated with the terms "sect" and "cult." Some scholars continue to use sect and cult as technical terms to distinguish types of NRMs. Stark and Bainbridge, for example, proposed a defini-tional distinction between church, sect, and cult based upon two vari-ables: degree of tension and ties to the religious traditions of the host society. According to this typology, sects and cults can be distin-guished from churches as religious groups that exist in a relatively high state of tension with their surrounding sociocultural environ-ment. Whereas sects represent schismatic movements that have sepa-rated themselves from another religious organization within the soci-ety, cults represent something new, whether a foreign import or a domestic innovation.[9]

In this context, I have chosen to adopt the less specific term NRM for a number of reasons. It avoids any confusion with the more gen-eral usage of sect utilized throughout the remainder of the text. More-over, the church/sect/cult typology poses some problems in terms of classification, when applied to a specific, empirical case such as Obaku. Depending on whether one focuses on historical links be-tween religious groups or perceived newness, Obaku may be classified as either a sect or a cult in the context of seventeenth-century Japan.

Scholars most commonly apply the term NRM to groups that emerged in the West since the Second World War, although the phe-nomenon of new religious groups is by no means confined to the West-ern world or to this century. Indeed, the landscape of Japanese religion in the nineteenth and twentieth centuries has been significantly altered by the emergence of wave upon wave of so-called new religions. Schol-ars generally regard these new movements as "religious responses to the crises of modernity."[10] Obaku bears little resemblance to these movements, developing according to a different religious and social dynamic and responding to distinctly different social circumstances. As a NRM, Obaku appears more in the form of a revival movement within the Lin-chi/Rinzai tradition, with elements regarded as new or innovative in the Japanese Zen context.

In readings on NRMs for an unrelated project, I have often seen

parallels between Obaku in early Tokugawa Japan and certain NRMs
in nineteenth- and twentieth-century America. In its manner of introduction and spread, its relations with established religious groups,
and its pattern of growth into a recognized religious tradition in its
own right, Obaku shares much in common with NRMs in other times
and places. Even the rhetoric employed by the modern anti-cult movement shares many common themes with early anti-Obaku tracts. I believe that looking at Obaku as a NRM will be more enlightening for
the study of its development in Japan than more standard approaches
to it as an established tradition transplanted from its native China.

In suggesting that Obaku be regarded as a NRM in seventeenth-
century Japan, I would like to highlight three issues regarding its development in the early stages. First, Obaku represented an innovation
within the world of Japanese Buddhism, especially within the Zen
community. Obaku masters introduced new forms of ritual and promoted a style of Zen practice distinct from the familiar norms of Rinzai and Sōtō. Even aspects of Obaku practice that were not innovative
in any deep sense appeared to be new, given Obaku's preference for
maintaining Chinese language and dress. It should be noted that references to newness or innovation in regards to any NRM are relative
within the context of time and space. Obaku styles of practice were
not new in any absolute sense; in China, the same practices would
have appeared commonplace, perhaps even normative.

Second, as is the case with most NRMs, Obaku experienced varying degrees of tension in its relations with the broader society and
other religious groups. Tensions between Obaku and the Japanese
government, which caused numerous early difficulties, eased rather
quickly. Having once overcome the bakufu's initial suspicions, Obaku
monks gained significant levels of support from government officials.
Tensions between Obaku and other Buddhist sects took an opposite
course, increasing over time as the Obaku lineage became more firmly
established and began to flourish. As is often the case with NRMs,
Obaku's fiercest detractors came from within its nearest relative,
Rinzai.

Finally, in the early decades of its development, Obaku lacked a
stable institutional base in Japan. As a new movement trying to establish itself, it needed to attract monastic disciples, to build up membership and support among lay followers, to acquire or build temples,
and to secure its financial standing. The chapters that follow will chart
the progress Obaku made in accomplishing these aims. Its success was
such that the very notion of looking at Obaku as a NRM may strike

some readers as strange. Obaku is an example of a "successful NRM," in the sense that it survived, grew to a size rivaling other Rinzai groups, and eventually became an accepted sect of Japanese Buddhism. Nevertheless, even in the modern period, remnants of its struggles to become an acceptable form of Zen Buddhism remain.

Current literature on the relative success or failure of NRMs suggests that, in order to be successful, a movement must maintain a balance between continuity with the host culture and moderate levels of tension with the same.[11] Without sufficient continuity, a NRM would be asking potential converts to reject their culture and religious heritage wholesale. This, in turn, would marginalize members and the group as overly deviant, thus raising the cost of membership beyond acceptable limits. As a form of Zen Buddhism, Obaku enjoyed a relatively high level of continuity with Japanese religion. It would have appeared sufficiently familiar to most Japanese to avoid the suggestion of deviance. Within the world of Japanese Buddhism, it was able to tap into an existing mood favoring restoration and to establish connections with leading proponents of the Rinzai revitalization movement, thus gaining its initial monastic foothold in Japan. In addition, Obaku's cachet as the most recent Chinese import in a long history of borrowing from Chinese Buddhism, allowed the sect simultaneously to capitalize on qualities of familiarity and freshness. That is, while having the advantage of being comfortably familiar, it could still market itself as new.

Moderate levels of tension with the outside culture and/or external religious groups help NRMs to create clear boundaries that define their movement over against existing religious institutions. Studies of recent NRMs show that external opposition, so long as it is not overwhelming, actually strengthens commitment rather than weakening it.[12] Obaku's retention of Chinese styles of dress, liturgical language, and custom would have promoted a strong sense of community and self-identification among the early generations of Japanese monks by clearly demarking the group as distinct from other Zen communities. The high levels of excitement in the early generations, witnessed by effective recruiting and fund-raising efforts, would have been enhanced rather than diminished by the opposition and criticism the unique Obaku practices provoked. It may be noted that successive generations of Obaku monks adopted more obviously Japanese styles of dress and custom in the period after Obaku's most significant growth, at a time when the group was already firmly established.

After the easing of tensions with the government that allowed

Obaku to begin the process of establishing itself in Japan, tension with the Buddhist community rose sharply. As is often the case with NRMs, apparent success precipitates a backlash against the group from the established religious community. In Obaku's case, much of the tension took the form of boundary disputes with Rinzai, which in fact served to strengthen both religious communities. On the one hand, external rejection by elements within the Rinzai monasteries tended to strengthen loyalties to the new sect. In turn, Obaku provided Rinzai leaders a foil against which to define a developing sense of orthodoxy and a means for rallying its own loyalties.

Much like modern anti-cult literature written from within the normative Christian community in the West, anti-Obaku materials stressed certain familiar themes: the motivations of its leaders, the propriety of its beliefs and practices, and the mental state of its converts. Yin-yüan and other early Obaku leaders came under special scrutiny and were often criticized. In particular, anti-Obaku texts call into question the sincerity of the leadership's religious purposes, suggesting that other motivations, such as personal safety, fame, and fortune, lay at the root of their activities in Japan. The teaching and ritual practices of the Obaku community were evaluated and rejected as departures from Rinzai orthodoxy as defined by the existing Rinzai community in Japan. Japanese converts were sometimes portrayed as fools who had been duped by the new movement. Details of the anti-Obaku Buddhist response will be addressed in Chapter 7.

Obaku's Self-Understanding

Based on internal sectarian terminology, it would appear that Obaku today posits for itself a kind of dual identity as both Rinzai-shū and Obaku-shū. These identities are perceived as overlapping and can be observed to encompass both the notion of *shū* as an independent institution and *shū* as valid Dharma lineage. First, under Japanese law, Obaku identifies itself as an independent sect, distinct from the Rinzai sect as a whole. As such, it is not to be confused with any of the various Rinzai *ha,* which are legally registered as subdivisions within the Rinzai sect. At the same time, Obaku conceives of itself as an authentic Rinzai lineage descending from the T'ang dynasty master Lin-chi through its founder Yin-yüan.

Obaku's claim to the Rinzai lineage is embodied in the designation *Rinzai shōshū,* or "True Heirs of the Lin-chi Lineage," which the Chinese founders first introduced. Successive generations of Obaku monks have continued to use this name to identify Obaku down to the present time. Chinese antecedents of the Obaku sect first coined the name *Rinzai shōshū* in a Chinese context. It was therefore not originally intended as a slight against existing Rinzai lineages in Japan. Nevertheless, it represented from the beginning an explicit religious claim to authentic Dharma transmission, which Obaku still maintains. To distinguish themselves from other lineages of Rinzai Zen already established in Japan, however, Obaku monks found it convenient to adopt early on the alternative designation Obaku-shū after the mountain name of the head monastery. Without abandoning their claim to the Rinzai lineage, Obaku followers have chosen to refer to their own branch of Rinzai as the Obaku lineage.

The nature of Obaku's dual identity as both Rinzai and Obaku is further evidenced by the manner in which the sect identifies its founder. In Obaku versions of their Dharma lineage, Yin-yüan typically receives dual recognition as the thirty-second-generation descendent of Lin-chi and the first generation of the Obaku lineage in Japan. While it is theoretically possible to identify any Dharma heir in the Obaku sect in a comparable dual manner, in practice the honor is generally reserved for the founder. In this way, Yin-yüan is presented as a pivotal figure in the history of Zen, much like Bodhidharma, who bears the double designation of Twenty-eighth Indian Patriarch and First Chinese Patriarch.

Yin-yüan and his Chinese disciples emigrated to Japan with the view of themselves as legitimate heirs to the Rinzai legacy. It seems likely that the term "lineage" comes closer to capturing Yin-yüan's understanding of Obaku's identity than other English constructs such as school, sect, or NRM. He and the other early Obaku leaders conceived of their movement more as an alternative lineage of Zen that was preserving a particular style of Zen practice than as an independent religious institution. The Obaku style was not in Japan long before the process of preserving the Dharma style became entwined with issues of institutional definition and survival.

THREE
Beginnings

In writing a history of the Obaku sect in Japan the first issue is where to locate its beginning. As is often the case with historical phenomena, upon reflection the choice is not obvious; several possibilities exist. While each choice has some validity, some basis in historical fact, each one also involves an interpretation of those facts that may ally one, wittingly or not, to some sectarian apologia or polemic. As Herman Ooms observes in his introduction to *Tokugawa Ideology:* "Beginnings pertain to an epistemological order rather than the order of things. To talk of a beginning is to engage in a highly interpretive discourse, and a very problematical one. . . . Such talk of beginnings often serves concrete interests and is thus itself ideological."[1] Rather than accepting one option without examining its interpretive implications, I shall begin by setting out the several possibilities and considering the purposes they may serve.

Four basic options for the beginning point of the Obaku sect can be drawn from existing historical accounts:

1. The work of Obaku's founder, Yin-yüan Lung-ch'i (1592–1673; J. Ingen Ryūki) in China, which represents the culmination of the restoration of the temple Huang-po-shan Wan-fu-ssu in Fukien province. The restoration process continued under three successive masters, Yin-yüan being the third, whose stated purpose was to revitalize the Ch'an style of the T'ang period Ch'an master Huang-po, who had resided on the mountain for some time and took his name from it.[2] Their restoration work began in the late sixteenth century and ended when Yin-yüan left for Japan in 1654.

2. The arrival of Yin-yüan Lung-ch'i in Japan in 1654. From the time he entered the gate of Kōfuku-ji in Nagasaki in the seventh

month, he immediately assumed the leadership of a community comprising both Chinese and Japanese monks.

3. The founding of the main temple of the sect, Obaku-san Mampuku-ji in Uji in 1661. Yin-yüan served as founder and first abbot, modeling his new temple on Huang-po Wan-fu-ssu in design and organization.

4. The official recognition of Obaku as an independent sect, separate from the Rinzai sect, by the Meiji government in 1876.

It is not uncommon for brief accounts of Obaku Zen to speak of its transmission to Japan from China in such a way as to leave the distinct impression that the sect existed in some form on the Asian mainland.[3] Although Obaku clearly has its roots in Ming period China, to claim that the sect began in China is overly simplistic and poses a host of problems. Strictly speaking, there never was an Obaku sect in China that distinguished itself from the rest of the Lin-chi (J. Rinzai) tradition and as such developed an independent institutional structure. The founding monks of the Obaku sect represented a specific line within the Lin-chi lineage whose headquarters was the monastery Huang-po Wan-fu-ssu. On the other hand, locating Obaku's beginning in China does serve to emphasize the strong Chinese character of the sect at a time when Zen in Japan had otherwise become thoroughly Japanese.

Yin-yüan taught a style of Zen advocated by his two predecessors at Huang-po Wan-fu-ssu, his master Fei-yin T'ung-jung (1593–1661; J. Hiin Tsūyō) and Fei-yin's master Mi-yun Yüan-wu (1566–1642; J. Mitsuun Engo). Culminating with Yin-yüan's efforts as abbot, these three men rebuilt the temple and consciously sought to restore the classical Lin-chi style of Ch'an.[4] On departing for Japan, Yin-yüan left behind a large group of Dharma heirs and disciples in China, and his line continued to thrive there for some time. The Chinese community at Wan-fu-ssu contributed to Yin-yüan's endeavors in Japan for years after he left, providing crucial support for the successful transmission of the line to Japan, where it became known as the Obaku sect. Any complete portrait of Obaku must include this Chinese background, but few scholars would refer to the Lin-chi lineage that practiced on Mount Huang-po as the "Obaku sect." The sectarian divisions characteristic of Japanese Buddhism were never as sharply drawn in China, even in the Ch'an context where lineage was a crucial means of legitimization. Moreover, the Lin-chi line from which Japanese Obaku descended cannot be singled out as independent from other Lin-chi lines of the time. It represents one form of Ch'an practice in late Ming China, but it never stood alone as a third sect of Ch'an over against the Lin-chi and Ts'ao-tung (J. Sōtō) schools. It would therefore be an anachronism to speak of an Obaku sect in China. Nonetheless, the origin of the Obaku Zen style lies in the late Ming style of the three masters from Wan-fu-ssu.

Scholars sympathetic to Obaku, such as Washio Junkei, often refer to Yin-yüan's arrival in Japan as the beginning of the Obaku sect in Japan.[5] This position is accurate in the sense that from the very beginning of his teaching in Nagasaki at Kōfuku-ji and Sōfuku-ji,[6] Yin-yüan's influence extended beyond the Chinese community of Nagasaki to the larger world of Japanese Zen. Many of the earliest Japanese converts to Obaku, such as Tetsugyū Dōki (1628–1700) and Tetsugen Dōkō (1630–1682), went to Nagasaki and joined the community there upon hearing of Yin-yüan's arrival. Many other Zen practitioners also paid their respects or practiced under Yin-yüan for periods of time without permanently joining the Obaku community. Having accepted Japanese monks and lay people as his disciples, Yin-yüan began to teach them in a manner familiar to the Chinese members of his group. One cannot argue, however, that in so doing he had any intention or awareness of founding a new, independent Zen sect. In the eyes of Yin-yüan himself and of those who came to practice under him, he was a Rinzai master, albeit from an alternative lineage to those represented in Japanese Rinzai. Positing this as the beginning of the Obaku sect suggests a degree of institutional independence and philosophical distinction from Rinzai Zen that did not yet exist. Identifying Yin-yüan's arrival as the beginning of the Obaku sect may serve certain purposes for those within the sect who continue to defend themselves against various negative stereotypes. Specifically, by presenting Obaku as an independent entity from the time of Yin-yüan's arrival, they reject any characterization of Obaku as a peripheral or even heterodox form of Rinzai, which was later rejected by the orthodox Rinzai community.

Currently, most scholars writing about Obaku prefer to associate the beginning of the Obaku sect with the date of the founding of Obaku-san Mampuku-ji in 1661.[7] At about that time, the term "Obaku-shū" first came into general use,[8] although the alternative designation, Obaku-ha, appears to have been equally common. The Japanese name obviously refers back to the mountain name of the temple in China, as well as the name of the new headquarters in Uji.

Earlier in the seventeenth century, the Edo bakufu had mandated that all temples be organized under a main temple/branch temple system. It was then common to identify divisions within the various sects and schools of Buddhism according to officially recognized main temples. In this usage, lines of Rinzai were designated as Myōshin-ji-ha, Daitoku-ji-ha, and so on, and the Obaku line was referred to as the Obaku-ha. As discussed above, the usage of the terms *ha* and *shū* was never precise, and the exact relationship between Obaku and Rinzai remained legally undefined until the modern period. Nevertheless, by granting Yin-yüan official permission to found a new main temple, the Edo bakufu conferred on the Obaku line an official degree of independence to govern itself and follow its own form of the Buddhist monastic code. Under the eyes of the law, from the time the main monastery, Mampuku-ji, was founded, Obaku-ha enjoyed the same degree of independence as its main rival, Myōshinji-ha. As a Rinzai lineage, one can still say that it was a part of the Rinzai school, but its differences from existing Japanese Rinzai lines in style and belief already tended to set it apart from the rest as a distinct sect.

In the strict legal sense of the term *shū*, defined only in the modern period, Obaku cannot be said to have existed as an independent sect alongside Sōtō and Rinzai until the Meiji government officially recognized it as such in 1876. Previous to 1876, the government had defined Obaku first as a *ha* within the unified Zen sect, and subsequently as a *ha* within the newly independent Rinzai sect. Parties within the administrative structure of both the Rinzai and Obaku communities petitioned the government for a revised legal definition that would reflect more accurately the groups' self-definitions as distinct and independent entities.[9] Obaku scholars reject the fourth option of using 1876 as the beginning of their sect, because they see this as a way of disparaging Obaku. By dismissing Obaku as "just a part of Rinzai," it has been possible until very recently to write histories of Japanese Zen without so much as mentioning the existence of a third sect.

The Restoration of Huang-po Wan-fu-ssu

The resurgence of Buddhism in late Ming China is also evidenced by the restoration of the temple on Mount Huang-po in Fukien province of southern China.[10] The temple was originally founded in 789 by Cheng-kan (n.d.), a monk in the Sixth Patriarch's line, who called his meditation hermitage Po-jo-t'ang. It was soon enlarged and renamed

Chien-fu-ssu. During the T'ang dynasty, the famous master Huang-po Hsi-yün (d. 850) took his vows there and later named his more famous temple in Kiangsi Huang-po-ssu after the mountain in Fukien.[11] The temple was restored early in the Ming dynasty in 1390 by the Ch'an master Tai-hsiu (n.d.), but was burned to the ground in 1555 during a period of civil unrest. Master Cheng-yüan Chung-t'ien (n.d.) tried to restore the temple during his tenure as abbot, from 1567 through 1572. The bulk of his efforts centered on obtaining a copy of the Chinese Buddhist canon for the temple from the authorities in Peking rather than rebuilding the physical structure of the monastery. His petitions to receive a Tripitaka remained unanswered at the time of his death, but two of his leading disciples, Hsing-shou Chien-yüan (n.d.) and Hsing-tz'u Ching-yüan (n.d.), determined to fulfill the master's mission. After repeated requests to the authorities and several trips to the capital, they were successful. The temple received an edition of the Chinese Tripitaka in 1612.

Mi-yün Yüan-wu began the actual physical restoration of temple buildings and grounds when he became abbot in 1630. Yin-yüan was Mi-yün's disciple and came to the mountain with him to serve as his attendant. In 1633, Mi-yün retired and his Dharma heir Fei-yin became abbot. Fei-yin appointed Yin-yüan to the post of head disciple. In 1637, Yin-yüan succeeded Fei-yin and became abbot for the first time. He served from 1637 until Mi-yün's death in 1642, when he resigned to fulfill the obligations of mourning his deceased master. He later served a second term from 1646 until his departure for Japan in 1654. The bulk of the restoration work was completed under his direction. During his tenure, some thirty buildings were erected and hundreds of disciples were said to have gathered at the temple to practice under his guidance.

The abbots of Wan-fu-ssu sought not only to restore the physical and economic structure of the temple, but to revitalize the Ch'an style of their Lin-chi lineage. They made use of those elements characteristically associated with the Lin-chi style, koan, slaps, and shouts. However, in keeping with the dominant syncretic nature of Chinese Buddhism, they also made use of a variety of Pure Land, T'ien-t'ai, and folk religious practices.[12]

Mi-yün, Fei-yin, and Yin-yüan regarded themselves respectively as the thirtieth-, thirty-first-, and thirty-second-generation descendents from Lin-chi.[13] They referred to their specific line as the Lin-chi chēng-tsung (J. Rinzai shōshū) or Lin-chi cheng-ch'uan (J. Rinzai shōden), reflecting their belief that they were heirs to the orthodox or true lineage from Lin-chi.[14] Indeed, their lineage claims at times extended beyond an evaluation of their own authenticity to a position challenging the validity of other lines. Fei-yin, in particular, became embroiled in arguments over Ch'an lineage then raging in China. He wrote his major work, the *Wu-téng yen-t'ung* (The exact lineage of the five lamps; J. *Gotō gentō*), in response to these arguments. In it, he set forth his own and Mi-yun's understanding of Ch'an lineages extending from the seven Buddhas of the past through the late Ming period. By doing so, Fei-yin not only sought to rectify lineage problems within his own school but to evaluate lineages from other schools as well. He invalidated the lineage claims made by several prominent Ch'an monks of the period, including Han-shan Te-ch'ing (1546–1623; J. Kanzan Tokusei) and Yun-ch'i Chu-hung (1535–1615; J. Unsei Shukō), who were by then deceased. In effect, Fei-yin used the concept of valid Dharma lineage as a polemical device to undercut the claims of rival lineages. By invalidating the claims of previous masters, he challenged the qualifications of their living descendents to preserve the Dharma and participate in valid transmission through the training and acknowledgment of Dharma heirs. Not surprisingly, the publication of the *Wu-téng yen-t'ung* in 1653 set off heated opposition from other groups. The dispute eventually lead to a public debate before government officials between Fei-yin and a Tsao-tung master, Yung-chüeh Yüan-hsien (1578–1657; J. Eigaku Genken). As a result of the judgment against Fei-yin at the debate, the original woodblocks of the *Wu-téng yen-t'ung* were destroyed in 1654, a few months after Yin-yüan left for Japan. Yin-yüan retained his copy and eventually republished the work in Japan in 1657.

Social Conditions in Late Ming China

During the years in which Wan-fu-ssu was being restored, the Ming dynasty was crumbling and Ch'ing forces established a new dynasty.[15] The late Ming emperors were ill-equipped to deal with the crises facing their empire. Manchu invasions from the north and rebellions from within left the country torn apart by war. Political and social discord was compounded by a series of natural disasters that lead to famine in various parts of the empire. Even the wealthy southern coastal regions such as Fukien, which had been successful in overseas commerce from the 1590s onward, were hard hit by skyrocketing rice prices, famine, and the resulting rioting and banditry during the 1640s.

On April 25, 1644, the Ch'ung-chen emperor committed suicide in the face of advancing rebel troops. Most historians use this date as the end of the Ming period and regard Ch'ung-chen as the last Ming emperor. In actuality, the political situation was quite complicated, and it was almost twenty years before the Ch'ing dynasty had completely suppressed the last of the Ming resistance. This period, from 1644 until 1662, is sometimes known as the Southern Ming, as the Ming loyalists maintained a stronghold south of the Yangtze River.

Within a few weeks of Ch'ung-chen's death, Manchu forces had taken the city of Peking and made it the capital of the Ch'ing empire, which they had proclaimed eight years earlier in 1636. The Manchus first proceeded to suppress the internal rebellions that had torn apart Ming China for decades and then moved south to quell the resistance movements of the last of the Ming loyalists. Ming forces continued to resist the "barbarian invasion" under the banner of a succession of Ming emperors until 1662, when the Manchus finally captured and executed the last claimant to the Ming throne, Yung-li, and his heir.

Throughout the Southern Ming period, the heart of Ming resistance was situated in Fukien province. The resistance was led by Cheng Chih-lung and his son Cheng Ch'eng-kung (1614–1662; J. Tei Seikō).[16] Cheng wealth and power were based upon the family's dominance in Fukien maritime commerce, and the Chengs used that power to oppose the Ch'ing. The Chengs first supported the prince of T'ang, who assumed the title of Emperor Lung-wu in 1645. Lung-wu adopted Ch'eng-kung and named him as his heir. When the senior Cheng, Chih-lung, surrendered to Ch'ing forces after his defeat in Foochow in 1646, Ch'eng-kung refused to follow his father's lead. He took control of his father's position as maritime leader in Fukien. He then consolidated his position so securely in Fukien that he was able to lead an offensive drive northward into Ch'ing territory between 1655 and 1659. When that movement failed, he and his forces fled to Taiwan in 1661.

As leaders in the Chinese sea trade, the Chengs had strong connections to the Chinese merchant community in Nagasaki as well as with local Japanese leaders. Ch'eng-kung was actually born in Japan to a Japanese mother, a connection that proved advantageous in his commercial dealings with the Japanese. Using their connections in Japan, the Chengs initiated a series of requests between 1645 and 1647, seek-

ing military support from the Tokugawa government in the name of
the Ming emperor.[17]

The Chinese Community in Nagasaki

Starting in the late sixteenth century, Chinese merchants began actively participating in overseas commerce. Although trade between
China and Japan had been officially banned by both countries, Chinese ships regularly came to port in Nagasaki, one of the region's leading trade centers. Long before Japanese national isolation laws limited
Chinese traders to that city in 1639, Nagasaki had a thriving Chinese
community. This merchant community later became the conduit for
bringing Chinese Ch'an masters to Japan, and Nagasaki served as a
way station for contacts between the Obaku sect in Japan and the
original community on Huang-po Wan-fu-ssu far into the Tokugawa
period.

As the Tokugawa bakufu became progressively more secure in its
power in the seventeenth century, Japanese laws regulating international trade and domestic religious practice began to impinge on the
Chinese traders, especially the expatriate merchant community in port
cities like Nagasaki. The regulation of Japanese religious practice began before the Tokugawa family established its reign. Starting in 1587,
Japanese military leaders began promulgating laws that prohibited
Christianity. Initially these laws did not directly affect commercial activities and, in any case, were not systematically enforced. The founder
of the Tokugawa shogunate, Tokugawa Ieyasu (1542–1616), pursued
policies intended to eliminate Christianity from the country without
harming international trade. However, the second Tokugawa shogun,
Hidetada (1579–1632) and his successor, Iemitsu (1603–1651), later
turned to a policy approaching national isolation that combined restrictions on religion, foreign trade, and international travel for Japanese. Under their leadership, bans on Christianity were strictly enforced, and by 1639 all Western nationals except the Dutch were
banned entirely from entering the country, even for purposes of trade.
Japan's international trade partners were thus effectively limited to the
Dutch, the Chinese, and the Koreans. The Tokugawa bakufu further
consolidated its control over international trade by limiting these remaining foreign contacts with Japan to Nagasaki, a city falling directly under bakufu rule. Although Dutch and Chinese merchants
were still welcome in Nagasaki, their living quarters were limited to

prescribed areas within the city; travel to other areas of the country was strictly forbidden.

In spite of these growing restrictions, Chinese trade with Japan increased throughout the first half of the seventeenth century, and Chinese merchants became a significant minority group in Nagasaki. Although many of the Chinese were Buddhist, as was the Japanese host community, they felt the need to construct temples of their own as their presence in the city became more established.[18] Chinese merchants from different geographical (and cultural) areas of China banded together and built three Chinese temples. Merchants from the Yangtze river basin built Kōfuku-ji in 1623, and it became known popularly as Nanking Temple, for the largest city in the region. Fuku-sai-ji was constructed in 1628 by people from the Chang-chow area of Fukien, and was therefore dubbed Chang-chow Temple. In a similar manner, Sōfuku-ji is known as Foochow Temple after the people who constructed it in 1635.

At this early stage in their history, the three Chinese temples may be identified as Ch'an temples, although this should not be interpreted necessarily to imply any strict sectarian identification. The temples were in no way affiliated with any Japanese Zen sect. They remained independent institutions until later becoming subtemples within the Obaku hierarchical structure under Mampuku-ji. A fourth Chinese temple, Shōfuku-ji, was built in 1677 by people from the Canton area. It is not always included in treatments of the other Chinese temples, as it was founded by a disciple of Yin-yüan and was a branch temple of Obaku-san Mampuku-ji from the start. All four of these temples still exist and remain Obaku branch temples. Only Fukusai-ji was destroyed completely by the atomic bomb in 1945; the others have buildings, images, and art dating back to the early seventeenth century.

Scholars believe that the Chinese Buddhist temples actually began as shrines to Chinese folk deities, especially Ma-tsu (J. Maso), the protective goddess of seafarers.[19] Chinese seaman customarily carried an image of Ma-tsu with them on board ship. They paid homage to the image throughout the journey, praying to it for a safe voyage. Upon arrival at their destination, they would take the image ashore and enshrine it temporarily, making offerings of thanksgiving for their safe passage. Upon their departure, they would once again install the image on board ship. Although the Chinese traders may at first have used their own residences as temporary shrines, it was more traditional to use a small community shrine, and soon such shrines were built in Nagasaki. All of the Chinese Buddhist temples in Nagasaki include a Ma-tsu hall among their buildings, a feature unique to them in Japan.

At first, the Chinese temples served only the most basic religious needs of the community, primarily the conducting of funeral and memorial services. Reflecting the eclectic nature of Ming religion, the temples included elements of Chinese folk religion that were unfamiliar to Japanese Buddhists but were common to any Chinese temple of the time. In addition to the Ma-tsu shrines, the temples included shrines dedicated to such Chinese folk deities as Kuan-ti, who was closely associated with merchant life. Kuan-ti was a historical military leader from the Three Kingdom period (220–280 C.E.) who was originally worshiped as a warrior deity. Gradually he became associated with financial success and by the Ming period became a common deity for the merchant class.[20] Although the practice of incorporating these folk deities into Buddhist temples is not at all unlike the Japanese custom of building a Shinto shrine within temple grounds, images of gods unknown to the Japanese caused some problems for the Chinese expatriates at this time. During the worst of the Christian persecutions, and especially after the Shimabara revolt of 1638, the Chinese apparently felt a special need to assert their Buddhist identity. It has even been suggested that the three Nagasaki temples were built primarily to demonstrate to the Japanese authorities that the Chinese expatriates were indeed Buddhist.[21]

The Chinese expatriate community extended invitations to Chinese monks from their home regions to come and serve as founders and abbots of the new temples. The early Chinese monks who made their way to Nagasaki were not masters of great distinction. Their primary concerns were twofold: performing funerals and memorial services for resident Chinese and their families, and officiating at Chinese-style ceremonies marking important calendrical holidays, such as the Buddha's birthday and P'u-tu (J. Obon). It is commonly believed that most of the Chinese clergy came to Japan to escape from the civil unrest in Ming China. The sole purpose of their religious activity in Japan was to serve the expatriate Chinese community. There is no indication that any of the early arrivals were Ch'an masters qualified to lead others in meditation or to acknowledge Dharma heirs. They did not seek a foothold in establishing new schools of Buddhism within the Japanese community. In this early stage, the Chinese temples and their monks had little or no influence on Japanese Buddhism. The situation changed when monks of higher caliber came over from China and attracted Japanese disciples.

Tao-che, the Forerunner of Obaku

The first monk with an established reputation to come to Nagasaki was Tao-che Ch'ao-yüan (1602–1662), known to the Japanese as Dōsha Chōgen.[22] Tao-che was a native of Fukien province and came from the same Dharma lineage as Yin-yüan. Tao-che's master was Keng-hsin Hsing-mi, a direct Dharma heir of Fei-yin, making Yin-yüan his Dharma uncle. Tao-che arrived in Nagasaki in 1651 and took up residence at Sōfuku-ji, where he served as abbot until 1655. He was the first Chinese monk to spread the Zen style of the Huang-po Wan-fu-ssu masters in Japan, and his work eased the way for Yin-yüan, who would follow a few years later.

News of Tao-che's arrival in Nagasaki quickly spread in the Japanese Zen world, and several Japanese monks came to practice under his guidance at Sōfuku-ji. The majority of Tao-che's Japanese disciples seem to have been monks from the Sōtō school,[23] but some Rinzai monks joined his assembly as well. A short list of monks who visited or practiced under him includes Dokuan Genkō (1630–1698), Gesshū Sōko (1618–1696), Tesshin Dōin (1593–1680), Kengan Zen'etsu (1618–1690), Egoku Dōmyō (1632–1721), Chōon Dōkai (1628–1695) and Unzan Guhaku (1619–1702). Tao-che is probably best known, however, for his relationship with the Rinzai master Bankei Yōtaku (1622–1693). Bankei had heard of Tao-che's arrival and joined his assembly in 1651, staying for perhaps a year. Bankei received Tao-che's *inka*, but he does not seem to have been completely satisfied with the master's abilities and did not perpetuate Tao-che's Dharma line.[24]

Although Tao-che taught numerous Japanese monks and bestowed *inka* on several of them, he was not successful in establishing his line in Japan. This was due in large part to his abrupt return to China in 1658, the reason for which is unclear. There are several stories and theories, but none is certain. By all accounts, Tao-che left after some sort of friction between himself and Yin-yüan's disciples.[25] When he left, most of his disciples turned to other masters, including some like Dokuan who had already received *inka* from him. The majority became disciples of Yin-yüan or one of the other leading Obaku masters. For this reason, Obaku scholars commonly regard Tao-che as a forerunner of the Obaku sect, who helped to prepare the Japanese community to be receptive to Yin-yüan and his movement.

Yin-yüan's Move to Nagasaki

By the middle of the seventeenth century, it had become common practice for the Chinese lay believers in Nagasaki and/or the Chinese monks who served them to send invitations to particular monks in China when one of their temples required a new abbot. In 1651, Sōfuku-ji was in need of an abbot, and the community sent an invitation to one of Yin-yüan's leading disciples, Yeh-lan Hsing-kue (1613?–1651; J. Yaran Shōkei).[26] Yeh-lan had entered monastic life in 1630 at Wan-fu-ssu and practiced under Mi-yun, Fei-yin, and Yin-yüan. He became Yin-yüan's Dharma heir in 1646 and had been serving as the abbot of Feng-huang-shan when he received the invitation from Sōfuku-ji. He accepted the offer and soon set sail for Nagasaki with Yin-yüan's approval. During the crossing, his ship broke up on a reef. Although many other passengers and crew survived the wreck, Yeh-lan was lost at sea. Yin-yüan seems to have been deeply affected by this loss, and later indicated that it was a primary factor in his own decision to leave for Japan.

Less than a year after Yeh-lan's death, I-jan Hsing-jung (1601–1668; J. Itsunen Shōyū), the abbot of Kōfuku-ji, began a campaign to bring Yin-yüan himself to Nagasaki.[27] Until that time, no prominent monks approaching Yin-yüan in stature had come to serve at the Chinese temples there. I-jan sent a series of four invitations to Yin-yüan between 1652 and 1653.[28] Although Yin-yüan at first refused these invitations on the grounds of his advanced age, he was eventually moved by the repeated requests. He himself seems to have been inclined to accept the offer from the start, but initially deferred to the wishes of his master Fei-yin. According to a letter later written by Yin-yüan addressed to Fei-yin, Fei-yin objected to Yin-yüan undertaking such a dangerous voyage when he was needed by the assembly in China.[29] Finally, after receiving the fourth letter from I-jan, Yin-yüan agreed to undertake the journey, writing his acceptance in the twelfth month of 1653.

Preparations for the crossing took some time, and Yin-yüan was not ready to depart until the sixth lunar month of 1654. His disciples pleaded with him to change his mind, but Yin-yüan felt that he could not disappoint the people waiting for him in Nagasaki. Based on let-

ters he wrote later, it seems that he promised the monks at Wan-fu-ssu
before he left that he would return to China after three years in Japan.
He appointed his Dharma heir Hui-men Ju-p'ei (1615–1664; J. Emon
Nyohai)[30] as his successor at Wan-fu-ssu and departed with a company of some twenty or thirty monks.[31] Most of these monks were
young and not especially advanced in their practice. Half of them remained with Yin-yüan in Japan, and the others returned to China after about a year in Nagasaki. Yin-yüan left behind his most advanced
disciples, including Mu-an Hsing-t'ao (1611–1684; J. Mokuan Shōtō)
and Chi-fei Ju-i (1616–1671; J. Sokuhi Nyoitsu), both of whom later
joined him in Japan.

Yin-yüan's Motivations

Scholars have paid a great deal of attention to Yin-yüan's reasons for
leaving China and settling in Japan. Determining the actual motives of
a historical figure is always problematic, but all of the modern scholars who discuss Obaku feel compelled to express an opinion on the
matter. This is perhaps because the issue of Yin-yüan's motivations for
going and settling in Japan has been under debate since at least the
early eighteenth century, when it was first raised in polemical texts at-
tacking the sect. Discussions about a founder's motivation can be
strong weapons in religious polemics, and arguments about Yin-
yüan's purpose in coming to Japan often reflect sectarian biases. In
some cases, it appears that scholars honestly striving to maintain nonsectarian objectivity have become unwitting participants in polemical
debates. Since a discussion of this type has been a standard feature in
the Japanese literature to date, a summary of the interpretations of
Yin-yüan's intentions is given here, with special attention devoted to
the polemical and apologetic tendencies of each.

Hirakubo Akira provides the most complete review of the various
theories developed by other scholars and analyzes most of the primary
source materials supporting each of them.[32] Based on his presentation,
one can divide the explanations into four basic types with minor variations: (1) Yin-yüan came to Japan to escape the turmoil and hardship
in China; (2) he came to spread the Dharma in Japan; (3) he came in
response to invitations from Japan; and (4) he came to complete his
disciple Yeh-lan's mission.

Starting with Tsuji Zennosuke, the majority of modern scholars
support the theory that Yin-yüan came to Japan, at least in part, to es-

cape the serious social and political upheavals in China at that time or because he could not reconcile himself to Ch'ing rule of China.[33] It is worth noting that Tsuji regards all of the monks, scholars, and artists who came to Japan in the seventeenth century as refugees from the chaos in China. His list of fifty-three such individuals extends well past the Southern Ming period to include individuals who emigrated as late as 1719.[34] Many of the monks from the later period emigrated at the invitation of Obaku-san Mampuku-ji to serve as its abbot, since the temple's monastic rule specifically required a Chinese monk to fill that post.

When Yin-yüan left China in 1654, Ming loyalists were still fighting the Ch'ing army, and his native region of Fukien remained a loyalist stronghold. Certain Buddhist monks from Fukien are known to have settled themselves deep in the mountains in order to escape the turmoil and practice in peace. Yeh-lan, for example, lived in seclusion in the mountains for two years, from 1647 until 1649. No doubt other monks chose to emigrate to Nagasaki for much the same purpose. It is believed that many of the expatriate Chinese merchants living in Nagasaki were there to escape the violence, so it would not have been strange if Yin-yüan had similar motivations. Hirakubo and other Obaku scholars, however, take offense at the suggestion that this was a primary motivation for Yin-yüan. They believe the argument relegates Yin-yüan's intention to spread the Dharma in Japan to the level of a secondary concern, a mere afterthought to the issue of his own comfort and safety.

Tsuji supports his contention that Yin-yüan was fleeing the violence by suggesting that evidence in Yin-yüan's *nempu* (year-by-year biography) indicates that the master himself experienced hardships and injustices while in China.[35] In response to Tsuji, Hirakubo denies finding any such evidence in his own exhaustive research on Yin-yüan's life. While Hirakubo acknowledges that Yin-yüan moved around during the worst years of the fighting, he argues that this activity was not directly related to the war. He provides examples from the *nempu* to show that Yin-yüan witnessed firsthand the suffering of other people in Fukien, but was not himself a victim.[36] What is obvious from Yin-yüan's writings is that he grieved for the fall of the Ming empire and abhorred the injustices and violence inflicted on the Chinese people during the difficult years of transition. Yin-yüan and other monks at Wan-fu-ssu were personally acquainted with members of the Ming resistance and sympathized with their cause. They held memo-

rial services for casualties in their area, especially after the fall of Foochow in 1647, when thousands of people were said to have been
killed.[37]

One can find some support for Tsuji's theory in the *Obaku geki,*
one of the earliest accounts of the establishment of Obaku in Japan.
The *Obaku geki* was written by the Myōshin-ji scholar Mujaku
Dōchū in 1720. Although the document is polemical in tone, it provides a good general outline of Yin-yüan's early years in Japan. The
manuscript circulated among monks in the Myōshin-ji line and seems
to have been intended for internal consumption. It contains a series of
episodes that show Yin-yüan and other Obaku monks in an unfavor-
able light.[38] The episode in question would have occurred in 1654,
two months after Yin-yüan's arrival in Nagasaki.

> On the ninth day of the ninth month, when Master Jikuin was liv-
> ing at his retreat at Zenrin-ji, Yin-yüan came there one morning
> while he was still asleep accompanied by seven or eight disciples. . . .
> Jikuin sat up in bed and said, "Why have you come so early in the
> morning?" Yin-yüan replied, "Although I thought I should return
> to China, the Ch'ing Dynasty has not yet quelled the rebellion.
> Since Japan is a country where the Buddhist Dharma flourishes, I
> think that I should stay here if I can. Since you know many of the
> *daimyō,* perhaps you would act as my intermediary and I could
> build a two-mat hut and hang out my Dharma banner."[39]

If accurate, this episode would indicate that conditions in China
were indeed a crucial factor in Yin-yüan's thinking from the outset
and were specifically relevant to his decision to remain permanently in
Japan. On the other hand, the *Obaku geki* is by no means an unbiased
history of Obaku Zen, and one cannot naively accept everything
recorded in it as factual. One must first bear in mind that Mujaku was
writing nearly seventy years after the fact and that he himself was not
a witness to this episode. The first parts of the *Obaku geki* were based
largely on what Mujaku learned from his master, Jikuin Somon
(1611–1677), deceased some thirty-three years before Mujaku recorded his version of events. It is also important to bear in mind that
Yin-yüan and Jikuin parted on bad terms in 1656 or 1657, so that
Mujaku's source was hardly impartial. Of greater importance, his purpose in writing the piece as a whole was to criticize Yin-yüan and his
Obaku line, so he included as many unflattering details as possible. In
the case of this particular episode, for example, there is reason to
doubt that Yin-yüan actually decided to remain in Japan at such an

early juncture. He subsequently expressed his desire to return to China several times over the years that followed, and his Japanese supporters certainly seem to have taken those feelings seriously.[40] It is therefore difficult to gauge the accuracy of the above episode.

Another version on the same theme can be found in a second eighteenth-century document, the *Zenrin shūhei shū*,[41] written by Keirin Sūshin (1652–1728), a monk from the Myōshin-ji line. According to this account, Yin-yüan and his disciples fled China because their lineage had been discredited when Fei-yin suffered his humiliating defeat in the public debate concerning the *Wu-téng yen-t'ung*. In this interpretation of Yin-yüan's motives, Yin-yüan and other Obaku monks were fleeing, not social and political upheaval, but the failure of their own lineage in China. In Yin-yüan's case, at least, the actual chronology of events does not support this argument, as he left China a few months before Fei-yin's unsuccessful debate in 1654. Interestingly, the *Zenrin shūhei shū* concedes that Chinese monks of Yin-yüan and Mu-an's stature had not previously come to Nagasaki but specifically denies that they came out of dedication to spreading the Dharma. The text thus stands in direct contradiction to the second type of theory about Yin-yüan's motives that stresses his commitment to spreading Buddhism.

The second interpretation maintains that Yin-yüan went to Japan primarily for the purpose of spreading the Dharma. For those inside the Obaku tradition, this theory is obviously more congenial. As Hirakubo points out, this explanation is based directly on some of Yin-yüan's personal reflections found in his recorded sayings, and this was the view taken by Yin-yüan's immediate disciples.[42] Over the years before he emigrated, Yin-yüan was in contact, directly and indirectly, with the Chinese expatriate community in Nagasaki. He knew that the Buddhist monks and lay people at the Chinese temples there sought his guidance, and he had heard glowing reports of Japanese dedication to Buddhism. He had reason, therefore, to believe that he would be greeted by a receptive audience and be able to contribute something to the advancement of Buddhism in Japan. He was, in fact, successful in spreading his Zen style in Japan, and firmly established his Dharma line with both Chinese and Japanese Dharma heirs. Even if escaping the political turmoil was one of his motivations for leaving China, once in Japan he certainly dedicated his life to teaching.

There are at least three distinct versions of the third theory, which attributes Yin-yüan's decision to emigrate to the invitations he received from Japan. First, as already described, the abbot of Kōfuku-ji sent Yin-yüan four invitations, and Yin-yüan finally accepted the fourth. In the most literal sense, I-jan's invitation was the immediate catalyst for Yin-yüan to sail for Nagasaki. It has also been suggested in early modern and modern sources that either the emperor Gomizunoo or, alternatively, the fourth Tokugawa shogun Ietsuna were actually responsible for commissioning I-jan to extend the invitation. Depending on the source, one or the other secular authority is supposed to have requested that a prominent Chinese Ch'an master be brought to Japan in order to provide a spark to revitalize Japanese Rinzai.

The earliest example of this type of argument is found in the *Nagasaki jitsuroku taisei* (Compilation of historical accounts from Nagasaki), compiled in 1760. According to its version of events, Ietsuna wanted to follow the example set by the Ashikaga shogun and build a great Zen temple. He ordered I-jan to invite a prominent Chinese monk to be its founder, and this resulted in Yin-yüan being invited. This story was then repeated in Obaku materials published during the Edo period.[43] Stories circulating during the Tokugawa period generally focused on the shogun as the primary agent. It was only after the Meiji Restoration that newer versions emerged replacing the shogun with the emperor in the role of patron.[44] There is no historical evidence to support either of these claims. Although neither leader was involved in the plans to bring Yin-yüan to Japan, these stories have been used by scholars to foster the idea that Obaku was a sect marked out for special favor either by the Tokugawa shogunate or by the emperor.

Finally, the claim that Yin-yüan went to Japan primarily to complete the mission of his disciple Yeh-lan represents Yin-yüan's own explanation for his decision to leave China. As noted earlier, Fei-yin did not approve of Yin-yüan making the trip to Japan, but ultimately Yin-yüan disappointed his master and left. Once he was in Nagasaki, Yin-yüan tried to explain his decision to Fei-yin in a New Year's greeting sent from Japan in 1655. The letter reads in part: "Originally, Yeh-lan was invited to Japan, but he did not fulfill his vow. Since he lost his life, I couldn't ask anyone else. [I came myself,] like a father paying his son's debt. Previously I had written to refuse their [invitation], because I had acquiesced to your stern admonition. . . . When they invited me a fourth time, I was moved by the sincerity of those far away and promised them [I would come]."[45] The needs of the Nagasaki community and their persistence obviously influenced Yin-yüan's decision, but by his own estimation the crucial factor was his feeling of responsibility toward Yeh-lan. Although one cannot claim that this explanation exhausts the relevant conditions leading up to Yin-yüan's decision to leave China or to settle permanently in Japan, as his own version of events it should carry special significance.

Historical inaccuracies in some variations not withstanding, all four of the theories concerning Yin-yüan's motivations appear plausible as explanations for his emigration to Japan. Perhaps all four motivations were operative to some degree in his decision-making process. None by necessity invalidates any of the others. One need not argue, for example, that concern over social conditions in China precludes sincere dedication to spreading the Dharma. It seems unlikely that a monk of Yin-yüan's advanced years and stature would undertake the journey without numerous motivations and factors coming into play. Ultimately, of course, internal motivations cannot be established with any certainty. Whatever his reasons, Yin-yüan did undertake the journey to Nagasaki. The next chapter will continue the narrative from the time of his arrival in Japan.

FOUR

Laying the Foundation

The Welcome in Japan

When Yin-yüan and his disciples arrived in Nagasaki in the seventh month of 1654, it was not only Chinese expatriates who came out to greet them. Thousands of people are said to have gathered to hear Yin-yüan preach at the official ceremony, where he assumed the position as abbot, only twelve days after he arrived.[1] Throughout his stay in Nagasaki, numerous Japanese officials and other prominent individuals came to pay their respects to the Chinese master.[2] In addition, approximately seventy Japanese monks joined Yin-yüan's entourage of twenty Chinese monks to participate in his first winter retreat, held three months after his arrival.[3]

In the months after Yin-yüan's acceptance letter arrived, word had spread throughout the Japanese Zen Buddhist world that the prominent Chinese master was coming. Several factors contributed to the enthusiasm with which he was welcomed. First, the Japanese had traditionally looked to China as the source of renewal for Buddhist teaching and practice, much as the Chinese Buddhists had looked to India and Central Asia. Like other forms of Buddhism brought to Japan in earlier periods, Zen was transmitted through the efforts of Japanese monks who visited China and studied under Chinese masters and of Chinese monks who emigrated to Japan in the twelfth, thirteenth, and fourteenth centuries. During nearly four hundred years prior to the Edo period, however, contact with Chinese Buddhism had been severely limited, and it was only in the mid-seventeenth century that renewed contact became practical. In the early seventeenth century, several Japanese monks expressed a desire to travel to China to study there as a means of renewing Buddhism in their own country, but na-

42

tional isolation laws precluded that option. The arrival of Chinese masters like Tao-che whetted the Japanese interest, but Yin-yüan represented the first Chinese master of high reputation to come to Japan. Many Japanese Buddhists were eager to see firsthand what his Zen style would be like. Of course, the changes that had occurred in Chinese Buddhism, especially in Ch'an, during the intervening centuries proved a shock to many Japanese, but that will be addressed later.

The early decades of the Edo period were a time of excitement and growth in the Buddhist world. Despite the period's reputation for stagnation and degeneracy, Buddhist sects were taking advantage of the existing political stability, building new monasteries or restoring old facilities as allowed by the government, developing new systems of education for their monks, rediscovering sectarian texts of earlier periods, and establishing formal networks of temples and monasteries. Many Rinzai and Sōtō Zen monks called for reform of their respective monasteries and sects at this time, and sectarian scholarship flourished. One such reform movement took root at Myōshin-ji, one of the leading Rinzai monasteries of the day. Certain monks within the movement looked to Yin-yüan as a possible resource in their plans to revive Rinzai Zen at Myōshin-ji.

By the beginning of the Tokugawa period, the *gozan* Zen temples, which had been the dominant force in Rinzai Zen in earlier centuries, had declined in vitality and were eclipsed by the independent temples Daitoku-ji and Myōshin-ji. These temples had the reputation for promoting strict Zen practice, rather than the more artistic and literary pursuits favored at *gozan* temples. They enjoyed strong financial support from *sengoku daimyō* during the sixteenth century and were the most influential Zen centers during the seventeenth century.[4] Myōshin-ji is also the monastery that had both the greatest contact with Obaku and came into the sharpest conflict with it.

Myōshin-ji was established as a Rinzai temple by the emperor Hanazono in 1337; Kanzan Egen (1277–1360), a disciple of Shūhō Myōchō (better known as Daitō Kokushi, 1282–1338), served as its founding abbot. Although the monastery never became a part of the *gozan* system of prominent Rinzai temples, it became one of the leading centers for Rinzai practice before its destruction during the Onin War. The monastery was restored and came to its greatest prominence during the Tokugawa period, when a majority of the leading Rinzai scholar-monks of the day came from its lineage.

Monks favoring reform at Myōshin-ji disagreed about the best means to revive the sect, and they split into two factions. One faction favored a strict interpretation of the monastic rule and the other a less literal interpretation, stressing the spirit rather than the letter of the law.[5] Gudō Tōshoku (1577–1661), one of the most influential Zen monks of the day, led the latter faction. Ultimately, Gudō's faction won and became the dominant force at Myōshin-ji in the generations that followed.[6] Leadership of the former faction included Isshi Monju (1608–1646) and Ungo Kiyō (1582–1659),[7] as well as such men as Ryōkei Shōsen (1602–1670), Tokuō Myōkō (1611–1681), and Jikuin Somon (1611–1677), all of whom played major roles in bringing Yin-yüan to Kyoto and in the establishment of Obaku-san Mampuku-ji. Ryōkei was at one time abbot at Ryōan-ji, an important Myōshin-ji branch temple, and later served two terms as abbot of Myōshin-ji, first in 1651 and then again for a short time in 1654. It was in his capacity as abbot the second time that he extended an invitation for Yin-yüan to visit Myōshin-ji. Ryōkei and his supporters planned to install the Chinese master as abbot at Myōshin-ji. Although none of them had ever previously met Yin-yüan, they were familiar with his teaching through volumes of his writings that circulated in Japan sometime before 1651.

According to the *Obaku geki,* three years before Yin-yüan came to Japan, Tokuō chanced to purchase two volumes of Yin-yüan's writings from a book dealer in Kyoto. He read the works and recommended them to Ryōkei, who then borrowed and read them as well. Ryōkei was equally impressed.[8] Additional information about the circulation of these volumes is not available, but it seems likely that other Rinzai monks in the Myōshin-ji line gained some access to them through Tokuō's generosity. When Ryōkei and Tokuō heard that Yin-yüan planned to come to Kōfuku-ji, they were pleased at the prospect of meeting the man himself and began to plan their invitation. Since Yin-yüan took a strict view of the monastic rule throughout his teachings, Ryōkei and the others viewed him as a new and powerful ally for their cause.

In the end, inviting Yin-yüan to Kyoto did not prove an easy task, much less installing him as abbot at Myōshin-ji. First, the logistics of obtaining permission for Yin-yüan to travel to Kyoto were complicated because as a Chinese national Yin-yüan did not enjoy freedom of movement within Japan. Ryōkei, Tokuō, and Jikuin undertook the lengthy process of formally petitioning the appropriate governmental authorities to secure the necessary travel papers. In addition to these external complications, they faced formidable opposition to their plans from within the Myōshin-ji community. Gudō Tōshoku and his faction took exception to the plan and effectively blocked any hope of a unanimous welcome at Myōshin-ji.

Yin-yüan's Move from Nagasaki to Kyoto

After arriving in Nagasaki, Yin-yüan took up residence as abbot at Kōfuku-ji where he sought to establish a higher level of Zen practice than had previously been known there. For the first time, the practice of meditation under a prominent Zen master and the active pursuit of enlightenment within the context of strict monastic discipline became the primary focus of concern at the Chinese Buddhist temples. To the extent possible under crowded conditions, Yin-yüan fashioned arrangements within the Kōfuku-ji community after the style of Wan-fu-ssu, employing the same monastic code and the same general pattern of ritual and meditative practice. In addition to the warm welcome extended by the Chinese expatriate population, Yin-yüan received hundreds of Japanese visitors from all ranks of society. His assembly soon included a large number of Japanese monks. Exact numbers are unclear, but the community expanded so rapidly that tight finances and overcrowding became major concerns during the first winter retreat. In the spring of 1655, the community at Kōfuku-ji managed to finance a much needed expansion of the temple living quarters and meditation halls to relieve the overcrowding. It is not clear how the temple acquired the funds for this project, but the extent of the renovations suggests that the financial constraints of the first months had eased. At about the same time, in the early months of 1655, Yin-yüan received an invitation from a group of Chinese lay believers to come to Sōfuku-ji; there he assumed the post of abbot that his disciple Yeh-lan had originally accepted. From then on, he simultaneously served the two temples, holding a joint summer retreat for the two assemblies that year.

One of the many Japanese monks who came to pay his respects and remained at the temple to practice under the master was Kyorei Ryōkaku (1600–1691), a Rinzai monk from Zenrin-ji in Hiroshima. Kyorei was from the Myōshin-ji line and a close friend of Tokuō. At Tokuō's suggestion, Kyorei made the short journey from Hiroshima to Nagasaki just a month after Yin-yüan's arrival. Yin-yüan must have been impressed by Kyorei, because he quickly invited him to stay on

at Kōfuku-ji to direct the Japanese monks during the first winter retreat. Kyorei's letter to Tokuō written during the retreat gives a surprisingly candid account of his observations.

> There are now about seventy Japanese monks and more than thirty
> Chinese monks. Yin-yüan opened the winter retreat on the fifteenth
> day of the tenth month, and the monks will meditate until the
> fifteenth day of the first month. The rule is being strictly observed.
> Japanese and Chinese monks are mingled together, but they cannot
> communicate. Moreover, both the Japanese and the Chinese monks
> are highly conceited, and there have been occasional incidents. I am
> troubled as you can well imagine. However, things are generally
> tranquil now. . . .
>   This is Master Yin-yüan's first retreat in Japan, and he is some-
> what nervous. He entrusted the Japanese assembly to me, and con-
> cerns himself with the harmony of the whole assembly.[9]

Taken as a whole, the letter is an excellent resource for understanding
the initial impression that Yin-yüan and his Zen style would have
made on a sympathetic Japanese observer. In the course of the letter,
Kyorei spells out more fully the causes for the tensions he alludes to
in the above passage. Since he was well aware of plans to invite Yin-
yüan to Myōshin-ji, he may well have been thinking ahead to the possible consequences of such an undertaking. Kyorei goes on to report
that he had already passed along to Yin-yüan messages of welcome
from Tokuō and Ryōkei. Presumably these messages expressed their
desire to invite him to Myōshin-ji in the near future. Kyorei indicates
that Yin-yüan seemed amenable to the idea. While voicing his own
support for the plan, Kyorei expresses doubt that the assembly at
Myōshin-ji would ever be able to come to a consensus and agree to
the move.

The internal problems at Myōshin-ji alluded to in Kyorei's letter
proved insurmountable, and Ryōkei and the others never realized
their dream of installing Yin-yüan as abbot at Myōshin-ji. Although
Ryōkei extended his invitation to Yin-yüan in his official capacity as
abbot at Myōshin-ji, he did not remain in the post for more than a few
months. Opposition to the invitation may well have played an important role in his decision to resign so quickly. His successor was Gudō
Tōshuku, the powerful leader of the rival faction at Myōshin-ji and
Ryōkei's primary adversary in the reform debate. Gudō bitterly opposed the plan to invite Yin-yüan and fought it as a direct threat to
the preservation of the Myōshin-ji line. He maintained that Myōshin-

ji should exclusively limit the abbot's chair to members of the lineage descended from the founder, Kanzan Egen (1277–1360). Gudō argued, therefore, that as an outsider Yin-yüan could not rightly be considered as even a potential candidate.[10] Although Gudō did succeed in blocking Yin-yüan's invitation to Myōshin-ji, he could not prevent his eventual move to Kyoto. Ultimately, the exclusion of Yin-yüan from Myōshin-ji led to the founding of Mampuku-ji, and with it the establishment of Obaku as an independent sect.

Faced with the failure of their original plan, Ryōkei and his supporters changed their tactics. They decided instead to invite Yin-yüan to take up residence at Ryōkei's own small temple, Fumon-ji in Settsu,[11] and initiated the official procedures necessary to carry out the revised plan. According to the *Obaku geki*, Jikuin played the primary role in obtaining official permission for Yin-yüan to travel outside of Nagasaki for an extended visit. In this regard, Jikuin seems to have been acting on behalf of his superiors, Ryōkei and Tokuō. Jikuin began the process by consulting with the shogunate's governor in Kyoto *(Shoshidai)*, Itakura Shigemune (1586–1656).[12] On Itakura's recommendation and with his financial assistance, Jikuin made his way to Edo and submitted an official petition to the bakufu signed by Ryōkei, Tokuō, and himself.

While in Edo, Jikuin gained the support of two leading bakufu officials, Great Counselor Sakai Tadakatsu (1587–1662) and Senior Counselor Matsudaira Nobutsuna (1596–1662).[13] According to the *Obaku geki*, Matsudaira built Ryūge-in, Jikuin's subtemple at Myōshin-ji, at this time in order to bolster Jikuin's social status and thereby improve the chances for the petition's approval. As a young and unimportant monk without a temple of his own, Jikuin did not have the prominence necessary to gain the council's trust. When the petition came under consideration by the council, these two men spoke in its favor and eventually secured its approval in the fifth month of 1655.[14]

Initially, the council was suspicious of Yin-yüan and believed that he might be a Ming spy. The bakufu had received repeated requests for military aid from the Ming loyalists, and Yin-yüan was known to have connections with them. In fact, it was the leader of the loyalists, Coxinga (Cheng Ch'eng-kung) himself who had provided Yin-yüan and his entourage passage to Nagasaki. So, in granting permission for Yin-yüan to visit Fumon-ji, the council remained extremely cautious and severely limited his access to Japanese society. It did not yet grant

Yin-yüan permission to stay on in Japan indefinitely, nor did it grant him freedom of movement in the country. While his case remained under consideration, the authorities simply allowed him to move from the confines of Nagasaki to the grounds of Fumon-ji, where he would live under conditions tantamount to house arrest.

Having gained official permission to invite Yin-yüan to Fumon-ji, Ryōkei, Tokuō, and Jikuin drafted an invitation. Jikuin once again traveled to Nagasaki to deliver the letter in person. Initially, Yin-yüan declined the invitation, indicating that for a man of his age he had already traveled far enough. Jikuin repeated his requests to the master and enlisted the help of the bakufu administrator in Nagasaki, Kurokawa Masanao (1602–1680) to intercede as well.[15] Between them they seem to have persuaded Yin-yüan, as he eventually accepted the offer. Yin-yüan left Kōfuku-ji in the eighth month of 1655 accompanied by a number of his Chinese disciples. They arrived at Fumon-ji about a month later.

Life at Fumon-ji

Under the conditions arranged with the shogunate, Yin-yüan initially lived at Fumon-ji under house arrest until his case could be heard and decided by the bakufu council. He was not allowed to leave the temple compound for any reason, nor were any visitors allowed entry to see him. Jikuin once again turned to his friend Itakura Shigemune for assistance in ameliorating the situation. Itakura came to Fumon-ji to meet with Yin-yüan in person, hoping to assess his character as a monk and his motives for visiting Japan. Itakura had already retired from his post as governor in Kyoto, but used his influence to have the constraints loosened somewhat so that a few visitors could enter.[16] Unfortunately, permission was delayed and did not arrive before the installation ceremony. On 11/4/1655 Yin-yüan conducted the opening ceremonies at which he formally assumed the post as abbot. Ryōkei, Tokuō, and Itakura were the only dignitaries in attendance.

According to an account in the *Obaku geki,* word spread quickly that a Chinese monk was living at Fumon-ji, and the restriction that only a few visitors at a time were allowed to enter the temple soon became meaningless. A group of Shinshū believers, attending services commemorating the anniversary of Shinran's death at a nearby True Pure Land temple, crowded the gates of Fumon-ji, eager for a glimpse of the foreigner. The monks at Fumon-ji were unable to maintain control of the crowd and the situation got out of hand. When word of the incident reached government officials, Jikuin was summoned by Shigemune, who demanded an explanation.[17] Although Shigemune severely reprimanded Jikuin for the episode, he apparently accepted Jikuin's apology. No steps were taken to impose tighter restrictions.

In 1656, Yin-yüan expressed his intention of returning to China. Around that time he received several letters from Wan-fu-ssu requesting that he return home. Yin-yüan had been absent for almost three years, and his disciples in China reminded him of his earlier promise to limit his stay in Japan to a three-year time span. In his reply, Yin-yüan explained that he found it impossible to refuse Ryōkei's hospitality at Fumon-ji, but that they could expect his return sometime after the new year, in 1657. For their part, Ryōkei and the other Japanese disciples, who had gone to great lengths to secure Yin-yüan's invitation to Kyoto, wanted to prevent or at least postpone Yin-yüan's return to China. They petitioned the bakufu once more with greater urgency, requesting that Yin-yüan's case be settled immediately and that all the restrictions of house arrest be lifted. This time, the bakufu's response was far more positive, retaining only a modicum of caution.

Yin-yüan was granted freedom of movement within certain limits, and the rules of isolation were greatly eased. In an official letter dated 7/26/1656,[18] the bakufu spelled out the following terms: (1) Yin-yüan could travel freely within the Kyoto region (including the cities of Kyoto, Nara, Osaka, Sakai, and Ōtsu) for periods of up to ten to twelve days with the escort of Ryōkei, Tokuō, or Jikuin. Travel outside of that area would require special permission from government authorities. (2) Yin-yüan could establish a monastic community under his direction at Fumon-ji consisting of up to two hundred Japanese monks. (3) Lay people could meet with Yin-yüan at the discretion of Ryōkei and Tokuō, but only Zen believers were to be admitted. The merely curious were still banned from entry.

Yin-yüan first exercised his new freedom to travel in the autumn of 1656 when he made a tour of Kyoto. He visited several of the major Zen temples in the city, including Myōshin-ji. There is no way of knowing how many Japanese monks actually joined Yin-yüan's assembly at Fumon-ji. From his recorded sayings and other contemporary sources, it is clear that many monks from Kyoto, including a number from Myōshin-ji, took advantage of the new opportunity to visit Yin-yüan. Some of these individuals stayed to practice at Fumon-ji for either a summer or a winter retreat.

The same letter that granted Yin-yüan new freedoms rejected the request that his leading Chinese disciple, Mu-an Hsing-t'ao, be allowed to join him in Kyoto. Mu-an had arrived in Nagasaki in 1655/7, just a few months before Yin-yüan left for Fumon-ji. He made the journey to Japan at Yin-yüan's suggestion and became the abbot of Fukusai-ji. Mu-an was not able to leave Nagasaki until 1660, when Yin-yüan's relations with the bakufu were completely normalized. He then joined Yin-yüan at Fumon-ji and accompanied him to Obaku-san Mampuku-ji when it opened.

At about this time, relations between Ryōkei and Jikuin deteriorated, culminating in Jikuin's withdrawal of his support for Yin-yüan. According to the *Obaku geki,* the final break with Ryōkei was precipitated by a dispute concerning a purple robe[19] that Ryōkei had procured for Yin-yüan without proper permission.[20] The deeper cause for Jikuin's alienation from Yin-yüan seemed to be his growing sense that Yin-yüan preferred Ryōkei, who, with his higher status, was better able to secure for him the trappings of high rank: a purple robe, a large temple, and an audience with the shogun. The scholar Ogisu Jundō suggests that although Jikuin had done more work than anyone else to bring their plans to fruition, Ryōkei and Tokuō took all the credit for the younger man's efforts, hastening a breakdown in relations.[21] In any case, Jikuin officially resigned, notifying the bakufu in person that he would no longer be representing Yin-yüan.

After Jikuin's resignation, Ryōkei began to handle direct dealings with the bakufu personally. He was seriously concerned that Yin-yüan would decide to leave Japan, and he took immediate action in the hope of preventing that possibility. In 1657, he made two trips to Edo in an effort to settle the matter once and for all before the bakufu council. He intended to improve Yin-yüan's circumstances in Japan significantly and thus dissuade him from returning to China. On his first trip to Edo, Ryōkei failed in his request for a purple robe for Yin-yüan, but managed to acquire a monthly government stipend of fifteen *koku* of rice (enough to support approximately a hundred people) for the community residing at Fumon-ji. It was becoming clear to Ryōkei that the bakufu would never fully accept Yin-yüan unless the authorities could evaluate his character for themselves. On his second trip he arranged for an official summons that called Yin-yüan to Edo to meet with the council and to have an audience at Edo castle with Ietsuna, the fourth shogun. Ryōkei then promptly returned to Kyoto to convince Yin-yüan that the long trip to Edo would be worthwhile. In a now familiar pattern, Yin-yüan was at first disinclined to go but eventually acquiesced. He wrote to his disciples in China, once again postponing his return, this time indefinitely. At this point, he made no indication to them that he had decided to remain permanently in Japan.

The trip to Edo, which took place at the end of 1658, was a great success. Connections established at that time with leading members of the bakufu led directly to the founding of Obaku-san Mampuku-ji. Yin-yüan seems to have made a very favorable impression on the young shogun, who was then only eighteen. In addition, he secured the patronage of the powerful high counselor Sakai Tadakatsu, who became his closest ally. Sakai demonstrated his respect for the master by asking Yin-yüan to perform the memorial service for the thirty-third anniversary of his father's death during his stay in Edo. After returning to Fumon-ji, Yin-yüan continued to exchange letters with Sakai, and through him remained in contact with the shogun.

In 1659, Yin-yüan wrote to Sakai and announced his intention to return to China, in effect asking the shogun for permission to leave the country. Sakai's response, dated 5/3/1659, indicated that Yin-yüan's visit to Edo had significantly changed his standing with the bakufu. The promises made in this letter precipitated Yin-yüan's decision to stay on permanently in Japan. Sakai wrote that he fully understood Yin-yüan's feelings of longing for home and that he had tried to convey them to the shogun. According to Sakai, the shogun responded in the following manner: "What Yin-yüan says is truly understandable. His moral character affected me when we met. Moreover, he is old, and there are [dangers] of storms on the long journey [to China]. I will be uneasy unless he remains in this country. Therefore, let him choose some land in the Kyoto area, and I shall grant it to him as temple grounds." [22]

The shogun's promise of land and permission to build a new temple convinced Yin-yüan to stay in Japan. He composed a grateful acceptance to Sakai and drafted a letter of apology to his disciples in China, explaining that he would not be returning home. Meanwhile, in Nagasaki, Mu-an wrote a letter to Wan-fu-ssu explaining his perception of the situation. He stated quite frankly that he believed that Yin-yüan did not have the freedom to leave Japan. Apparently, Mu-an and Chi-fei Ju-i, another leading disciple residing in Nagasaki, both feared that Yin-yüan was being held against his will. They were not convinced otherwise until after they were reunited with Yin-yüan and spoke with him directly. [23]

Bakufu's permission was essential for building a new temple, since the laws governing Buddhist temples and clergy *(jiin hatto)* strictly forbade any unauthorized construction. The government likewise retained the exclusive right to bestow land grants, which were officially documented with the bakufu's red seal certificate. Official documentation granting ownership of the land followed several years later, but as a result of the shogun's offer Yin-yüan immediately began searching for an appropriate site. It is not known for certain whether or not Ryōkei planted the idea for the shogun's offer or had petitioned for permission to open a new temple for Yin-yüan in earlier negotiations. Some secondary sources suggest that this is a possibility, but they offer no concrete evidence to support the contention.

The Foundation of Obaku-san Mampuku-ji

Yin-yüan first expressed an interest in rebuilding Jikishi-an, a small temple in northern Saga, an area to the north and west of Kyoto. Although a True Pure Land temple today, Jikishi-an was then affiliated with Myōshin-ji. Its abbot was the Rinzai monk Dokushō Shōen (1617–1694), a disciple of Takuan and Isshi Monju. Dokushō inherited the temple when Isshi died in 1646. During the period when Yin-yüan was in residence at Kōfuku-ji, Dokushō traveled to Nagasaki and became one of his attendants.[24] The basic problem with adopting Jikishi-an as the site for Yin-yüan's new monastery seems to have been its proximity to Daitoku-ji, another major Rinzai Zen temple. The idea was dropped due to objections raised by the community at Daitoku-ji.

Yin-yüan eventually chose a plot of land to the southeast of Kyoto, in the hills of Yamashiro province, known for the excellent tea grown in the region. The land was situated in the Owada district within the small city of Uji. It belonged to the Konoe family, members of the imperial *(kuge)* class. The Konoe had controlled the land since the Heian period, and their rights to it had been confirmed by Oda Nobunaga, Toyotomi Hideyoshi, and the Tokugawa shogunate. Although it is not at all clear whether or not the Konoe family or the imperial court had any involvement in the choice of land, much was later made of the imperial connection. Emperor Gomizunoo's mother resided at an imperial retreat on these grounds, and it was said that she voluntarily withdrew as an expression of her personal support for the founding of Mampuku-ji. In any event, when the bakufu exercised its right to transfer the ownership of the land to the temple, the Konoe family was duly compensated with a deed to land in the Settsu province taken from the bakufu's holdings. The land transfer involved a parcel in Uji valued at a total of 1,400 *koku* of rice annually. From this parcel, Mampuku-ji received a portion valued at 400 *koku* (approximately 72 cubic meters or 2,048 bushels), while the bakufu retained the balance. The official red seal certificate granting the land to Mampuku-ji, dated 7/11/1665, deeded an area of 90,000 *tsubo* of land (approximately 8,900 hectares or 22,000 acres) to the temple and included a yearly stipend of 400 *koku* of rice (theoretically, enough to support four hundred people for one year).[25]

Building began in the fifth month of 1661, and the dedication ceremonies were held in the first month of 1663. Yin-yüan and his disciples actually took up residence in the autumn of 1661 in order to oversee the work, long before the opening ceremonies. Construction continued steadily for about eighteen years, with the bulk of it taking place under the guidance of the second abbot, Mu-an.[26] The monastery received financial support for the project from both government and private sources. The shogun personally donated 20,000 *ryō* of silver and 450 teak trees, and provided the services of his own administrator of construction, Aoki Shigekane (1606–1682), and the Akishino carpenter clan.[27] Sakai Tadakatsu willed the temple 1,000 *ryō* for the construction at his death in 1662.[28]

From the beginning, Yin-yüan intended to model the temple, in the layout of the buildings and grounds and in its administration, on his home temple in China, Huang-po Wan-fu-ssu. He symbolized this by giving the new temple the same mountain and temple names, pronounced in Japanese Obaku-san Mampuku-ji.[29] In nearly all respects, Mampuku-ji was built as a Ming-style temple. Yin-yüan and his successors commissioned Chinese artisans to carve the images found throughout the temple buildings. He and his fellow monks contributed their skills as calligraphers and painters, and samples of their work can be seen on the temple sign boards and adorning the walls.[30] Yin-yüan produced his own version of the monastic code for the governance of life and practice at Mampuku-ji to ensure that the Ming tradition would survive after his passing. Particularly crucial was the code's explicit stipulation that all future abbots be Chinese.

For Yin-yüan and the Japanese monks who sponsored him from the time of his arrival in 1654, the foundation of Obaku-san Mampuku-ji may have seemed the culmination and fulfillment of years of labor. Yin-yüan and other Chinese masters who joined him in Japan now had a proper headquarters from which to propagate their teachings. Japanese monks and laypersons could visit the monastery and feel that they were entering a Chinese enclave, one in which Zen ritual and meditative practice retained a distinctly Chinese flavor. From the perspective of establishing Obaku as a viable new sect in the world of Japanese Buddhism, however, the founding of Mampuku-ji was only the first step.

Even if one accepts the founding of Obaku-san Mampuku-ji as the institutional beginning of the Obaku sect in Japan, the new movement still faced many challenges before it could attain stability and acceptance. In 1663, Obaku possessed only a minimal network of temples and had recruited only a few permanent Japanese converts. Besides the new headquarters at Mampuku-ji, the permanent network of Obaku temples included only the three Chinese monasteries in Nagasaki. Most of the Japanese monks who joined Obaku assemblies did so for brief periods of time, only to return to their home Rinzai or Sōtō temples. Over the decades that followed, Obaku experienced remarkable growth. By 1745, for example, Obaku could claim some 1,043 temples in fifty-one provinces throughout the country on its official roster of main and branch temples.[31] The Chinese founders and the first generation of Japanese converts together laid a firm foundation for the movement and began the process of extending it beyond the confines of Mampuku-ji.

FIVE

The Chinese Founders

Yin-yüan Lung-ch'i has rightly received a prominent place in the history of Obaku Zen as the founder of the sect. In this study, however, the founding generation will be extended to include Mu-an and Chi-fei, two of Yin-yüan's Chinese disciples who acted as key figures in the successful establishment of the Obaku movement in Japan. Both Mu-an and Chi-fei came to Japan at Yin-yüan's behest, in order to assist him in his endeavors in the new and foreign environment. Although neither of these younger monks equaled Yin-yüan in stature when they first arrived, they nonetheless already qualified to serve as Zen masters in their own right, and their reputations continued to grow in Japan. Mu-an and Chi-fei were, in fact, the only other Chinese emigré monks affiliated with the Obaku movement who came to Japan already designated as Dharma heirs.[1] Other Chinese disciples who contributed to the early development of Obaku and might otherwise be counted in the founding generation have been excluded because they completed their training in Japan after the establishment of Obaku-san Mampuku-ji.

Representing different generations in terms of lineage and chronological age, Yin-yüan, Mu-an, and Chi-fei played somewhat different roles in the drama. As the most prominent Chinese Obaku master to emigrate to Japan, Yin-yüan served as the charismatic center of the new movement. Through his teaching and his reputation (and assistance from his prominent Japanese sponsors), he gave shape to the central core of the new sect. As Yin-yüan's immediate successor, Mu-an oversaw the institutional development of the movement, guiding Obaku through its most crucial period of growth and stabilization. Yin-yüan and Mu-an can be juxtaposed as embodiments of the development from the charismatic beginnings of the movement to the institutionalization of Obaku as a sect. The third member of the founding generation of Chinese masters, Chi-fei, did not choose to assume an official leadership role at Mampuku-ji. Nevertheless, his charismatic teaching style drew significant support to the sect, and his Dharma heirs and grandchildren represent some of the most important lines within the overall lineage. Chi-fei left a deep mark on the Obaku sect out of all proportion to the shortness of his career. The following sections will describe the contributions of the three founders in terms of the physical and material growth of the movement and the training of disciples, especially Dharma heirs who carried on the work of the new sect.

Yin-yüan Lung-ch'i (1592–1673)

Yin-yüan's contribution to the initial establishment, recounted in detail in the previous chapter, need not be repeated here. His reputation and writings inspired many interested Japanese to investigate the Obaku movement. The vast majority of Japanese laypersons and Buddhist clergy who visited Obaku temples in the early years of the movement came specifically to see Yin-yüan. A relatively small number of Japanese were drawn by his teachings, which had circulated in the Zen community. Most of the others were likely attracted by Yin-yüan's prominence as a high-ranking Chinese master, what one might call the charisma of office. Although only a small percentage of those individuals who came into contact with Obaku stayed on to become permanent converts to the community, Yin-yüan was successful in retaining a core group of Japanese followers who became the foundation for later growth. Indeed, Yin-yüan's success in impressing prominent Japanese Zen monks and members of the governing class led directly to the founding of Obaku-san Mampuku-ji. As founder of the large main monastery, Yin-yüan established the physical heart of the Obaku sect. In addition to the main monastery, the *Kinsei Obakushū matsujichō shūsei* credits Yin-yüan with founding fifteen other Obaku temples in Japan.[2] The exact number of temples founded by Yin-yüan, or by any other Obaku monk, cannot be accurately determined by the lists provided in the *Kinsei Obakushū matsujichō shūsei*. It was common practice for monks to designate their master as founding abbot *(kaizan)* when they assumed the position as first head monk or abbot. Lists may, for example, designate Mu-an as the founder of some temples that were in fact built by patrons of Tetsugyū, Chōon, or another of his disciples.

Yin-yüan's immediate Dharma heirs quite naturally represent a significant segment of the early core leadership of the Obaku sect. The second, third, and fourth abbots at Mampuku-ji emerged from that group. Throughout his career, Yin-yüan designated a total of twenty-three Dharma heirs, of whom twenty were Chinese nationals and the remaining three Japanese. Among the Chinese heirs, Yin-yüan recognized fifteen disciples while still in China before he departed in 1654. Thirteen of these monks never visited Japan, although they did in some cases send disciples there. (This number includes Yeh-lan, who died attempting to cross over to Japan.) A number of younger Chinese disciples from Wan-fu-ssu accompanied Yin-yüan to Japan, and perhaps ten to twenty of the original group remained there permanently. In the years following the founding of Mampuku-ji, five of these disciples became Yin-yüan's heirs. Yin-yüan's Japanese Dharma heirs included Ryōkei Shōsen (1602–1670), Dokushō Shōen (1617–1694), and Dokuhon Shōgen (1618–1689), all prominent members of the Rinzai community who were able to assist Yin-yüan in building the Obaku sect.[3]

Already advanced in age at the time of his arrival in Nagasaki, Yin-yüan soon passed the mantle of leadership to his leading disciples after the opening of Mampuku-ji. In 1664, only a year after the dedication ceremony, Yin-yüan retired in favor of Mu-an, his senior disciple in Japan. By that time, Yin-yüan was seventy-four years old, and certain duties of the office had become too strenuous for him. In particular, the abbot of Mampuku-ji, as head of the Obaku sect, was required to travel regularly to Edo to fulfill his obligations to the shogun and other bakufu officials. Never eager to travel long distances, Yin-yüan happily entered into the quiet of retirement at Shōin-dō, a small subtemple within the Mampuku-ji complex.

Throughout his decade of retirement, Yin-yüan remained directly involved in the general affairs of the monastery. He continued in his role as primary formulator of the monastic code, composing many of the texts found in the *Obaku shingi* during this period. The rigors of everyday management and institution building, however, fell to younger men. His senior disciple, Mu-an, arrived in Japan in 1655 at the age of forty-four, in the prime of his life and poised to begin his career as a Zen master.

Mu-an Hsing-t'ao (1611–1684)

Mu-an received Yin-yüan's *inka* while still in China in 1650 and came to Japan at Yin-yüan's request in 1655. In Nagasaki, he served the Chinese expatriate community for several years, awaiting permission to travel freely in Japan. In 1660, he joined his master at Fumon-ji and from that time on was able to participate in all the plans for building Mampuku-ji. When Mu-an assumed the office of second abbot at Mampuku-ji from Yin-yüan, he thereby acquired formal authority as the leader of the Obaku sect as a whole. In this capacity, Mu-an carried out the more strenuous tasks of overseeing the institutional construction of the new sect and assumed responsibility for dealing with bakufu officials. Under his guidance, both the physical and the human structures of the sect were stabilized and greatly extended. On several occasions Mu-an visited Edo when summoned by the shogun and also established the sect's headquarters in the capital.

During his tenure as abbot, Mu-an directed the ongoing construction projects at Mampuku-ji from 1664 until their completion in 1679. When he assumed leadership, Mampuku-ji comprised only the bare bones of a functioning monastery. At that time, only six temple buildings stood completed: the Dharma Hall (Hōdō), the Eastern and Western Residence Halls (Tōzai no hōjō), the meditation hall (Zendō), the kitchen *(chūdō)* and the bathhouse *(yokudō)*. Mu-an received a donation of 20,000 *ryō* of gold and a shipment of teak from the shogun Ietsuna in 1667. With this support he constructed several new buildings, including the Shakyamuni Treasure Hall (Daiyūhōden), the Guardian Kings Hall (Tennōden), the dining hall (Saidō), the bell tower *(shōrō)* and the drum tower *(korō)*. In addition to his work at the main monastery, Mu-an also founded a number of temples throughout the country, primarily as a result of his dealings with high-ranking bakufu officials and other samurai. The *Kinsei Obakushū matsujichō shūsei* credits him with founding some twenty-four Obaku temples. Among these, the most important for the sect as a whole was Zuishō-ji, which became Obaku's headquarters in Edo.

In 1674, Mu-an held Obaku's eight-day ordination ritual *(sandan kaie)* at Zuishō-ji.[4] This established the temple as the only site outside of the ordination platform *(kaidan)* at Mampuku-ji for full ordination into the Obaku order. In addition to conferring full ordination on monks and nuns at these large precept ceremonies, Obaku masters made use of these elaborate ritual occasions to spread Obaku's teachings to large numbers of laypersons. By holding the ceremony in Edo, Mu-an extended Obaku's outreach to the capital's high population, most of whom would never have an opportunity to participate in the ordination ceremony in Uji. The massive crowd who attended the first *sandan kaie* in Edo no doubt included large numbers of samurai, individuals who could potentially render support to the new sect. Mu-an's biography claims that three thousand participants received the Bodhisattva precepts on that occasion, and an astounding five thousand people received Dharma names at Zuishō-ji![5]

Mu-an contributed to the human growth of the Obaku institution in other ways as well; his Dharma heirs alone constitute a significant legacy to the sect's future. While Obaku sources emphasize Mu-an's role in building up the physical resources of the sect,[6] his Dharma heirs arguably represent his largest contribution to securing the institutional base for the Obaku movement. Mu-an designated forty-six heirs, including forty-three Japanese and Japanese-born monks.[7] The descendents of these individuals represent eleven of the twenty-three major sublines of transmission within the sect. Within the overarching Obaku lineage *(shū)*, there are eleven major lines *(ha)* of transmission and twenty-three sublines *(ge)*.[8] Ten of the eleven *ha* were founded by Yin-yüan's immediate Dharma heirs; the eleventh was founded by Kao-ch'üan. Mu-an himself founded two of the eleven, namely the Manju-ha and the Shiun-ha. Eleven of his Dharma heirs are regarded as the founders of sublines.[9]

In evaluating the circumstances that contributed to Mu-an's prolific career as a Dharma master, the length of his career and his position relative to Yin-yüan seem to be the most significant factors. In the first place, Mu-an served as abbot of Mampuku-ji for seventeen years, much longer than any of the other early abbots. During that time, he assumed primary responsibility for the majority of the monks practicing at the main monastery. In addition, Yin-yüan began to entrust many of his own students, especially the Japanese disciples, to the younger man's care as early as 1655. For this reason, Mu-an had a large pool of disciples, a group that would probably have included many of the more talented converts to the new movement. While the sheer number of Mu-an's Dharma heirs has led some members of the Zen community to question his abilities as a master,[10] it bears witness to the significant role that Mu-an played as institution builder.

Despite Yin-yüan's appeal as a Zen master, he retained primary responsibility for the training of only a small minority of the Japanese converts who joined the Obaku assembly. Though the majority entered the community hoping to practice directly with Yin-yüan, only a few worked with him for an extended period of time. Beginning in 1655 at the time of Yin-yüan's departure from Nagasaki for Settsu, Mu-an began to assume responsibility for the training of the majority of Yin-yüan's Japanese disciples. This pattern of delegating responsibility to the younger master continued after the founding of the main monastery, especially once Mu-an inherited the position as abbot. As a result, Yin-yüan ultimately recognized only three Japanese Dharma heirs, a mere fraction of Mu-an's forty-three. In all, at least eighteen of Mu-an's Japanese heirs met with, and in most cases practiced under, Yin-yüan before coming under Mu-an's guidance. This means that nearly half of Mu-an's Dharma heirs originally practiced with Yin-yüan.

A careful analysis of the biographical data for Yin-yüan's and Mu-an's respective Dharma heirs reveals that a distinct pattern in the training responsibility for Japanese disciples developed based on the age and seniority of the Japanese disciples at the time they entered the Obaku community. While the data do not provide adequate evidence to argue that this pattern necessarily represents a conscious decision implemented by the founders, they do present clear distinctions between the two groups of heirs. It would seem that Yin-yüan retained the chronologically older and institutionally more senior converts, whereas Mu-an took on the younger and less prominent men.

Among Yin-yüan's three Japanese heirs, the average age at which they first came into contact with the Obaku community was forty-three, a full sixteen years older than the average age of twenty-seven seen in Mu-an's group. This latter figure is based on twenty-two cases for whom age at first contact can be determined. Biographical data is not available for all forty-three of Mu-an's heirs. In addition, all three of Yin-yüan's heirs had achieved a relatively high level of prominence before joining Obaku. For this reason, they were able to be of service to Yin-yüan during the initial period of the movement's formation. Two of the three had previously received *inka* from another Zen master and had inherited temple holdings, which they could bring to Obaku. Very few of Mu-an's heirs had attained comparable levels of achievement, and none had previously received *inka*. It should be noted that this pattern of distribution effectively preserved the natural distinctions of chronological generations within the framework of monastic generations. In other words, older monks of the same chronological age and generation as Mu-an and Chi-fei remained disciples of Yin-yüan and eventually assumed their place in the Obaku lineage as Mu-an and Chi-fei's Dharma brothers. Younger converts became Mu-an's heirs, and thus Yin-yüan's Dharma grandchildren.

Chi-fei Ju-i (1616–1671)

Chi-fei arrived in Japan in 1657, at the age of forty-two. Although he never played a formal leadership role within the Obaku institution comparable to that of Mu-an, he did contribute to the quality of the movement through his influence as a Zen teacher and through the productivity of his Dharma heirs. Chi-fei recognized only five Dharma heirs during his fifteen years in Japan, but many more Japanese disciples came to him to practice under his guidance. Indeed, of the three founding Chinese masters, Chi-fei enjoyed the highest reputation for skill in directing students. Numerous leading Japanese Obaku converts such as Tetsugyū, Egoku, Etsuden, and Tetsugen passed at least one seasonal retreat in his assembly.

As seen in sectarian biographies and stories recounting the early years of the Obaku movement, Chi-fei and Mu-an apparently represented quite different styles of Zen leadership. Not only did Mu-an assume the more formal role as abbot who directed the institutional growth and stability of the sect, he appears in the texts as a relatively serious and formal presence in the ritual life of the community. Chi-fei, on the other hand, suggests something of the freedom and spontaneity associated with the Ch'an masters of the classical period. The following anecdote illustrates this distinction.

> On one occasion at Obaku-san [Mampuku-ji], they held the consecration service *(kaigen)* for the images of the sixteen arhats. That day, the images were divided into two sections, one set to the east and the other to the west. Zen Master Mu-an and Zen Master Chi-fei were conducting the consecration ceremony of the images. Mu-an was a stern but gentle person. One by one he opened the [arhats'] eyes, politely offering incense, bowing and reciting the Dharma words. Chi-fei, however, without offering incense, without bowing, and certainly without reciting the Dharma words, abruptly raised an iron fist and *bang bang* struck each image right between the eyes, saying, "This monk's eyes are already open." [11]

Like Ch'an masters of old, Chi-fei is said to have once publicly and dramatically destroyed examples of his calligraphy in order to demonstrate graphically that words cannot convey the Dharma. [12]

Unlike Yin-yüan and Mu-an, Chi-fei did not decide to remain permanently in Japan, although circumstances prevented his return to China. His original purpose for making the journey appears to have been to honor Yin-yüan's request that he come. Once in Japan, he was determined to stay until he could visit with his master. When Chi-fei first arrived in Nagasaki, Yin-yüan was already in residence at Fumon-ji in Settsu. As Chi-fei did not have permission to travel freely, he was unable to complete his objective for several years. In the meantime, he took up the position as abbot at Sōfuku-ji, serving the expatriate community in that capacity for six years. During that time, Chi-fei grew increasingly concerned that Yin-yüan was being held in Japan against his will. Despite Yin-yüan's letters to the community in China assuring them of his eventual return, the date was set forward on a number of occasions. Chi-fei planned to speak directly with Yin-yüan to ascertain the constraints of the situation. He would then accompany the master home to China, if that were his actual preference.

Chi-fei finally received government permission to travel in the eighth lunar month of 1663. He sailed to Uji and joined Yin-yüan at the newly dedicated Mampuku-ji later the same year. Relieved that his master was not in fact being held hostage, Chi-fei decided to return to China alone. He first spent some time touring the Kyoto and Nara area and then passed a summer retreat at Mampuku-ji. In the autumn Chi-fei set sail for Nagasaki, where he would seek a passage home.

Chi-fei never sailed for China. On his journey back to Kyūshū various events delayed his plans. First, he gained the patronage of the local daimyo, Lord Ogasawara, whose permission he required in order to leave the country. Chi-fei and Ogasawara had previously become acquainted when they were both touring Kyoto. At that time Ogasawara became Chi-fei's lay disciple. Pleased at the opportunity to renew the relationship, Ogasawara only reluctantly granted Chi-fei permission to depart. He extended an invitation that Chi-fei postpone his journey home and serve for a time as the founding abbot at a new temple, Fukuju-ji in Kokura. Chi-fei remained in residence at Fukuju-ji for three years, until after his patron's death. He then resumed his original journey to Nagasaki in 1668.

In Nagasaki, Chi-fei once again took up residence at Sōfuku-ji, although this time he did not plan to stay for long. Ill health and the demands of his disciples and the local community once again delayed his journey. While Chi-fei had not expected to gather an assembly and resume his former role as Zen master at the monastery, he was soon overwhelmed with requests that he do so. Out of consideration for his disciples, he agreed to postpone his plans for a year or two. In the autumn of 1670, Chi-fei took ill, never fully to recover. He passed his final years at Sōfuku-ji, dying at the age of fifty-six.

Other Prominent Chinese Masters

When Mu-an retired as abbot at Mampuku-ji in 1680, he appointed another of Yin-yüan's Dharma heirs, Hui-lin Hsing-chi (1609–1681; J. Erin Shōki), as his successor. As determined by Yin-yüan in the *Obaku shingi*, leadership would pass from one immediate Dharma heir to the next, in order of seniority, before moving on to the next generation of Dharma grandchildren. Seniority was based upon the date of formal recognition as a Dharma heir. With Chi-fei already deceased, Hui-lin ranked as the next Chinese monk in order of seniority. Hui-lin had originally accompanied Yin-yüan to Nagasaki and from there moved on with him to Fumon-ji and to Mampuku-ji. Among the more mature monks in the entourage, Hui-lin served as one of Yin-yüan's senior assistants. He received Yin-yüan's *inka* in 1661, the first Dharma heir to be designated in Japan. Hui-lin was already old and ailing when he assumed the position of abbot, and he served less than one year. His short tenure did not allow him time to make a significant mark on the temple. He designated only six Dharma heirs, all of them Japanese. He is recognized by the sect as the founder of the Ryūkō subline.

In due course, Hui-lin recommended Tu-chan Hsing-jung (1628–1706; J. Dokutan Shōkei) to succeed him. Tu-chan had likewise accompanied Yin-yüan to Nagasaki at the age of twenty-seven and remained with him throughout the years at Fumon-ji and Mampuku-ji. According to Kyorei, Tu-chan was among the more promising of the younger Chinese monks. Although he presents a somewhat controversial figure in the sectarian view, Tu-chan did contribute to the spread of Obaku in Japan, and his influence was probably more extensive than Obaku scholars currently acknowledge.

Tu-chan received *inka* from Yin-yüan in 1664 and went on to recognize some thirty-nine Dharma heirs of his own. The vast majority of Tu-chan's disciples were Japanese, and he recognized thirty-eight Japanese monks as heirs. While only one Dharma heir, Yüeh-feng Tao-chang (1655–1734; J. Eppō Dōshō), was Chinese, several subsequent abbots were Tu-chan's descendents through this line. This suggests that Tu-chan had a more lasting influence on the sect than

Obaku sources recognize. He is officially acknowledged as the founder of the Shishirin line, and three of his disciples founded sublines. Tu-chan served as abbot at Mampuku-ji for ten years, from 1682 until 1692. He is credited with founding nineteen Obaku temples.

Tu-chan does not receive much acknowledgment in sectarian sources for his contributions to the Obaku sect because of his controversial teaching style and his unsuccessful involvement in an intrasectarian dispute. Tu-chan became popularly known in his day as "Nembutsu Dokutan," apparently because he advocated a style of *nembutsu* practice more in keeping with Japanese Pure Land sects than with the Zen style of Yin-yüan and the other Obaku masters. Modern Obaku scholars stress that Tu-chan represents an exception in this regard, not the norm. For this reason, they regard his years as abbot as a period of decline for the temple.[13] Tu-chan was eventually forced to retire as abbot after losing a dispute with Kao-ch'üan Hsing-tung (1633–1695; J. Kōsen Shōton) that centered around the naming of posthumous Dharma heirs for Ryōkei.[14] The bakufu became involved in the affair and settled it in favor of Kao-ch'üan, who then succeeded Tu-chan as the fifth abbot.

Kao-ch'üan came to Japan from Wan-fu-ssu in 1661. As a young monk, he served as an attendant to Yin-yüan in China. After Yin-yüan departed, he practiced under Yin-yüan's successor at Wan-fu-ssu, Hui-men Ju-p'ei (1615–1664). He was eventually designated Hui-men's Dharma heir in 1661, making him Yin-yüan's Dharma grandchild. Hui-men commissioned Kao-ch'üan to travel to Japan and convey to Yin-yüan good wishes for his seventieth birthday from all monks at the home monastery in China. The real purpose of the visit seems to have been for him to escort Yin-yüan home to China. Despite his mission, Kao-ch'üan too decided to remain permanently in Japan. He took up residence at Mampuku-ji and became one of Yin-yüan's closest assistants in his last years. Kao-ch'üan served as abbot at Mampuku-ji for only four years, but he had a lasting influence on Obaku Zen.

Kao-ch'üan designated sixteen Dharma heirs and became the founder of one of the eleven primary Obaku lines, the Bukkoku-ha. In this regard, Kao-ch'üan stands out as the only founder of a primary line who was not a direct Dharma heir of Yin-yüan. He wrote extensively and was highly regarded for the quality of his prose. He was often asked to write introductions and postscripts for editions of recorded sayings by other monks, and Yin-yüan had him compose a number of pieces. His writings include a reworking of Yin-yüan's monastic code, the *Obaku shingi,* into its present form, a series of biographies of the Chinese Obaku masters who had come to Japan, and even a biography of famous Japanese monks.[15]

Kao-ch'üan was the last of the fully qualified Ch'an masters to come over from China. After his death, the Obaku sect continued to select Chinese monks to serve as abbot at Mampuku-ji for several generations, but they left behind little more than their names. In most cases, the later abbots were brought over to Japan as young monks and trained at one of the Chinese temples in Nagasaki and at Mampuku-ji. The bakufu cooperated with sect officials in making the arrangements for travel papers and the like. It gradually became more difficult to find qualified Chinese candidates, and the century-old practice came to a close late in the eighteenth century. Since the death of the twenty-first abbot in 1784, all of the abbots at Mampuku-ji have been Japanese.

Even in the first few decades of Obaku's development in Japan, however, it is not enough to concentrate exclusively on the Chinese founders of the sect. Without the cooperation and hard work of their Japanese disciples the Obaku sect would not have emerged. To complete the picture of the first decades of growth and development, one must turn to the first generation of Japanese Obaku masters such as Ryōkei, Tetsugyū, and Chōon to understand Obaku's vitality and its successful integration into the world of Japanese Buddhism.

SIX

Japanese Converts

In drawing a general portrait of the first generation of Japanese Obaku converts, the first step is to define the group to be so designated. One standard approach would be to include all individuals who became associated with the Obaku movement within a specified period of time. Unfortunately, this ideal presents far too many practical difficulties in terms of available data to be a viable possibility. This study concentrates instead on a more limited target group: those Japanese disciples who received formal recognition of enlightenment (*inka*) from one of the three founding Chinese masters, Yin-yüan, Mu-an, or Chi-fei. Reasons for limiting the study to this group include: (1) considerations of overall impact on the success of the Obaku sect; (2) date of entry into the Obaku monastic community; and (3) availability of relevant and reliable biographical data.

All of the names of the individuals included in the study appear in the *Obakushū kanroku,* a text of two fascicles originally written by Kao-ch'üan to be an official lineage chart for the Obaku sect. Kao-ch'üan began the record in 1692 and the text was first published in 1693. Kōdō Genchō (1663–1733) compiled the next major segment of the text in 1726. Later editions updating the lineage appeared in 1790, 1917, and 1936. The text traces the Obaku lineage back to the seven so-called historical Buddhas, the twenty-eight Indian Patriarchs, and the six Chinese Patriarchs. It continues tracing the background Rinzai lineage from the Sixth Patriarch through Lin-chi and down to the founder, Yin-yüan, who is regarded as thirty-second generation after Lin-chi. Yin-yüan simultaneously represents the first generation of the Obaku lineage in Japan, serving as the pivotal figure in the transition from Rinzai to the Obaku sect proper. The first fascicle covers the Obaku lineage from the time of Yin-yüan through the Bunsei era

(1818–1830). The second fascicle continues mapping the lineage through 1887. Although the *Obakushū kanroku* is not exhaustive,[1] it does serve as an official catalogue of the Obaku sect's Dharma lineage and is the most complete listing of Dharma heirs in the Obaku sect. The relevant list of Japanese converts drawn from the *Kanroku* comprises a total of forty-nine names, including three disciples of Yin-yüan, forty-three of Mu-an, and three of Chi-fei. It should be noted that all these individuals were monks, although not all of them were ordained when they first became associated with Obaku.

The Japanese Dharma heirs represent an elite subgroup within the Obaku ranks of monastic and lay followers. These monks had the institutional status necessary to serve as abbot or head monk at Obaku temples, to accept disciples of their own, and to designate Dharma heirs who would carry on the tradition. No doubt they enjoyed greater prestige among lay supporters because of their close association with the founding Chinese masters. In terms of human and economic factors, these individuals contributed more to the growth of Obaku in the early years than any other group within the Obaku community. They broadened the appeal of Obaku to a wider audience of Japanese, thus attracting lay patrons and supporters who strengthened the financial basis. They brought to the order monks and nuns who formed the human capital of the sect. Their activity accounts for a large percentage of the temples the fledgling sect acquired in the early decades, some newly founded and others drawn in from other sects.

Nearly all of the Japanese Dharma heirs of the founding generation of Chinese masters became associated with Obaku very early in the movement's history. When looking at the dates of entry into the Obaku community, one finds that the vast majority initiated contact with a Chinese master before the founding of Mampuku-ji in 1663. Nearly 80 percent practiced at one of the Chinese temples in Nagasaki under Yin-yüan or Mu-an, or joined Yin-yüan's assembly in Tonda.[2] Japanese who entered the group after the founding of Mampuku-ji may have had some opportunity to practice under the founding generation for a short period of time, but they typically received *inka* from subsequent Chinese abbots. While there would be some justification to define this later group of Japanese as first-generation converts, for practical purposes (primarily related to availability of data) they are not included in the present study.

In most cases, one may anticipate that a certain amount of biographical information regarding recognized Zen masters will be preserved. The Zen school maintains a lively interest in those individuals regarded as authentic transmitters of the Dharma, as evidenced by the familiar genre of biographical compendia, often relating the life stories of masters within a specific Zen sect or lineage. After a prominent monk's death, it is common practice for a leading disciple to compile the master's written works and sermons and to compose a brief biography. It is not surprising, then, that biographical information is available for thirty-five of the forty-nine first-generation Japanese Obaku monks included in this study. Only three of these thirty-five monks died without designating at least one Dharma heir. In sharp contrast, of the fourteen monks for whom we lack significant biographical data, seven apparently died without any heir at all. The only data available for these fourteen individuals, all Dharma heirs of Mu-an, are their Dharma names, the date on which *inka* was conferred, and any subsequent Dharma heirs they recognized.

Were access to reliable data not a problem, inclusion of a much broader group of Japanese Obaku disciples and sympathizers would be desirable. Ideally, the first generation would be extended to include all of the Japanese disciples who approached the Chinese founders for guidance, male and female, lay and ordained, as well as supporters who provided financial assistance to the Obaku monastic community. Such a project, a standard feature in studies of contemporary NRMs, cannot be undertaken for the Obaku sect in Tokugawa Japan. With the exception of the formally acknowledged Dharma heirs and a few prominent lay supporters of the founding Chinese masters, little information can be found.

Of special interest in this regard would be a study of those who converted to Obaku for a period of time and later exited. In studying new religious movements, alienated members, sometimes referred to as apostates, often provide extensive information on the group's beliefs and practices based on their personal experience. Although this information cannot be taken at face value, given the biases often associated with leaving a religious group, it nevertheless can provide alternative perspectives to sectarian literature. In the case of Obaku, an accurate listing of apostate members cannot be constructed. An account of Obaku's early history based on the knowledge of one prominent apostate, Jikuin Somon, however, is available secondhand in the *Obaku geki*. That material will be the topic of extensive analysis in Chapter 9.

Temple records include the names of other monks who practiced within various Obaku assemblies and were appointed to various monastic offices. A list of these monks would include at least two categories of individuals: the less prominent Obaku disciples who remained within the ranks but never attained status as Dharma heirs and visiting clergy who stayed temporarily and then returned to their home temples. One may also assume the existence of still other disciples whose names are completely lost. Local records, for example, provide tantalizing hints about individual nuns who took up residence in small meditation retreats outside the bounds of various Obaku temples.

Creating a listing of lay Obaku disciples and supporters poses more serious complications. The names of prominent laypersons who visited the Chinese founders or who requested their instruction often appear in the masters' published writings (J. *goroku*) and biographies (J. *nempu*). It would not be reasonable, however, to regard all such individuals as lay disciples or even supporters. The encounters with the Chinese monks were often social calls fulfilling little more than the social requirements of etiquette, or perhaps sating the curiosity of individual Japanese. As often as not, no lasting relationship was established by these meetings. In the case of other, less prominent laypersons, no historical record may survive at all. In particular, accurate estimates of the numbers of lay disciples and supporters from the commoner classes cannot be undertaken.

The majority of the biographical material upon which the following general characterization of the first generation of Japanese Obaku converts is based was drawn from the individual listings found in the *Obaku bunka jinmei jiten*. This dictionary of early Obaku monks and supporters represents a basic resource in the field. Its authors, Obaku scholars Otsuki Mikio, Katō Shōshun, and Hayashi Yukimitsu, bring together information gleaned from a wide variety of source materials, including some rare sectarian texts, such as the biographies and recorded sayings of lesser-known Obaku monks, as well as material drawn from more readily available primary and secondary texts. In certain cases, particularly for Ryōkei Shōsen, Tetsugen Dōkō, Chōon Dōkai, Tetsugyū Dōki, Egoku Dōmyō, and Hōshū Dōsō, additional source materials were used to supplement the information available in the dictionary.

The biographical material preserved for each of the thirty-five monks is not completely consistent in regard to the amount of data available. More prominent masters quite naturally received more attention in Tokugawa sources and in later secondary research. Consequently, the data are skewed in their direction. In compiling statistics related to social class, age at entry, age at *inka,* and so on, the number of monks falling under the rubric "unknown" or "uncertain" ranges from the minimum of fourteen (the number for whom no data exists) to twenty-three, depending on the category.

General Portrait

Based on an analysis of biographical information including family names, the breakdown by social class of the first generation of Japanese converts shows that the vast majority of the Obaku study group, 80 percent of the known cases, came from the upper classes (samurai and *kuge*). Although statistics are not readily available for other Buddhist groups, this pattern of monastic membership likely parallels that found in other Zen monastic communities in Japan of the day. The Japanese upper classes enjoyed greater access than other segments of the population to wealth and education, both necessary prerequisites for a successful career as a Zen monk. The monastic practice of Zen traditionally includes extensive study of texts written in classical Chinese. For this reason, entry into the monastery, a theoretical possibility for anyone requesting ordination, was in actuality a practical possibility only for the educated minority. Although literacy rates did rise among all social classes throughout the Tokugawa period, one may assume relatively low levels of literacy among the commoner classes during the period under question, the latter half of the seventeenth century. In the case of the early Obaku community, fluency in reading and writing Chinese would have been even more essential, since communication between Japanese disciples and Chinese masters initially hinged on written skills in Chinese shared by the two cultural groups.

Among the thirty-five first-generation Japanese Obaku monks whose biographies are available, something is known of the family history of twenty-five individuals. Within this subgroup, twenty (80 percent) have surnames and family backgrounds clearly indicating roots in either the samurai class or the nobility. Among the remaining 20 percent, all five cases present special circumstances, making their social class ambiguous. Most appear to have come from educated or wealthy families. While some of these individuals may be regarded as commoner class, not surprisingly none came from peasant families in rural villages. Two of the study group were born into clerical families from the True Pure Land tradition. These monks received at least a basic education in their home temples and had participated in formal study of classical Buddhist texts prior to joining the Obaku community.[3] Two other monks were born to Chinese fathers from the expatriate community living in Nagasaki.[4] These two spoke both Chinese and Japanese fluently, effectively bridging the language gap in the early community. In addition, one of the two received a formal education in classical Chinese. In the latter case, insufficient biographical material exists to determine the family's social class, although the monk's paternal family possessed a surname, an indication of either wealth or prestige if not upper-class status.[5]

Certain biographical patterns, such as birth position and the experience of parental loss, occur with sufficient frequency to suggest that these factors contributed to the original decision to enter monastic orders for the first-generation converts. It should be noted that, in the majority of cases, ordination occurred before the first encounter with an Obaku master. For this reason, these factors probably did not contribute to the decision to join the Obaku movement. Several of the monks in the study group were born as second or third sons in a samurai family, a birth position that placed them at a disadvantage in terms of income and secure employment. Most samurai positions and stipends were hereditary, and inheritance typically followed a pattern of primogenitor. Second and third sons as a group could not anticipate inheriting their father's position and generally sought other options for their future.[6] Entering orders represented one viable option within a relatively limited field of socially acceptable possibilities.

Nine of the biographies indicate an early childhood experience of serious emotional trauma or loss. In one case, the family home was destroyed by fire and the entire family turned to the maternal grandparents for support. Eight other monks experienced parental loss in childhood. Such a loss, particularly if it occurs at an early age, may contribute to the decision to enter Buddhist orders for a variety of reasons. Buddhist texts often mention that intense experiences of loss engender a poignant awareness of the transient quality of human life. Such feelings may serve as motivation to leave the secular life and seek the relief promised by Buddhist practice. Economic factors may also play a role, as the death of parents or the loss of the family home may limit the options available to young children. Finally, orphaned children may take the tonsure, whether encouraged to do so by others or not, in order to fulfill the obligations of filial piety. Offering the merit of ordination for one's deceased parents has long been seen as a commendable practice in Buddhist East Asia.

In most cases, the first generation had already taken the tonsure before encountering the Obaku movement. Among the twenty-nine monks for whom previous affiliation can be established, twenty-five (86 percent) were ordained before their first contact with Obaku. The other four came to the group as lay practitioners, receiving their first ordination from an Obaku master. Obaku clearly appealed most directly to members of the existing Zen community, since 79 percent of the known cases were Zen monks at the time of first contact. Of the twenty-three Zen monks who converted to Obaku, seventeen were previously associated with Rinzai Zen, and ten of this number can be definitely identified as coming from the Myōshin-ji line. This means that a full 34 percent of the known cases, lay and ordained, were converts from the Myōshin-ji. Only four of the ordained converts were Sōtō monks. In the remaining two cases, the exact Zen affiliation is unclear. These numbers bear out the argument that Rinzai in general and Myōshin-ji in particular had ample reason to perceive Obaku as a drain on human resources.

An issue closely related to Obaku's drain on the existing Zen communities is the stature of the individuals being drawn away from them. It is quite difficult to establish a meaningful measure of the loss of talent the first generation represented, because perceived loss may exceed any external factors. For the purposes of this study, however, two external factors were singled out for special attention in determining prominence: appointment to a monastic position of high status within a Zen monastery and designation as the head monk or abbot at a smaller branch temple or family temple *(bodaiji)*. Of the study group, seventeen monks had attained some level of prominence based on these two criteria. Two had previously served as abbot at Myōshin-ji, and two others attained the rank of high seat at the same monastery. Eleven monks were clearly not prominent based on these criteria, and the remaining twenty-one monks fall into the category of unknown status.

The above figures suggest that approximately 35 percent of the first-generation converts were prominent members of the Zen monastic community before becoming Obaku monks. More prominent monks represented a more obvious loss to their former community. Some of these individuals would have brought branch temples with them when they converted to Obaku. Virtually all of them received significant lay patronage after their conversion, serving as founding abbots and restorers of numerous temples added to the Obaku roster of affiliated temples. Patronage on this level extends the drain on previous affiliations to include economic and material considerations. Not surprisingly, the more prominent converts came under attack for their decision. Tannen Dōjaku (1629–1679), a former Sōtō monk who had already served as head monk at a Sōtō temple, Chōfuku-ji, came under harsh criticism when he returned his Dharma certificate after accepting Mu-an's *inka*. Etsuden Dōfu, then serving as head seat at Myōshin-ji, made his first contact with Yin-yüan in secret, perhaps to avoid causing overt problems for himself in the already tense environment of the Myōshin-ji community.

More than half of the study group joined the Obaku community while they were still young men in their late teens and twenties. Under most circumstances, individuals in these younger age ranges would not have attained much prominence within the Zen hierarchical structure. From the perspective of the previous affiliations, these younger monks represent more a drain in terms of future potential rather than realized status. In a number of cases, the biographies indicate that previous masters displayed great reluctance to allow their young disciples to make contact with the Obaku masters. For their part, the younger monks who had attained less status were therefore freer to move among Zen communities; they were risking less than their more advanced Dharma brothers in joining a new movement. The high percentage of younger individuals suggests that many of the early Obaku converts came to Obaku in search of something lacking in their home temples. Some came on pilgrimage *(angya),* seeking a teacher with whom they could establish a productive working relationship. Others may have been interested in experiencing a strict style of Zen practice or the exotic thrill of a Chinese environment.

As a whole, the first generation appears to have been first attracted to the Obaku community by the reputation and writings of Yin-yüan. Of the thirty known cases, seventeen of the first-generation monks (57 percent) made their first contact with Yin-yüan himself. Even those who met first with Mu-an or Chi-fei may have been drawn by Yin-yüan's reputation. There are recorded cases of individuals outside the study group who went to Nagasaki in the hope of visiting with Yin-yüan but arrived too late. After Yin-yüan's departure for Settsu in 1655, Japanese did not have free access to meet with him for several years due to government restrictions. During that time period, many Japanese established relations with Yin-yüan's leading Dharma heir, Mu-an. Although none of the biographies explicitly indicates this, it is possible that some members of the study group had a similar experience.

After Yin-yüan, the largest percentage of the study group made their first contact with Mu-an. Six of the thirty known cases, or 20 percent, became Mu-an's disciples without meeting Yin-yüan first. Four others initially practiced Zen under other Obaku leaders, Chi-fei, I-jan, or Tetsugen. Among the study group, three monks (10 percent of the known cases) originally practiced under the Chinese master Tao-che's guidance. All three later became disciples of Mu-an sometime after Tao-che returned to China. Scholars have long recognized Tao-che as a forerunner of the Obaku movement, and the data regarding first contact among the first generation of converts bear this out.

Whatever drew the first generation of converts to Obaku, the individuals in the study group remained inside the Obaku community and attained a significant degree of prominence as the Dharma heirs of the founding generation of Chinese masters. Relevant biographical data is available for the thirty-two individuals regarding age, date of entry, and years of practice leading to recognition as a Dharma heir. These thirty-two monks averaged 14.5 years of practice under the guidance of their respective Dharma masters before receiving *inka*. Although the age at which they received formal recognition varied greatly, ranging from the youngest at twenty-eight to the oldest at sixty-three, the majority received *inka* during their forties. The median age at the time of *inka* for the group of thirty-two known monks is forty-five and a half. The pattern differs significantly, however, when comparing the Dharma heirs of Yin-yüan with those of Mu-an and Chi-fei. Yin-yüan's three Dharma heirs were significantly older on average than the other two subgroups, both in terms of age at first contact and age at *inka*. They ranged in age from fifty-five to sixty-three at the time of *inka*, averaging fifty-eight. As mentioned earlier, Yin-yüan's Japanese heirs represent an elite subgroup of older and more accomplished monks whom Yin-yüan did not pass along to practice under the younger Chinese masters.

Contributions of the First Generation of Japanese Obaku Masters

Certain individuals among the first generation of Obaku converts made outstanding contributions to the growth of Obaku as a movement and to its successful establishment as an independent sect of Zen Buddhism in Japan. Ryōkei Shōsen, the first Japanese heir of Yin-yüan, acted as the prime mover in establishing cordial relations between Yin-yüan and the bakufu and between the Obaku movement and the imperial family. He thus deserves much of the credit for enabling the foundation of the main monastery and providing a much needed resource of prestige. Tetsugyū Dōki, Egoku Dōmyo, and Chōon Dōkai continued in the footsteps of their master, Mu-an, in promoting the institutional growth of the sect. Between them, they founded a vast number of new Obaku temples and designated some 123 Dharma heirs. Tetsugen Dōkō, another disciple of Mu-an, contributed to the reputation and popularity of the Obaku sect through his publication efforts and social welfare work. Tetsugen, with the assistance of many Obaku monks and lay followers, produced the first complete woodblock edition of the Chinese Buddhist scriptures in Japan.

The following sketches discuss the individual contributions made to the growth of Obaku Zen by these five prominent examples of early Japanese converts. Special attention is given to their early careers and the circumstances related to their joining the Obaku movement. These specific examples may provide a sense of the individual concerns suggested in more general terms in the above patterns of affiliation.

Ryōkei Shōsen (1602–1670)

Ryōkei Shōsen was born in 1602 in Kyoto, the second son of Okamura Seiichirō. His father became seriously ill while he was a young child and came close to death. The family credited his recovery to moxa treatments provided by a mendicant Buddhist monk, and they therefore dedicated Ryōkei to the monastic life. He entered Tō-ji, the Shingon headquarters in Kyoto, at age eight, and began his Buddhist education studying Esoteric Buddhism. At age sixteen, he left Tō-ji and took the tonsure under the Zen monk Chūshitsu Genshō at Jiun-san Fumon-ji, a small Rinzai temple in the Tonda area of Settsu province. Ryōkei inherited the temple a few years later when Chūshitsu passed away, and became the fifth head monk at an unusually young age.

Soon after Chūshitsu's death, Ryōkei left his home temple to go on pilgrimage, traveling for many years. During this period he received Dharma transmission from Hakubu Eryō, a master from the Myōshin-ji line. When Hakubu died in 1629, Ryōkei succeeded him as head monk at a subtemple at Ryōan-ji. At about this time he was appointed head seat at Myōshin-ji. Thus, by his late twenties Ryōkei had already attained a position of moderate status within the Rinzai community.

In the autumn of 1651, Ryōkei was appointed abbot at Myōshin-ji and received a purple robe from the emperor. He soon retired from the office, but returned to serve a second time in 1654. It was sometime during the interval that Ryōkei first became familiar with Yin-yüan's teachings through his published works. He was therefore pleased to learn that Yin-yüan had decided to travel to Nagasaki. During Ryōkei's second tenure as abbot at Myōshin-ji, he made plans with a small group of like-minded monks within the assembly and began the long and complicated campaign to invite Yin-yüan to Kyoto. According to the biographical account in the *Obaku bunka jinmei jiten,* Ryōkei promoted Yin-yüan's cause because he still hoped to receive *inka* from a prominent master.

The details of Ryōkei's activities in securing Yin-yüan's place in the Zen community in Japan have been presented in the previous chapter and need not be reiterated here. Although Ryōkei failed to realize his dream of installing Yin-yüan as abbot at Myōshin-ji, he is largely responsible for the course of events that led to the founding of the Obaku sect as an independent institution in Japan. He secured bakufu permission for Yin-yüan to travel freely throughout the country and to remain indefinitely in Japan. Eventually, he acquired permission and funding for Yin-yüan to establish Obaku-san Mampuku-ji, the main monastery of the Obaku sect located in Uji.

In addition to ameliorating relations with the bakufu, Ryōkei likewise secured strong imperial support for the new sect. He instructed the retired emperor Gomizunoo in the teachings of Zen over a number of years. In 1666, he recognized the emperor as his first and only Dharma heir, a topic to be discussed at some length later. Ryōkei himself received *inka* from Yin-yüan in 1664, thus becoming the founder's first Japanese Dharma heir. Shortly thereafter, Gomizunoo appointed him restorer and head monk at Hōrin-san Shōmyō-ji.[7] In 1669, he received a formal transmission robe from Yin-yüan and the honorific title Daishūshōtō Zenji from the retired emperor.

Ryōkei died in Osaka in 1670, under somewhat unusual circumstances. He had received an invitation from lay patrons to give a series of Dharma talks in the eighth lunar month of that year and was staying at Reiki-san Kyūshin-in in Settsu. On August 23, a combination of extremely high tides and heavy rainstorms caused the Kizu and Yasuhara rivers to flood. The temple grounds were engulfed in the flood waters and the buildings destroyed. Although the head monk and several other monks were able to take shelter in time, Ryōkei was trapped inside by the rising water. Unable to save himself, Ryōkei took up a brush and recorded his death poem. The poem was recovered later, preserved in his box.

Tetsugyū Dōki (1628–1712)

Tetsugyū Dōki was born in Nagato province on 7/26/1628. His father's family name was Masuda, and his mother's Nagatomi. A fire left the family destitute when Tetsugyū was only seven. The entire family moved to Tottori Inaba and there took up residence with his mother's natal family. Tetsugyū received a monastic education, starting at age eleven, and took the tonsure at age fifteen. During his late teens he suffered eye problems attributed to his voracious reading of the sutras. He remained partially blind for a period of three years. After recovering his sight, Tetsugyū began to travel on pilgrimage for several years. In the autumn of 1648, he entered the assembly at Myōshin-ji and attended various lectures in Kyoto.

Tetsugyū began to attract some attention from lay patrons as a promising Zen monk even before he entered Myōshin-ji. Between 1648 and 1654, he received several invitations to serve as head monk at smaller temples in the Kyoto-Osaka region. Since he was not yet satisfied with his own spiritual progress, he either declined these offers or quickly resigned the position.

Tetsugyū regarded the opportunity to practice under one of the Chinese Obaku founders as a means of fulfilling his impractical desire to practice Zen in China. His superiors in the Myōshin-ji lineage seem to have regarded him as too promising a candidate to risk losing, and they twice refused him permission to practice under Chinese masters. His first request was rejected in 1654, when he hoped to go to Nagasaki and pay his respects to the newly arrived Yin-yüan. He was later denied permission to enter Mu-an's assembly at Fukusai-ji.

Tetsugyū did eventually reach Nagasaki in 1655, where he took up residence at Zenrin-ji, a Myōshin-ji branch temple. He received some brief instruction from Yin-yüan before the master's departure for Fumon-ji later that year. Frustrated by the second refusal from his superiors denying him permission to practice with Mu-an, Tetsugyū decided to leave Nagasaki and return to the Kyoto area. Lay patrons, including the Nagasaki *bugyō*, interceded on his behalf. He finally gained entry to Mu-an's assembly and soon attracted his favor. He was quickly appointed by Mu-an to serve as *jisha*. He later spent a winter retreat under Chi-fei's guidance at Sōfuku-ji.

Practice under Obaku masters did not initially necessitate that Tetsugyū sever all ties with Myōshin-ji. Before Obaku acquired distinct institutional independence, relations remained ambiguous. In the autumn of 1659, for example, Tetsugyū was appointed head seat at Myōshin-ji. His involvement in the new movement, however, continued to deepen. Throughout this period, Tetsugyū regularly visited the Obaku masters at Fumon-ji and later at Mampuku-ji. He participated in several seasonal retreats and related ritual events. Growing tension between Myōshin-ji and the Obaku movement after the opening of Mampuku-ji may have precipitated Tetsugyū's final decision in 1664. His full entry into the new sect was formalized in the autumn of that year, when he received the precepts from Mu-an, then second abbot of Mampuku-ji, at the second ordination ceremony *(sandan kaie)*.

Mu-an recognized Tetsugyū as his first Dharma heir in 1667, when Tetsugyū was forty years old. During the winter retreat of 1666, Tetsugyū experienced *satori* when hearing the bell announcing the fifth watch at about 6 A.M. He submitted a verse to Mu-an, and Mu-an summoned him to Mampuku-ji for confirmation of the experience. He initially received a *hossu* (ritual whisk) as a symbol of Dharma transmission, and later was granted a formal transmission robe in 1671. On several counts, Tetsugyū can be regarded as Mu-an's leading Dharma heir. His position as the first Dharma heir in chronological terms gave him seniority over the long series of heirs who followed. Mu-an appointed him to serve as the second abbot at Zuishō-ji, the sect's major monastery in Edo, in 1675. In that capacity Tetsugyū had the authority to hold official Obaku ordination services *(sandan kaie)*. When Mu-an died in 1684, Tetsugyū conducted the memorial services and acted as chief mourner.

As the highest-ranking Obaku monk in Edo, Tetsugyū had some dealings with the Tokugawa bakufu. He was summoned to Edo castle by two successive Tokugawa shoguns. In 1676, he had an audience with Ietsuna, and over a period of months from 1694 to 1695 he gave a series of lectures for Tsunayoshi at the Edo castle. In addition, he had extensive relations with other high-ranking samurai. Through their patronage, he founded numerous temples, which helped to extend the financial basis of the new sect. He is listed as the founder or restorer of at least twenty temples in the *Kinsei Obakushū matsujichō shūsei*.

Like his master Mu-an, Tetsugyū contributed to the institutional growth of the Obaku sect in both human and material terms. When he died at age seventy-three in the eighth lunar month of 1700, he had already designated a total of thirty-four Dharma heirs. He is regarded as the founding patriarch of the Chōshō line, one of Obaku's liveliest sublineages.

Egoku Dōmyō (1632–1721)

Egoku Dōmyō was the fifth child of the Oda family, retainers of the daimyo of Nagato province. His mother died when he was a small child, and he was raised by an uncle. At age nine he was sent into monastic life at a small Rinzai temple and took the tonsure at age seventeen. In 1650, Egoku heard that Yeh-lan, Yin-yüan's Dharma heir, was coming to Japan, and he accompanied Jikuin to Nagasaki to greet him. Along the way, Egoku encountered Tao-che at an inn. He followed Tao-che back to Sōfuku-ji and entered his assembly. Egoku spent three years at Sōfuku-ji. According to his biography, he abruptly left the Chinese temple after hearing what he regarded as a slanderous remark: a Chinese merchant commented that Japanese monks enjoyed practicing at Chinese temples because there they did not suffer from constant hunger. Egoku left the temple in a rage and lived the mendicant life for several months in order to disprove the slander. He then returned to Nagasaki and resumed his practice with Tao-che.

Egoku did not make contact with the Obaku founders for many years after Tao-che left, perhaps due to the same discord that had caused his master's departure. According to the tradition, Tao-che instructed his Japanese disciples to seek out the guidance of Yin-yüan as a part of his deathbed request in 1662. Egoku complied in 1663, when he visited Obaku-san Mampuku-ji with a group of some twenty disciples and called on both Yin-yüan and Mu-an. Egoku subsequently received the precepts at the Obaku ordination ceremony in 1665. He spent several retreats at Mampuku-ji, serving in various temple offices. He also practiced under Chi-fei for a time.

Egoku received Mu-an's *inka* in 1671, becoming his second Dharma heir. He received a formal transmission robe in 1674. He founded numerous temples, including his primary temple, Daihō-san Hōun-ji in Kawachi province. The *Obakushū matsujichō shūsei* lists him as founder or restorer of twelve temples. He served as abbot at Zuishō-ji in 1687, the highest Obaku position then open to Japanese monks. In that capacity, he bestowed the precepts on 2,000 people who attended the *sandan kaie* of 1691. He designated a total of forty-two Dharma heirs throughout his long career and is regarded as the founding patriarch of the Shōringe subline. He died in 1721 at the age of ninety.

Chōon Dōkai (1628–1695)

Chōon Dōkai was born on 11/10 of 1628 in Hizen province. His family name was Kusuda. After his mother died when he was five years old, he was raised by his paternal grandmother. He began studying at a local Buddhist temple at age nine, and took the tonsure at thirteen. When he was seventeen, Chōon secretly left his home temple and began to travel. He planned to study Confucianism in Kyoto and at the same time to take full advantage of the many Zen centers in the region. He visited with several well-known Zen masters and attended lectures and sermons. During his time in Kyoto, Chōon first became acquainted with the teachings of the Yüan dynasty master Chun-feng Ming-pen (1263–1323; J. Chūhō Myōhon). Hoping to practice under a descendent of that lineage, he sought out Isshi Monju at Eigan-ji. Much to his disappointment, Chōon arrived after the master's death in 1646. Nevertheless, he took up residence there and practiced for a time with one of Isshi's disciples. According to biographical accounts, this experience initiated Chōon's career as a serious student of Zen meditation. He worked diligently for the next several years, living most of the time in a small hermitage.

In 1654, Chōon returned to his native Kyūshū and entered Tao-che's assembly at Sōfuku-ji. During this period, he also spent a winter retreat at Kōfuku-ji under Yin-yüan, but did not then establish an enduring relationship with the Obaku master. Chōon continued to practice under various masters for several more years, traveling extensively. He did not again approach the Obaku founders until 1661, when he read Fei-yin's *Wu-téng yen-t'ung* (J. *Gotō gentō*). Realizing for the first time that Yin-yüan was actually a descendant of Chun-feng Ming-pen, he made his way to Mampuku-ji, then under construction. Chōon met with Yin-yüan, but was initially denied permission to join the assembly. Through the intercession of his old friend Tu-chan (J. Dokutan), he was eventually admitted.

Chōon received the precepts from Yin-yüan at the first *sandan kaie*, held at Mampuku-ji in 1663. During his first years at Mampuku-ji, he practiced under the guidance of all three of the founding Chinese masters. He served in a number of monastic offices, advancing through the ranks. In 1665, he accompanied Mu-an to Edo for an audience with the shogun. Perhaps it was at that time that he established connections with high-ranking samurai in Edo. He was invited back the following year by lay patrons and soon served as head monk at several small family temples. In 1671, Mu-an commissioned him to oversee the construction of Zuishō-ji, Obaku's main monastery in Edo. When the work was completed, he then served there as *saidō* during the first seasonal retreat.[8] Later the same year, he received Mu-an's *inka*. Over the next several years, Chōon received invitations from numerous high-ranking samurai and served as founding abbot for several new Obaku temples. In all, he is credited with founding twenty-two temples, located predominantly in the provinces of Kōzuke and Shinano.

Chōon's intellectual interests extended beyond Zen Buddhism to include Shinto thought and ancient Japanese history. He studied extensively Shinto texts, including the Seventeen Article Constitution *(Kenpō hongi)*, attributed to Shōtoku Taishi, and the *Taishi kuji hongi*, to which lay patrons granted him access. He gave a number of public lectures on Shinto texts and authored commentaries on them. Chōon's involvement in the area of Shinto learning eventually lead to his being embroiled in a minor public controversy. In 1679, he received permission to publish a woodblock edition of the *Sendai kuji daiseikyō*. Some years later, in 1682, officials from Ise Shrine lodged a formal complaint with government officials maintaining that the text was a forgery. The bakufu responded by banning the text and ordering the woodblocks destroyed. It also punished Chōon for his involvement in the episode by placing him under house arrest at Kōsai-ji. The mother of Tokugawa Tsunayoshi interceded on Chōon's behalf, and his sentence was reduced to fifty days of house arrest.

In addition to his dealings with the samurai class, Chōon was active as a promoter of Buddhism among the commoner classes. On numerous occasions he held precept ceremonies to bestow the precepts on the fourfold assembly (monks, nuns, laywomen, and laymen). According to the *Zenrin shūheishū*, Chōon traveled about in rural areas, setting up temporary sites for his precept ceremonies.[9] Pro-Obaku materials suggest that Chōon bestowed the precepts on approximately a hundred thousand lay people throughout his career.

Chōon was an outspoken critic of the Zen practice of his day. His arguments will be taken up in more detail in a later chapter but may briefly be said to center on two issues. First, Chōon rejected the Rinzai style of koan practice typical of his day. He regarded it as formalistic and debased, dismissing it as a form of "counting practice." In a similar manner, he took a highly critical stance regarding certain patterns of Dharma transmission, then accepted in various parts of the Zen community, which did not require face-to-face transmission between master and disciple. Like many of his fellow first-generation converts, Chōon came to Obaku seeking a vibrant and rigorous style of Zen practice within the context of a Zen lineage that he regarded as valid.

Tetsugen Dōkō (1630–1682)

Tetsugen Dōkō is perhaps the most famous Japanese Obaku monk. His name became widely known as a result of his major publication project, which produced a complete woodblock edition of the entire Chinese Buddhist Scriptures produced in Japan, sometimes referred to as the Tetsugen edition (J. Tetsugen-ban).[10] In a number of ways, however, Tetsugen stands out as atypical of the first generation of Japanese converts. First, he came from relatively humble origins and began his religious career as a Jōdo Shinshū priest. Unlike the other disciples of Mu-an discussed above, Tetsugen contributed a relatively small number of new temples to the sect, founding only seven in his short career. In sharp contrast to Tetsugyū, Egoku, and Chōon, Tetsugen designated no Dharma heirs at all. His legacy to the sect rests largely on his publishing activities.

Tetsugen was born into a clerical family surnamed Saeki in the Mashiki region of Higo province (now Kumamoto prefecture). His father served as a shrine monk *(shasō)* at the local Hachiman-gū shrine. Tetsugen took the tonsure at age thirteen at a nearby Jōdo Shinshū temple. He soon became the disciple of Saigin (1605–1663), a prominent Shinshū scholar, and followed him to Kyoto in 1647. There Tetsugen studied at the Shinshū seminary (later to become Ryūkoku University) for several years.

Tetsugen broke from Shinshū during 1654 or 1655. His decision appears to have been motivated in part by a sectarian dispute that led to the temporary closure of the seminary and the dismissal and banishment of his teacher Saigin in 1654. Tetsugen left Kyoto and returned to his native Kyūshū in 1655. Having heard about Yin-yüan's arrival, he went directly to Nagasaki and gained admission to Yin-yüan's assembly at Kōfuku-ji. Tetsugen was among the group of early Japanese disciples whom Yin-yüan entrusted to Mu-an's guidance when he departed for the Kyoto area. In Tetsugen's case, the transition was not an easy one. Initially denied entry by Mu-an, Tetsugen sought further guidance from Yin-yüan in Tonda before returning to Kōfuku-ji and formally entering Mu-an's assembly. Tetsugen had the opportunity to practice under all three of the Chinese founders, later spending at least one seasonal retreat with Chi-fei. He received Dharma transmission from Mu-an in 1676.

Tetsugen shared with several of the other first-generation converts a common interest in strict adherence to Buddhist monastic precepts. He lectured publicly on the topic on many occasions and discussed related issues in his writings. His perspective on the issue of monastic discipline was no doubt influenced by his own experience as a Shinshū monk.[11] Indeed, it is quite possible that Tetsugen was married as a young monk, a practice officially permitted at the time only within the Shinshū order. Given his strong words on the topic, Tetsugen probably left Shinshū in large part because he disapproved of its understanding of monastic discipline.

Tetsugen also found in Obaku a receptive audience for his proposed scripture project. With the active support of several Chinese and Japanese Obaku monks, Tetsugen began a full-scale effort to produce a complete woodblock set for the entire Chinese Buddhist Scriptures in 1669. He traveled the country, preaching at local temples in order to raise funds for the project. A large portion of the funding came from small donations made by individual samurai, commoners, and lay cooperative groups.

Tetsugen is also known in Japan for his social welfare efforts undertaken during a period of serious famine in the Osaka-Kyoto region in 1681 to 1682. When the famine was growing to crisis proportions, Tetsugen was in Edo seeking official bakufu permission to publish his scripture collection. Hearing of the suffering, Tetsugen rushed home in 1682 to oversee relief efforts centered at his home temple Zuiryū-ji in Tamba, Osaka. Tetsugen held public lectures to raise funds, much as he had done to fund the scripture project. He and his disciples distributed rice and money to thousands of men, women, and children on a daily basis for several weeks. It is said that they saved as many as a hundred thousand people from starvation. Eventually, Tetsugen fell ill and died of a fever contracted as a result of his daily contact with famine victims during the relief effort. He was fifty-three years old.

This chapter has described the contributions made by the Chinese founders of the Obaku movement who gave it shape and by the early generation of Japanese converts who spread the movement throughout the country. The cooperative efforts of both Chinese and Japanese monks helped to promote Obaku from a small new religious movement to a viable sect of Zen Buddhism. Using data drawn from the *Obakushū kanroku,* the official sectarian lineage chart, one can map out the exponential growth of the Obaku movement over its first century in human terms. Yin-yüan is recognized as the thirty-second-generation descendent of Lin-chi and the first generation of the Obaku sect. The second generation, that of Yin-yüan's immediate disciples such as Mu-an, Chi-fei, and Ryōkei, numbered only ten Dharma heirs. By the third generation, when Japanese converts already far outnumbered their Chinese counterparts, the number of Dharma heirs had grown to 123; the fourth generation to 564; the fifth to 962. The sixth generation, which dates to approximately one hundred years after the founding of Mampuku-ji, was the largest in the sect's history, numbering 1,014 Dharma heirs.[12] (It should be noted that these numbers do not reflect the total number of Obaku monks, only those individuals specifically recognized as Dharma masters in their own right.) What remains to be seen is what drew Japanese converts to Obaku and how the community conceived of itself. In the next chapter, attention will be shifted to the style of Zen practiced within the Obaku community and to the teachings and tendencies that made it unique within the world of Japanese Zen.

SEVEN
Obaku's Monastic Style

Obaku scholars often introduce their comments on the distinctive aspects of Obaku practice with the observation that Obaku Zen has much in common with Rinzai Zen. The reason for this is obvious; as a line descending from Lin-chi I-hsuan (d. 866; J. Rinzai Gigen), the Obaku sect inherited much the same tradition as the lineages of Japanese Rinzai established in Japan several centuries earlier. Most of the differences between the two schools can be attributed to changes that occurred in Ch'an practice and thought in China after the Yüan dynasty, when contact between the Chinese and Japanese Zen communities diminished. Neither remained static. Both the Chinese and Japanese traditions continued to develop separately, in ways appropriate to their respective cultural and historical contexts. For all the differences, however, what they shared remained more substantial than what separated them.

As a tradition of Zen Buddhism, the Obaku sect regards meditation as the central feature of its practice.[1] Obaku may find a different balance between the elements of monastic practice—meditation, ritual observance, and scholarly pursuit—than do the other Zen schools, but it shares with them the common basis of meditation as its primary concern. Moreover, Obaku practitioners describe their purpose in familiar Zen terms, such as "seeing nature and becoming a Buddha" (*kenshō jōbutsu*). Like the other Zen lineages, Obaku makes use of such images as direct transmission of the Dharma from mind to mind (*ishin denshin*), a special transmission outside of the written scriptures (*kyōge betsuden*), to describe itself. For this reason, the practice of Obaku Zen participates in the typical Zen format of masters directing the progress of a group of disciples, with special emphasis on transmission from master to disciple.

As the descendents of Lin-chi, Obaku masters use the same teaching methods that one associates with any monastic Zen practice. Glancing through their biographies or recorded sayings, one finds frequent use of shouts and slaps in encounters between master and student. Masters give their disciples koan to use as meditative devices; they engage their students in *mondō* (question and answer encounters) to evaluate their progress; and they confer *inka* on select individuals to certify their enlightenment experience and acknowledge their competence to teach others. Obaku masters make use of the same Zen corpus of literature for their instructions as do other Zen masters, especially the *Record of Lin-chi* (J. *Rinzai roku*), *The Blue Cliff Record* (J. *Hekigan roku*), *The Gateless Barrier* (J. *Mumonkan*), *Lankavatara Sutra* (J. *Ryōga-kyō*), and so on. The teachings of individual Obaku masters are recorded in the Zen genre of published writings (*goroku*) and Dharma talks (*hōgo*), forming a subcorpus specific to the Obaku sect.[2]

Obaku masters in the early period appear to have regarded the relative importance of the texts from the Zen corpus in a manner somewhat distinct from their Japanese Rinzai counterparts. Whereas Rinzai masters tended to favor composite texts such as the *Mumonkan* or *Hekigan roku*, Obaku masters preferred to study and comment upon *goroku* texts. Yin-yüan, for example, used the *Rinzai roku* as the basis for many of the lectures represented in his own recorded sayings. Yanagida Seizan argues that Yin-yüan's direct use of the *Rinzai roku* had a direct influence on Japanese Rinzai. Before the introduction of Obaku Zen, the *Hekigan roku* had been the more influential text in Japanese Rinzai, but, following Yin-yüan's lead, the Japanese rediscovered the original text and came to prefer the direct study of the *Rinzai roku*.[3]

Similarities do not arise exclusively from the common historical heritage from China shared by Obaku and Rinzai Zen. Once the Obaku movement was established in Japan and contact thus reestablished between Chinese and Japanese Rinzai styles, a certain degree of mutual influence became inevitable. Based on the pattern of Japanese adoption and adaptation of earlier influxes of Chinese Buddhism, one would expect to find a gradual process of enculturation of Obaku Zen into the existing world of Japanese Zen—a Japanization of it, as it were. To some extent this did occur. Obaku scholars today recognize the influence of Hakuin's Zen style, as well as that of other Japanese Rinzai and Sōtō masters, on their sect. As things stand now, Obaku monks regularly get their academic training at Rinzai universities, especially Hanazono University in Kyoto, thus reenforcing the common bonds.

The current generation of Obaku scholars wish to minimize the differences that exist between Obaku and Rinzai in the present as well as those that existed historically. This sectarian preference compounds the difficulties inherent in any attempt to evaluate the common elements and differences as they existed in the mid-seventeenth century or to trace the actual pattern of historical change within Obaku practice. There is a wealth of textual evidence, however, upon which to begin the process. This evidence is basically of two types: internal Obaku texts and external texts, predominantly of a critical nature, reflecting Japanese reactions against Yin-yüan and his school. A full evaluation of all this textual material would require a detailed study far beyond the scope of this project. This chapter will merely suggest the general contours of the issues involved. It will focus primarily on internal Obaku sources, allowing Obaku's image of itself to emerge whenever possible. Where appropriate, however, external documents will be used to complete the picture.

Most treatments of Obaku's characteristics begin with a discussion of its combination of Zen and Pure Land practices. Although such a combination certainly sets Obaku apart today and has lead to its identification in the popular mind as "Nembutsu Zen," this is not the dominant theme found in the early writings of members of the sect. Nor, as it happens, did outside commentators make much of Obaku's inclusion of Pure Land elements in the early decades of the sect's development in Japan. I will begin, therefore, with the definition of Obaku Zen practice as seen in the work of the founding generation of Chinese monks.

Yin-yüan seems to have recognized the inevitability of enculturation and sought to preserve the distinctly Chinese qualities of his Dharma style. To this end, toward the end of his life, he wrote instructions to guide his disciples after his passing, particularly for the sake of the generations who would come after his immediate heirs were themselves gone. These instructions form the basis of the Obaku monastic code, known as the *Obaku shingi* (Pure rule of the Obaku sect).[4] Since this text became the guiding blueprint for the newly established sect, any consideration of unique characteristics should begin with a brief review of it. By means of it, the first generation of Chinese masters, especially the founder Yin-yüan, preserved the distinctive characteristics that set Obaku apart from other Zen schools of the time.

The *Obaku shingi*

The *Obaku shingi* was first published in 1673, the year of Yin-yüan's death. Although commonly attributed to Yin-yüan, the actual history of the text is somewhat more complicated. As the text itself indicates, it was revised by Mu-an and compiled by Kao-ch'üan Hsing-tun. In actual fact, the bulk of the text was written by Kao-ch'üan, although tradition maintains that he was following Yin-yüan's own instructions and recorded matters previously determined by the master. Yin-yüan did directly author portions of the text, including the *Yoshokugo*, a set of instructions that he wrote as an independent document in 1671, when he was eighty years old. This document, consisting of an introduction and ten articles, is included in the *Obaku shingi* as an appendix under the same title. Other portions of the text directly attributed to Yin-yüan include the preface, dated 1672, and the postscript.[5]

The *Obaku shingi* belongs to the genre of Chinese and Japanese monastic codes (*shingi*, literally "pure regulations") written specifically for Zen monasteries. The history of Zen codes is a complex topic and has been the subject of some scholarly debate.[6] A few words about the genre and its history will be helpful in understanding the *Obaku shingi*. In general, although Zen monastic codes detail such elements as daily manual labor, which we associate specifically with Zen monastic practice, they do not diverge radically from the more general Buddhist monastic codes of the earlier Indian and Chinese traditions. Chinese monastic codes built upon the earlier Vinaya tradition, taking for granted its existence and its enduring importance. Ch'an monks, for example, were traditionally ordained using the same sets of precepts (e.g., the 10 precepts for novices and the 250 for monks) as found in the Vinaya texts. While Sōtō and Rinzai follow Japanese patterns for ordination and depart somewhat from the traditional style of ordination, Obaku maintains the practice of ordaining monks with the full Vinaya code.

According to traditional accounts, the T'ang master Pai-chang Huai-hai (720–814; J. Hyakujō Ekai) wrote the first Zen code, the *Pai-chang ch'ing-kuei* (The pure rule of Pai-chang; J. *Hyakujō shingi*), and thus established the institutional independence of the Zen school in China. Although no such document ever likely existed,[7] most of the codes compiled from the Sung dynasty on refer to it as their basis. The oldest extant example of the genre dates from the Sung dynasty, the *Ch'an-yüan ch'ing-kuei* (The pure rule of the Zen monasteries; J. *Zen'on shingi* or *Zennen shingi*), compiled in 1103.[8] This monastic code became the basis for numerous later editions in China and was transmitted to Japan sometime around 1200. It was especially important for Eisai (1141–1215) in his efforts to establish Rinzai temples according to the tradition he observed in China.

The *Obaku shingi* itself is based more closely on a Yüan dynasty text, the *Ch'ih-hsiu Pai-chang ch'ing-kuei* (The Pure Rule of Pai-chang compiled by imperial command; J. *Chokushū Hyakujō shingi*),[9] compiled between 1336 and 1343. Although the title suggests that this text is based on Pai-chang's code, it was actually derived from various Sung dynasty texts. As the title indicates, it was compiled under imperial auspices and was intended as a guide for all Ch'an temples of the day. By the Yüan dynasty, Buddhist temples in China had come under closer governmental supervision, and this is reflected in the first and third sections, which express gratitude and loyalty to the imperial court and obligations of service to the state.

The *Obaku shingi* represents a subcategory in the genre of Zen monastic codes designed to govern the conduct of individual temples rather than to serve as more general guidelines, such as the *Ch'an-yüan ch'ing-kuei* and the *Ch'ih-hsiu Pai-chang ch'ing-kuei*. It was common practice for founders or restorers of Zen temples in Japan to write such specialized codes, designed to meet the specific needs of their assembly. The *Obaku shingi* was intended to regulate life at the head monastery, Mampuku-ji, and was later applied to its branch temples, with appropriate modifications. The monastic life described in the code sounds very much like life in any Zen monastery: The monks rise early and begin the day with the morning services before dawn. Then they meditate until breakfast is served at about sunrise (literally, when the cook can see his hand). Meals are simple affairs, with rice and vegetables as the staples; the monks eat communally and in silence. (The Chinese style of food known in Japan as *fucha ryōri* for which Obaku is famous is not the norm for the monks themselves except on special occasions or when a benefactor sponsors a vegetarian feast.) After the first meal, they return to the meditation hall until lunch is served at noon. During the day each monk engages in some form of manual labor—cutting grass, raking the grounds, begging in the city, and so on. In the late afternoon, they gather again for the evening service. They then have another session of meditation at this point, and the students have the opportunity to meet with their master until it is time to retire at 9:00 P.M.[10]

The main body of the *Obaku shingi* has ten chapters, loosely patterned after the *Ch'ih-hsiu Pai-chang ch'ing-kuei,* but much shorter and more specific than the latter. The *Ch'ih-hsiu pai-chang ch'ing-kuei* consists of four (or sometimes eight) fascicles, divided into nine sections. It is considerably longer than the *Obaku shingi,* which consists of only one fascicle. Since it provided a general monastic rule for use in various Zen monasteries throughout Yüan China, it is much less specific in its regulations than a text composed for an individual monastery such as the *Obaku shingi.* For example, in the fourth section, it indicates that memorials should be celebrated honoring the monastery's founder and the abbot's Dharma master, mentioned by title only, along with specific memorials for Bodhidharma and Pai-chang. The *Obaku shingi* makes explicit reference to Yin-yüan as founder, along with references to Bodhidharma, Pai-chang, and Lin-ch'i in its comparable third section. The correspondence between sections of the two documents is not exact. The first four sections of the *Obaku shingi* correspond in title and subject matter with the first, third, fourth, and fifth sections respectively of the *Ch'ih-hsiu pai-chang ch'ing-kuei.* After that, although they cover similar matters, the parallels break down.

The following is a section-by-section synopsis of the *Obaku shingi:*

Section 1, *Shukuri,* gives instructions for offering prayers and blessings to the ruler and high officials for their protection of the Buddha's Dharma.

Section 2, *Hōhon,* compares the debt of gratitude owed to the Buddhas with that owed to one's parents and spells out the prayers of thanksgiving used to commemorate events from the life of the historical Buddha, his nativity, realization of the Buddhist path, and final entry in Nirvana, as well as the nativity of two bodhisattvas, Avalokitesvara and Maitreya. The inclusion of Avalokitesvara and Maitreya reflects the popularity of these two bodhisattvas in China; by the Ming period, they were included in the ritual practice at most temples.[11]

Section 3, *Sonso,* provides memorial verses for Bodhidharma, Pai-chang, Lin-chi, and several special memorials for Yin-yüan as founder of the monastery.

Section 4, *Jūji,* determines the daily responsibilities of the abbot as the guardian of the Dharma.

Section 5, *Bongyō,* stresses the importance of keeping the precepts, that is, living by the "pure practice" (*bongyō*), lest the monks lose sight of their primary purpose. This section includes long, detailed instructions for the Obaku service of conferring the precepts on novices and advanced monks, known as the *sandan kaie,* literally "the three platform ceremony for conferring the precepts."

Section 6, *Fuju*, describes the order of the morning and evening services, determining the sutras and *dharani* included, the details for use of bells and drums, and movements of the monks. Both the content and the style of these services show some Pure Land influences. Not only are Pure Land sutras included among the sutras for daily recitation, along with the Heart sutra, but the monks are instructed to chant the *nembutsu* at these services as they enter and leave the hall. The section also provides instructions for other, less regular, services such as the small *segaki* (ceremony for feeding hungry ghosts, usually held at Urabon-e), known as the *shōsejiki,*[12] releasing live animals, making offerings on behalf of petitioners, chanting for the dead, and so on.

Section 7, *Setsujo*, gives a listing of seasonal events and celebrations month by month, with detailed instructions following. These include the summer and winter retreats, the celebratory rituals and memorials listed in Sections 2 and 3, and other major events such as Obon. Some of these events are unique to Obaku in Japan, although they may have been common in Ming China; for example, the *kanrinbō*, a ceremony conducted for the sake of the departed, is held in the temple cemetery on the fifteenth day of the seventh month.

Section 8, *Raihō*, describes the behavior appropriate to the monastery grounds. It includes instructions for entering and leaving the hall, behavior inside the hall, special instructions for the first and fifteenth days of each month, rules pertaining to the bath, the proper manner for admitting novices, proper seating order within the dining hall, and a listing of temple offices. There are separate rules governing the sick room (*shōgyōdō*) and procedures for the head of the novices when lecturing in the abbot's stead (*rissō hinpotsu*). Inserted into this section is a text written by Mi-yun Yüan-wu, one of Yin-yüan's predecessors at Wan-fu ssu, advocating strict adherence to the precepts.

Section 9, *Fushin*, explains the meaning of manual labor in the monastery.

Section 10, *Senge,* describes matters related to the death of a monk.

There are, in addition to these chapters, several appendices attached at the end, including a series of illustrations of Obaku musical instruments, religious implements, signboards, and so on. Many of these articles differ significantly from their Japanese counterparts, in common usage at the beginning of the Tokugawa period. The most important of the appendices is Yin-yüan's *Yoshiyokugo*, which explicitly sets out his wishes for the monastery and sets in action a system that preserved the Chinese quality of Obaku practice that exists even today.

The *Yoshiyokugo* consists of ten articles, many of them general in nature. In them, Yin-yüan stresses such themes as mutual coopera-tion, continued preservation of the Obaku Dharma style, and the im-portance of strict observance of the precepts. Most important from a historical perspective, however, is the passage in which Yin-yüan gives detailed instructions for the selection of future generations of abbots. When Yin-yüan wrote this document in 1671, he had already named Mu-an as his successor and had been living in retirement for seven years. By means of this final testament, he extended his control over the choice of future abbots for several generations.

> Select the third abbot and so on from among my Dharma heirs according to their rank. After they have served in turn, go on to the next generation of disciples [literally, Dharma grandchildren]. By all means, select virtuous monks already deserving of esteem who will successfully promote the Dharma style. . . .
>
> Historically, when one looks at the Dharma heirs of the succes-sion of founders who came over from China in the past, after three or four generations the line ends and the founder's place is left va-cant. Previously, the lay believer Sakai [Tadakatsu] suggested an idea to defend our sect [from this eventuality]. He said that from now on, when there is no one [qualified] at the main temple, we should invite someone to come from China, so that the Dharma line will never be cut. This suggestion is quite appropriate. Future gen-erations should act accordingly.[13]

Yin-yüan's instructions in this regard were followed, and Mampuku-ji continued to have Chinese abbots for as long as it was possible to find qualified Chinese monks to come to Japan. For over a century, until the last Chinese abbot died in 1784, Mampuku-ji received a lim-ited influx of new Chinese monks who maintained the Chinese cul-tural influence on the sect. This allowed for a remarkable continu-ity regarding a number of Chinese elements in both the Dharma style and everyday life at the monastery that might otherwise have been lost in the face of the dominant Japanese cultural and religious envi-ronment. Details pertaining to purely cultural elements such as lan-guage, clothing, food, and so on will be discussed later, but one finds here the basis for their perpetuation. Yin-yüan thus preserved what is in general terms the most outstanding characteristic of Obaku Zen, its Chineseness.

Recognizing that the *Obaku shingi* is fundamentally similar to other Zen codes, one can still find in it elements indicating Obaku's unique characteristics vis-à-vis Japanese Rinzai. First, in the daily services one sees Pure Land influences foreign to Japanese Zen. Next, in the religious calendar are certain ceremonies, such as the *sandan kaie,* unknown or rare in Japanese Zen temples. One can also identify a number of tendencies not unique to Obaku Zen but nonetheless characteristic of it in the relative emphasis they receive. Those worthy of mention include the positive attitude toward the sutras and academic pursuits, encouragement of monks to work among the common people, and the strict observance of the precepts. None of these elements would have set Obaku Zen apart in Ming China, but taken as a whole they were sufficiently distinctive to contribute to the process of Obaku becoming a separate Zen sect in the Japanese context.

Before turning to look at these characteristics in more detail, a brief note on the influence the *Obaku shingi* had on other Japanese monastic codes of the time is in order. Because the Obaku founders brought their style of practice from China to Japan, the school faced unique problems inherent in transcultural situations. I have therefore preferred to present the *shingi* as a means of preserving the Chinese character of the school in the Japanese context. When one is working within the framework of a single culture, monastic codes are more often indicative of reform movements. As such, they may set one monastery or movement in a sect apart from other elements in the same sect. During the period following Obaku's transmission to Japan, in the late seventeenth and early eighteenth century, we find monastic codes playing just such roles.

Several monks from both the Rinzai and the Sōtō sects became interested in writing new monastic codes or publishing and studying older codes in order to restore discipline and direct the development of the tradition. Within the Sōtō school, for example, Sōtō monks published an edition of the *Eihei shingi* (T. [Taishō daizōkyō], vol. 82, no. 2584), a compilation of writings composed by Dōgen in the thirteenth century, in 1667. The Sōtō monk Gesshū Sōko (1618–1696) wrote and published his own code for Daijō-ji, the *Undō jōki,* in 1674. In 1679, he produced the first published edition of the *Keizan shingi* (T. vol. 82, no. 2589), attributed to Keizan Jōkin (1264–1325). Gesshū's disciple Manzan Dōhaku (1636–1715) republished the *Keizan shingi* in 1682 and produced his own study of monastic codes, the *Shōjurin shingi,* between 1680 and 1691. In the Rinzai school,

Mujaku Dōchū wrote codes for individual temples and produced his own major commentary on the *Ch'ih-hsiu pai-chang ch'ing-kuei,* known as the *Chokushū Hyakujō shingi sae* or the *Hyakujō shingi sakei,* in 1718.

This renewed interest in monastic codes was one facet of the growing reform movements characteristic of the late seventeenth and early eighteenth centuries. It is a prime example of the vitality that characterized the Zen community of that time. Not only can the Obaku code be seen as a part of this general trend, it also contributed directly and indirectly to the work of several monks. Gesshū and Manzan, for example, were both influenced by the work of Obaku masters, and drew directly from the *Obaku shingi* in addition to relying upon existing Sōtō codes. The later Sōtō reformer Menzan Zuihō (1683–1769) specifically criticized Gesshū and Manzan for this. Menzan sought to restore a purely Sōtō code, devoid of Obaku accretions. In a similar manner, Mujaku Dōchū used his own work with historical monastic codes as a means to purify Japanese Rinzai of any Obaku influences.

The *Sandan kaie*

The *Sandan kaie* (Triple Ordination Platform Ceremony), described in section five of the *Obaku shingi,* combines the final ordination of Obaku monks with a service for conferring the precepts on lay believers.[14] The ordination portion of the ceremony follows a general pattern common within the Mahayana tradition. Monks are ordained first by accepting precepts from the Vinaya tradition of Theravada Buddhism, the shorter set of novice precepts and the longer set of precepts for the fully ordained monk; eventually they receive their final ordination with their acceptance of the Bodhisattva precepts, a specifically Mahayana development.

There is a long history in Mahayana Buddhism of spreading the Dharma through the bestowal of a smaller set of precepts on lay believers. Laypersons were typically encouraged not only to keep the most basic Buddhist precepts against killing, stealing, lying, sexual misconduct, and drinking liquor, but to take on more stringent practices similar to those of monks and nuns for limited periods of time. The tradition designated specific times each month when laypersons were invited to participate more fully in monastic life.

In the Mahayana traditions of China and Japan, it became common for Buddhist masters to confer the precepts on large numbers of people at public lectures and similar gatherings. In Japan, the practice was generally associated with so-called Vinaya or *ritsu* movements, which arose in various Buddhist sects and sought to restore discipline within the Buddhist Sangha as well as to strengthen the faith of lay Buddhists.[15] While Obaku was not a *ritsu* movement in the literal sense, and never identified itself as such, it shared with them the basic approach of reviving Buddhism and preserving the Dharma through strict observance of the precepts. We know from anecdotal evidence that Japanese Obaku masters sometimes held more impromptu precept ceremonies to bestow the precepts on the common people. Biographical material on the early Japanese masters occasionally specifies places were such ceremonies were held and the approximate numbers of laypersons who participated. In addition, the *Zenrin shūhei shū* includes a story about Chōon Dōkai holding these popular ceremonies while traveling through country villages. In this case, the story is told to discredit Chōon, for it claims that he performed the ceremony for money.[16]

The Obaku *Sandan kaie* can be seen as a related tradition, and as such is not unique in Japan. The Obaku practice is, however, more closely related to a tradition from Chinese Ch'an temples of the T'ang and Sung periods than to *ritsu* movements seen in Japan. The Obaku ceremony is a highly structured ritual performed according to detailed instructions. Moreover, it combined bestowal of the precept on lay believers with the formal ordination ceremony for Obaku monks.

Obaku masters were the only Buddhists in Japan to perform the *Sandan kaie* ceremony, and for this reason it may be regarded as a unique characteristic of the sect. The ceremony does not seem to have been unique to their line in China, nor was it originally developed by them. The community at Wan-fu-ssu held the ceremony regularly, and Yin-yüan led it at least sixteen times while serving there as abbot. It is not known who first introduced the ceremony at Wan-fu-ssu; since it was a late Ming development, it was probably introduced by Yin-yüan or one of his immediate predecessors. When Yin-yüan realized that the Japanese had never seen or heard of the ritual, he thought it would be a shame for them not to experience this beautiful ceremony. He therefore composed and had published a text, the *Gukai hōgi,* describing the *Sandan kaie* in some detail. He also made available in Japan the existing Chinese textual source that he used as the basis for his own work.[17] The instructions from the *Gukai hōgi* were then incorporated into Obaku's monastic code in abbreviated form as a permanent part of Obaku practice.

The Obaku sect has not continued to hold the *Sandan kaie* cere-

mony as Yin-yüan seems to have intended.[18] Therefore, the exact procedure for the *Sandan kaie* is no longer completely understood. Directions given in the *Obaku shingi* would normally have been aug-
mented by an oral tradition preserving practical details not provided
in the written text. Without that oral tradition, Obaku scholars cannot even be certain about the proper interpretation of the written instructions; thus their descriptions of the ceremony are usually quite
vague. The following description, based on the day-by-day instructions found in the *Gukai no nittan* portion of Section 6 in the *Obaku
shingi*,[19] must be regarded as tentative.

The ceremony took place over the course of eight days. The first
two days were dedicated to bestowing the precepts on the broader
Buddhist community; both laypersons and monks took refuge in the
Three Treasures—the Buddha, the Dharma, and the Sangha—and
then received the Five Precepts, the Eight Precepts, and the ten precepts for novices. Although they are listed separately, these sets of precepts are all related. The ten precepts for novices (*shami jikkai*) are to
refrain from: (1) killing living things; (2) stealing; (3) sexual misconduct; (4) lying; (5) drinking liquor; (6) eating after noon; (7) going to
see dancing, singing, and shows; (8) adorning the body with perfumes,
jewelry, and other finery; (9) sleeping in a high bed; and (10) receiving
money. The Five Precepts (*gokai*) are the first five of these, which lay
people are expected to observe on a daily basis. There are some practical differences, of course, since the ban on sexual misconduct implies
refraining from fornication and adultery on the part of laypersons,
rather than all sexual activity, as it does for monks and nuns. The
Eight Precepts (*hakkai*) usually refer to the first nine of the novices'
precepts, with (8) and (9) combined. Laypersons could undertake the
observation of these stricter conditions on specific days of the month.

On the third and fourth days of the *Sandan kaie*, the monastic community formally accepted novices who had previously been accepted
by individual teachers. During these two days, novices received their
robes and bowls, took the ten precepts for novices, and were lectured
on them. All of the events of the first four days comprise the first platform. The *Obaku shingi* does not describe the ordination of nuns. In
most parts of the Buddhist world, the procedure is somewhat different, with nuns accepting additional precepts as novices and fully ordained nuns. It seems likely that the many nuns who joined the Obaku
order participated only in the first two days of the ceremony. If they
received the precepts for novices, it would have been done privately
from their respective teachers.

The next two days of the ritual were dedicated to the full ordination of monks according to the Vinaya code,[20] which was designated as the second platform. On the fifth day, the leader of the ritual, usually the abbot of Mampuku-ji, lectured on the four kinds of refuge for sentient beings (*shie*). *Shie* can mean a variety of things, including the four kinds of practices appropriate for monks. In this case, however, it refers to the four kinds of things that all sentient beings can rely upon, namely the Buddha, the Dharma, the Sangha, and the Precepts. On the sixth day, the participating monks received the 250 precepts of a fully ordained monk.

On the seventh and eighth days of the ceremony, the third platform, the Bodhisattva precepts (*bosatsukai*) were explained, and then the monks mounted the ordination platform and received them. The Bodhisattva precepts are generally divided into ten heavy and forty-eight light precepts (*jūjūkai shijūhachikyōkai*). While the precepts for novices and the 250 precepts for fully ordained monks are based on the Theravada tradition, the Bodhisattva precepts are specifically Mahayana in origin.[21]

Based on biographical accounts of the first generation of Japanese Obaku monks, it appears that the *Sandan kaie* may have served more than one purpose for the monastic community. In addition to representing the formal locus for ordination of new Obaku monks, it also functioned as a conversion ritual for previously ordained monks. Monks who had attained some position of seniority within another Buddhist sect and who did not need to receive the precepts on Obaku's *kaidan* in order to be formally acknowledged as fully ordained, nevertheless participated in the *Sandan kaie*. It provided for them a public and ritual context in which to affirm their affiliation with the Obaku sect.

Yin-yüan may have conferred precepts on his Japanese disciples in a less formal manner on earlier occasions, but he held the first *Sandan kaie* in Japan at Mampuku-ji during the winter retreat of 1663. He held the ceremony twice more after his retirement, in the second month of 1665 and again in the second month of 1670. After that time, Mu-an and successive abbots of Mampuku-ji continued the tradition for some time. It was normally expected that novices would have already received the ten precepts from their master when they first joined the order. Full ordination was then granted only at the *Sandan kaie*, which was to be held every three to four years at the discretion of the abbot. Initially, the ceremony was limited to the main temple Mampuku-ji, and monks had to travel there for ordination.

However, after 1675 when Mu-an held the service at Zuishō-ji, the new Obaku headquarters in Edo, both sites were used.[22]

The *Sandan kaie* was designed not only for ordaining Obaku monks, but as a means to spread the Dharma among the common people. Obaku abbots used the ceremony to popularize Obaku Zen and to create or strengthen its ties with lay believers. Dating back to the T'ang and Sung periods, Ch'an monasteries in China regularly used ceremonies conferring the Bodhisattva precepts on laypersons in much the same way,[23] as had the Zen sects in Japan.[24] Obaku's success in promoting itself through this ritual is hard to evaluate, as no records were kept of the ceremony and no exact figures are available. We have only the anecdotal evidence from biographies and recorded sayings to provide information. According to references made in Yin-yüan's biography, five hundred people participated each of the first two times he led the service, and over a thousand the third time.[25] When Mu-an held the ceremony in 1677, 1,200 people were said to have participated, and when Kao-ch'üan led it in 1695, another 1,100 people came.[26] These figures are approximate at best. Nonetheless, they do indicate significant interest in the ceremony among lay people in Kyoto and Edo. Not only could lay believers renew their ties with the Buddhist Sangha and gain merit from taking the precepts, but it was also a novel opportunity for ordinary Japanese to watch in person an elaborate Chinese ritual.

The Maintenance of Chinese Cultural Identity

Life at Mampuku-ji and other Obaku temples differed from that found in other Japanese temples because certain distinctive patterns of Ming monastic life were maintained in such areas as ritual language, musical instruments, religious implements, food, clothing, personal appearance, and temple architecture. These differences created a special atmosphere at Obaku temples and made for the appearance of a distinctive Chinese style of Zen. In actuality, these differences were external, more closely related to cultural and ethnic identity than to differences in Buddhist teaching. Nevertheless, Zen monastic practice encompasses all aspects of daily life, and Zen codes prescribe appropriate behavior even on seemingly trivial levels. For this reason, the preservation of cultural differences did take on a religious quality for the Chinese Obaku masters. Conversely, these differences prompted Japanese Rinzai masters to criticize Obaku Zen as ritually incorrect.

During the early years when the majority of the Obaku community were Chinese, it was perfectly natural that they would continue to use their own language in daily and ritual life. From the start, this created special problems for relations between the Chinese masters and their Japanese disciples. Fortunately, they all shared the written language of classical Chinese to bridge the gap, and there were interpreters to help in formal situations. Apparently, Yin-yüan never felt comfortable speaking Japanese when he received important guests, but he and the other Chinese monks did learn to communicate in Japanese for everyday purposes. Some Japanese disciples also made an effort to learn to speak Chinese in the Fukien dialect of their masters.

All Obaku monks, as well as other monks visiting for extended periods of time, were expected to learn to chant the sutras and other prayers of the daily services in Fukien dialect Chinese. Although Japanese naturally became the dominant language over the years, the custom of chanting in Fukien dialect in ritual contexts has been preserved down to the present day. Large portions of the *Obaku shingi* include Japanese markings in the phonetic syllabary (*furigana*), indicating a Japanese approximation of Fukien pronunciation. Obaku monks still chant everything according to this style, known in Japanese as *Obaku bonbai* or *Obaku shōmyō,* and learning to do so is among the first priorities for novices.

Obaku masters brought with them the musical instruments and other religious implements they used in China. These are depicted in an appendix to the *Obaku shingi,* and thus knowledge of them has been preserved down to the present. Indeed, they remain in use throughout all Obaku temples. Some of these instruments, which have subsequently become commonplace in Japanese temples of all sects, were unknown or uncommon in Japan before the establishment of Obaku temples. For example, the drum known as *mokugyo,*[27] used as an accompaniment to chanting the sutras, is said to be a Ming instrument first imported to Japan by Obaku masters.[28]

The Ming style of Buddhist monastic services, including the specific uses of the various musical instruments, are also preserved in the ritual directions in the main body of the Obaku monastic code. The original musical quality of the services has also been maintained by an unbroken chain of oral tradition within the sect. The combination of drums, bells, and hand chimes, along with the rhythms of the chanting, create an overall effect more closely resembling esoteric services than those of other Japanese Zen sects. We know from Tokugawa period comments that the music sounded exotic to the Japanese who heard it, and in some cases distinctly unpleasant.[29]

Obaku temples have likewise preserved certain culinary customs from Ming China. Monks at Mampuku-ji are required to eat together in the dining hall and share a common serving pot in the Chinese manner. It was Yin-yüan's explicit wish that the monks not divide up into smaller cliques at mealtimes, and he specifically called for monks living in their own subtemples within the monastery precincts to gather for meals with the whole assembly.[30] In addition, Obaku is known for its Chinese vegetarian cuisine, called *fucha ryōri* in Japanese. This distinctive cuisine was originally prepared as festival food at the temple and has never been daily fare for the monks. Visitors to Mampuku-ji can still partake of a meal served in the traditional fashion. The monastery provides *fucha ryōri* to the public not only as a means to raise funds but also to promote public awareness of the sect.

Obaku monks were harshly criticized by Japanese monks in the Tokugawa period for their eating habits. Comments were often made to the effect that Obaku monks were fat, that they ate throughout the day in obvious violation of the basic Buddhist code.[31] The criticism may well have had some basis in fact, as Zen temples in China and Japan did serve evening meals, euphemistically called *yakuseki*, or "medicinal stone." The practice is said to be medicinal in the sense that it wards off illness associated with insufficient diet. *Yakuseki* is first mentioned in Ch'an monastic codes in the *Ju-chung jih-yung ch'ing-kuei* (J. *Nyusshu nichiyō shingi*), published in 1209.

Another cluster of Obaku customs relates to the dress and personal appearance of the monks. First, Chinese monastic robes worn by Obaku monks were somewhat different from Japanese robes. We know from the *Obaku geki* that Japanese tailors had trouble producing these robes and that one tailor in Kyoto came to specialize in making them.[32] The Chinese also wore shoes rather than the straw sandals customary in Japan, and also a different sort of cap. We know from criticism in the *Zenrin shūheishū* that Chinese etiquette related to the wearing of the cap differed from Japanese custom, and that this caused a certain misunderstanding. The topic of the sixth section of the first fascicle of the *Zenrin shūhei shū* concerns wearing the cap incorrectly. It mentions that Ming monks ignored the proper etiquette for caps prescribed by the *Ch'ih-hsiu Pai-chang ch'ing-kuei* and wore their caps out of season. This improper usage was said to create the false impression that the caps served some symbolic function other than the practical purpose of keeping the head warm in winter. The text specifically mentions that the founder of the Obaku line wore the cap out of season in order to conceal his worldly appearance, a reference to Chinese monastic hair styles, which allowed for longer growth between shavings.[33]

Chinese monks typically shaved their heads according to a different schedule than the Japanese, so that it was not uncommon for them to have as much as two inches of hair. This gave them a somewhat worldly appearance in the eyes of their Japanese critics. We know from portraits that Chinese monks also grew their nails quite long, sometimes extending for several inches, as was the Chinese custom of the day. Although it was natural for the Chinese Obaku monks to maintain these Chinese styles, their Japanese disciples adopted the same customs as a part of their monastic discipline. Even previously ordained monks from other sects were expected to change from Japanese to Chinese robes when they came to practice Zen for extended periods of time. Portraits of the early Japanese masters clearly show their full adoption of Chinese dress and personal appearance. It was this latter development that particularly caused resentment among some Japanese, who felt that it indicated a lack of respect for Japanese customs. Since many of these customs were not specifically prescribed in Obaku's monastic code, some were gradually replaced by Japanese monastic styles.

Other Characteristics

While not unique to Obaku Zen, there are three other characteristics that do help to define the Obaku style of Zen: its attitude toward the sutras and teachings, its stress on strict observance of the monastic code, and its strong tradition of work among the common people. Each of these tendencies has a basis in the *Obaku shingi* and represents an area of emphasis within Yin-yüan's teachings. One may also observe similar tendencies in other Ming period masters such as Chu-hung and in some Tokugawa period Japanese masters. These are the characteristics that probably struck the deepest chords in the Japanese monks who joined Obaku in the early years of its development in Japan.

In some cases, Zen masters have taken a radical position toward the sutras (and the Buddhist teachings they represent) and have called for their destruction. One may well argue that statements of this sort, like the instruction to kill the Buddha, are intended symbolically and are not meant to be fulfilled literally. Nonetheless, they do represent a strong emphasis within Zen Buddhism to value personal experience over scholastic pursuit. Zen masters speak of the direct transmission of the Dharma from mind to mind, not the transmission of a written tradition. There is a strong bias in the teachings of many Zen masters against a bookish understanding of Buddhism. Other Zen masters, however, take a more positive attitude toward the sutras and teachings, arguing that the teachings and meditation are one (*zenkyō itchi*). They recognize that the truth one encounters in the sutras is ultimately the same as what one experiences through meditation. Obaku Zen generally takes this latter, positive attitude toward the written tradition.

In Yin-yüan's early years of practicing Zen, when he first began studying the sutras, he is said to have observed to a friend that grasping the essential meaning of the sutras is like being shown the correct road to follow—one must still follow the road for oneself in order to reach the goal.[34] Nevertheless, Yin-yüan inherited a tradition of deep respect for the sutras that typified monks at Wan-fu-ssu, where earlier abbots had taken great pains to acquire a copy of the Chinese Buddhist Scriptures for the monastery. According to Yin-yüan's biography, he read the entire collection during his tenure as abbot at Wan-fu-ssu. In the entry for Yin-yüan's forty-seventh year, the biography says that he spent a thousand days reading the sutras in order to commemorate the eighty-second anniversary of the first petition made by the former abbot Cheng-yüan Chung-t'ien to government authorities requesting a copy.[35] The biography incorporates a brief history of the three earlier abbots, including Cheng-yüan, who dedicated their lives to obtaining a copy of the Chinese Buddhist Scriptures for the monastery. Yin-yüan continued to read and study the sutras throughout his life and encouraged his disciples to do the same.

Obaku Zen does not regard sutra study as sufficient in and of itself, but it does consider study and reverence for the scriptures as an essential part of monastic life. Naturally, Obaku favors the writings of the Zen patriarchs and certain sutras that have traditionally been associated with Zen thought, just as other sects give priority to some sutras over others. The Obaku sects' positive attitude toward the sutras as a whole is manifested in their production of the Obaku edition of the Tripitaka. Yin-yüan carried his copy of the Chinese Tripitaka with him to Japan as a part of his personal library. He later passed the volumes on to Tetsugen, and they became the basis for the majority of the volumes in the Obaku edition. Although Tetsugen rightly deserves the bulk of the credit for completing this project, Yin-yüan and the entire community contributed their skills and resources to support him. In a very real sense, Obaku made the Tripitaka readily available to any temple in Japan for the first time in the history of Japanese Buddhism.[36]

Even before Yin-yüan came to Japan, he was known to the Japanese for his strict attitude toward observance of the precepts. He believed that the renewal of Rinzai Zen could be achieved only through a return to monastic discipline. The Japanese disciples who gathered around him shared in this conviction. Men like Ryōkei and Tetsugen left their previous affiliation to join Obaku largely because of their deep commitment to strict observance. With its emphasis on meditation and the sudden achievement of enlightenment, Zen has sometimes been interpreted as bypassing or transcending monastic discipline. Obaku Zen takes much the opposite approach. The attitude that monastic discipline is a necessary basis for Zen practice permeates the *Obaku shingi*. For example, in the fifth section on pure practice, the text reads: "Students of the way must first of all keep all of the precepts, the ten precepts of the novice, the two hundred fifty precepts of the monk, and the ten heavy and forty-eight light precepts of the Bodhisattva. . . . If you do not keep the precepts, then you cannot meditate. If you cannot meditate, then you cannot attain wisdom."[37] Obaku Zen thus portrays itself as using the traditional divisions of the Buddhist path, discipline, meditation, and wisdom. As in traditional formulations, disciples of Obaku Zen begin with discipline and, building on it, progress through meditation to wisdom.

Among the features of Obaku practice that can be considered under the rubric of strict monastic discipline is their attitude toward the summer and winter retreats (J. *ango*). The custom of keeping a retreat dates back to Buddhist practice in India, when monks were expected to remain settled in one location and not travel during the rainy season, a period of three months during the summer. In Ch'an temples in China, this custom developed into two yearly retreats: the summer retreat, observed from the fifteenth day of the fourth month through the fifteenth day of the seventh month; and the winter retreat, observed from the fifteenth day of the eleventh month through the fifteenth day of the first month of the new year. These periods of retreat became intense sessions of meditation practice for disciples under a master's guidance.

Yin-yüan and the other Obaku masters strictly observed the regulations governing these retreats. We know from Kyorei's letter, for example, that Yin-yüan held his first retreat in Japan in the winter of 1654–1655, and Kyorei specifically mentioned that the assembly kept the rule strictly. Yin-yüan saw to it that the practice of keeping the summer and winter retreats would be preserved at Obaku monasteries by having them clearly regulated by the *Obaku shingi*.[38] All disciples were expected to participate in the sessions, and special permission had to be granted by the master to excuse an individual. Disciples had more freedom of movement during the months between sessions, and it was during the off months that they were expected to carry out their other projects.[39] At this time, Japanese Rinzai monasteries held retreats at the discretion of the master who served as abbot, but it was not necessarily a regular feature of their practice. The holding of scheduled retreats was among the features of Obaku practice that attracted Japanese Zen monks in the early years of its development in Japan. This practice no longer distinguishes Obaku, as Rinzai monasteries also regularly keep the retreats as a result of reforms implemented in the eighteenth century by Hakuin.[40]

The summer and winter retreats served an important purpose in the practice of Zen meditation; these were periods when students made great progress in their practice because they could meditate intensely and meet with their master on a regular basis. They also provided opportunities for individual monks to experience the leadership of another master. As with the other sects of Zen, Obaku monks habitually traveled to study under different masters, usually with their own master's consent. Monks from other Rinzai lines and from the Sōtō sect often joined an Obaku assembly for one of these sessions, and it was in this way that firsthand knowledge of Obaku practice spread throughout the Zen world in Japan. This free exchange between monasteries had been the pattern of Zen practice in Japan and China for generations. Before Myōshin-ji posted new regulations in 1665 that banned their monks from taking part in retreats outside their lineage, monks from the Myōshin-ji line participated with some frequency.

A final attitude that characterizes Obaku Zen is its dedication to work among the common people. Buddhist monks have always served as religious teachers for lay believers, and Obaku masters also fulfilled this role. Examples of this kind of service are innumerable. Obaku monks wrote letters; composed lessons on Buddhism (*hōgo*), sometimes in the vernacular (*kana hōgo*); and preached sermons for the sake of lay believers. Yin-yüan tried to set an example of Buddhist compassion to laypersons by regularly holding the ceremony for setting living creatures free. He had a pond called Hōjōchi (Pond for releasing living things) constructed at Mampuku-ji specifically for this purpose.

Obaku masters sometimes went beyond the role of teacher to provide for the physical needs of the common people. Normally these activities would be the domain of lay believers, but lay people did not always have the expertise or the resources to meet immediate physical needs, especially in times of crisis. For example, Tetsugyū worked among the common people in the countryside and became well known for building bridges and reclaiming swampland for farming; he spent most of his time working with the merchant classes in the urban centers and was known for distributing food and monetary aid during periods of severe famine. These two Japanese Obaku masters stand out in their dedication to relieving physical distress, but they are only the most prominent examples of this kind of public service within the sect.

The distinctive characteristics of Obaku monastic practice described in this chapter may be summarized as falling under three broad headings. First, ritual practices such as the *Sandan kaie* set out in the *Obaku shingi* that preserved elements of Chinese monastic ritual of the Ming period. Second, a number of elements have been characterized here as representing a preservation of Chinese life and cultural influence. This category includes the Chinese pronunciation of sutras and other prayers that constitutes Obaku's unique ritual language, the musical instruments and other ritual implements newly imported by the Ming founders, Chinese styles of monastic robes and personal grooming, and Chinese monastic food. Third, certain elements, while not unique to Obaku belief and practice, do represent the particular balance early Obaku masters struck within the general scope of the Zen teachings. This category includes Obaku attitudes toward the sutras, Zen literature, and other written materials; the early generation's stress on strict observance of the monastic code; and the high value they placed on work among the common people. The following chapter will address the influences of Pure Land Buddhism and other religious and philosophical teachings on Obaku belief and practice.

EIGHT

Pure Land Outside, Zen Inside

Obaku Zen has unmistakable elements of Pure Land influence in its practice, and this was obvious from the very beginning to the Japanese monks who encountered Obaku masters. Kyorei, the Myōshin-ji line monk who wrote the earliest report on Obaku practice in Japan, noted, "if one looks closely, the outer form looks like the Pure Land school, but the inner looks like the Zen school."[1] Kyorei provided a relatively kind and sensitive interpretation of what he had seen. Not all observers would be so generous. The combined practice of Zen and Pure Land caused Obaku Zen considerable trouble in Japan, and indeed still does so. Such a combination appeared largely foreign and sometimes even abhorrent to Japanese Zen monks, reacting as they naturally would from their own knowledge and experience of Japanese Pure Land. Combined practice would have appeared quite different to a Chinese monk than to his Japanese counterpart due to the historical and cultural differences in the Buddhism practiced in their respective countries.

To the Japanese, Zen and Pure Land appeared as opposites, the former advocating self-reliance in the quest for enlightenment and the latter promoting total dependence on the power of the Buddha Amida. The Chinese, in contrast, had a long history of combined practice, and its absence, particularly in the context of Ming Buddhism, would have seemed far stranger to them than its inclusion. It is important to bear in mind, however, that Japanese Zen monks came to draw the opposition between the two traditions much more sharply after the mid-eighteenth century, following the lead of reformers such as Hakuin. It is from the retrospective view that the greatest contrast exists between Obaku and the rest of Japanese Rinzai in terms of Pure Land practice, as "purity" became a major issue only in the later Tokugawa and modern periods.

To understand Obaku's use of Pure Land teachings, one must first comprehend the history of combined practice in China and the methods for reconciling apparently contradictory concepts and practices. On the other hand, to comprehend the Japanese reaction, one must also bear in mind the history of Zen and Pure Land in Japan before the arrival of Obaku masters. A great deal of scholarly work has been done on these topics and related issues, and it would be redundant to repeat those efforts here.[2] Therefore what follows is a brief review of the salient points of the history and theory behind joint practice, leading up to a detailed description of Obaku's use of Pure Land teachings.

A history of combined practice ought properly to include two different aspects of the tradition, those approaches taken to reconcile practice from the Ch'an side and those from the Pure Land side. Few individuals transcended these traditional divisions so thoroughly as to allocate equal status to the two types of practice. Most Buddhists who advocated dual practice were either Ch'an masters who in some way incorporated Pure Land teachings into their Ch'an practice or Pure Land masters who advocated the use of Ch'an meditation in addition to the central practice of the *nembutsu*. This review will stress the former approach, that is, the Ch'an perspective, as the more relevant to Obaku Zen. It is actually possible to extend the history of joint practice back to the fourth century, long before one can properly speak of either the Ch'an or the Pure Land school in any meaningful sense.[3] The early material, however, is sparse and uninstructive for the present purposes.

In discussing the attitude of Ch'an toward Pure Land teachings, one may begin with the teachings found in *The Platform Sutra*, traditionally attributed to Hui-neng (638–713), the sixth patriarch of Ch'an. Hui-neng's fundamental criticism of Pure Land belief was that it encouraged believers to seek for a means of salvation external to themselves instead of turning their focus inward to examine the self. Once, when Hui-neng was asked by a visitor to comment on rebirth in the Pure Land, he replied:

> At Sravasti the World-honored One preached of the Western Land in order to convert the people, and it is clearly stated in the sutra, "[The Western Land] is not far." It was only for the sake of people of inferior capacity that the Buddha spoke of farness; to speak of

nearness is only for those of superior attainments. . . . The deluded person concentrates on Buddha and wishes to be born in the other land; the awakened person makes pure his own mind. If only the mind has no impurity, the Western Land is not far. If the mind gives rise to impurities, even though you invoke the Buddha and seek to be reborn [in the West], it will be difficult to reach.[4]

Starting with this text, it has been argued that the classical Ch'an tradition took the basic attitude that while Pure Land practice may be appropriate for those of lesser capacities, in fact it has little real value in moving an individual along on the path to enlightenment. Any teaching that focused one's attention outward was actually guiding one in the wrong direction.

Before Hui-neng's time, there is some evidence that this attitude had not yet become firmly established. The fourth patriarch, Tao-hsin (580–651; J. Dōshin), was the earliest Ch'an master to describe something resembling the practice of the *nembutsu* in his writings. He identified the mental state resulting from that practice with the state of no-thought attained through Ch'an meditation.[5] The fifth patriarch, Hung-jen (601–674; J. Gunin), did not follow Tao-hsin's lead, but later descendents in Tao-hsin's line did, and they developed a Ch'an practice based on this similarity. Two generations later, if one follows the line through Chih-hsien (609–702; J. Chisen) and Ch'u-chi (648–734; J. Shojaku) rather than the sixth patriarch, we come to a Korean master named Musang (684–762; J. Musō). Although a Ch'an master, Musang actually taught a form of *nembutsu* that used gradual modulations in the voice as a device to induce meditative states.[6]

Examples like this in the early tradition are sporadic and do not by any means represent the central thrust of the tradition at that time. Nor do these individual masters constitute anything like a movement. The closest thing to a movement advocating dual practice of Ch'an and Pure Land to be found in the classical period are two successive masters from the Ox-head school, Fa-chih (635–702; J. Hōji) and his disciple Chih-wei (646–722; J. Chii). Their line soon died out, and after that one finds little evidence of dual practice by Ch'an masters through the T'ang (618–907) and early Sung (960–1279) periods. It is very difficult to assess the level of dual practice during these periods, and it is possible that later generations altered the texts to suit their own agendas.[7]

A self-conscious movement advocating dual practice did not really emerge until sometime after the tenth century, when Yung-ming Yen-shou (904–976; J. Yōmei Enju) provided a theoretical basis for it.[8] Yen-shou extended his syncretic efforts toward the harmonization of all schools of Buddhism, but made special efforts to demonstrate the compatibility of Ch'an and Pure Land. At that time, most masters who advocated either Ch'an or Pure Land practice were highly critical of one another. Ch'an masters tended to regard Pure Land believers as incapable of progressing along the steep Ch'an path; Pure Land advocates accused Ch'an practitioners of being selfishly intent on their own enlightenment and lacking in the Buddhist virtue of compassion.[9] Yung-ming Yen-shou is said to have transcended these divisions in both his practice and his thought.[10]

Yen-shou used philosophical categories to harmonize the two schools of thought, basing his argument on the nonduality of dichotomies such as the absolute (*li*) and the phenomenal (*shih*).[11] On a practical, soteriological level, Yen-shou taught that Ch'an and Pure Land were not only compatible but mutually beneficial for believers. He wrote, "If there were Ch'an but not Pure Land, then nine out of ten people would stumble along the way. . . . If there were no Ch'an and only Pure Land, then 10,000 out of 10,000 practitioners would see Amida, so they would not be concerned about their not attaining enlightenment. When there is both Ch'an and Pure Land, then like horned tigers, people become masters in this life and Buddhas in the next. If there were neither Ch'an nor Pure Land, then [caught] between the anvil and the post for 10,000 kalpas and one thousand lifetimes, there would be nothing on which to rely."[12]

By the Yüan dynasty (1280–1368), textual materials clearly indicate widespread dual practice throughout Chinese Buddhism. This is one of the primary reasons many Japanese and Western Zen scholars refer to this period as a time of gradual decline for Ch'an Buddhism in spite of the fact that it grew in sheer numbers.[13] This evaluation appears to be based on a later construction of Zen purity rather than on the vitality of the tradition or other neutral criteria. Throughout the Ming period, dual practice continued as the norm throughout the world of Chinese Buddhism. All of the prominent masters of the period, including the four restorers of Buddhism in the later years of the Ming dynasty, Yun-ch'i Chu-hung (1535–1615), Tzu-po Chen-k'o (1543–1603), Han-shan Te-ch'ing (1546–1623), and Ou-i Chih-hsu (1599–1655) advocated some form of dual practice.[14]

The understanding of Pure Land teachings, including the goals and the specific practice referred to as *nembutsu,* varies between schools of Chinese Buddhist traditions. The term *nembutsu* can be understood as meaning a variety of meditative techniques, from visualization of the Buddha and his Pure Land to the verbal invocation of the Buddha's name, and can also refer to a variety of practices based on interpretations of different sutras. The Buddhist master Tsung-mi (779–841; J. Shūmitsu), regarded as both a Hua-yen master and a Ch'an master, categorized these practices into four types. Roughly speaking, they are (1) vocal invocation of the Buddha's name, (2) concentration on a physical representation of the Buddha, (3) mental visualization of the Buddha, and (4) identification of the self with Amida Buddha. Tsung-mi set out this categorization in his *Hua-yen ching hsing-yüan p'in shu-ch'ao.*[15]

Within the Hua-yen and T'ien-t'ai schools, the *nembutsu* practice is one among the many kinds of meditation employed, not intended to be an exclusive practice. In the context of Esoteric Buddhism, the term *nembutsu* normally refers to a form of meditation in which the believer focuses on Amida Buddha, using techniques of mental visualization; the goal of this form of concentration is the resulting state of *samadhi.* This interpretation of *nembutsu* practice is based on the *Visualization Sutra* (J. *Hanju zammaikyō*).[16] By contrast, the practice commonly identified by Japanese Buddhists with the institutional distinct (Japanese) Pure Land school is based on Shan-tao's (618–681; J. Zendō) interpretation of the three Pure Land Sutras.[17] The latter tradition stresses oral invocation of Amida Buddha's name rather than visualization. The goal of practitioners is rebirth in the Pure Land in the next life. For believers of this type, the *nembutsu* is an expression of faith and gratitude for Amida Buddha.

Of these two general approaches to Pure Land thought found in China, the esoteric and Shan-tao's, the esoteric interpretation would clearly be more amenable to Ch'an masters and more fruitful for harmonization from the Ch'an perspective.[18] It should be noted, however, that even in the case of the Pure Land tradition based on Shan-tao's understanding, some ground remained for combined practice. While the Pure Land school in China tipped the balance between reliance on other-power (*tariki*) and reliance on self-power (*jiriki*) heavily on the side of other-power, it did not completely reject all elements of self-power.

Whether using the term *nembutsu* in reference to meditation on the Buddha or to invocation of the name, Buddhist teachers have long rec-

ognized that the practice has calming effects on the mind that can lead
to a state of *samadhi* in which the distinction between subject and
object is transcended. For example, the great T'ien-t'ai master Chih-i
(538–597; J. Chigi) included meditation on the Buddha Amida among
the methods for attaining *samadhi*.[19] The twelfth-century Ch'an master Ch'ang-lu Tsung-tse (n.d.) recommended the practice of *nembutsu*
for purposes of calming the mind both to beginners and to those individuals facing immanent death.[20] As noted above, Wusang and his disciples used vocal invocation for the same purposes. Based on this kind
of observation and the philosophical basis developed by Yen-shou,
various Ch'an masters during the late Sung and early Yüan, including
the dominant master of the age, Chung-feng Ming-pen (1262–1323;
J. Chūhō Myōhon), argued that Ch'an meditation and Pure Land
practice lead to the same or similar results.[21]

In some cases, these Ch'an masters encouraged their students to use
the *nembutsu* in much the same way they would use a koan or a
mantra. They recommended chanting the name without advocating
belief in Amida Buddha or rebirth in the Pure Land, since it was the
resulting meditative state and not faith in Amida's vow that they believed had efficacy. In fact, they reinterpreted Amida and the Pure
Land in Ch'an terms, speaking instead of the "Pure Land only in the
mind" (*yuishin jōdo*) and "the Amida within the self" (*koshin no
Mida*). In this way, faith that a Pure Land believer would direct outward toward an external power (*tariki*, other power) was directed inward toward the true self (*jiriki*, self-power). Eventually, this kind of
instruction was taken one step further and developed into what became known in the Ming period as the *nembutsu kōan*. Ch'an monastic codes included recitation of Amida's name as a part of funeral
services for monks and, more importantly, during times of serious illness,[22] as did many of the Japanese codes modeled after them.

The precise origin of the *nembutsu kōan* is unclear, but by the
Ming period it had come into common usage. Unlike most other
koan, the *nembutsu kōan* has no roots in the classical Ch'an corpus
and takes on any number of variations. Its most basic form is the question "Who is it who chants the *nembutsu*?" Generally speaking, a
Ch'an master would give this koan to a lay disciple, usually one who
already practiced the *nembutsu*. The master would encourage the student to meditate on this question while going about his usual practice
of chanting Amida's name. The basic purpose of the exercise was to
turn the believer's focus away from a purely Pure Land recitation

based on faith toward a more Ch'an understanding of it. The masters believed that the *nembutsu kōan* could engender in a Pure Land believer the same feeling of doubt that the koan did in Ch'an practitioners, and thus lead to an enlightenment experience.[23]

Ch'an masters used this exercise as a sort of bridge between the steep path of Ch'an and the easy path of Pure Land. By doing this, they hoped to reach out to people of average and below average abilities who might find Ch'an meditation too difficult. This was consistent with the strong Ming emphasis on lay Buddhism. It does not seem that masters commonly used this exercise with their disciples inside the monastery. This is not to say that monks themselves did not practice the *nembutsu,* as we know of several examples of monks who did. However, the *nembutsu kōan* was primarily a way for Ch'an masters to serve the needs of lay believers and not a practice for those who had dedicated their lives to religious practice.

Dual Practice in Japan

Dual practice of Zen and Pure Land was introduced in Japan during the Kamakura period in the late thirteenth century (late Sung/early Yüan dynasty in China) by Japanese monks who had studied at Ch'an monasteries in China and by Chinese monks who fled the chaos in their native land during the change of dynasties and settled in Japan. The most prominent Chinese Ch'an master of the time, Chung-feng Ming-pen (1263–1323; J. Chūhō Myōhon), was himself a proponent of dual practice, and most of the Pure Land influence on Japanese Rinzai at that time can be traced to him. This was the case because a great many of the Japanese monks who traveled to China sought him out, and some of his Chinese disciples later made their way to Japan.[24] For a variety of reasons, however, these Pure Land influences did not endure in Japanese Zen as they did in China.

First, the general tendency of Japanese Buddhism during the Kamakura period moved in exactly the opposite direction from the Chinese. While Chinese Buddhism grew increasingly syncretic and combined concepts and practices from different Buddhist schools of thought, including Hua-yen, T'ien-t'ai, Ch'an, and Pure Land,[25] the Japanese were continuing to divide into distinct sects and were moving toward single, exclusive practices. This trend can be seen in all of the new Japanese schools of the period, the Pure Land sects (Jōdo-shū, Jōdo shinshū, and Ji-shū), the Nichiren sect, and the two Zen sects,

Rinzai and Sōtō.[26] Buddhist practice introduced in the Heian period by Shingon and Tendai had been characterized by a high degree of ritual and complex thought requiring extensive training. The new Kamakura schools each sought in its own way to simplify Buddhist practice by focusing on a single form: the Pure Land sects relied on recitation of the *nembutsu,* the Nichiren sect on reciting the title of the *Lotus Sutra,* and the Zen sects stressed meditation. Although it would be an oversimplification to say that even these schools completely abolished all other forms of practice for their adherents, they were all moving away from syncretism.

Not only was the intellectual and religious climate of the time not conducive to any form of multiple practice, specific developments within Japanese Pure Land and Zen propelled them further apart than they had ever been in China. The two dominant Pure Land schools, Jōdo-shū and Jōdo shinshū, under the guidance of their founders, Hōnen (1133–1212) and Shinran (1173–1262), had taken the Pure Land tradition of Shan-tao to its logical limit, denying any validity to practices other than chanting the *nembutsu.* They taught that in the final age of *Mappō* people could only attain salvation through the vow of the Buddha Amida and called for total reliance on Amida's power (*tariki*). This made all practices other than reciting Amida's name obsolete. In fact, the Japanese Pure Land sects maintained that any other form of Buddhist practice would actually cause the believer harm, because it implied trust in one's own efforts (*jiriki*) rather than absolute reliance on faith in Amida. For philosophical reasons, then, Pure Land believers in Japan could not argue, as some of their Chinese counterparts would, that Zen meditation and Pure Land practice had the same result.

For their part, Zen masters were highly critical of Pure Land practice in Japan. Not only did they regard reliance on an external Buddha as misguided, they found the monastic practices of Japanese Pure Land, particularly True Pure Land, completely unacceptable. As salvation by faith alone implied that keeping the precepts was no longer a necessary part of Buddhist practice, True Pure Land monks were allowed and even encouraged to marry and eat meat. Chinese Pure Land masters had never taken reliance on the power of Amida to this extreme, and they had never advocated rejection of the common Vinaya tradition shared by all the Buddhist clergy. Under these circumstances, Zen Buddhists in Japan came to regard Pure Land Buddhism as a perversion of the tradition.

Earlier examples of Chinese Ch'an masters promoting dual practice were largely forgotten during the centuries when contact with China diminished, and the gulf between the Zen and Pure Land schools remained intact until the arrival of Obaku masters. Japanese Zen masters came to see any Pure Land influence on their Zen practice as a form of contamination. There are a few examples of Japanese Zen masters like Suzuki Shōsan (1579–1655) and Ungo Kiyō (1583–1659) who advocated dual practice of Zen and Pure Land, though they regarded it primarily as a means to reach the laity. Shōsan was an independent, one might even say marginal, figure in the Zen tradition; he did not function within the bounds of institutional Zen, and his ideas had little or no influence on other Zen Buddhist masters of the day.[27]

In contrast to Suzuki Shōsan's position as a relative outsider to the institutional Zen world, Ungo was a prominent figure within the Zen hierarchy and for a time served as abbot at Myōshin-ji. As a senior master in the Rinzai school, Ungo took two stands that were somewhat controversial at Myōshin-ji. First, he was an outspoken advocate of strict monastic discipline as the proper means to reform the sect. Second, even while abbot at Myōshin-ji, he continued to promote the practice of *nembutsu* among lay believers. His ideas were rejected by the majority of the other monks at the temple, and he was effectively forced out of office. His teaching has been denigrated within the mainstream of the Rinzai tradition as an inferior form of "Nembutsu Zen" and it has not been influential. In this sense, like Shōsan, Ungo is regarded as a marginal figure in the Rinzai tradition.[28]

When the Obaku masters came to Japan and their Zen style displayed obvious Pure Land influences, such as chanting the *nembutsu* and including Pure Land sutras as a regular part of daily services, most Japanese monks could only associate this with the dominant Pure Land tradition familiar to them in Japan. Even committed Obaku supporters from Myōshin-ji like Ryōkei had trouble reconciling themselves to this aspect of Obaku practice. It is said that when Yin-yüan was residing at Fumon-ji and acting as abbot, Ryōkei did not participate fully in the Obaku-style services that Yin-yüan held in the morning and evening. He refrained from actively participating in those elements of the services that showed direct Pure Land influence. For example, he would remain seated while the other monks entered and exited the hall, chanting the *nembutsu* as they went. The Japanese response to this characteristic will be treated in more detail in the next chapter.

Obaku Zen's Dual Practice of Zen and Pure Land

The teachings of the Obaku masters fell squarely within the Chinese syncretic tradition and would not have seemed in any sense extraordinary in a Ming Chinese context. The Chinese founders approached the dual practice of Zen and Pure Land from the Zen perspective, and it was clear where the balance lay between the two teachings. They were Zen masters who made some use of Pure Land practices within a Zen context, reinterpreting them in terms of Zen conceptualization. Obaku's dual practice falls into two basic categories: use of the *nembutsu kōan* with Pure Land lay believers and the ritual use of Pure Land sutras and the chanting of Amida's name within the monastery. Most modern scholarship has focused its attention on the former category, perhaps because it is more easily reconciled with the Rinzai tradition.[29] Based on the historical sources, however, it is much more likely that Japanese monks in the Tokugawa period were responding to the latter when they reacted against Obaku Zen as an impure Zen style.

Based on the recorded sayings of Yin-yüan, Mu-an, Chi-fei, and other early Obaku masters, one can say that Obaku followed the Chinese pattern of using the *nembutsu* primarily with lay believers, reinterpreting it in Zen terms as a koan. Looking at Yin-yüan's extensive writings as the primary resource for understanding Obaku's Zen style, one finds only a handful of references to chanting the *nembutsu*. In each instance, Yin-yüan was approached by a Pure Land believer who already used the *nembutsu* as his or her primary Buddhist practice. Yin-yüan encouraged each of them to reflect on some form of the question "Who chants the *nembutsu*?"[30] Like other Zen monks before him, Yin-yüan sought to reach out to people at their current level of Buddhist understanding and then to inspire them to move forward, toward a Zen approach to Buddhist practice. He did this by giving them a koan-like problem to contemplate while they continued in their regular Pure Land practice. I have found no evidence to suggest that Yin-yüan ever encouraged a strictly Pure Land approach to the *nembutsu*, such as stressing the efficacy of chanting the name in faith, without steering the believer toward a Zen reinterpretation of it. Nor is there reason to believe that he gave the *nembutsu kōan* to anyone other than committed Pure Land practitioners; there are no instances recorded in his works of the master recommending the *nembutsu kōan* to any of his Zen followers, lay or monk.

In this regard, Yin-yüan's teaching style is not unlike that of the Rinzai master Hakuin. Despite Hakuin's harsh criticism of dual practice in the Zen monastic setting, he took a much softer, more conciliatory tone when writing to Pure Land believers. In the *Orategama zokushū,* for example, he wrote, "It must be understood that the koan and the recitation of the Buddha's name are both contributing causes to the path that leads to the opening up of the wisdom of the Buddha."[31] Hakuin did not believe that the two practices were equally beneficial by any means, but he recognized the benefits of Pure Land practice for lay people of lesser abilities. In much the same way, Yin-yüan adjusted his approach to suit his audience but always maintained his basic Zen orientation.

One does find an obvious exception to the typical Obaku pattern of dual practice among the early masters, namely, the fourth abbot of Mampuku-ji, Tu-chan Hsing-jung. Tu-chan seems to have been a strong believer in the Pure Land teachings and regularly practiced the *nembutsu* himself, especially later in his life. For this reason, he became known as "Nembutsu Dokutan," an epithet used not without scorn by those within the Obaku tradition. By the accounts of Obaku scholars themselves, Tu-chan crossed the line from dual practice in the traditional Chinese Zen sense to a pure Japanese style of Pure Land practice. For this reason, Tu-chan is regarded within the tradition as a marginal figure, and his teachings are not considered by Obaku scholars today to be representative of Obaku Zen.[32]

Obaku masters of the Tokugawa period made no apparent attempt to justify their use of the *nembutsu kōan* with lay followers, but modern apologists within the sect have done so. In one defense of Obaku's Zen style, Akamatsu Shinmyō argued, for example, that through their openness to Pure Land beliefs, Obaku masters reunited the gradual and sudden practices of Buddhism. He concluded that, far from producing an impure form of Zen, Obaku's style of dual practice makes Zen accessible to people of high, middle, and low capacities. Akamatsu maintains that when Zen excludes other teachings, specifically Pure Land beliefs and sutra study, then it becomes one-sided and excludes the practice of compassion.[33]

The inclusion of Pure Land elements in the ritual practices at Obaku temples clearly set Obaku Zen apart from Japanese Rinzai and Sōtō Zen.[34] As noted above, Obaku monks chant aloud Pure Land sutras along with a variety of other scriptures at daily services, and they recite Amida's name as a form of walking meditation when they enter and leave the hall. The exact order of services is found in Section 6 of the *Obaku shingi*.[35] For the morning service, the monks chant the *Sūramgama dharani* (from the *Sūramgama sutra*)[36] and the *Heart Sutra*. For the evening service they chant the *Amida Sutra*, the *Heart Sutra*, the *Ojōju*,[37] and other *dharani*. The full name for the *Ojōju* is *Batsu issaigosshō kompon tokushō jōdojinshu*; it is generally associated with funeral services, as it requests rebirth in Amida's Pure Land. (Other rituals, such as the *Hōjō gishiki*, the ceremony for releasing living animals, may also display some Pure Land influences.) It is important to bear in mind that the Pure Land elements represent only a small portion of the daily services and are by no means the central feature of Obaku ritual.

I have found no explicit explanation of any sort for these ritual practices in the primary sectarian literature of the Tokugawa period. This lacuna suggests that the practices were so common in Ming China that the early Obaku masters felt no need to explain or justify their existence. Since the order and contents of the daily services were prescribed in the sixth section of the *Obaku shingi,* they have been preserved down to the present and pose a continuing challenge for modern Obaku apologists. Hayashi Bunshō, now abbot at Mampuku-ji, explains somewhat defensively in his writings that Amida is not the only Buddha mentioned in the daily services, as one would expect to find in a Pure Land temple. He argues that whether one thousand or ten thousand Buddhas are mentioned it does not matter, because they are all names for the true self.[38] I have also had this matter explained to me by one of the scholar-monks at Mampuku-ji after observing one of the services. My informant explained that he had been taught that the Obaku style of *nembutsu* practice was a form of meditation and that it had nothing to do with a Buddha outside himself. He pointed to his solar plexus and indicated that during that exercise Obaku monks concentrate on the Amida within themselves and try to realize the Pure Land inside.

In popular and scholarly writings alike, the common perception of Obaku is that it represents a form of "Nembutsu Zen." Contempo-

rary Obaku scholars are extremely sensitive to this charge because the
term is often used in a derogatory manner. It generally implies a perversion of the Zen approach to Buddhist practice that somehow combines two contradictory sets of beliefs. While Obaku scholars do not
deny the Pure Land influence on their school, they reject the characterization of their Zen style as Nembutsu Zen. Unlike their Edo period
forebears, present-day Obaku monks feel the need to explain explicitly the presence of Pure Land elements in their rituals. They take the
position that Obaku's use of Pure Land belief is more like that found
in the Tendai and Kegon traditions than that of the native Japanese
Pure Land schools, Jōdo-shū and Jōdo shinshū. Some scholars suggest
that the misperception of Obaku as Nembutsu Zen was actually encouraged by Obaku monks themselves in the Meiji period in a misguided attempt to popularize the sect and broaden its economic
base.[39] Whether or not that is in fact the case, the Pure Land influence
on Obaku today is clearly not as strong as is popularly believed.

Other Influences on Obaku Zen

Evidence of Chinese folk religion on early Obaku practice is hard
to trace, as it was never described in the written documents. It is likely
that folk practices would have occurred quite naturally when the
Obaku masters were serving the needs of Chinese expatriates in Nagasaki, and some of these practices may have been retained as Obaku
spread to other parts of the country. As described earlier, the Obaku
temples in Nagasaki (the three Chinese temples founded before Yin-
yüan came to Japan and those originally founded as branch temples
of Mampuku-ji) all had halls dedicated to the Chinese folk deity Ma-
tsu, whose image was temporarily enshrined there while Chinese sea
merchants were in port. Obaku temples in other localities do not have
Ma-tsu halls, no doubt because Chinese traders were not allowed
access to other Japanese cities.

There is some evidence to suggest that other Chinese folk deities
may have been venerated at Obaku temples at one time, since other
folk images can be found. For example, the folk deity Kuan-yü, more
commonly known in the West as Kuan-ti, is enshrined as the main image in the Garan-dō, one of the lesser halls at Mampuku-ji. Although
worshiped originally as a warrior deity, Kuan-yü was popularly regarded as a guardian god who warded off evil spirits. By the late Ming
period, he was also associated with financial success and became a

special favorite among Chinese merchants. How his image came to be enshrined at Mampuku-ji is not certain. Whether or not the Chinese monks observed any folk rituals at Obaku temples during the Edo period is not known. Today, Obaku temples maintain ties with immigrant Chinese communities in some cities and provide a locus for traditional folk festivities. During the celebration of Chinese Obon in September and October, Chinese students set up the traditional altars for the dead at Obaku temples, which include images from Taoist and other folk-religious pantheons.

One expects to find evidence of Confucian and Taoist influence on any Ming period Buddhist group, and Obaku is no exception. The belief that the three teachings, Buddhism, Confucianism, and Taoism, were one and harmonious (sankyō itchi) remained widespread among Buddhists in China at the end of the Ming dynasty.[40] This view was promoted by almost all of the prominent Buddhist masters of the day, though naturally from a Buddhist perspective.[41] Yin-yüan and the other Chinese masters would have been quite unusual had they not held similar views. In Japan as well, Buddhists living at the beginning of the Edo period had, by necessity, to come to grips with Neo-Confucian thought, as it permeated and dominated the intellectual discourse of the secular world. Nonetheless, very little is said about Confucian and Taoist influence in any secondary literature on Obaku Zen. Nor has any work been done to ascertain the attitude that individual Obaku masters took toward those schools of thought. This alone suggests that the syncretic movement to harmonize the three teachings was not central to the thought of Yin-yüan and the others. However, there are several directions that research could take to evaluate their positions vis-à-vis Confucian and Taoist thought.

First, there is a certain amount of material in Yin-yüan's collected works related to Confucianism and Taoism. For example, one finds among his poetry in praise of various Buddhist masters a few verses extolling the Taoist master Lao-tzu and one verse stating that Buddhism and Confucianism are compatible.[42] Yin-yüan extolled the Confucian virtues in general, and filial piety was a special theme in much of his teachings and writings.[43] There may well be other, less obvious passages in Yin-yüan's collected works with Taoist or Confucian themes, especially in letters to lay believers. It is worth noting in this context that the biographies of Obaku masters, Chinese and Japanese alike, tend to stress their strong filial devotion. Yin-yüan's biography explains that he deferred entering the monastic life for many years until his mother died in order to fulfill his deep sense of filial piety toward her, and other biographies develop similar themes. Evaluation of all this material would require a more lengthy study of Yin-yüan's recorded sayings and the biographies than is appropriate here but would provide a good basis for a study on Confucian and Taoist influences on Obaku Zen.

Furthermore, it is important to remember that Yin-yüan did not forbid his disciples from reading extensively in non-Buddhist writings once they had advanced sufficiently in their practice. This attitude is reflected in the fifth section of the *Obaku shingi* devoted to a description of correct practice. After warning that no amount of book learning will avail if the monks do not persevere in keeping the precepts and in their practice of meditation and good works, permission is nonetheless granted for the master to allow disciples to read as extensively as they please. "So long as it does not interfere with their meditation, monks who have mastered the sutras and recorded sayings [of Zen masters] may read as widely as they like in any books."[44]

Yin-yüan himself kept an extensive personal library, which he brought with him from China. This library included a large number of non-Buddhist writings, among them Confucian and Taoist texts. A catalogue of Yin-yüan's private library was compiled a few months after his death. The list is divided into three sections, Buddhist scriptures; Buddhist texts, including those produced by Obaku masters; and secular writings. The third section is the smallest, but includes sixty-one items. Many are poetry collections, but there are a number of Taoist writings, such as the Inner Chapters of Chuang-tzu, and Confucian texts, such as the collected writings of Wang Yang-ming.[45] A thorough review of the titles would perhaps offer clues as to which aspects of non-Buddhist thought were especially appealing to Yin-yüan.

Although not directly relevant to the issue at hand, it is interesting to note that Japanese Confucian scholars were known to have cultivated friendships with Obaku masters and to have studied the Chinese language with them.[46] Scholars such as Itō Jinsai (1627–1705) and Ogyū Sorai (1666–1728) preferred to read the Confucian classics in the original Chinese rather than by translating them into Japanese, using *kambun* markings. In order to do this properly, they endeavored to master the Chinese language, both written and spoken. For these scholars and others like them, Obaku masters were a living resource of Chinese language and culture that was otherwise unavailable to them, living as they did under conditions of national isolation.

The elements of religious influence from outside the Zen tradition—the inclusion of Pure Land belief and practice, Chinese folk religion, and perhaps the ready incorporation of themes from Confucian and Taoist teachings—have sometimes been labeled as Obaku's syncretic tendencies. They may be alternatively identified as Obaku's preservation of Ming Chinese religious culture. While practices of this sort may have appeared somewhat distinctive in a Japanese Zen context, they would probably not have distinguished the practice at Wan-fu-ssu from other Chinese Buddhist monasteries. In the broadest terms, what made Obaku Zen unique in Japan was its Chineseness. Obaku presented a foreign face in Japan, not only in external aspects such as food and dress, but in internal patterns of thought and belief as well. Indeed, Obaku's early success in Japan depended largely on its identity as a Chinese movement that so clearly distinguished it as an alternative tradition from other mainline Japanese Buddhist groups.

NINE

Obaku in the World
of Japanese Zen Buddhism

Most scholars who write about Obaku Zen in the context of Tokugawa Buddhism remark that it deeply influenced early modern Buddhism, especially Zen Buddhism. Yet they have rarely commented in
concrete terms on the nature of that influence or given detailed information on the Obaku sect's relations with other schools of Zen in
Japan. This chapter will explore these subjects in an effort to portray
Obaku's position in the world of Japanese Zen during its first century
in Japan, beginning with the initial rush of interest at the arrival of the
founder, Yin-yüan, and extending through the period of reform
within the Rinzai sect under Zen Master Hakuin and in the Sōtō sect
under Menzan. These are crucial years for the formation of Zen as it
is known today in Japan, and Obaku did indeed play a role as a catalyst for reform. In fact, its influence on reform was in some respects
direct and positive in nature, as it contributed specific elements and
tendencies from its Zen style to the Japanese world of Zen. In other
respects, Obaku had an indirect influence on the established sects as
they rejected Obaku practices or, in some cases, rejected what they
took to be Obaku practice.

Obaku contributed as a positive influence on Japanese Zen in such
areas as the movement for monastic discipline as a means of reform
and renewed interest in reading and studying the original Zen records
of the masters, such as the *Rinzai roku,* rather than compilations like
the *Hekiganroku.* Concrete examples of positive influence, however,
appear to be somewhat limited. Rather, Obaku primarily influenced
Japanese Zen in an indirect manner. In response to a style of Zen quite
foreign to that known in Japan, Japanese Rinzai masters, and to a
lesser extent Sōtō masters, were stimulated to redefine and sharpen

their own sense of what Zen practice ought to be. For the most part, Japanese Zen masters from other lineages objected to Obaku masters wielding much influence over their disciples; other lineages took steps to guard against the possibility that reform movements developing within the Rinzai and Sōtō sects would ultimately follow Obaku patterns.

Initial Responses to Obaku Zen

As discussed in the historical sketch of Obaku in Chapter 4, Yin-yüan's arrival in Japan was anticipated by elements within the world of Japanese Zen, especially the monks at Myōshin-ji who were already familiar with his writings. After his arrival, numerous monks and lay believers made the journey to Nagasaki to meet the master and pay their respects. In many cases Rinzai and Sōtō monks joined his assembly and practiced under his direction for a summer or winter retreat before returning to their home temples. This early stage in Obaku's history in Japan has been called "the Ingen boom" because of the magnitude of the Japanese excitement at the arrival of a prominent Chinese master. None of the earlier Ming arrivals had engendered such a response, but neither had they attained the stature in China that Yin-yüan enjoyed as the abbot of Wan-fu-ssu. From 1654 to 1656, there was no reason to believe that Yin-yüan would be staying on permanently in Japan, and this no doubt contributed to the flood of visiting monks interested in observing firsthand a Chinese style of Zen.

The Japanese monks who visited at one of the Obaku assemblies had no basis for anticipating the changes in the overall Chinese Zen style that had occurred since regular contact with Chinese Zen masters had ceased some two or three centuries previously. None of them had personal experience traveling in China as Japanese masters from earlier centuries sometimes did. This left them somewhat unprepared for the culture shock inherent in entering an essentially foreign environment. For that, in effect, was what they were doing when they joined Yin-yüan's assembly. Yin-yüan and his company maintained their usual patterns of life and kept to the monastic rules they had followed in China. Japanese monks thus encountered any number of new and unfamiliar practices and customs. They would have found themselves strangers in their own country, since it was they who were expected to adapt to Chinese ways in order to practice under Yin-yüan.

In many cases they were surprised, sometimes even shocked, by what they observed in the daily practice of the Chinese assembly, including the incorporation of Pure Land practices into the daily Zen rituals.

Evidence for this kind of response to the cultural and religious differences of Obaku practice is found in the writings of visiting monks. Among these, the finest and most detailed example is a letter from the Rinzai monk Kyorei in which he reported his impressions of Yin-yüan and the Chinese assembly at Kōfuku-ji during the winter retreat of 1654–1655.

> Zen Master Yin-yüan arrived as anticipated. As for me, I arrived in Nagasaki at the beginning of the eighth month [of 1654] and met with Master [Yin-yüan]. When I was about to ask [permission] to return home, Yin-yüan detained me. Since the shogunate's administrator [of Nagasaki] and the assembly also requested me to remain for a little while, I have stayed on at Nan-king Temple [Kōfuku-ji]. The year is almost at an end, so I plan to return to Hiroshima in the middle of the first month next year.
>
> Master Yin-yüan is in good health. There are now about seventy Japanese monks and more than thirty Chinese monks. Yin-yüan opened the winter retreat on the fifteenth day of the tenth month, and the monks will meditate until the fifteenth day of the first month. The rule is being strictly observed. Japanese and Chinese monks are mingled together, but they cannot communicate. Moreover, both the Japanese and the Chinese monks are highly conceited, and there are occasional incidents. I am troubled as you can imagine. However, things are generally tranquil now. With my present detachment, I understand that it is not so unusual. I am very relieved. This is Master Yin-yüan's first retreat in Japan, so he is somewhat anxious [that all go smoothly]. He entrusted the care of the Japanese members of the assembly to me, and concerns himself with the harmony of the assembly as a whole.
>
> I conveyed Tokuō's [message] to Yin-yüan and had it translated. He also received Master Ryōkei's [message] and was pleased.
>
> It is reasonable to expect me to come down next spring, but there are various difficulties at the temple, so it would be better if I didn't go far away. There is an unusual need for money. . . .
>
> As for inviting Yin-yüan to Myōshin-ji, I heard from the *shuso* Shin[1] that Tokuō and Master Ryōkei and others have each taken steps [to invite him to serve as abbot]. I would truly like to do the same, but I don't think that the assembly [at Myōshin-ji] is in accord. If the whole monastery were in agreement, then he could be invited with official government permission. Master Yin-yüan

would very much like to meet Master Ryōkei. If the process of the invitation proceeds, then Yin-yüan should be able to go to Kyoto. . . .

Shin has already told you about the monastic code, but I will comment briefly. It is very different from the one followed in Japan. – Meals are three times a day. Early in the morning and at noon time there is rice gruel as usual. Again in the late afternoon there is rice gruel, and then in the evening there are tea and cakes. This is the daily routine. Between times, there are tea and cakes at odd hours. Some days they may even eat six times! The monks have fat bellies. This is very different from Japan.
– After the morning service, the assembly proceeds to the abbot's quarters and bows three times. This is not done in Japan and is truly a splendid custom.
– Entering the hall is quite inferior to the [manner followed] at Myōshin-ji.
– At the end of the morning service, the assembly chants *Namu Amida Butsu* while entering and exiting [the hall] (*gyōdō*). The bells, drums, and *mokugyo* have an interesting rhythm, but it is an inappropriate ritual for Japan. Every day it grates on one's ears. There are various other customs that I cannot remember, and so cannot recount them.

The manner of doing *zazen* seems very commendable. In general, if one looks closely, the outer form looks like Jōdo-shū, but the inner looks like Zen-shū. This is probably the pattern for monastic life [in China].

Among Yin-yüan's attendants, there is no one outstanding. The *seidō* Dokuō (Ch. Tu-ying)[2] is said to be clever. Next, the scribe (*shoki*) named Dokuchi (Ch. Tu-ch'ih)[3] is said to be well liked in China. Other than that, there is the attendant (*jisha*) Ryōen (Ch. Ken-yen)[4] who behaves well. The one named Dokutan[5] works at his koan single-mindedly, and even Yin-yüan is impressed by him. The others are of little talent, but they are conceited in a way unknown among Japanese. They have no sense and are unpleasant people.

Next year, one or two of Yin-yüan's Dharma heirs will be coming to Japan. It is rumored that twenty or thirty men will accompany them. Perhaps you could come down to Nagasaki once and see conditions for yourself.[6]

Kyorei's description suggests that the tensions that arose between Chinese and Japanese monks in these early days of enthusiasm for the Obaku movement were largely the result of cultural differences. As he explains it, not only could the two groups not effectively communicate with one another, but both sides displayed unreasonable pridefulness. More than just spoken language divided them; the customs, manners, and assumptions that make up the unspoken language of the two cultures were in conflict. The theme of cultural tension underlies much of the interaction between Obaku and Japanese Rinzai throughout the first century of contact. Cultural differences may well have been more crucial than differences in Zen practice and teaching in determining Obaku's place in Japanese Buddhism.

Kyorei was a close friend of Tokuō and was regarded as an ally of the faction at Myōshin-ji that favored a strict adherence to the monastic code. He was therefore probably predisposed to appreciate Yinyüan's Dharma style, and he tempers his negative remarks with several positive comments about his experience. This lends a balance to his observations not found in later Rinzai texts, which are one-sidedly negative in tone. Kyorei expresses concern about four basic topics, concerns that recur again and again in later Rinzai discussions of Obaku practice. The primary problem that Kyorei mentions is the difference between monastic codes followed by the Ming Chinese and the Japanese forms of Rinzai. He specifically refers to the Chinese practice of taking three meals each day, including one after the noon hour, a breach of the basic Buddhist precepts taken by all monks, including novices. The Japanese regarded such eating habits as detrimental to meditation, as a full stomach tends to make one sleepy.[7] Second, Kyorei observes that the monks practiced a form of chanting the *nembutsu* as a regular part of their morning service. He makes an accurate assessment that this combination of an external Pure Land veneer over a solid Zen core is the Chinese pattern of Ch'an in the Ming dynasty. It was this incorporation of the *nembutsu* into monastic practice, rather than the use of the so-called *nembutsu kōan* among lay disciples, that would later draw the most caustic criticism against the Obaku style from Rinzai masters. Kyorei raises a third concern about the distinctive qualities in Obaku music and chanting that he regards as inappropriate in a Japanese Zen context. The fourth issue raised is the generally low level of ability that Kyorei observed among Yinyüan's Chinese disciples. Kyorei mentions that a few of Yin-yüan's Dharma heirs were expected to come at a later time, suggesting that more talented disciples than those included in the first group existed. The early arrivals were not an especially advanced group, and none had received Yin-yüan's *inka* before they left China. More advanced disciples, particularly Mu-an and Chi-fei, who had become Yin-yüan's Dharma heirs before he left China, emigrated later. These individuals did, in fact, prove to be more impressive to Japanese visitors and converts. Nonetheless, a theme of disappointment subtly underscores most later Rinzai commentary related to Obaku; the Chinese masters of the Ming period never quite measured up to Japanese expectations. The general conclusion reached within the Japanese Zen community was that, by the Tokugawa period at least, Japanese Zen masters had surpassed their Chinese counterparts.

As Kyorei's letter indicates, only a few months after Yin-yüan's arrival in Japan, the assembly at Myōshin-ji was already divided over what attitude the temple should take toward him and his Zen style. Histories of Myōshin-ji and biographies of the anti-Obaku participants, notably those of the master Gudō, agree that this issue split the assembly at Myōshin-ji into two factions.[8] Ryōkei Shōsen, Tokuō Myōkō (1611–1681), and Jikuin Somon (1610–1677) were the core of the pro-Obaku party that supported inviting Yin-yüan to become abbot at Myōshin-ji. Gudō Tōshoku (1577–1661) and Daigu Sōchiku (1584–1669) led the opposing faction, which vehemently rejected such an action. The latter faction succeeded in blocking the invitation and subsequently became the dominant party at Myōshin-ji. The pro- and anti-Obaku factions of the late 1650s follow the contours of a preexisting division within the temple concerning the appropriate interpretation of the monastic code in the Rinzai school. Both factions sought the same end, the restoration and revitalization of Rinzai, but disagreed as to the best method for attaining their goals. One may regard this division as a variation of the recurrent tension between Zen freedom and the limitations of maintaining the precepts that arose throughout Zen history and indeed throughout Buddhist history.

All schools of Buddhism share a common tradition of monastic discipline based originally on the *Vinaya* texts, the monastic code set out in the early Buddhist scripture. In the case of Chinese Buddhism, the monastic code took on the form of a distinctive genre of literature known as "pure rules" (Ch. *ch'ing-kuei;* J. *shingi*). Despite the extensive development of this genre in China and its deep historical importance to the practice of Zen in Japan, portions of the Ch'an/Zen tradition have at times taken aim against any reliance on external codes of conduct in much the same way that elements within the community caution against reliance on an external Buddha or external scriptures. The Sixth Patriarch, Hui-neng, for example, conferred the "formless precepts" (*musōkai*) on his disciples. By redefining concepts such as the precepts in this manner, Hui-neng sought to elevate the discussion above the literal.[9]

> If in your own mind you rely on truth [the Dharma], then, because there is no falseness in successive thoughts, there will be no attachments. . . . If in your own mind you rely on purity [the Sangha], although all the passions and false thoughts are within your own natures, your natures are not stained.[10]

Based on this and similar passages, the tendency to uphold the freedom of enlightenment in opposition to any external monastic code emerged within Zen Buddhism. In some extreme cases, this led Zen masters to blatantly break precepts in order to illustrate their point. It is best to bear in mind that these extreme ideas and actions were situated within the context of monastic discipline. They were intended less as absolute denials of the precepts than as shocking reminders to disciples that even subtle attachments to the Dharma may prove a hindrance. Even those Zen masters who stressed the transliteral meaning of the precepts continued to use those precepts to govern their monastic life.

The Rinzai sect in Japan was torn by an eruption of the recurring dispute over the proper understanding of the precepts early in the Tokugawa period. Once in Japan, Obaku masters became embroiled in the dispute, which predated their arrival. The Chinese masters attracted to their ranks many Japanese monks who shared their view that the precepts had to be strictly preserved and agreed that this was the best method for reviving the Rinzai sect. Opponents in the dispute, likewise dedicated to reviving Rinzai, favored a less literal interpretation of the precepts. Nonetheless, neither party advocated a literal rejection of the precepts in practical terms, since both sides continued to live and practice in basic accordance with the monastic codes.

The pro-Obaku faction included those monks who preferred a strict interpretation of the monastic code and regarded monastic discipline as the best means to reform Rinzai. This position was referred to derisively by its opponents as *Jikai Zen*, "maintain the precepts Zen." Jikai Zen was championed earlier in the seventeenth century by such Myōshin-ji masters as Ungo Kiyō and Isshi Monju. Neither Ungo nor Isshi became involved in the later Obaku dispute. Isshi died in 1646, some eight years before Yin-yüan's arrival. At least one of his former disciples, Dokushō Shōen (1617–1694), who shared Isshi's views on strict monastic discipline, actively participated in the pro-Obaku faction and later became a Dharma heir of Yin-yüan. Ungo served as abbot of Myōshin-ji for a brief time in 1645 but soon retired from that post under unfortunate circumstances. Ungo actively advocated the use of the *nembutsu* as an appropriate device for lay practice. Although his position was not Pure Land in the strict sense, it scandalized members of the Myōshin-ji community to such an extent that there was a movement among them to defrock him for bringing shame on Rinzai Zen with his Pure Land contamination.[11] Opposition to Ungo was led by Gudō and Daigu, central figures in both the anti-Obaku party and the faction opposed to strict interpretation of the precepts. Long before Yin-yüan and Obaku Zen came on the Japanese scene, Myōshin-ji had begun its struggle over strict monastic discipline and inclusion of Pure Land elements in Rinzai teachings.

Gudō Tōshuku lead the opposition to the Obaku movement at Myōshin-ji. Gudō served as abbot at Myōshin-ji for three separate terms. It was from his line that the great eighteenth-century reformer Hakuin would descend. Gudō and his supporters regarded strict interpretations of the precepts as a formalism inappropriate to the Zen context. They took an attitude described as "preserving the precepts from a position without precepts" or "formless precepts of the mind" (*musō shinchi kai*).[12] It was their contention that adherence to the precepts was a natural result of enlightenment but that preservation of the Patriarch's Zen style required a transcendence beyond formalistic adherence.[13]

In a practical sense, the lines regarding Obaku had already been drawn long before Yin-yüan left China, since both sides were aware of his position on this issue through their familiarity with his writings some years prior to his emigration. Yin-yüan and his predecessors at Wan-fu-ssu advocated a strict interpretation of monastic discipline, which made him the natural ally of the one faction and an adversary to the other. Ryōkei and his group hoped to strengthen their position at Myōshin-ji by inviting the prominent Chinese master to be abbot. Gudō and his party recognized this possibility for the threat that it was and vigorously opposed all of Ryōkei's plans as they emerged. Gudō developed a purist position regarding Myōshin-ji, claiming that the temple was reserved exclusively for direct descendents of its founder, Kanzan Egen. Gudō argued that Myōshin-ji monks could not serve as abbots at temples affiliated with other Dharma lines, nor could Dharma heirs from other Rinzai lines serve as abbot at

Myōshin-ji line temples. Gudō based this argument on the *Shūmon shōtōroku* written by Tōyō Eichō (1429–1504), the founder of the Tōyō line of the Myōshin-ji lineage from which Gudō descended.[14]

Even after plans to invite Yin-yüan to serve as abbot were abandoned and he was invited instead to Fumon-ji in Settsu, Gudō remained inflexible in his opposition to Yin-yüan. Despite Yin-yüan's high status, Gudō never made the trip to Settsu to greet him. According to a passage in the *Obaku geki*, he felt that it was Yin-yüan's place, as a visiting foreign monk, to approach him, the highest-ranking Rinzai monk in Japan.[15] Gudō knew quite well that Yin-yüan was being held at Fumon-ji under house arrest and could not make the short trip to Kyoto. A few years later, however, when Yin-yüan was finally granted some freedom of movement and made a tour of the temples in Kyoto in 1659, he did stop at Myōshin-ji. On that occasion, Gudō, then abbot, refused to greet him formally. The two men apparently exchanged unpleasantries indirectly through intermediaries. According to Myōshin-ji accounts, their exchange lead to Yin-yüan's abrupt departure.[16] During the visit, Yin-yüan did pay his respects to Kanzan at the founder's pagoda but otherwise stayed at Jikuin's subtemple, Ryōge-in, for three days in all.

Gudō's rejection of Yin-yüan's Zen style extended beyond the issue of monastic discipline. As with his opposition to Ungo's teaching, Gudō objected to the inclusion of Pure Land elements in Obaku practice. According to Gudō's *nempu*, when Jikuin came to him seeking permission for Yin-yüan's above-mentioned visit to Myōshin-ji, Gudō asked whether it was true or not that Yin-yüan practiced the *nembutsu*. According to the text, Jikuin hesitated when he saw Gudō's stern expression. Thinking better of stating the truth directly, Jikuin demurred and denied that Yin-yüan made use of the *nembutsu*. Gudō replied, "Ungo chanted the *nembutsu*, and now Yin-yüan does so as well. Even were I to fall to the lowest of the 80,000 hells, deep down I would still adhere to Patriarch Zen. We do not yet know whether Yin-yüan's Zen will prove to be a help or a detriment to our sect in the future. It is difficult to argue the point, so I will just leave it up to the assembly."[17]

Relations with Myōshin-ji after the Founding of Mampuku-ji

When Yin-yüan was granted permission by the Tokugawa bakufu to build a new temple and then received both the land and the fund-

ing to do so, the direct threat of Obaku having undue influence on
Myōshin-ji seemed to have been averted. Obaku would become an independent sect or lineage in Japan without direct links to Myōshin-ji
line temples. Yet tensions between the two groups did not ease. In fact,
they escalated. The existence of Obaku-san Mampuku-ji posed a new
and different kind of threat to Myōshin-ji, and the Myōshin-ji leadership responded in even sharper terms.

To understand the nature of Obaku's threat, several facts must be
borne in mind. First, Obaku received strong backing from the government on both national and local levels. That is to say, Obaku monks
and temples enjoyed the patronage of the bakufu in Edo as well as of
various local daimyo who governed the provinces. The retired emperor Gomizunoo also seemed to favor Yin-yüan's line, probably because of his established relationship with Master Ryōkei. The newly
founded Obaku line was thus in a strong position politically. As will
be seen later, Myōshin-ji monks criticized Obaku for its political connections, perhaps because these connections made its growth possible.
Furthermore, the new line almost immediately gained a small but increasing number of branch temples. These included the three existing Chinese temples in Nagasaki as well as some former Myōshin-ji
temples, such as Ryōkei's own Fumon-ji in Settsu.[18] Supporters of the
new sect, many of them former members of the Myōshin-ji line such
as Ryōkei, Chōon, and Tetsugyū, set out to spread the Obaku movement by establishing new temples.[19] Since bakufu regulations prohibited building new ones, this often took the form of changing the
affiliation of an existing temple from its previous main temple to
Mampuku-ji. Studies of Edo period temple listings would have to be
done on a case-by-case basis to determine the exact numbers, but
many of the early Obaku temples were originally branch temples
of Myōshin-ji. This was only natural, as the former Myōshin-ji line
monks who joined Obaku had strong connections with them. Obaku
therefore represented a significant drain on Myōshin-ji's material and
human resources.

Myōshin-ji took steps to stem the tide of defections to Obaku. For
example, two or three monks from Ryōan-ji, a branch temple where
Ryōkei had previously served as abbot, were placed under house arrest for one hundred days and not allowed any contact with the
outside world during that time as a punishment for their association
with the Obaku movement.[20] Gudō intended to expel anyone who
had taken up residence at an Obaku temple and did not return imme-

diately to Myōshin-ji when summoned. The most obvious target of
the new policy was Ryōkei. He was, after all, the most prominent
member of the Myōshin-ji community to support Yin-yüan, and consequently came under the fiercest attack. It is not clear whether or not
Gudō's threat to expel the pro-Obaku monks actually contributed
to the eventual return of several individuals, including Jikuin and
Tokuō. In their cases, the timing of their return to Myōshin-ji suggests
that it may have influenced their decision. Jikuin broke with Ryōkei
first and returned to Myōshin-ji before Yin-yüan's trip to Edo in
1658. If one follows the account in the *Obaku geki*, Tokuō would
have left Yin-yüan's assembly the following year in order to participate in the three hundredth anniversary celebration of the founding of Myōshin-ji by Kanzan.[21] According to Kawakami's history of
Myōshin-ji, however, Tokuō did not actually return to Myōshin-ji
until 1662, a year after Gudō's death. At that time, Tangetsu (1607–
1672), a master more sympathetic to Obaku, was serving as abbot.[22]
Tangetsu greeted the Chinese master with great pleasure. He initiated
contact with Yin-yüan during his early days in Nagasaki and remained
in correspondence with him over the years. Although Tangetsu never
became directly affiliated with Obaku and retained his allegiance to
the Myōshin-ji line, he remained on cordial terms with various Obaku
monks.

Gudō's intention to expel monks who were associated with Obaku
took on concrete form only after his death, when the assembly at
Myōshin-ji took decisive action in 1665. Ryōkei became Yin-yüan's
Dharma heir in the first month of 1664 and officially changed his
Dharma name from Sōsen to Shōsen.[23] During the following year,
Myōshin-ji rewrote its posted regulations (*hekisho*) to explicitly prohibit its monks from practicing at other temples. At the same time, the
assembly formally decided to expel Ryōkei, defrocking him as a
Myōshin-ji line monk.[24] Given the timing and wording of the new reg-
ulations, Ryōkei's defection seems to have been the final straw that
precipitated the formal action taken at Myōshin-ji.

The revised regulations were posted at Myōshin-ji on 7/11/1665.
They read:

> It is an old temple rule that monks in our founder Kanzan's line-
> age do not hang their staffs [i.e., enter to practice] at other temples.
> Recently, there have been several people who have gone to other
> temples to practice, have changed their robes, altered their appear-
> ance, or changed their Dharma names. These monks have forgot-

ten their debt of gratitude to their [original] master and lost their sense of gratitude toward their home temple. Since this is not appropriate behavior for a monk, they will not be permitted to return to their home temple.

In recent years, [monks] at various branch temples of [Myōshin-ji] have wrongly performed the rituals of other temples, rituals of a kind that have never been heard in the three hundred years [of Myōshin-ji's existence]. Those who have forgotten their home temple's old ceremonies and have turned their backs on the strict procedures of our tradition are sinners against our sect. Henceforth they must promptly desist.

The above matter should be regarded as a firm rule to protect the home temple. Hereafter, anyone who violates it will suffer the calamity of expulsion.[25]

Although the regulation does not explicitly mention Obaku temples or specific monks, it was obviously designed to punish monks such as Ryōkei who had gone to Obaku temples to practice under Yin-yüan and the other Obaku masters. The first clause seems to describe Ryōkei in particular, since it mentions changing the Dharma name. The mention of changing robes and appearances would have been a more general reference, since all Japanese monks who entered Obaku assemblies were expected to change to Chinese robes and to follow such Chinese practices as shaving their heads less frequently and letting their nails grow long.

Ryōkei and another Myōshin-ji monk, Teijū Ezen (1592–1668), met and designed a response to the revised regulations, which they jointly issued in 1667. Teijū was among those punished by the assembly at Myōshin-ji based on the revised wall code. In his case, he was reprimanded for implementing portions of the Obaku monastic code along with elements of the Obaku style of ritual and practice at his temple, Ryūhō-ji, in Tottori. The second clause of the posted regulations was probably written specifically to address his case. Teijū composed the response and sent it anonymously to four officials at Myōshin-ji. The text begins by praising Yin-yüan and extolling his arrival in Japan as a special opportunity for Japanese Zen. It then replies to the points made in the posted regulations one by one. The heart of Teijū's argument was that the new regulations would prevent Japanese Rinzai from reaping the benefits of contact with Yin-yüan's Zen style. Teijū points out that Kanzan himself changed teachers and Dharma names during his own search for enlightenment, and that to prohibit individual monks and branch temples from enjoying the

benefits of contact with other teachers defied the original purpose of
Rinzai Zen.[26]

Myōshin-ji answered this anonymous letter with the *Takkyaku-mon*, a counterresponse written by the monk Mumon Genshin (1627–
1686).[27] Mumon called those who objected to the old rules of
Myōshin-ji and/or its Zen style traitors. He argued that in Japan there
was a Japanese Buddhist Dharma, and that Chinese robes, music, and
the like were disruptive to it. Therefore, he concluded, it would be a
terrible error for Myōshin-ji monks to regard Yin-yüan as a model to
be imitated. When in Japan, Chinese monks should conform to Japanese norms. Although Mumon claimed that Myōshin-ji's relations
with Yin-yüan were friendly and that the temple only wanted to prevent its members and subtemples from committing the error of as-
similation to a foreign Zen style, that was not the case. Relations between the two temples remained tense for many years, and monks
from Myōshin-ji continued to compose texts critical of Obaku and
its monks.

The *Zenrin shūhei shū*

In 1700, one such critical text, the *Zenrin shūhei shū*, was published
for the stated purpose of exposing the persistent evil habits that the
author believed threatened the continued health of the Zen sect.[28] The
text comprises two fascicles including a total of thirty-seven sections.
The second fascicle bears the title *Zoku zenrin shūhei shū*; it follows
precisely the same format and displays the same writing style as the
first. Scholars believe that both portions were written by the same
author and generally refer to the two volumes as a single work. The
preface to the first fascicle refers to the author as "an anonymous descendent of Hanazono" (*Hanazono no matsuyō mumyōshi*), and it is
generally accepted that Keirin Sūshin (1652–1728), the 313th abbot
of Myōshin-ji, actually composed the piece. Each of the thirty-seven
sections evaluates one evil practice or problematic text that the author
regards as harmful in some way to the Zen sect. Written under the
guise of exchanges between a student and his master, each section follows the format of question and answer.

The majority of the subjects covered by the *Zenrin shūhei shū*
relate directly to Rinzai Zen. It is obvious from the author's discussion that he regarded Obaku as a lineage falling under the general
rubric of Rinzai Zen and not as a completely separate institutional

entity. Nevertheless, his purpose is to protect Rinzai from any possible contamination from the Ming style of Zen represented by the Obaku masters. In addition to Rinzai and Obaku materials, the author made use of Sōtō resources whenever he deemed them applicable or useful. Indeed, the preface indicates that the author took an all-encompassing view of Zen. The text opens with the comment "There are some twenty lines of Zen [in Japan], from those of the forerunners Dōgen and Eisai down to the rear guards Yin-yüan and [Hsin-yueh] Hsing-ch'ou."²⁹

Although it is not its sole object of criticism, a large proportion of the *Zenrin shūhei shū* relates to Obaku Zen, either directly or indirectly. In some sections, the author mentions individual Obaku monks by name. More commonly, he makes general references to "Ming monks" who came to Japan. There are also a few specific cases where the subject matter strongly suggests criticism of individual Obaku monks or practices, but the author makes no direct reference to them as such. In all, seventeen sections are critical of Obaku Zen, eleven out of the twenty-two sections in the first fascicle, and six out of the fifteen in the second. For the sake of analysis, I have divided the criticisms against Obaku into four categories: (1) criticism leveled indirectly; (2) criticisms based on differences in Zen style; (3) defensive responses to implicit Obaku criticisms of Japanese Rinzai; and (4) criticisms against specific individuals.

The first two sections of the *Zenrin shūhei shū* make no direct mention of Obaku Zen, neither referring to Obaku monks by name nor using the more generic reference to "Ming monks," but the nature of the evil practices discussed suggests that Obaku is among the intended targets.³⁰ Section 1 discusses the proper use of offertory incense (*shihōkō* or *hōkō*) that a master offers to express gratitude to his Dharma master. The text argues against the practice of dividing up the offertory incense to recognize one's debt of gratitude toward various other masters, not just the Dharma master from whom one has inherited the Dharma. According to the writer, this practice is disrespectful and indicates that the monk has forgotten his *on,* the debt of gratitude owed to his Dharma master. This section may well be aimed at Ryōkei and others like him who, figuratively if not literally, divided their loyalties when they accepted Dharma transmission from Obaku masters.

The second section criticizes the practice of inappropriately taking up residence at a temple affiliated with another lineage. Such behavior is said to slight one's own Dharma lineage. In this case, the author specifically refers to the Sōtō practice of changing lineage whenever becoming abbot or head monk at a temple related to a different line (*in'in ekishi*), which became the norm in Sōtō Zen temples two hundred years earlier. At the time of the *Zenrin shūhei shū*'s publication, the Sōtō reformer Manzan was leading a movement against this practice. Keirin Sūshin, the author of the *Zenrin shūhei shū*, subsequently became involved in the Sōtō dispute in 1704, when he wrote a tract defending the position Manzan took in the *Shūtō fukko shi*. In the same context, Keizan refuted the *Shōbō Tekiden Shishi Ikkushū*, the work of Manzan's detractor, Jōzan.[31] It is quite possible that the movement of Rinzai monks from Myōshin-ji line temples to Obaku temples motivated Keirin to take a stand against the Sōtō practice.

The issue of moving between temples and switching Dharma lineages was a general topic for debate throughout the Zen world at that time. Neither Rinzai nor Obaku accepted the practice of *in'in ekishi* within their own lineages, but evidence suggests that it did sometimes occur. The posted rules at Myōshin-ji explicitly forbade monks to cross over between lineages, strong indication in itself that the practice was not unknown. The first-generation Japanese convert to Obaku, Chōon, is known to have fought against related abuses of Dharma lineage within the Obaku sect.[32] The author of the *Zenrin shūhei shū* may have intended his criticism of the Sōtō practice to apply equally to monks who crossed over from one Rinzai lineage to another, specifically from Myōshin-ji to Obaku. He may well have had Ryōkei's acceptance of Yin-yüan's Dharma specifically in mind, although Ryōkei's case was somewhat different from the Sōtō practice, which was the institutional norm and could involve several changes during a monk's career.

The second set of criticisms found in the *Zenrin shūhei shū* relates to differences in Zen style that existed between Japanese Rinzai and the Ming style represented by Obaku. The author of the *Zenrin shūhei shū* regards these differences as evidence of deterioration in Ch'an practice in China where, he explains, abuses of the accepted monastic code had become the norm. In most cases, these criticisms reflect changes in monastic practice that occurred in China between the Sung dynasty when Zen was transmitted to Japan and the late Ming period when Obaku masters emigrated. For example, the seating order of the monks customary in Obaku temples is based on the so-called uncle-nephew (*shukutetsu*) system commonly used in Ming China. Following this protocol, monks are ranked according to both their years of individual practice and their sublineage's relative standing in the overall Obaku lineage. The *Zenrin shūhei shū* dismisses this alternative system of etiquette as "a wicked habit of these latter days." In the Japanese context, it may well have appeared to be an innovation. Zen temples in Japan traditionally preferred an arrangement based exclusively on the individual's years of practice and personal advancement, the system introduced at the Japanese Gozan temples sometime during the thirteenth or fourteenth century.[33] In a similar manner, changes that occurred in the use of celebratory incense and the introduction of prayer amulets between the early Sung and the late Ming are said to be the result of debasement in the Ch'an style in China. Had contact between the Chinese and Japanese Zen communities not been severely limited for two to three centuries, the Japanese would have been exposed more gradually to changes in Chinese practice. Perhaps under these circumstances the discontinuity between Obaku and Rinzai practices would have seemed less abrupt and Obaku would have appeared less foreign to Japanese observers.

In several sections, the *Zenrin shūhei shū* echoes themes first introduced in Kyorei's early report on conditions within Yin-yüan's assembly at Kōfuku-ji. First and foremost, it discusses various alternatives (regarded in the text as changes) in the monastic code observed at Obaku temples. In a number of sections, these changes are interpreted as Ming departures from a "pure" and universal Zen monastic code that was preserved in Japan but was either corrupted or totally lost in China. For example, the Obaku style of ritual music and chanting, which clearly offended many Japanese Rinzai monks, is said to be the result of Ming Zen having "forgotten the eternal rule of Pai-chang."[34]

The differences held up for censure range in nature from relatively major changes in ritual observance to minor issues such as alterations in the names of temple buildings and the proper wording inscribed on temple sign boards. In a section dedicated to listing a number of these smaller examples, the author suggests that the underlying reason for all of the many minor abuses of Zen etiquette and custom is that Ming monks were not sufficiently familiar with the standard Zen code. The text reads:

> They have not memorized the rule, so they think that the style in [Japanese] Zen monasteries is not correct. . . . I heard that once Yin-yüan had come to Japan, he began to read the *Pai-chang ch'ing-*

kuei. He said that in Ming China it had been lost for a long time, but fortunately in Japan he could read it and thereby emerge from the mists of ignorance. How true![35]

It is not at all clear to which version of the Pai-chang code the author is referring here. Most likely he alludes to the *Ch'ih-hsiu Pai-chang ch'ing-kuei* (J. *Chokushū Hyakujō shingi*), a Yüan dynasty text then commonly assumed to be an edited version based on Pai-chang's original code. This text had already been transmitted to Japan in the fourteenth century, and also remained extant in Ming and Ching dynasty China. Ming editions of the Chinese Buddhist Scriptures included the text, and it is well established that Obaku masters had access to a complete copy of the scriptures at Wan-fu-ssu. Indeed, Yin-yüan brought his own complete copy of the Chinese scriptures with him to Japan, later used as the basis for the Obaku-ban. The *Ch'ih-hsiu Pai-chang ch'ing-kuei* appears as text number 1636, volumes 1 and 2 in box number 263 in the Obaku-ban. In any event, given Obaku's dedication to strict monastic discipline, the suggestion that Obaku masters did not fully understand the classical Zen monastic code or had lost it altogether is an especially severe criticism. It undermines one of the basic characteristics of Obaku's Zen style. There is a strong sense here that the author of the *Zenrin shūhei shū* believed that the true practice of pure Chinese Ch'an was preserved only in Japanese Rinzai temples and not in the contemporary Chinese style of Obaku Zen.

The author of the *Zenrin shūhei shū* comes very close to saying precisely that in a section on proper etiquette for wearing the Zen monk's cap (*mōsu*). Having quoted a passage from the *Ch'ih-hsiu Pai-chang ch'ing-kuei* that prescribed the appropriate times to remove the cap, he observes, "Fortunately, this kind of old rule still exists in the Zen monasteries of Japan today and can still be observed."[36] What follows is a rather strange discussion of Ming etiquette, with explicit references to the Obaku line, presumably designed to show that, unlike the Japanese, the Chinese had corrupted the Zen code. Although he never explicitly explains what differences exist in the Chinese behavior, he offers a variety of possible explanations for them: the Chinese monks may be imitating popular secular custom; they may wish to disguise their worldly appearance;[37] or they may mistakenly believe that monks' caps serve the same purpose as the headdress of government officials, and so on. It seems likely that the underlying issue in this section is the offensiveness of the overtly Chinese appearance retained at Obaku temples, where Chinese dress and grooming remained the norm.

In a related section, the author identifies running quickly during *kinhin*, the walking meditation performed as a break during sessions of seated meditation, as a late development introduced to Japan by Ming monks. He decries the fast-paced *kinhin* as a form of lunacy rather than a true Zen practice. It is interesting that, in this case, the writer has actually given precedence to the Sōtō manner of meditation and, appropriately, selects a passage from a Japanese Sōtō text, the *Keizan shingi*, to defend the superiority of slower-paced *kinhin*.[38] Once again, the author provides an explanation for the Ming innovation.

> I personally believe that the Zen style of contemporary Ming China has degenerated. They don't even keep the fast! Noon and night they eat whenever they feel like it. They are always sated. Therefore, when they sit in meditation, their minds sink into darkness and sleep can easily overtake them. Even if they raise their body and shift their legs, they still don't wake up. Therefore they are trying to focus their attention by walking fast and running around. Is this skill in *samadhi*? It is not. It is a crazy practice. It cannot rightly be called *kinhin*.[39]

In this passage, the author of the *Zenrin shūhei shū* argues that a breach in the most basic rules for novices regarding mealtimes inevitably results in a decline in meditative practice. The Chinese overeat, so they must resort to running to stay awake during meditation sessions. Here the eighteenth-century text raises a theme first mentioned by Kyorei but develops it much further and in more negative terms. While Kyorei praised the meditation he observed at Kōfuku-ji, the *Zenrin shūhei shū* implies that Obaku's departure from the monastic code severely undermines the monks' ability to meditate.

A third group of criticisms represents Japanese responses to explicit and implicit Obaku criticisms of the Rinzai style dominant in Japan. Obaku masters made extensive use of the recorded sayings (*goroku*) of earlier Zen masters, especially the *Rinzairoku*. These original texts were given preference over the major collections of koan such as the *Hekigan roku* that were more influential in Japan than in Ming China.[40] Obaku masters encouraged the study of these Zen texts in a manner not commonly seen in Japanese Rinzai temples before Obaku influence. They sought not to use small portions of them as koans, although that practice was not unknown in Obaku, but rather to read and understand the text as a whole. Yin-yüan and other Obaku masters based their own lectures on these original texts, explaining or applying them to the immediate context concerning their disciples. According to Yanagida Seizan, Japanese Rinzai typically relied upon the *Hekigan roku* as its guiding text until influenced by the Obaku preference. Yanagida suggests that it was Yin-yüan who inspired the movement toward undertaking direct study of the original Zen literature, especially the *Rinzai roku,* that began during the Tokugawa period. Early on, Obaku's alternative emphasis was seen as an implicit criticism of Japanese Rinzai for its reliance on koan collections rather than the reading of recorded sayings in their entirety. Although the *Zenrin shūhei shū* section that discourages the use of Zen texts for study rather than practice contains no direct reference to Obaku, explication of recorded sayings was so closely associated with Obaku monks that it is regarded as a criticism of Obaku.

The *Zenrin shūhei shū* becomes overtly defensive when it examines two Obaku texts that explicitly expressed criticism of the Japanese use of koan collections, the *Bukai nanshin* (sometimes read *Mukai nanshin*) of Chōon Dōkai (1628–1695), and Ryōkei's *Shūtōroku.*[41] It should be noted that both of these texts were written by Japanese Obaku masters who had originally studied under Japanese Rinzai teachers. They both had a firsthand familiarity with the approach to koan practice then prevalent throughout the Japanese Rinzai world. As the *Zenrin shūhei shū* explains, the Rinzai system was based on a series of three hundred koan, with the one hundred cases from the *Hekigan roku* forming the heart of the process.[42] The relevant passage reads, "If Nanshin [Chōon] wants to know about our three hundred koan cases [they include the following:] First of all, the one hundred cases in the *Hekigan roku* are known as the main practice. Then there are, in addition, one hundred cases of prior practice known as the Pre-Hekigan (*hekizen*) and the later one hundred cases known as the Post-Hekigan (*hekigo*)."[43]

While it is difficult to know exactly how koan were used by the early Obaku masters, they were probably not as dependent on the traditional koan collections as were their Japanese counterparts. It is said that in addition to assigning more traditional cases, Obaku masters often invented koan spontaneously for their students to suit a specific situation. According to Furuta Shōkin, for example, Chōon was attracted to Obaku in large part because its basic approach to Zen practice did not focus exclusively on traditional koan cases. Yin-yüan and his predecessors Fei-yin and Mi-yun were said to have revived the T'ang style of Zen, which stressed an immediate form of interaction between master and disciple rather than relying upon traditional koan cases, as became the norm from the Sung dynasty onward.[44] The master Chi-fei, under whom Chōon studied for a time, was said to be especially talented at inventing koan to meet the specific needs of his students. Chōon's experience with Chi-fei may have contributed to his negative appraisal of the Japanese system of koan study.

Chōon wrote the *Bukai nanshin* in 1666 as a *kana hōgo*, a Buddhist sermon composed in vernacular Japanese, for a laywoman who lived in Edo. The text maps out a form of Zen not based on koan practice at all, but rather formatted upon the four Bodhisattva vows: (1) to save all sentient beings; (2) to extinguish all the afflictions; (3) to study all Buddhist teachings; and (4) to attain the supreme Buddha way and the six perfections (charity, observance of the precepts, perseverance, energy, meditation, and wisdom).[45] In the passage from the *Bukai nanshin* quoted by the *Zenrin shūhei shū*, Chōon attacks the fossilized practice of koan that he had experienced as a Rinzai monk in his youth.

> They just memorized the koans of the ancient masters and reduced the practice of Zen to written language and conversational language. Or they would choose from the three hundred cases in the *Hekigan roku* and take that to be koan practice. As the secular proverb says, they were keeping count. They kept careful count of their comings and goings and called that the Great Awakening of Enlightenment.[46]

Chōon describes here a form of koan study then prevalent in Japan in which the Zen student mastered the literary content of the classical Chinese koan without necessarily seeking to penetrate any one of them for an enlightenment experience. In this approach, the master need not be enlightened himself but only to have gone through the same regimen of study.[47] Obaku masters like Chōon were not alone in criticizing the Japanese system. Japanese Rinzai masters also realized that there was a basic problem in the Rinzai practice of koan in the early Tokugawa period, and one of the reforms attributed to the eighteenth-century Rinzai master Hakuin was the revitalization of the koan system.[48] Hakuin's own critical view of the koan practice that had existed before his time may have been somewhat akin to Chōon's, as he himself developed a more dynamic approach.

The passage quoted from Ryōkei's *Shūtōroku* in the *Zenrin shūhei shū* presents a critical appraisal of his contemporaries' reliance on the *Hekigan shū*. In the passage, Ryōkei explains that the version of the text in common use is a muddled patchwork of the original; plagued as it is with extensive corruptions, the text is difficult to decipher, let alone understand.[49] Ryōkei admits that, with careful study, one may benefit from reading it but wonders whether it deserves the high reputation it enjoys.

> The text has words missing, and correct and incorrect [sections] are mixed together and muddled. If one works at it, one can distinguish the gist of our sect's teaching within it. Still, is it appropriate to call this kind of leftover food and soured rice The Blue Cliff of [Zen Master] Bukka [Engo]?[50]

In particular, Ryōkei seems to doubt the value of investing as much energy in writing commentaries on the text as Chinese and Japanese continue to do. Without a study of the full text of the *Shūtōroku*, it is hard to know how Ryōkei intended these remarks. Like Chōon, Ryōkei may have been objecting to the literary and academic exercises based on the *Hekigan roku* that passed for koan practice at the time. The *Zenrin shūhei shū*'s response is not enlightening, since it is primarily ad hominem in nature.

Although Chinese and Japanese monks shared the written language of classical Chinese, the language barrier created many difficulties in the early encounters between Obaku masters and Japanese monks. In some respects, even the common written language seems to have been a source of tension. One of the implicit criticisms that the *Zenrin shūhei shū* addresses is the Chinese contention that the Japanese did not generally have a firm mastery of classical Chinese. It may be difficult to pinpoint examples in which Obaku masters denigrated Japanese abilities in the written language, but it is obvious that Japanese monks felt that this had occurred. Japanese and Chinese styles of written Chinese do differ. The Japanese tend to use more particles, indicating various verb inflections characteristic of Japanese. This allows a text to be more readily rendered into Japanese according to *kambun* markings. The Obaku masters used Ming colloquial expressions unknown to the Japanese that differed from the older style of written language with which the Japanese were familiar.

During centuries leading up to the Tokugawa period when exchange with China was limited, Zen monks served as advisors to various Japanese rulers because of their education and literary ability in written Chinese, the language of official discourse down to the modern period. This remained the case in the early Tokugawa period until Confucian scholars began to fill the roles previously held by Zen monks. Zen temples had long been the guardians of culture, and were among the only sources of education available in Japan until the rise of neo-Confucian schools during the Tokugawa period.[51] Language ability in written Chinese was a source of pride for many Japanese monks, and it would be only natural for them to perceive native speakers as a kind of threat to their status in the intellectual world. This was no doubt intensified by the fact that many intellectuals came to view the Chinese Obaku masters as a resource for recovering the spoken language and improving their written skills as well.

In the section in the *Zenrin shūhei shū* related to differences in Chinese and Japanese pronunciation, the initial question strikes just such a note of appreciation for the reintroduction of spoken Chinese by the Obaku masters. The author's response exemplifies the defensive attitude that may have been common among Japanese monks.

> When the Dharma descendents [of Chinese masters] brought the teachings of all the sects [to Japan], they brought all the sutras and dharani, but the Chinese pronunciation was lost. Recently, Ming monks have come to Japan and once again we can hear the Chinese pronunciation. Isn't that fortunate?
>
> Reply: That is extremely foolish! Not only do you (*nanji*) not know Chinese pronunciation, you don't know Japanese pronunciation either![52]

The section continues with an extended explanation of *on* and *kun* readings of Chinese characters (pronunciations said to reflect the original Chinese word and the indigenous Japanese equivalent, respectively). It identifies the former as authentic Chinese pronunciation and the latter as Japanese. It concludes with a denial that the language spoken by the Ming monks was actually Chinese.

> As you know, in their country ever since the Yüan and Ming dynasties, the Mongols have ruled the country, so the [Chinese] tattoo their bodies and cut their hair [like the Mongols]. Their language and literature have also been greatly altered by these northern barbarians. Therefore, what the Ming monks say is Chinese isn't really Chinese. It's Ming and therefore Mongol.[53]

According to the *Zenrin shūhei shū*, Japanese sinophiles would do better to work on their own than to study the language with the Obaku emigrés!

One of the final sections of the *Zenrin shūhei shū* presents a concluding defensive argument against any possible revitalizing role that some Japanese hoped Obaku Zen would fill. This concluding topic probably represents the strongest reaction against Obaku in Japanese

Rinzai. The idea that Yin-yüan's Zen style could revitalize Japanese
Rinzai was circulating among some Rinzai monks even before Yin-
yüan left China. The Japanese monks who joined Obaku assemblies
were not alone in their belief that Japanese Rinzai needed to take steps
to improve the level of its practice and discipline. Other movements
for reform arose at Myōshin-ji in the seventeenth century and culmi-
nated in Hakuin's work in the eighteenth. The other movements, however, strongly opposed the suggestion that Obaku held any answers to
the problems plaguing Japanese Rinzai.

The *Zenrin shūhei shū* responds to the suggestion that Obaku
held a key for revitalizing Rinzai by first calling into question the motives that had brought the Obaku founders to Japan. According to the
text, they came, not as "men who have forgotten themselves for the
sake of the Dharma," as some believed, but rather out of a sense of
despair. The passage briefly recounts the unsuccessful public debate
of Yin-yüan's master and predecessor at Wan-fu-ssu, Master Fei-yin
T'ung-jung. Fei-yin had challenged the validity of the lineages of certain of his contemporaries in his compilation of Zen biographies,
entitled *Gotō gentō* (The exact lineage of the five lamps), published in
1653. Fei-yin's charges had extended beyond the confines of Lin-chi
Ch'an and called into question a number of Ts'ao-tung lineages. This
caused considerable opposition from Ts'ao-tung adherents, leading
eventually to a public debate before the secular authorities between
Fei-yin and the Ts'ao-tung master Yung-chüeh Yüan-hsien (1578–
1657; J. Eigaku Genken). The debate took place a few months after
Yin-yüan had departed from China in 1654. Fei-yin lost the debate,
and as a consequence the authorities ordered the destruction of the
original woodblocks of the *Gotō gentō*.[54] The *Zenrin shūhei shū* claims
that Fei-yin's defeat caused the whole Obaku line to lose heart and
thus to accept the invitations that they come to Nagasaki. The actual
timing of Yin-yüan's departure for Japan vis-à-vis the public debate
and defeat of Fei-yin obviously undermines this claim. Nevertheless,
the thrust of the argument remains that Yin-yüan and his followers
came to Japan first and foremost to escape misfortune, not to spread
the Dharma.

It is somewhat ironic that the *Zenrin shūhei shū* goes on to criticize
the Obaku sect for arbitrarily limiting the abbots at the three Nagasaki temples to direct disciples of Yin-yüan's line. By the time of its
writing, the three original Chinese temples in Nagasaki were all affiliated with Obaku as branch temples under the head temple, Mam-

puku-ji. These temples not only continued to serve the ritual needs of the Chinese expatriate community in Nagasaki, they also provided a staging post for fresh talent from China who could serve at Mampuku-ji and other major Obaku temples. The abbots at the Nagasaki temples were generally Chinese monks from Wan-fu-ssu, but there is no clear documentary evidence to corroborate the claim that this was required. The passage harkens back to Tao-che's departure from Sōfuku-ji (at which time he was replaced by one of Yin-yüan's disciples). It suggests that, although Tao-che came to Japan fully qualified to serve as abbot (literally, with a master's whisk in hand), he was not permitted to serve at any of the three Nagasaki temples because he did not belong to Yin-yüan's immediate lineage. If the Nagasaki temples had limited the ranks of monks who could serve as abbot in this manner, they would have matched similar limitations that applied to all Myōshin-ji line temples.

The final words of the section indicate just how offensive the author found the suggestion that Obaku could revitalize Rinzai:

> The [Chinese] merchants mistakenly brought over ordinary monks who did not [qualify to carry a master's] whisk. They came and soon called themselves fully qualified masters. For five to seven years they closed their gate and engaged in pen and ink *samadhi*. And by doing that they plan to reform the Zen community! Oh, it won't be so difficult! This is another bad Dharma habit that the Ming monks have augmented in recent years.[55]

The reference to pen-and-ink *samadhi* (*hikken sammai*) is not completely clear. It may refer to the practice of using written exchanges between Japanese disciples and Chinese masters, who shared only the written language. Alternately, it may be an attack on Obaku's Zen style, suggesting that it focuses on artistic pursuits or a literary understanding of Zen texts rather than on attaining enlightenment.

Several Obaku masters come under severe personal attack in the *Zenrin shūhei shū*, and these ad hominem criticisms form the fourth and final category to be considered here. As seen above, questioning the motives of the Chinese masters forms one type of personal attack. "I have heard that Yin-yüan, Mu-an, Chi-fei, and Kao-ch'üan were truly the foremost [monks] from contemporary Ming China. Be that as it may, it happens that, to a man, they came to this country and are not at all [the type of] men who have forgotten themselves for the sake of the Dharma."[56] The depth of the Obaku founders' understanding is likewise questioned in another section:

When the founder of the Obaku [line] first arrived in Japan, people had not yet fathomed the shallowness of his enlightenment. There were a number of people such as Bankei [Yōtaku], Kengan [Zen'etsu], and Ran from the Myōshin-ji line and some Sōtō monks such as [Unzan] Guhaku and [Dokuan] Genkō from Higo and Hizen who did not completely agree with him. When it came to the second abbot [of Mampuku-ji] Mu-an Hsing-t'ao, people half believed and half doubted him. By the time you reach the third and fourth generations, [the Obaku abbots] were already completely debased (*shichirei hachiraku*). Even if there were one or two of them capable of spreading their own position, none of them had so much as tasted the spittle of our secret practice of Zen. Although one cannot be sure about the founder, when one considers the fact that the [line] after him was completely debased, one wonders if perhaps the founder also failed to fathom his origin.[57]

To devalue the understanding of the founder and his immediate successor quite naturally debases the entire lineage. The harshest words in the *Zenrin shūhei shū*, however, are reserved for those Japanese Rinzai monks who left the Myōshin-ji line in favor of Obaku.

Monks such as Ryōkei and Chōon were perceived by many as traitors to their original Dharma lineage. Ryōkei represents a special case among the monks who converted to Obaku, because none of the others had approached his rank and stature within Japanese Rinzai before they changed affiliation. Most of the converts were young men like Chōon and Tetsugyū who had not yet received *inka*, let alone a purple robe or the position of abbot at Myōshin-ji. The *Zenrin shūhei shū* singles out Ryōkei as the worst offender against Rinzai Zen, using unusually strong language.

> Ryōkei had long since received *inka* from Master Hakubu Eryō. He had accepted the imperial command and succeeded to [the position of abbot] at Myōshin-ji. Then later he traded his inheritance and changed his robes. Not only did he deceive himself and others, he betrayed his debt of gratitude [to his Dharma line] and scorned the imperial command. One can say that he is the greatest sinner among monks and lay people alike. His acts of flattery would cause a wise man shame.[58]

Because Ryōkei had attained a high rank within the Myōshin-ji hierarchy, the *Zenrin shūhei shū* regards him as the lowest sinner. Ryōkei's unfortunate death in a flood tide in Osaka in 1670 is even represented as the karmic retribution for his sins against the Zen community. Other Rinzai texts went so far as to refer to the flood tide as "Kanzan's wave," indicating that it brought retribution from Kanzan Egen, the founder of Myōshin-ji, against Ryōkei for his defection.[59]

Chōon was a younger, lower-ranking monk when he joined Obaku, so he did not incur the same wrath as Ryōkei. Nonetheless, he was a prolific writer and influential in spreading Obaku teachings, and so an obvious target for criticism. The author of the *Zenrin shūhei shū* begins his assessment of the *Bukai nanshin* with a story designed to show the debased level of Chōon's character and thus discredit his writing. The author recounts his own chance meeting with the Obaku monk when on pilgrimage some years earlier:

> Quite unexpectedly, [Chōon] rented a cottage and set up an ordination platform. He played on an instrument and so summoned the foolish men and women from the neighboring houses. He made it into a place of practice (*dōjō*) for repenting and receiving the precepts. He accepted a fee [for conferring] the precepts. Then he left and went to another inn, and then another. Each day he took in some money in this manner and then would take a rest. Truly, he resembled a performer who dances mime or does tricks with a lion.[60]

The historical accuracy of the charge that Chōon inappropriately accepted funds for bestowing the precepts like a traveling minstrel is unknown. One would hardly expect to find corroboration for this practice in the Obaku literature, since it is a clear breach of the monastic code. Obaku sources do confirm that Chōon sometimes performed a precept ceremony for lay people as a part of his public teaching. It is equally clear that he traveled throughout Japan, as is evidenced by the number of temples that he founded in various provinces.

The *Obaku geki* of Mujaku Dōchū

The second Rinzai text to be considered here is the *Obaku geki,* written by one of Myōshin-ji's finest scholars of the early Tokugawa period, Mujaku Dōchū (1653–1745). The text is divided into two distinct sections. The first portion provides a narrative account of Yin-yüan's early years in Japan, giving extensive information about the role played by Myōshin-ji monks in gaining official permission for him to remain permanently in the country. Mujaku wrote this section in Japanese, drawing on the recollections of his master, Jikuin, and other contemporaries, as well as some textual evidence. The second section of the *Obaku geki* comprises a series of short vignettes, each under a separate title, written in classical Chinese. These passages vary greatly in style and content, and seem to come from a variety of sources. The vignettes stand as independent units that Mujaku could not easily have tied together into a narrative. They do, however, share a common theme of presenting Obaku monks in a bad light. Throughout both portions of the text, Mujaku interjects his own reflections and conjectures, clearly marking these comments as such. In addition, he occasionally inserts a quotation from classical Buddhist sources that he finds in some way illuminating to the issue at hand.

Like the majority of Mujaku's works, the *Obaku geki* was never published in a woodblock edition for general circulation. Until quite recently, only a few original handwritten copies of the *Obaku geki* existed.[61] According to the listing in Iida Rigyō's biography of Mujaku, three original copies of the *Obaku geki* exist, one at Shunkō-in at Myōshin-ji, a second at Nagasaki's historical museum, and a third at Tokyo University.[62] All comments made here are based on the Shunkō-in copy written in Mujaku's own hand. Given the paucity of copies, it seems likely that Mujaku intended the text for internal circulation within the Myōshin-ji community, not for the wider Zen community. Given the negative portrait that Mujaku drew of individual Obaku monks and the lineage as a whole, he may have intended the *Obaku geki* as a warning to any and all Myōshin-ji monks who still found the Obaku style of Zen appealing. He may also have hoped to clarify his master Jikuin's role in inviting Yin-yüan to Kyoto, in order to distance him from the likes of Ryōkei, already fully discredited in the eyes of many Myōshin-ji monks, and from others who persisted in their support for Yin-yüan.

There are a few problems with dating the *Obaku geki* as a whole. Some scholars have also questioned the authorship of portions of the text. At the end of the Japanese narrative, Mujaku signed his name, Dōchū of Ryūge-in, and recorded the date as the second day of the eighth lunar month of the year Kyōhō 5 (1720).[63] For this reason, most scholars regard the whole text as dating from that year. In fact, there is no way of knowing when Mujaku composed or added the Chinese sections. They are arranged as separate units and could have been written before or after the narrative, and may well have been collected over a period of several years. An episode recounted in the final Chinese vignette reportedly dates from the year Genbun 4 (1739), so at the very least the final episode was added on much later than 1720.[64] In addition, whereas Mujaku's signature makes the author-

ship of the Japanese portion obvious, some scholars, notably Minamoto Ryōen, have questioned the authenticity of the Chinese portion, which bears no such mark.[65]

Minamoto conjectures that another monk either edited or composed the Chinese section, basing his findings on a number of observations. First, he notes that the interspersed comments identify the
speaker alternatively as Dōchū or Hōu. Based on his own impressions
of the content and style of these comments, Minamoto believes the
names refer to two different people. In point of fact, however, Hōu
was one of Mujaku's pen names, which he used in many other of his
writings. A careful study of the usage of the two names in the *Obaku
geki* itself shows that Mujaku consistently refers to himself as Dōchū
in the Japanese portion of the text and Hōu in the Chinese sections.
The single occurrence of the name Hōu found in the Japanese narrative appears in a Chinese passage, one that Mujaku inserted into the
Japanese narrative as part of his editorial remarks.[66] Minamoto explains that in the copy of the text he consulted, a note was written in
the margin by a Chinese monk to the effect that Mujaku always wrote
in *kana* because he did not know Chinese. (No comparable remark
appears in the Shunkō-in copy.) Minamoto makes no attempt to evaluate this comment but simply quotes from it. The remark has no basis in fact. Mujaku displayed an impressive grasp of classical Chinese
in the many volumes of scholarship he composed in that language, especially in his lexicons of Zen terms drawn from the Chinese Ch'an
corpus, which are still highly regarded by scholars today.

Minamoto's doubts about the authorship of the Chinese segments
may well have arisen because of problems related to the copy of the
Obaku geki he consulted. Minamoto does not identify which of
the three existing originals he used, but it could not have been the
Myōshin-ji copy preserved at Shunkō-in. Yanagida Seizan, one of
Japan's leading experts on Mujaku, positively identified the Shunkō-
in copy as an example of Mujaku's own handwriting.[67] It does not
contain any marginal notes of the type mentioned above. Furthermore, Minamoto refers to a vignette, apparently written in Chinese,
which does not appear in the Shunkō-in copy.[68] It appears that
Minamoto may be correct in assuming that the copy he examined
was edited by a later monk. This is not, however, the case with the
Shunkō-in copy; both the Chinese and the Japanese portions of that
text were written by Mujaku himself.

Since the material in the *Obaku geki* is primarily anecdotal in nature, its criticism of Obaku Zen centers on stories about individual Obaku monks. Most of the material focuses on Yin-yüan and Ryōkei, but a few sections discuss the activities of anonymous Obaku monks of later generations. I shall first examine the portraits drawn of individual monks before moving on to evaluate the general criticisms of Obaku implicit in the text.

Mujaku overtly represents Yin-yüan as a degenerate monk who sought his own fame and fortune rather than serving the cause of the Dharma. In fact, the Yin-yüan depicted in the *Obaku geki* manipulated the very practice of spreading the Dharma as a means to achieve his own personal ends.

> I knew from his first words that he was that kind of monk. When Yin-yüan first turned to my teacher Jikuin, he said, "Since you know many of the daimyo, if you were to act as intermediary in building me a two-mat grass hut, I could set up my Dharma banner." When he said that, I knew for certain that he was a monk [seeking] fame and fortune. In ancient times, truly worthy teachers would never have said such a thing even by mistake, because it wouldn't have entered their minds in the first place. As you might expect, his followers are fools taken in by his deceiving spirit. They fan the fire of decadence all the more. The nation is full of lawless and debauched men who add and subtract from the teachings and do not preserve the precepts at all. Although people say that he will rekindle Japanese Zen, one would better say that he will corrupt it.[69]

Mujaku further illustrates this point by mentioning two other inappropriate actions taken by or for Yin-yüan that led to Jikuin withdrawing from Yin-yüan's cause. First was the episode involving a purple robe improperly procured for Yin-yüan.[70] On one occasion when Jikuin happened to visit a tailor's shop in Kyoto that specialized in making Chinese-style monastic robes, he came across a purple robe made up in the Chinese fashion. He inquired about it and learned that it was intended for Yin-yüan. Fearing the worst, Jikuin rushed to Fumon-ji to confront Ryōkei about the methods by which the robe had been obtained. Actively seeking the honor of a purple robe was offensive enough to Jikuin in purely religious terms, but to do so without following proper procedure could have brought grave political consequences on the fledgling Obaku movement and the entire Rinzai sect. Myōshin-ji was one of two Zen temples embroiled in the so-called Purple Robe Affair earlier in the century. Members of the temple had been stripped of imperial honors, including purple robes, when the bakufu took action against the emperor's involvement in Buddhist affairs. Myōshin-ji monks were therefore somewhat sensitive about the issue.

Yin-yüan's second serious breach of Buddhist conduct was actively to seek an audience with the shogun Ietsuna. Mujaku quotes Jikuin as having said, "The illustrious monks of antiquity were sometimes summoned by the king or a minister, but they would not go. Still less would they themselves have desired an audience. It is entirely wrong for this bearded Chinese to act as if he wants an audience. Yin-yüan has lost his morals."[71] Once again Jikuin took action, this time informing the bakufu of his official resignation as Yin-yüan's representative. Mujaku obviously concurred with his master's assessment of Yin-yüan's behavior. By presenting Obaku's founder in this light, Mujaku hoped to defend Japanese Rinzai from any contaminating Obaku influences that others misguidedly took for reform.

Ryōkei participated actively in the above two episodes, using his considerable influence as a former abbot of Myōshin-ji to gain advantage for Yin-yüan with both the bakufu and the court. Mujaku paints an ambiguous portrait of Ryōkei, one that is basically free of the baser motivations seen in Yin-yüan's words and deeds. In marked contrast to the *Zenrin shūhei shū*, the *Obaku geki* contains only one example of direct criticism of Ryōkei. In one of the vignettes recorded in Chinese, Gudō criticizes Ryōkei's close association with Yin-yüan: "And as for that Ryōkei, he's bald and wrinkled. He's old enough to know better. But when he encounters something new he gets himself turned upside down and loses his head. He really should be pitied."[72] This remark seems to capture Mujaku's implicit opinion of Ryōkei, who appears in the text as an eager and somewhat naive supporter of Yin-yüan. Ryōkei seems more of a dupe who falls under the spell of the manipulative Chinese monks than a villain himself. Even in the episode that describes Ryōkei presenting a Zen master's whisk to Emperor Gomizunoo as a symbol of Dharma transmission, Ryōkei is not portrayed as the real villain. Rather it is Kao-ch'üan who comes across as the truly guilty party who lied about the emperor's final wishes in order to usurp the imperial name exclusively for Obaku.[73] As is often the case in literature critical of new religious movements, the founders of the movement, in this case the Chinese monks, are cast as unscrupulous individuals with irreligious ulterior motives while their followers are portrayed as misguided souls.

From the viewpoint of the *Obaku geki,* the early Japanese supporters of Obaku, represented by Ryōkei, Jikuin, and Tokuō, seem to
have made the mistake of trusting the Chinese master Yin-yüan before
they really knew him. They were attracted by the unknown, a trait
shared by many Japanese living in the closed world of Tokugawa
Japan. In at least two scenes, Mujaku mentions that crowds of ordinary Japanese gathered to catch a glimpse of Yin-yüan, drawn by the
novelty of seeing a Chinese. In much the same way, Ryōkei was fool-
ishly intrigued by the exotic Chinese style of Zen, but he did not truly
understand Yin-yüan's character. Those who were able to see through
to the truth either broke with Yin-yüan or never supported him in the
first place. In one episode, which Mujaku recounts only to dismiss
later as fallacious, a government official wisely refused to support
Yin-yüan sight unseen. The official observed that even after knowing a person for a number of years one may not really know what is
in another's heart, much less understand the motivations of a total
stranger.[74] In Mujaku's account, the government officials who eventually made the decision enabling Yin-yüan to remain in Japan and to
found a large monastery based their judgments upon the reliability
and character of the Japanese monks in Yin-yüan's service, and not on
their direct knowledge of Yin-yüan himself. Mujaku glosses over the
changes that occurred in the bakufu's attitude after the shogun and
councilors had met Yin-yüan for themselves.

The *Obaku geki* probably served as a warning to the innocent
monks at Myōshin-ji who might be swept up in the excitement and
novelty of the new religious movement. As Mujaku pointed out, however, not only the innocent ran that risk: monks with similarly debased
characters would naturally be attracted to Yin-yüan and gravitate toward Obaku as well. Mujaku provides a specific example of this by
recounting a later event involving Egoku Dōmyō (1632–1721), another former Myōshin-ji line monk.[75] Egoku apparently requested an
audience with the daimyo of Kaga province in order to preach the
Dharma. Himself being well versed in the Zen tradition, the daimyo
publicly embarrassed Egoku by making the following observation:
"Illustrious monks of the ancient past refused to go even when they
had been invited by officials. Egoku seeking an audience now, without
my even inviting him, is at odds with the illustrious monks of the
past." The daimyo's caustic remark caused Egoku to withdraw. Mujaku inserted this episode into the narrative immediately following the
account of Yin-yüan requesting an audience with the shogun as part

of his own commentary. He concluded that Egoku shared Yin-yüan's degenerate desire for fame and fortune. Like his master Yin-yüan before him, Egoku had put himself forward in a manner unbefitting a Zen monk.

Mujaku concludes the *Obaku geki* with two further examples of unnamed, wicked Obaku monks who between them committed murder and theft, and broke the precept against sexual relations.[76] All of these later examples stand as Mujaku's evidence that Yin-yüan's original degeneracy bred further degeneracy in his lineage; the wickedness within the Obaku line clearly descends directly from its founder. As Mujaku put it, the later examples are "also evidence of the lingering style of Yin-yüan."[77]

Mujaku has surprisingly little to say directly about Obaku's Zen style or the ritual distinctions that dominated both Kyorei's letter and the *Zenrin shūhei shū*. He makes no mention at all of Obaku's inclusion of Pure Land elements, nor does he comment on Obaku departing from the traditional Zen monastic code in any other respect. This is mildly surprising, as Mujaku himself was one of the leading experts of his day on Zen monastic codes (*shingi*) and is known to have composed several of them for individual temples.[78] He provides only a few anecdotal references to Obaku's Zen style, leaving the weight of his argument to rest on the degenerate character of the Chinese masters as seen in the various narrative selections provided.

In the opening scene of the narrative, Mujaku recounts a story about Yin-yüan releasing living creatures, a Buddhist practice known in both the Chinese and the Japanese traditions. While residing in Nagasaki, Yin-yüan apparently accepted a monetary donation from the local daimyo. He used the money to buy live fish, which he then released into a pond. To everyone's dismay, all the fish died and immediately came floating to the top of the pond. Mujaku himself refrained from commenting on the event, but he quoted Yin-yüan's interpreter as saying: "The Japanese will never believe in you if you do this sort of thing. Isn't there some other way to spread the Dharma?"[79]

A second unfortunate incident, recounted in the Chinese portion of the text, occurred during Yin-yüan's tenure at Fumon-ji in Settsu.

> Master Daishun Gentei [said] that some days when Master Yin-yüan was at Fumon-ji in Tonda, he hung up his staff and mingled with the monks. At lunchtime one day, Gentei was serving the others. He lost his grip and dropped the rice bucket. The rice scattered all over the floor. Yin-yüan saw this from a distance, laughed, and

said, "Did the bottom drop out of the bucket? Did the bottom drop out of the bucket?" [80]

Yin-yüan refers here to a line from Hsüeh-feng I-ts'un's (822–908; J. Seppō Gison) recorded sayings, in which the experience of enlightenment is compared to the bottom suddenly falling out of a bucket.[81] In sympathetic hands, this story might easily be used to illustrate Yin-yüan's wit and familiarity with the classical Zen sources. One might even argue that it demonstrates his ability to apply the sayings of the old masters to daily life in an attempt to impel a disciple toward enlightenment. Mujaku, however, came to a far different conclusion, "I say that frivolity of this sort shows the vacuity of Yin-yüan's Zen style." [82] Mujaku set a stern tone here that Japanese assumed fairly often regarding the Ming Chinese masters, who were accused of behaving in a frivolous manner because they used a great deal of humor in their daily life, unfamiliar perhaps in the more restrained atmosphere of a Japanese Zen monastery.

There is one rather cryptic passage in the Chinese section of the *Obaku geki* that may have been intended as a criticism of Obaku's principal method of propagating the sect throughout the country. Mujaku mentions that there are Obaku monks who claim to transmit the Dharma but have no home temple of their own. He says that they "are all over the city, in front of shops and behind them." [83] This may refer to the large number of Obaku monks who did not initially possess temples. Their number grew so rapidly that it quickly surpassed the number of Obaku temples available to them. In addition, the early generations of Japanese Obaku monks regularly traveled and gave lectures to spread their teaching in different cities and towns where there were no Obaku temples. Thus, Obaku monks did not initially enjoy an existing network of temples throughout the country. Often they stayed at Sōtō temples, where they were more warmly received than in Rinzai monasteries. There are numerous examples of communities that were sufficiently impressed by these traveling Obaku monks to raise the funds to restore a dilapidated temple and then invite the visitor to stay on there and serve as resident monk.

Implicit throughout the *Obaku geki* is the perception that Obaku monks were overly proud and not respectful enough of their Japanese hosts. One cannot be certain whether or not the Chinese monks were intentionally haughty toward their Japanese peers or in what ways they manifested such behavior. They may well have behaved in a superior fashion, as the Japanese report. Certainly Kyorei had observed pride as a contributing factor in the tensions arising between Chinese and Japanese practitioners. Alternatively, it is possible that the Chinese were conforming to the code of monastic etiquette as they knew it, and that cultural differences led to a perception of rudeness. In any event, ample evidence exists to demonstrate that, whether the Chinese were intentionally disrespectful or not, offense was taken by many Japanese.

In the Chinese section of the *Obaku geki*, one of the vignettes relates to Gudō's complaints against Yin-yüan, including his lack of due respect and courtesy. In particular, Gudō expressed his displeasure at Yin-yüan's behavior, which he found presumptuous for a foreign guest in Japan.

> To begin with, Yin-yüan does not understand courtesy. I am the highest-ranking monk in the Zen monasteries of Japan. If he wants to spread his Dharma in Japan, then he should first come and consult with me. After that, there would be time enough to save sentient beings according to their capacity. If I went to Ch'ing China, then I would do as much.[84]

Gudō knew that Yin-yüan was under house arrest at the time and thus not free to make such a courtesy call. Still, he expected some recognition of his status as the abbot of Myōshin-ji, the main temple under which Fumon-ji officially fell.

According to Mujaku's accounts of Yin-yüan's behavior, on several occasions the Chinese monk took actions that would almost certainly have appeared rude and offensive to the Japanese present. When preparing for his audience with the shogun, for example, Yin-yüan refused to bow three times, as Japanese custom dictated and as the councilors specifically requested. Mujaku explained that Yin-yüan's refusal caused considerable distress to Ryōkei and Tokuō, who had to negotiate a compromise between Yin-yüan and the councilors. In the end it was agreed that Yin-yüan would bow only once while his Japanese escorts would bow three times in his stead. When the audience finally took place, Yin-yüan entered the shogun's hall and sat down directly opposite the young shogun, as if in the presence of an equal. At one point during the meeting, Yin-yüan rose and started to walk directly toward the shogun. Ryōkei was forced to restrain him in order to prevent any further misunderstanding or embarrassment.[85]

Later in the text, Mujaku raised the complaint that, although Yin-yüan spoke Japanese at least passably well with his own attendants, he refused to do so in the presence of honored guests. In these more formal situations, Yin-yüan relied upon the services of a simultaneous translator and spoke in his native tongue. Mujaku interpreted this as Yin-yüan's way of belittling his Japanese guests. (Those of us who have struggled with foreign languages may take a more sympathetic view!) Mujaku also mentioned in the same context that Yin-yüan's dying instructions mandated that Mampuku-ji must always invite Chinese monks to serve as abbot. In Mujaku's opinion, this practice served to perpetuate the pattern of disrespect throughout the entire Obaku sect.[86]

For both Mujaku Dōchū and the author of the *Zenrin shūhei shū*, the ultimate conclusion about Obaku Zen was that it posed a clear and immediate danger to Japanese Rinzai. For practical reasons, they hoped to stem the flow of human and material resources that was draining Rinzai of talented men, valued temples, and external monetary support. But their concerns ran much deeper than these practical concerns, extending to issues related to proper Rinzai practice. Both feared that, in spite of expectations to the contrary in some quarters, Obaku would have a corrupting influence on their own sect's teachings and practices. The arrival of Obaku masters and the establishment of the Obaku sect in Japan motivated a reexamination on the part of Japanese Rinzai masters of what exactly they believed should constitute Rinzai belief and practice. Some Obaku tendencies did find their way into Japanese Rinzai temples; the most obvious examples of this are the renewed interest in reading and studying the original texts in the Zen corpus and a restored dedication to observing the winter and summer retreats as communal events. These tendencies were in harmony with movements arising within Japanese Buddhism and the wider intellectual world of Tokugawa thought. Other Obaku tendencies, however, were flatly rejected as inappropriate or impure. Foremost in this category is the combined practice of Zen meditation and *nembutsu*, which ran counter to the Japanese tendency toward pure—that is, exclusive—practices.

Hakuin and Obaku Zen

The mid-Tokugawa era master Hakuin (1686–1769) is known as the restorer of Japanese Rinzai, and his teaching and Zen style form the basis of modern-day Rinzai Zen in Japan. His influence is so far-reaching that it is not at all uncommon to refer to modern Rinzai Zen as Hakuin Zen. Hakuin sought to revitalize Rinzai practice in his day by returning to the style of the Sung dynasty, when Ch'an was at its zenith in

China and was first transmitted to Japan. For this reason, he focused on koan study as the central feature in Zen practice. He advocated the continuation of that study throughout one's life, not just during the training years before one's enlightenment experience had been acknowledged. Concomitant with his work to restore the Sung style of Zen were Hakuin's efforts to purify Zen of all that he regarded as contaminating influences that had accumulated over the centuries following the Sung period. In this regard, he singled out two types of Zen practice for special censure, silent-illumination Zen (*mokushōzen*) and the combined practice of Zen and Pure Land. Hakuin never explicitly mentioned Obaku Zen in his writings. Because Obaku Zen advocated a form of dual practice of Zen and Pure Land, however, one can discern something of his attitude toward Obaku by looking at his views of combined practice.

First, Hakuin did not object to Pure Land practice in and of itself. He recognized it as an appropriate practice for believers of medium- or low-level abilities. In several places in his writings he indicates respect for Pure Land as an alternative path leading toward enlightenment. "It must be understood that the koan and the recitation of the Buddha's name are both contributing causes to the path that leads to the opening up of the wisdom of the Buddha." [87] This passage appears in one of Hakuin's letters, entitled the *Orategama zokushu,* in which he compared koan practice with the practice of *nembutsu.* Such positive evaluations generally appear in letters addressed to lay believers, especially those who have already expressed their devotion to Pure Land practice. Hakuin supported the wholehearted practice of the *nembutsu* for those lay people and monks who truly lacked the ability to undertake the "steep" path of Zen. On the other hand, he became incensed by attempts to incorporate Pure Land practice into Zen, especially within the confines of the Zen monastery.

Although Hakuin stressed in the *Orategama zokushu* that the practice of the *nembutsu* and the use of koan are both expedient means to a common goal, he by no means suggested that the two practices were equally effective. According to Hakuin, in comparison to the countless numbers who have attained enlightenment through koan study, only a few have ever benefited from practice of the *nembutsu.*[88] Moreover, using an appropriate beginner's koan such as the *Mu* koan of Chaochou (the first case from the *Mumonkan*) can lead to relatively quick results, while reliance on Pure Land practices may well take a lifetime and lead nowhere.[89]

Hakuin explains that before Ch'an began to decline in China, start

ing with the Indian and Chinese Patriarchs and continuing down to
the Yüan dynasty masters, Ch'an masters had never chanted the Buddha's name nor expressed a desire for rebirth in the Pure Land. They
retained the pure practice of the "steep way." According to Hakuin,
combined practice arose later, in the period of decline during the late
Ming dynasty, among men such as Yun-ch'i Chu-hung who were unable to progress in their Ch'an practice.[90] In Hakuin's judgment, these
later masters turned to Pure Land practice in the face of death out of
despair for their future lives.

> This is not meant to belittle the basic teachings of the Pure Land nor
> to make light of the practice of the calling of the Buddha's name.
> But not to practice Zen meditation while within the Zen Sect, to be-
> cloud the eye to see into one's own nature because of laziness in the
> study of Zen under a teacher and idleness in one's aspirations, only
> weakens the power to study Zen. People such as these end up by
> spending their whole lives in vain. . . . People of this sort, while
> within Zen, slander the Zen teachings. They are like those wood-
> eating maggots that are produced in beams and pillars and then in
> turn destroy those very beams and pillars.[91]

Hakuin thus traces the movement toward combined practice to personal weakness in the late Ming Zen masters. Once this contaminating dual practice entered the Zen monasteries, it spread like a disease.
"From that time on the monasteries all fell into line and marched
along behind this teaching; herein lies the basis for the deterioration
of the style of Zen."[92] In order to prevent the whole Zen community
from being similarly infected, the root cause had to be exposed and removed. For this reason, Hakuin attacked combined practice in the
harshest terms.

Hakuin did not directly identify the Obaku sect or Obaku monks
in his attacks on combined practice as he did the Ming master Chu-
hung. As the primary conduit of the debased Ming style of Zen, however, Hakuin certainly intended Obaku Zen to be one of the primary
targets of his tirades against combined practice. In a few passages the
identification of Obaku masters lurks just beneath the surface of the
text. For example, in the *Yabukōji,* where Hakuin allows his anger to
emerge almost unchecked, he alludes to Obaku's transmission to
Japan.

> A hundred years ago the true style changed and Zen followers
> adopted an obnoxious teaching. Those who would combine Pure
> Land and Zen are [as common] as hemp and millet. In olden times

the outward appearance was the *sravaka* practice, the internal mystery was the bodhisattva Way. Nowadays outward appearance is the Zen teaching and the inner mystery is the Pure Land practice.[93]

As Yampolsky points out in his related note, the time reference mentioned in this passage coincides precisely with the arrival of Yin-yüan in 1654. Moreover, Hakuin has neatly inverted here the observation first made by Kyorei that Obaku Zen is outwardly Pure Land and inwardly Zen. Whereas Kyorei's comments suggested the underlying worthiness of Obaku practice as a form of Zen, Hakuin's remark suggests that Obaku should be regarded as debased and without redeeming value as a form of Zen.

The verbal image that Hakuin evokes of the Zen masters who promote combined practice seems to depict the proud figures we find in Obaku portraits of the Chinese masters. They sit sternly and with dignity, wearing their silk caps and holding their whisks. "After all, they look like true living Patriarchs of direct descent in the lineage, people whom even a Buddha or a demon would not dare approach."[94] In even more subtle terms than those of Mujaku, Hakuin describes the dangers posed by the allure of the Chinese Zen masters. Looking the part of Patriarchs, they are assumed by many Japanese to be superior in ability; but on close inspection "they do not have the slightest capacity to see into their own natures."[95] In Hakuin's view, these masters take on the outward trappings of Zen while concealing their true dedication to Pure Land. Thus, their outward appearance poses a threat, as they may deceive the unwary and so spread contamination throughout Japanese Zen, just as it spread in Ming China. Hakuin makes the direst of predictions if this trend is allowed to continue. "The deterioration of Buddhism in Japan must not continue for long. . . . If Zen is combined with Pure Land, Zen cannot last for long and will surely be destroyed."[96]

Obaku and Sōtō Zen

The arrival of the Obaku masters from China and the establishment of the Obaku sect in Japan had the greater impact on Rinzai Zen, but it also affected the Sōtō school to a lesser extent. A thorough evaluation of Obaku Zen's influence on Sōtō Zen is beyond the scope of the present work. What follows here is a brief sketch of the relations between the two schools based on secondary literature written primarily by Sōtō scholars.

Sōtō monks were as interested as their Rinzai counterparts in seeing Chinese masters for themselves. Many made their way to Nagasaki to meet with Yin-yüan and his more prominent disciples, Muan and Chi-fei. A partial list of the prominent Sōtō masters who studied under the Obaku masters includes Unzan Guhaku (1619–1702), Yuie Dōjō (1634–1713),[97] Tokuō Ryōkō (1649–1709), Mutoku Ryōgo (1651–1742), Gesshū Sōko (1618–1696), and Manzan Dōhaku (1636–1715). Whereas relations with Rinzai were strained from the start, relations between Sōtō and Obaku were generally friendly during the first years of Obaku's development and remained cordial even after the founding of Obaku-san Mampuku-ji, when tensions with Rinzai escalated. This is not surprising, for Obaku could not pose the same threat to Sōtō as it did to Japanese Rinzai.

There are numerous examples of Sōtō monks practicing under Obaku masters for periods of time, but few of these men stayed on to become Obaku Dharma heirs. The majority returned to their Sōtō temples and, in some prominent cases, even adapted elements of Obaku ritual and regulations into the Sōtō framework. Without the pressures of institutional constraints such as the posted wall regulations at Myōshin-ji, Sōtō monks were free to learn from Obaku practice and to establish ongoing relationships with Obaku monks; many friendships developed between Sōtō and Obaku monks, especially with the first generation of Japanese converts such as Tetsugen, Tetsugyū, and Chōon. While Obaku motivated Rinzai masters to reevaluate their teachings predominantly for negative reasons, Sōtō masters were positively influenced. In a very real sense, contact with Obaku masters inspired Sōtō monks to undertake a reform of their own sect.

The response to Obaku within Sōtō followed a very different pattern from that seen in Rinzai circles. In Rinzai, the progressive party, represented by Gudō, resisted Obaku influences and therefore took issue with attempts made by the restoration party to welcome Obaku monks and adopt their customs. The two movements were at odds over Obaku from the first. By contrast, in the Sōtō case the progressive monks who welcomed Obaku influences were the very men who initiated the great Sōtō reform movement of the late seventeenth and early eighteenth centuries. It was only later that problems began to emerge between progressive and reform tendencies within the Sōtō sect, and concomitantly between Sōtō and Obaku. This can be illustrated by examining two of the great Sōtō reformers of the mid-Tokugawa period, Manzan Dōhaku (1636–1715) and Menzan Zuihō (1683–1769).[98]

Manzan concentrated his reform efforts in two directions. First, he strove to restore Dharma transmission through individual, personal contact between masters and disciples (*isshi inshō*), which he argued was Dōgen's original intention. Sōtō had developed an alternative form of transmission dependent on the temple of residence (*garanbō*), which necessitated changing one's lineage according to one's position as abbot (*in'in ekishi*). Manzan received encouragement and support for this effort from his longtime friend, the Obaku monk Chōon Dōkai. Chōon led a similar reform movement within the Obaku sect and was highly critical of the existing Sōtō practice.[99] Manzan did not, however, draw directly on Obaku texts as the basis for his argument on Dharma transmission but made creative use of Dōgen's works.[100] On the other hand, there is textual evidence of direct Obaku influence on Manzan's second sphere of action, the reform of monastic discipline.

Manzan undertook monastic reform by studying and publishing earlier Sōtō rules that had been almost lost over the centuries. He himself did not initiate this avenue of reform. His master Gesshū Sōko began to research the historical monastic codes composed as guidelines for Japanese Sōtō, specifically the *Eihei shingi* and the *Keizan shingi*. He also wrote a monastic code for his home temple Daijō-ji, entitled the *Undō jōki*. Gesshū studied under both Tao-che and Yin-yüan and was impressed by the Obaku monastic code. He published his own code in 1674, just two years after the *Obaku shingi* had appeared, and was inspired by it to some extent. Although Gesshū indicated that the *Undō jōki* drew on the two Sōtō codes, Sōtō scholars have noted the obvious reliance on the *Obaku shingi* as well. Gesshū encouraged Manzan to continue this research into Sōtō's historical monastic codes. It is said that Manzan fulfilled his master's dying request by writing the *Shōjurin shingi*, his own extensive study of existing Zen codes. Like Gesshū, Manzan not only extended his research back to traditional Sōtō sources but also took into account the *Obaku shingi*, and through it older Rinzai codes.

Over the course of the four centuries before Manzan's time, the traditional Sōtō codes had nearly been lost as resources for Sōtō practice, just as many of Dōgen's writings had been hidden and almost forgotten. Therefore, Gesshū and Manzan's efforts were important examples of sectarian scholarship that made the older texts accessible for the first time in generations. Although intended as codes for Daijō-ji, the *Undō jōki*, and to a greater extent the *Shōjurin shingi*, became influential throughout the Sōtō world and were widely adopted by other Sōtō temples. Like Gesshū, Manzan not only drew on the traditional Sōtō codes but made use of some elements of Obaku customs. For example, unlike the *Eihei shingi,* which mandates that the *sōdō* (monks' hall) serve as the locus for both meditation and meals, the *Shōjurin shingi* makes use of Obaku terminology and refers to the place for meditation as the *zendō* (meditation hall) and the place for meals as the *saidō* (dining hall). In Obaku temples there were indeed separate halls for sleeping, meditating, and eating, and Manzan's adoption of this terminology created the impression that his own Sōtō temple likewise had separate halls. In fact, the terms *zendō* and *sōdō* referred to the same building at Daijō-ji, but because of the terminology, it eventually became popular at other Sōtō temples to use three separate halls in the Obaku fashion. A second example of Obaku influence on Sōtō monastic codes is the alteration of the time of chanting at mealtimes. The *Keizan shingi* calls for chanting to be performed after the meal; Gesshū and Manzan changed this practice to comply with Obaku custom and shifted the chanting to before the meal. This particular change was first enacted by Gesshū in the *Undō jōki,* and Manzan followed suit.[101]

The reform movement begun by seventeenth-century Sōtō scholars like Gesshū and Manzan continued to bear fruit in the eighteenth century, particularly with the work of the most prominent sectarian Sōtō scholar, Menzan. As the reform movement progressed, the restoration of Dōgen's Zen style came to dominate the agenda. Sōtō scholars became increasingly intolerant of any accretions from other sources. As a result, the later Sōtō scholars came to criticize their predecessors for grafting Obaku customs onto Sōtō practice. Menzan was able to build upon the earlier generation's rediscovery of Dōgen's original writings and to produce his own extensive research in Dōgen studies, including his eleven-volume encyclopedia on Dōgen's terms, the *Shōbō genzō shōtenroku.*

Menzan agreed with Manzan's basic reform work regarding both Dharma transmission and monastic discipline, both of which were based upon rediscovering and reinstituting Dōgen's style of Zen. However, Menzan took issue with Manzan's reliance on the *Obaku shingi* in the *Shōjurin shingi* and the resulting alterations that occurred in Sōtō practice throughout Japan. In his works on Sōtō monastic discipline, the *Sōdō shingi gyōhōshō* (published in 1753 in five fascicles) and the *Sōdō shingi kōtei betsuroku* (published in 1755 in eight fascicles), Menzan criticized these foreign elements as inappropriate for Sōtō Zen and sought to expunge all traces of Obaku influence from Sōtō practice.

Obaku Zen entered Japan at an exciting time for Buddhism, when monks from various sects were actively engaging in sectarian research and publishing old texts and new commentaries. They were searching for answers to the problems their sects faced in the new era of peace and were considering methods to restore practice to the high level they believed had existed before the disruptions of the Warring States period. In Zen Buddhism, the nascent reform movements of the mid-seventeenth century were laying the groundwork that would support the more successful movements of the following century. During the first century of Obaku growth, the new sect did serve as a catalyst for change in both Rinzai and Sōtō Zen, in large part because the Japanese looked to it as such. As a form of Chinese Zen, the Obaku style naturally attracted attention and commanded a certain respect from the Japanese. Once the differences in its Zen style became apparent, Obaku offered Japanese Zen a range of new possibilities and provided access to older Chinese resources and patterns of practice that had not been fully utilized in Japan for generations. Obaku's unique characteristics also triggered negative responses that contributed indirectly to a process of redefinition of Zen practice in Japanese terms.

No small aspect of the division between Obaku and Japanese Rinzai were the cultural differences that exaggerated the real distinctions between the Chinese and Japanese approaches to Zen. Obaku's Chinese character and its dedication to maintaining that character made it difficult for the school to be assimilated immediately into Japanese Rinzai. It developed instead into a small but stable movement, independent from other Rinzai lines. Ultimately, its independence and differences were strong enough for it to constitute a third sect of Zen in Japan, despite its identity as a Rinzai lineage. Nevertheless, its ties with Japanese Rinzai have remained strong throughout its history. Not only did Obaku influence Japanese Rinzai in its early years, but Japanese Zen styles and movements had a strong impact on the Obaku sect over the years. In particular, the style of Zen developed by Hakuin influenced later Obaku masters. Hakuin and his disciples' growing impact on Japanese Rinzai corresponded with the decline in the flow of qualified Chinese abbots from China to Mampuku-ji in the mid-to-late eighteenth century. Obaku's internal vitality was diminishing by then, and the sect was ready for an influx of new ideas. By the end of the Tokugawa period, Obaku had become less distinctly Chinese and had adopted many Japanese customs and practices not expressly contrary to the Obaku monastic code. If the Chinese Obaku masters had once helped to reintroduce such basic Zen texts as the *Rinzai roku* into the Japanese scene, by the modern era Obaku students came to study that text under the tutelage of Rinzai scholars.

TEN

Obaku and the Secular Authorities

After an uneasy beginning, Obaku Zen enjoyed a constructive and beneficial relationship with various secular authorities during the Tokugawa period. The sect received support from elements within the ruling military government in Edo, from local provincial daimyo, and from members of the imperial family, all of which served to strengthen the new sect and encourage its spread. The secular authorities effectively created space for the new movement to find a secure niche in the world of Tokugawa Buddhism. In the modern period, scholars reflecting on the support Obaku received from secular powers have tended to stress either Obaku's dealings with the Edo bakufu or those with the imperial family, but not both. As a result, they often portray the Obaku sect one-sidedly as either a special favorite of the imperial family or as the Tokugawa bakufu's chosen Zen line. Both arguments have some basis in historical fact, but ideological concerns arising in the modern period seem to have determined the presentation and interpretation of historical facts.

Not surprisingly, Obaku scholars earlier in this century presented the facts surrounding Obaku's transmission and diffusion with a special emphasis on imperial favor. The historical sketches written in the 1930s by scholars such as Akamatsu Shinmyō, for example, convey the distinct impression that Mampuku-ji was founded under imperial direction.[1] While they do not deny bakufu involvement in the process of establishing Obaku, they largely ignore it, stressing instead the negative impact that bakufu regulations had on the emperor and the Buddhist world in general. Contemporary scholars, such as Takenuki Genshō, have done extensive work to bring to light the role played by the Edo bakufu in establishing and spreading Obaku Zen.[2] In this reworked version of Obaku history, Obaku is, in a sense, the creation of the Tokugawa bakufu as it searched for a way to imitate the earlier Ashikaga pattern of bakufu–Zen relations. In all fairness, the latter portrayal is more deeply rooted in the historical sources and reflects more accurately the impact of secular influence at the time. Because these accounts seek to balance the one-sidedly imperial focus of earlier works, however, the imperial connections, which also played an important part in Obaku's development, are conspicuously absent from more recent histories.

By the time Obaku masters first emigrated to Japan, the military government under the leadership of the Tokugawa family was secure in its authority and the emperor's powers had been clearly restricted in scope. In the most immediate terms, imperial favor would not have sufficed to ensure Obaku's success in Japan. Without bakufu permission, Yin-yüan and his Chinese disciples would never have been able to travel beyond Nagasaki, let alone found a new monastery of Mampuku-ji's size. Nevertheless, the emperor still proved to be a valuable ally in the cultural and religious spheres, where his influence remained strong. He continued to enjoy a significant level of authority among the Buddhist leaders in Kyoto, particularly at the dominant Rinzai Zen temples, Myōshin-ji and Daitoku-ji. Therefore, Obaku had much to gain from both of the two secular powers and managed rather successfully to balance its loyalties to each without becoming embroiled in the tension that existed between the two. The bakufu and the emperor, in turn, found their own reasons to sponsor Obaku in a manner appropriate to their respective powers. In general terms, the bakufu's interest was predominantly cultural rather than religious, and the emperor's more a matter of personal devotion to the practice of Zen. Both applauded Obaku's strict interpretation of monastic discipline and may have shared the hope that the sect could play a role in the growing vitality of the Rinzai school in Japan.

Tokugawa *Hatto* and the Purple Robe Affair

During the first fifty years of the seventeenth century, the Tokugawa bakufu enacted a series of laws (*hatto*) to govern the various elements in Japanese society as a part of its overall plan to consolidate its authority. In particular, it designed *hatto* to control the three portions of society that had possessed power in the past and therefore posed the greatest potential threat to the Tokugawa's continued dominance— that is, the military houses, the imperial court, and Buddhist sects.

Quite naturally, once Mampuku-ji was founded, Obaku also fell under the general laws governing Buddhist temples. These laws served first to regulate Obaku's relations with the Edo bakufu as well as its dealings with other Buddhist sects, the imperial household, and so on. The impact of the *hatto* on Obaku extended far beyond the immediate literal constraints they entailed. The temple laws, *jiin hatto,* had already determined the contours of the existing religious world in which Obaku had somehow to find its niche. These preexisting conditions severely limited the avenues open to the fledgling movement in its efforts to expand. In addition, incidents precipitated by the bakufu enforcing specific *hatto* designed to limit imperial relations with the Buddhist community that occurred earlier in the century, before Obaku came onto the scene, affected its relationship with the emperor.

One of the underlying principles operative in all of the various *hatto* was to separate groups from their traditional sources of power; for example, the military houses were divested of direct ownership of land and thus separated from direct control over the peasants who worked the land. In a similar manner, the laws governing the imperial court and Buddhist groups divided these two potential allies in a variety of ways. Because the emperor traditionally had a special relationship with certain temples, the bakufu took steps to bring this type of relationship under its direct control.

Buddhist monks were encouraged through a host of laws to limit themselves to scholarly and religious pursuits, thus reducing the Buddhist community's access to the political and military power that many sects had enjoyed during the period of civil unrest in the centuries immediately preceding the Tokugawa period. During the period of the Warring States, Buddhist temples had been among the strongest political and military powers, possessing land holdings and standing armies that, in some cases, rivaled the most powerful daimyo. Oda Nobunaga, Toyotomi Hideyoshi, and Tokugawa Ieyasu each took steps to control these temples and reduce their military and economic power as a crucial part of the process of unification.[3]

Relations between the imperial court and Buddhist leaders had influenced the Japanese political scene since the introduction of Buddhism in the sixth century. Japanese emperors generally acted as sponsors of Buddhist monks and temples, which then reciprocated by providing religious services of various kinds for the sake of the court and the nation. Although the military leaders of the medieval period are normally thought of as the sponsors for Rinzai Zen temples, the

emperor also enjoyed a special relationship with several of the leading Rinzai temples, notably Myōshin-ji and Daitoku-ji. When the
Tokugawa bakufu sought to assert its authority over both the imperial court and Buddhism, part of its plan was to create a barrier between
the emperor and these Zen temples. It accomplished this with two related set of *hatto* enacted in 1613 and 1615. The first were directed at
eight specified temples,[4] including Daitoku-ji and Myōshin-ji, and the
second extended similar restrictions to the main temples of all sects.
Before that time, the emperor possessed the official authority to name
the abbot of various temples, including Myōshin-ji and Daitoku-ji,
and to bestow such honors as the purple robe and honorific titles on
individual monks of any sect. With the *hatto* of 1613 and 1615, the
bakufu required that henceforth the emperor would appoint abbots
and grant imperial honors only with prior notification of the proper
bakufu authorities. This process was tantamount to the emperor having to request bakufu permission to fulfill his traditional role vis-à-vis
the Buddhist community. Although the emperor retained the nominal
authority to name abbots and bestow honors, his decisions were
placed directly under bakufu scrutiny and were subject to government
approval.

At the same time that it set controls on imperial–Buddhist relations, the bakufu took steps to limit the pool of qualified candidates
for the position of abbot at some of the more prominent Rinzai Zen
temples. It did this by determining an official set of qualifications of its
own devising: first, a Zen master was required to have practiced as an
ordained Buddhist monk for at least thirty years, and, second, he was
required to have studied at least 1,700 koan from the traditional Zen
sources in order to qualify for the post.[5] Daitoku-ji and Myōshin-ji
both received *hatto* specifying these qualifications for future abbots
in 1615.

Both of the bakufu's requirements may be regarded as external cre-
ations foreign to the internal development of the Zen tradition. The
tradition had no established rule designating a minimum number of
years of practice to qualify as abbot at a major temple, although the
posts were generally limited to advanced individuals with many years
of monastic experience. Nor had the tradition ever designated a series
as large as 1,700 koan as a set course of study for its monks. Smaller
sets of koan, such as the three hundred cases centered on the *Hekigan
roku* discussed previously, were in regular use at the time. The number
of koan prescribed by the bakufu regulations probably derived from a

mistaken understanding of the *Ching-té ch'uan-téng lu* (J. *Keitoku dentōroku*), often said to contain 1,701 biographies of Ch'an masters. The *Ching-té ch'uan-téng lu* actually contains approximately 960 biographies; the remaining number merely comprises a list of names.[6] While a majority of the koan traditionally used in the Zen sect can indeed be found within the text, the number of cases does not in fact approach 1,700.

Emperor Gomizunoo (1612–1629), known for his deep personal affinity with Zen Buddhism, was reigning at the time these *hatto* came into effect. Gomizunoo had a strained relationship with the Edo bakufu throughout his reign. Like his father Goyōzei (1587–1611) before him, Gomizunoo lived under the indignity of bakufu scrutiny. The shogunate maintained an official representative in Kyoto, the *Shoshidai*, whose responsibilities included overseeing the imperial court. (Tokugawa Ieyasu recreated the post in 1600 to govern the former capital and to keep an eye on the imperial court, the *kuge* class, and Buddhist temples in the Kyoto area. The official holding the post reported to Edo every five years to make his report.) In addition, Gomizunoo was obliged to marry the daughter of Tokugawa Hidetada, the second shogun. Eventually, it was the Purple Robe Affair (*Shie jiken*) that precipitated Gomizunoo's abdication in 1629, as will be seen, but that did not bring an end to his personal conflict with the Edo bakufu. Tensions continued into his years of retirement. The shogun Iemitsu insulted the retired emperor in 1634 when he publicly refused the honorific title of *Dajōdaijin* that Gomizunoo had privately proposed to confer upon him.[7]

It would seem that Gomizunoo was a man of considerable talent who resented the level of bakufu interference in court affairs and bridled under the new strictures successively placed upon him. On a number of occasions the emperor ignored the bakufu's determined procedure for conferring imperial honors, and his actions eventually provoked a response. The bakufu took action in order to assert its authority over the court by enforcing the *hatto* of 1613 and 1615. In 1627, it officially invalidated a number of imperial honors, including both honorific titles and purple robes, which had been granted without its approval. The resulting incidents within the Buddhist community are known in Japan as the *Shie jiken*, or Purple Robe Affair.[8]

Monks from both Myōshin-ji and Daitoku-ji were immediately affected by the invalidations of 1627, and both temples responded by protesting the government's decision. Takuan Sōhō (1573–1646), a

former abbot of Daitoku-ji, orchestrated the initial Zen response to
the bakufu's action. Takuan returned to Daitoku-ji and wrote the
Benmeiron, a highly critical appraisal of the original *hatto.* In the
Benmeiron, Takuan argued that the bakufu regulations were unreasonable in the light of practical considerations and concluded that
they must have been drawn up by an unenlightened individual who
did not properly understand Zen practice and training. For example,
it was Takuan's contention that the requirement that thirty years of
training be mandatory for a monk to qualify for the post of abbot
was both artificial in design and unnecessary in its restrictiveness. The
regulation would effectively waste the finest years of a master's life,
years when he should instead be busy guiding students. As for the requirement that the candidate for abbot have mastered 1,700 koan,
Takuan felt that this was excessive in the extreme and missed the true
intention of Zen practice. Enlightenment was not determined by years
of practice or number of koan studied. Moreover, these requirements
would make the continuation of Dharma transmission difficult or even
impossible. In 1628, Takuan signed the document along with two
other monks, Gyokushitsu Sōhaku (1572–1641), the current abbot at
Daitoku-ji, and Kōgetsu Sōgan (1574–1643), another former abbot.
They sent it to the Kyoto *Shoshidai,* who forwarded it on to Edo for
bakufu consideration.

The bakufu responded to the criticism from Daitoku-ji and
Myōshin-ji by formally recognizing as valid some of the imperial honors it had previously invalidated. Specifically, it reinstated those ap-
pointments of imperial honors bestowed according to proper form and
those granted to men above the age of fifty. But in return, the bakufu
demanded written apologies from both Daitoku-ji and Myōshin-ji for
their protests. The bakufu's decision sent the assemblies at the two
temples into confusion as to how best to respond. Moderate factions
at both temples preferred to compromise with the government and argued in favor of sending the formal written apologies. However,
Takuan and his group refused to concede to government demands. As
a result of their intransigence, the bakufu summoned to Edo the three
monks who had signed the criticism for censure. The government
punished Takuan and Gyokushitsu with banishment, but dealt more
leniently with Kōgetsu, who complied with its orders and apologized.

Angry over the bakufu's initial interference in his decisions and its
heavy-handed tactics with the protestors, Emperor Gomizunoo abdicated the throne in favor of his young daughter, Empress Meishō

(r. 1629–1643), in 1629. Lacking any real power to counter the bakufu's actions, abdication was the emperor's strongest available means of protesting. By abdicating, Gomizunoo contravened a specific request made by the third Tokugawa shogun, Iemitsu, that he remain on the throne.

The Purple Robe Affair was resolved a few years later when the banishments inflicted on Takuan and Gyokushitsu were lifted. The incident does not appear to have permanently soured the relationship between the protestors and the government. All three monks returned to bakufu favor, and all of them were eventually summoned to Edo castle to instruct the third shogun, Iemitsu.[9] The incident did, however, have lasting implications for the emperor's relations with the Buddhist world, which later affected his dealings with the Obaku sect.

Obaku Zen and the Emperor Gomizunoo

The emperor Gomizunoo's relationship with Ryōkei, Yin-yüan, and other Obaku monks forms an interesting chapter in Obaku's early history. Obaku Zen claims a very special relationship with Gomizunoo, whom they include on their genealogical charts as a full master in one of the sect's dominant Dharma lines. Gomizunoo appears as an Obaku master of the thirty-fourth generation (Yin-yüan is the thirty-second and Ryōkei the thirty-third) in the official record for the sect, the *Obakushū kanroku*.[10] Not surprisingly, Obaku's claim caused tensions with other Zen groups to escalate during the Tokugawa period. Even within the Obaku community itself the news elicited some controversy when it first became public knowledge. Despite the short-term difficulties that Obaku encountered on this account, the relationship between Gomizunoo and Obaku later proved a long-term asset of incalculable value. In the years following the Imperial Restoration of 1868, it became highly advantageous to have imperial credentials. Many of the details surrounding the emperor's relations with Obaku remain obscure. Accounts vary greatly depending on the nature of the source and the sectarian affiliation of the author. It is interesting, for example, that a recent biography of Gomizunoo entitled *Gomizunooin*, written by Kumakura Isao, provides almost no information regarding the emperor's practice of Zen or his relationships with Zen masters. Kumakura provides extensive coverage of various aspects of Gomizunoo's life, especially his dealings with the Tokugawa family and his artistic pursuits.

The Emperor Gomizunoo was born in 1596, the third child of Emperor Goyōzei. He ascended to the throne in 1611, reigning for nineteen years until his abdication in 1629. At the time of his abdication he was only thirty-four years old, and he lived a long life in retirement, dying in 1680 at the age of eighty-five. Even after his abdication, all sources indicate that Gomizunoo continued to fulfill the official duties of naming abbots and conferring purple robes and honorific titles. Tensions with the Edo bakufu did not ease completely even after the Purple Robe Affair was settled, although the situation was somewhat ameliorated by the common cause of repulsing Christianity. This cause successfully allied Buddhist leaders, the imperial court, and government officials during the 1630s. There are several examples, however, of continued tension with the bakufu related to the emperor's dealings with Buddhist leaders. Some of these directly relate to the history of Obaku Zen.

During Gomizunoo's reign, the emperor had contact with various Buddhist monks as a natural consequence of his position. Nevertheless, his interest in Zen at the early stages of his life may well have been largely cultural. Both the imperial family and many Buddhist masters, especially Zen masters, shared an abiding interest in such cultural pursuits as the tea ceremony, calligraphy, and poetry. In the pursuit of these common interests, Gomizunoo had extensive dealings with Zen monks such as Takuan, but he may well have regarded Takuan more as a tea master than as a Zen master. After his mother's death in 1630, however, Gomizunoo seems to have become more serious about his interest in Zen. At that time, he came to rely primarily upon the Rinzai master Isshi Monju as his guide. He continued to summon other Myōshin-ji masters to instruct him over the years, including Ungo Kiyō and Gudō Tōshoku. In fact, it was on the occasion of one of Gudō's sermon's at the palace that Gomizunoo first met Ryōkei. His relationship with Ryōkei later became the emperor's primary link with Obaku Zen.[11]

As has been mentioned in other contexts, Isshi Monju preferred a strict approach to monastic discipline. It is possible that Isshi's position on this issue influenced the emperor's understanding of Zen. Alternatively, the emperor may have preferred Isshi in part because his viewpoint on discipline suited the emperor's own proclivities. Whatever the case, over the years following Isshi's death in 1646 Gomizunoo continued to prefer advocates of strict adherence to precepts, including the Obaku masters.

Gomizunoo took the tonsure as a Buddhist monk in 1651 and was given the religious name of Enjō Dōkaku Hōō. As with his abdication, this action was regarded at the time as a protest against the Tokugawa shogun's treatment of him. Iemitsu had specifically requested that the emperor neither resign nor take the tonsure. Gomizunoo had resigned years earlier against the shogun's wishes, but he refrained from taking holy orders. His restraint did not extend to waiting a polite interval of time after news arrived of Iemitsu's death. Gomizunoo acted swiftly, taking the shogun's passing as an opportunity to fulfill this long-standing wish.[12] The emperor's action has generally been interpreted as an intentional affront to the Tokugawa shogun, as he waited only a few days after Iemitsu's passing before taking the tonsure. Iemitsu died on 4/2/1651, and Gomizunoo was ordained on 5/6, approximately two weeks later. When Gomizunoo publicly announced his ordination, the funeral services and mourning for Iemitsu were barely under way. Even if Gomizunoo intentionally timed his ordination to indicate his ongoing protest against Tokugawa interference in imperial affairs, his later actions nevertheless suggest that he was genuinely motivated to enter orders for religious reasons and that he did practice Zen meditation as a serious student.

Gomizunoo's relationship with Ryōkei developed gradually over a number of years, culminating, according to Obaku accounts, in the emperor receiving *inka* and inheriting Ryōkei's Dharma. The two men first met in 1636 when Ryōkei came to the palace as one of Gudō's attendants, and the emperor took notice of the young monk on that occasion. At about the time of his own ordination, the emperor conferred several honors on Ryōkei, naming him abbot at Myōshin-ji, first in 1651 and then again in 1654, and granting him the purple robe in 1651. These honors do not in themselves necessarily indicate that a deep personal relationship existed between the two men; indeed, that relationship seems to have developed years later. Ryōkei was summoned to the palace several times over the years to instruct the emperor in Zen teachings and practice; these visits became more frequent after 1655, when Ryōkei had begun his work for Yin-yüan in earnest. It seems likely that during the years 1655 through 1659, while Yin-yüan's case was still pending before the bakufu, Ryōkei approached the court to gain imperial support for Yin-yüan's cause. He may have recommended that Yin-yüan receive an imperial purple robe, which would perhaps have raised Yin-yüan's stature in the eyes of the shogun's counselors. In any event, Obaku sources regard 1657 as the point at which the emperor first became affiliated with Obaku Zen through his dealings with Ryōkei.[13]

Evidence in one episode of the *Obaku geki* concerning a purple robe suggests that Ryōkei made arrangements for the emperor to bestow the imperial honor on Yin-yüan without first seeking bakufu approval. According to Mujaku, Ryōkei acquired a purple robe for Yin-yüan through irregular channels, and Jikuin only learned of the plan by chance.

> In those days, there was a well-known tailor named Nihee (later called Sōkyū) of Yamagataya, a tailor shop on Sanjō Street [in Kyoto]. Other tailors couldn't make Chinese caps and robes, but this [tailor from] Yamagataya was skilled at making them after taking a single look at them. Therefore, he hung out a signboard saying "Chinese caps and robes" and made them exclusively. On one occasion, Jikuin walked into the shop and saw Nihei sewing a Chinese robe out of purple. Jikuin was shocked and asked, "Who is that for?" Nihei answered, "For the Zen master Yin-yüan."
>
> Then Jikuin went to [Fumon-ji in] Tonda to ask Ryōkei [about this]. Ryōkei said, "The Lady Enkōin in Hataeda (Emperor Gosai's foster mother)[14] made a request to the Retired Emperor Gomizunoo and then gave [the robe] to Yin-yüan." Jikuin said, "In Zen monasteries in Japan, one only wears a purple robe if one has received an imperial order from the court. One cannot be allowed to wear a purple robe without both the knowledge of the military government and permission from the imperial court."
>
> The monks on Ryōkei's side cried, "He will wear it!" Monks on Jikuin's side answered, "Just try it! We'll tear it off!"[15]

According to Mujaku, this event precipitated the final break between Ryōkei and Jikuin, and prompted Jikuin to withdraw his support from Yin-yüan's cause. Jikuin was shocked that Ryōkei and Yin-yüan actively sought imperial favors in a manner unworthy of Zen monks. If the account is factual, Jikuin was not only offended at the forwardness of Ryōkei's behavior in religious terms but was concerned about following the proper procedures determined by government regulation. According to the *hatto* of 1615, laws that were enforced by the bakufu on the earlier occasion of the Purple Robe Affair, bakufu permission for a such an honor was required in advance. Failure to acquire permission could bring censure on individual monks or an entire temple. The clear implication in the passage quoted above is that bakufu permission had not been sought and that Jikuin feared Ryōkei's actions would inevitably invite problems from government officials.

Gomizunoo never met face-to-face with Yin-yüan or any of the other Chinese Obaku monks. Apparently, Gomizunoo continued to observe a taboo, dating back to the emperor Go-uda (1274–1287), which forbade the emperor to meet directly with non-Japanese.[16] This prohibition did not prevent Gomizunoo from having extensive correspondence with Obaku masters such as Yin-yüan, Mu-an, and Kao-ch'üan, but he always maintained contact with them through a Japanese intermediary such as Ryōkei or by means of written exchange. The emperor heard a great deal about Yin-yüan from Ryōkei and through him knew about the founding of Mampuku-ji. Since Gomizunoo could not invite the Chinese master to court to instruct him in person, he made a special request through Ryōkei that Yin-yüan compose for him a lesson on Zen. Yin-yüan replied with a short lesson on the Dharma composed in Chinese (hōgo) in 1663.[17] This initiated an indirect relationship between the retired emperor and Yin-yüan that lasted until Yin-yüan's death in 1673.

Over the years, Gomizunoo was generous in his dealings with Yin-yüan and Mampuku-ji, demonstrating his respect for the master through his monetary donations, material gifts, and exchanges of poetry. In 1666, for example, Gomizunoo presented Yin-yüan with five Buddhist relics in a small jade pagoda and provided the funds to build the Shariden (Relic's hall) on the grounds of Mampuku-ji where the same relics were later enshrined. According to Obaku accounts, when Gomizunoo learned that Yin-yüan was on his deathbed in 1673, he sent a message conferring on the dying master the honorific title *Daikō fushō kokushi*. On that occasion, Gomizunoo is reported to have said, "The master is a National Treasure. If he could live longer, I would gladly take his place [in death]."

If this version of events is historically accurate, the Obaku sect showed great discretion about announcing the honorific title that Yin-yüan received on his deathbed. Yin-yüan's attendant Kao-ch'üan is said to have read aloud the emperor's letter, so the Obaku community was aware of the imperial honor, but the sect kept the title secret until some twenty-two years later. When Kao-ch'üan finally revealed it publicly, he did so with bakufu permission.[18] If this was the case, it seems likely that the earlier secrecy was maintained in deference to the bakufu's *hatto* governing imperial titles, because Gomizunoo would not have had sufficient time to obtain bakufu permission before Yin-yüan's death. It is, of course, possible that the title was actually acquired twenty-two years after Yin-yüan's death.

The Imperial Dharma Heir

During the period from 1661 until Ryōkei's death in 1670, he served as Gomizunoo's Zen master and their relationship developed fully. Before that time, Ryōkei had been working diligently on Yin-yüan's behalf and was traveling almost constantly. In 1661, when Mampuku-ji came under construction, Ryōkei had achieved his objective of establishing Yin-yüan in Japan. He then returned to his home temple, Fumon-ji, in Settsu. In 1664, Gomizunoo appointed Ryōkei abbot and restorer of Shōmyō-ji, a temple dear to the emperor. Shōmyō-ji is situated in Hino, in what is today Shiga prefecture. The original temple was built by Shōtoku Taishi, but the entire complex burned to the ground in the late sixteenth century and was not rebuilt until many years later. Gomizunoo undertook the restoration of the temple grounds and appointed its early abbots. The emperor originally expressed his intention that Isshi Monju serve as the founding abbot, but Isshi died before the work had progressed significantly. Other monks served as resident monk in the interim between Isshi's death in 1646 and Ryōkei's assuming the office in 1664. Official records designate Ryōkei as the founding abbot.[19] By the time Ryōkei became abbot at Shōmyō-ji, he had already received *inka* from Yin-yüan, and the temple officially became an Obaku branch temple.

Over the ten-year period from 1661 through 1670, Ryōkei often went to the palace to lecture on Zen to the emperor, his family, and his attendants. In 1665, he conferred the precepts on one of Gomizunoo's daughters. In the autumn of 1667, Ryōkei gave the emperor the Oak Tree koan (*teizen hakuju*) as his device for meditation. Sometime later, Ryōkei confirmed the emperor's enlightenment experience based on his response to the koan.[20] A letter of thanks from the retired emperor addressed to Ryōkei indicates that the emperor attained enlightenment under Ryōkei's guidance.[21] During the following summer, Ryōkei conferred the full Bodhisattva precepts upon the retired emperor. Obaku scholars interpret this to be a further indication of Ryōkei's Dharma transmission, since formal Obaku ordination at the *Sandan kaie* culminates with the Bodhisattva precepts.[22]

When Ryōkei died unexpectedly in a flood tide in Osaka in 1670, he had not yet transmitted the Dharma to any of his disciples aside from the emperor, who could not, in any case, function as a typical Dharma heir. The emperor mourned the passing of his teacher, not the least because Ryōkei's line had no other heir to carry on the Dharma and would therefore come to a premature end. Gomizunoo took the traditional steps necessary to honor Ryōkei as his Dharma master: He had three memorial pagodas built for him, one at Mampuku-ji, a second at Shōmyō-ji, and the third at Keizui-ji in Tonda; he saw to it that all the regular memorial services for Ryōkei were observed at Shōmyō-ji. Finally, when Gomizunoo was himself dying, he took steps to ensure that Ryōkei's lineage would continue after him. According to Kao-ch'üan's account of events, Gomizunoo wrote to Kao-ch'üan and entrusted to him a number of religious implements and pieces of poetry that the emperor had received from Yin-yüan and Ryōkei. The emperor requested that these articles be appropriately preserved by the sect. In addition, the emperor included a set of dying instructions, which he requested Kao-ch'üan to fulfill.[23]

Why the emperor chose to rely upon Kao-ch'üan rather than one of his several superiors at Mampuku-ji is not completely clear, but the decision did place the younger monk in a difficult position. Two possible factors in Gomizunoo's choice may have been the long-standing relationship between the emperor and Kao-ch'üan and the vacancy of the abbot's chair at Mampuku-ji. Kao-ch'üan had acted as Yin-yüan's assistant in his final years, writing several documents in his stead. This service first brought him into contact with the emperor when he wrote the thanksgiving record commemorating the construction of the Shariden. Following that occasion, numerous exchanges of gifts, poetry, and letters between the emperor and Kao-ch'üan preceded the emperor's final request, which arrived shortly after the emperor's death in 1680. Given the date of the emperor's death, the sect would not yet have had time formally to replace Mu-an, who died earlier the same year. Therefore, the emperor could not rely upon the abbot of Mampuku-ji, an otherwise obvious choice.

According to Kao-ch'üan's account, the emperor wanted to prevent the premature end of Ryōkei's Dharma line, so he requested that Kao-ch'üan take action as his proxy and appoint an heir. The emperor informed Kao-ch'üan that he had inherited Ryōkei's Dharma, providing both the master's whisk and a verse as evidence of this fact. As a retired emperor, Gomizunoo could not fulfill the normal duties of a Zen master. He could not accept and train students, activities that could, in due time, allow for the face-to-face transmission of the Dharma to a worthy disciple. Nor did Gomizunoo personally know Ryōkei's other disciples so that he might make an informed choice from among them. Gomizunoo therefore requested that Kao-ch'üan choose the appropriate individual from among that group, present him with the whisk, and thus transmit Ryōkei's Dharma in the emperor's name.

Kao-ch'üan was faced with something of a dilemma as to how to proceed. The situation posed difficult problems whatever course of action he might choose. According to Obaku practice, Dharma transmission should occur only after face-to-face encounters between a master and a student. When a master died unexpectedly, his disciples would seek out other Obaku masters to guide their practice and confirm their enlightenment experience. They would then become the new master's Dharma heirs. That is precisely what happened when Tetsugen died at the early age of fifty-three without having named any of his disciples a Dharma heir. Many of Tetsugen's disciples turned to Mu-an, including Hōshū, Tetsugen's leading disciple, who eventually received Mu-an's *inka* and is listed in his line.

Under normal circumstances, Ryōkei's disciples might reasonably have turned to Gomizunoo and perhaps become his Dharma heirs directly. The emperor's exalted social position set him outside the normal monastic life and made regular procedures impractical. At the same time, his unique status lent special weight to his unusual and otherwise unorthodox request. Kao-ch'üan consulted with his superiors at the head temple, including Tu-chan Hsing-jung who would soon become the fourth abbot at Mampuku-ji in 1682, and then showed great discretion in keeping his decision quiet. For five years, Kao-ch'üan took no public action to fulfill Gomizunoo's instructions, although it is said that he used that time period to evaluate Ryōkei's leading disciples to determine their level of understanding. Then, in 1685, he conferred *inka* on Kaiō Hōkō (1635–1712), officially naming him as Gomizunoo's successor. Kaiō received Ryōkei's whisk and the emperor's monastic robe and was appointed abbot at Shōmyō-ji. Obaku masters including Kao-ch'üan, Tetsugyū, Nan-yüan Hsing-p'ai (1631–1692; J. Nangen Shōha), and Dokuhon Shōgen (1618–1689) marked the occasion by composing celebratory verses.

Kao-ch'üan's decision was not greeted with universal applause. Criticism arose within the sect and from other Buddhist leaders, eventually leading to government involvement to settle the dispute. External criticism took two forms. On the one hand, some individuals accused Kao-ch'üan of delaying his decision for five years in order to accomplish his true purpose—namely, to cut off Ryōkei's Dharma line. On the other hand, other Rinzai monks took issue with Obaku's apparent attempt to stake an exclusive claim on the emperor's devotion. Mujaku Dōchū of Myōshin-ji took this latter approach in the

Obaku geki, in which he denied that the emperor had ever made such a request in the first place.

> After Gudō had passed away, the emperor summoned Ryōkei. After a time, Ryōkei offered the retired emperor one of his whisks. This meant that he wanted to place the emperor's name exclusively on the list of his Dharma heirs. The emperor looked upon [the whisk] as a worldly implement. Later, Ryōkei drowned to death in a high flood tide in Naniwa. When the emperor himself was facing death, he sent the whisk along with a message to Akenomiya (the emperor's daughter, who later became a nun and resided at Rinkyū-ji). [The message] said, "This is something for a monk to use; it is useless at the palace. It was originally Ryōkei's religious implement. Please have Kao-ch'üan return it to one of Ryōkei's disciples."
>
> After the emperor passed away, his daughter did exactly what he had requested. Kao-ch'üan accepted the whisk, but told a lie. He said that the emperor wanted to be Ryōkei's Dharma heir. (The emperor merely wanted to return the whisk to Ryōkei's disciples.)[24]

Mujaku is at pains here to deny that the emperor considered himself Ryōkei's Dharma heir, despite the fact that he possessed Ryōkei's whisk. In a rare slip, Mujaku contradicts himself within these few lines, giving two conflicting explanations. First he claims that the emperor regarded the whisk as a secular implement, an unlikely explanation for a devout Zen practitioner such as Gomizunoo. Then he suggests that, although the emperor recognized the whisk's religious meaning, he distanced himself from the obvious implication that he had become Ryōkei's heir. On a more subtle level, Mujaku argues against any exclusive claim to Gomizunoo's Zen affiliation by mentioning in the same context his deep connections with Gudō and Isshi, both monks from Myōshin-ji.

The internal dispute resulting from Kao-ch'üan's publicly naming Kaiō to be Gomizunoo's Dharma heir proved more serious in nature. It split the sect into two factions, pitting Kao-ch'üan and his supporters against the abbot Tu-chan and other senior monks at the main temple. Tu-chan and the others stressed that Obaku should not recognize Dharma transmission except through direct, face-to-face encounters between master and student. According to the *Obaku geki,* Tu-chan based his argument against Kao-ch'üan's decision on an incident that had occurred at Wan-fu-ssu some time earlier, presumably when Ch'an Master Fei-yin was abbot.[25] On that occasion, Fei-yin apparently expelled a monk for accepting Dharma transmission by proxy. Tu-chan understood this decision as a precedent that established a binding rule for the Obaku line. He absolutely refused to accept the indirect transmission to Kaiō as valid.

For his part, Kao-ch'üan defended his decision in light of the special circumstances related to the emperor's social status, stressing that his primary objective was to fulfill the emperor's final deathbed instructions. Of particular interest in this regard is Mujaku's description, albeit at third or fourth hand, of the contents of a letter Kao-ch'üan supposedly wrote to Tu-chan in his own defense. In the letter, Kao-ch'üan allegedly "quoted the emperor as saying, 'We take Yin-yüan to be Bodhidharma, Ryōkei to be the second Patriarch, and ourself to be the third Patriarch.'"[26] Mujaku denies that the emperor ever spoke or wrote these words. He maintains instead that Kao-ch'üan invented the saying in order to slander the emperor and mock the Japanese people.[27]

Arguments continued to plague the sect for a number of years, and all internal efforts to settle the dispute proved unsuccessful. Eventually, the case was decided by the bakufu when Tu-chan made an official petition requesting its determination of the matter. Ultimately, Tu-chan was unsuccessful in his efforts to invalidate Kaiō's reception of Gomizunoo's Dharma, and his petition to the bakufu brought about his own defeat. The bakufu decided that Kao-ch'üan had acted rightly, showing proper respect for the wishes of a Japanese emperor as befitted a visiting Chinese master. As a result of this decision, Tu-chan was forced to resign as abbot in 1691; he and his party left Mampuku-ji and retired to reside at other Obaku temples.

Following the accepted procedure for a retiring abbot, Tu-chan sent the bakufu a list of all candidates qualified to succeed him as abbot at Mampuku-ji, along with his own preference for his successor. In each of the previous transitions, the bakufu simply confirmed the retiring abbot's first choice. In this case, however, the government passed over Nan-yüan, Tu-chan's designated successor, in favor of Kao-ch'üan. Although not a direct heir of Yin-yüan, Kao-ch'üan also qualified, and his name appeared on the list of possible candidates. He became Mampuku-ji's fifth abbot in 1692, thus ending the so-called indirect transmission incident (*daifu jiken*, or *daifu ronsō*).

Obaku Relations with the Tokugawa Bakufu

The Tokugawa bakufu had initially taken a suspicious attitude toward Yin-yüan and his Chinese disciples when it first received petitions requesting permission for them to travel and reside outside of Nagasaki in 1655. Although Yin-yüan was a well-known Chinese monk and the petitions were filed by prominent Japanese Rinzai masters, Yin-yüan's connections with Ming loyalists still fighting in China caused Tokugawa government officials some concern. By 1659, the situation had been completely reversed. The bakufu not only became a full supporter of Yin-yüan, it would agree to sponsor the founding of the main temple Obaku-san Mampuku-ji, to provide a yearly stipend to finance its upkeep, and even to facilitate further emigration of Obaku monks from China to perpetuate the line. This change in attitude came about gradually over the four- to five-year petition process, but the most dramatic progress occurred in 1658 when Yin-yüan traveled to Edo for an audience at the castle. One can perhaps regard Yin-yüan's personal encounters with the shogun and his counselors during that visit as the turning point after which all residual doubts about his motives were laid to rest. The positive impression Yin-yüan made may explain the bakufu's willingness to grant him permanent status as a resident alien, but that alone does not seem sufficient to explain the bakufu's active involvement in establishing a new Zen sect. This is particularly the case when one recalls that bakufu policies were otherwise geared toward constraining Buddhism's growth. Under the circumstances, one must ask what the bakufu sought to gain from its arrangement with Obaku Zen and why Obaku was singled out for special treatment.

The Japanese scholar Takenuki has pointed out a possible parallel between the Tokugawa bakufu's relationship with Obaku Zen and that of other military houses to Rinzai Zen since the Kamakura period.[28] Takenuki provides ample evidence of bakufu sponsorship of Obaku, giving details as to who donated what and when. A brief listing of the larger donations follows. First, the bakufu provided the land and permission to build the new monastery in 1659. According to the red seal certificate that was first issued on 11/7/1665, the land granted to Mampuku-ji measured ninety thousand *tsubo* with an annual stipend of four hundred *koku* of rice.[29] Red seal certificates were issued to Mampuku-ji by every shogun beginning with Ietsuna down through the fourteenth, Iemochi (1846–1666). The grant of land and the stipend remained unchanged throughout the period. It should be noted that in granting permission to found a new temple the bakufu made an exception to its own order, enacted just the year before, in 1658, forbidding the construction of new temples. The senior counselor Sakai Tadakatsu, who became Yin-yüan's strongest supporter in the Edo government, left one thousand *ryō* of gold in his will for construction costs. In 1667, the shogun Ietsuna personally donated twenty thousand *ryō* of gold and four hundred and fifty teak trees. He assigned his own administrator of construction, Aoki Shigekane (1606–1682),[30] the daimyo of Kai province, to direct the project and provided the additional services of the carpentry clan Akishino. Having the shogun's support lent Obaku a high level of credibility among the other military houses, and many daimyo and *hatamoto* followed the shogun's lead by contributing to the construction projects at Obaku-san or by sponsoring Obaku temples in their home districts.[31]

Having illustrated his contention that Mampuku-ji was founded and built under strong bakufu sponsorship, thus supporting his comparison to earlier historical examples, Takenuki does not explore the implications of the comparison. Specifically, he never addresses the possible motives of the Tokugawa bakufu that the comparison may suggest. The following discussion will first consider additional elements that support the comparison and then move on to some contrasts, to see what the historical patterns may suggest. In both cases, the Kamakura and Tokugawa bakufu were relatively new military governments that supported new Zen lines by building large monasteries and appointing Chinese emigré masters as abbots. The Zen school held distinctive advantages from the perspective of these military governments. As Collcutt put it, "The Zen stress on active meditation, man-to-man debate, physical self-discipline, and practical rather than bookish experience, appealed naturally to the warrior spirit. . . . Furthermore, as a predominantly monastic form of Buddhism, Zen was socially stable, politically non-volatile, and as amenable to secular supervision and control in Japan as it had been in China."[32]

Certain characteristics in Obaku's Zen style may have further commended it to the bakufu as a good basis for "revitalizing" or, perhaps more accurately, controlling Japanese Rinzai in a manner beneficial to the Tokugawa system. Obaku's stress on monastic discipline and its positive attitude toward the study of scripture made it an appealing form of Zen, suiting the bakufu's general goal of reducing Buddhism's political threat by reaffirming monastic discipline and scholarship. It seems unlikely that the bakufu was otherwise interested in the details of Obaku's practice and thought as it compared to Japanese Rinzai. The Pure Land elements that offended Japanese monks and ultimately contributed to Obaku's independence as a third Zen sect were not an issue for the bakufu. Government officials were not concerned with the "purity" of Obaku versus Rinzai Zen practice. Nor did they become involved in any philosophical sectarian debates that did not cause a public disturbance.

Like Rinzai in the thirteenth and fourteenth centuries, Obaku represented a new style of Buddhism in Japan, one that was not yet coopted by any political power in Japanese society. Whereas the existing Rinzai monasteries had long-standing connections with the imperial court, as discussed above, Obaku did not. The Zen community of Kyoto included many individuals from the nobility who were not favorably inclined in their attitudes toward the military government in Edo. The Purple Robe Affair and the poor treatment the emperor received at the shogun's hands probably only exacerbated feelings of animosity. The bakufu may have deemed it advantageous to establish and maintain close ties with at least one influential Zen monastery in Kyoto. Chinese Obaku masters were likely allies since as foreigners they had no cultural biases against the military government. Indeed, in the Obaku case, the bakufu participated in the selection of successive abbots, a role reserved for the emperor in the case of most major Zen monasteries.

Tokugawa Ietsuna and his successor, Tsunayoshi, followed the example of the Ashikaga shoguns in patronizing Zen monasteries, in this case making significant donations to Mampuku-ji. Following the Ashikaga pattern, Tokugawa shoguns were far more interested in the cultural aspects of Zen than in actually practicing meditation for themselves. With a few notable exceptions such as Sakai Tadakatsu and Aoki Shigekane, Obaku Zen did not inspire great personal devotion among the bakufu and *han* officials who supported the new sect. Even in Sakai's case, there is no clear indication that he practiced Zen meditation under a master's guidance. Like most government officials, his religious concerns were centered on holding Buddhist memorial services for his deceased family members and earning personal merit through his monetary support of Buddhist monks and monasteries.

There is no way to be certain how many military houses became patrons of Obaku in the early years of the period. Official records for military families, *bukan,* did not record religious affiliation until the year Keio 2 (1866).[33] In the records for that year, Obaku is specifically listed as the primary affiliation for twelve individuals. In many other cases, the affiliation is noted simply as "Zenshū," and some of these individuals may have been Obaku believers.

In addition to the parallels noted above, there are contrasts between the Kamakura and Tokugawa situations that prove equally enlightening in understanding Obaku's role in Tokugawa society. Whereas the Ashikaga bakufu used Zen temples in the *gozan* system as a nationwide, quasi-political institution,[34] the Tokugawa bakufu had already coopted all existing Buddhist sects to serve the same purpose. Buddhist temples acted as quasi-governmental agencies in the *danka seido,* or parishioner system, requiring each family throughout the country to register its membership at a local Buddhist temple to prove they were not Christians. The Tokugawa bakufu did not need Obaku in particular to serve any such purpose. Rather, Obaku lent the Tokugawa bakufu an opportunity to provide Japanese society with one direct link with Chinese culture, especially the calligraphy, painting, poetry, and prose for which Obaku masters were well known. Just as the Tokugawa bakufu retained for itself exclusive control over international trade and affairs, so it maintained control over the limited immigration of Chinese monks who came to reside in Obaku temples. The bakufu thus preserved for itself the role as sole purveyor of Chinese culture in areas of the country outside of Nagasaki through its sponsorship of emigré monks in Kyoto, Edo, and other major cities.

Obaku's Growth within the Tokugawa Temple System

Obaku entered the scene in Japan five or six decades after Tokugawa Ieyasu had attained ascendancy and had unified the country under his control. By 1654 the bakufu already had a coherent policy for regulating Buddhist sects and temples. For this reason it is useful to consider first the situation prevailing before Obaku's founding. In dealing with Buddhist organizations, the bakufu had issued new laws regulating Buddhist temples and schools (*jiin hatto*) several times over the years. In keeping with long-standing sectarian divisions within Japanese Buddhism, the *hatto* were issued predominantly along sectarian lines. They formalized existing patterns in which temples within a given sect might be related in a hierarchical manner. The system of relating temples hierarchically as main and branch temples (*honmatsu seido*) had its roots in the Heian period but had never been formalized to incorporate all temples.[35] The new regulations mandated that every Buddhist temple should officially designate its affiliation with a sect headquarters and that each sect should clearly specify the internal relationships between its main and branch temples. This resulted in a formal system intended to incorporate every existing temple into an overarching hierarchical structure. Such a system was designed to facilitate governmental control over Buddhist temples, as officials would need to communicate directly with only a small, circumscribed set of main temples. The main temples were then responsible for conveying any government directives from above to their affiliated branch temples. In order to fulfill this responsibility, main temples were from the outset granted significant control over their branch temples in the overall system.

Although many temples already had preexisting lines of affiliation with a given sect or major temple, others did not. The process of registering main and branch temples required a certain amount of sorting out of the lines of association within sects, a process that inevitably precipitated some disputes among temples, as each one was forced to choose and formally state its affiliation. Any network intended to consolidate every temple within the entire country necessarily took time to materialize. Gradually, Buddhist groups took on a defined shape that approximated the sectarian pattern still familiar today. The first stages of the process are represented by the *Kan'ei no shoshū honji-chō*, a register of all main and branch temples compiled in 1632 and 1633. Registries of main and branch temples were then prepared at irregular intervals throughout the Tokugawa period in order to update the existing records. Obaku temples appear in later registries, beginning in the Enkyō years (1744–1748). Takenuki's *Kinsei Obakushu matsuji chōshūsei* provides detailed information about Obaku temples found in later registries. In all the records, Zen temples can be clearly distinguished as either Rinzai or Sōtō, based on the divergent history and practices of the two schools. Unlike Sōtō, however, Rinzai Zen temples were not united under a single superstructure. The Rinzai sect was traditionally divided into several lines associated with the larger temples, which include Myōshin-ji, Daitoku-ji, Nanzen-ji, and so on. The Obaku hierarchy of temples can be seen as a part of this latter pattern, all Obaku temples being associated directly or indirectly with Obaku-san Mampuku-ji and its official relationship with an overarching Rinzai school left somewhat ambiguous.

A new religious movement such as Obaku faced significant obstacles to growth as a result of the limitations inherent in this system. Despite its close relationship with the government, Obaku enjoyed no special status under the law. Like all existing sectarian networks within the hierarchy, Obaku was constrained by the regulations against building new temples and the regulations limiting the restoration of existing temples without bakufu permission. Unlike the older schools, however, Obaku did not already possess a large network of temples historically affiliated with the main temple, Mampuku-ji. Initially, Obaku was limited to just those temples that government officials sponsored with bakufu permission. It would have remained quite small had the regulations for temples not developed and changed in a manner that proved beneficial to its cause.

In 1665, the bakufu issued a new set of *hatto* applicable to all Buddhist sects that effectively altered the balance of power between main and branch temples. Main temples had previously held the upper hand as they were given official power to regulate their branch temples. Having once established the hierarchical pattern within the sect, branch temples did not have the freedom to change their affiliation without the main temple granting them permission, an unlikely event at best. Under the new laws, branch temples and their members were given the authority to determine their own affiliation; according to the new guidelines, the branch temples and their congregations gained control over the choice of abbot, which in turn determined the temple's affiliation. This left room for considerably more fluctuation in affiliation, a circumstance that directly benefited Obaku. Temples such as Fumon-ji in Settsu, which had previously been listed officially as Myōshin-ji branch temples, became Obaku branch temples by virtue of their abbot's affiliation. Other temples that had only weak connections with their main temples became prime targets for Obaku expansion. It is not known whether or not the bakufu designed these regulations with Obaku's interests in mind. The date for these new *hatto*, 11/7/1665, coincides precisely with the date for the first red seal certificate granted to Mampuku-ji. The timing suggests the possibility of a direct correlation, but there is no concrete evidence on which to rely. Nonetheless, whether intended to benefit Obaku or not, the new laws were among the more crucial steps taken by the Tokugawa bakufu that promoted the development of Obaku Zen, since they effectively created an opening in an otherwise closed landscape.

Obaku monks, especially the first generation of Japanese converts, developed a variety of strategies based on the new regulations for acquiring new temples for the new movement. For example, existing family temples in Edo or the provinces often became Obaku branch temples when the local daimyo or another high-level official invited an Obaku monk to serve as abbot. Obaku monks traveling through different regions of the country to spread the new Zen style among the common people also founded numerous temples with popular support. Obaku monks did not enjoy the benefit of an existing network of Obaku temples in which to stay for even short periods of time when traveling. They would therefore sometimes stop at a dilapidated temple or at one that no longer had a resident monk and use it for temporary shelter. If the local community responded positively, the Obaku monk might be invited to restore the temple and serve as its head. The members of the congregation could then switch the temple's official affiliation to Mampuku-ji or to another large Obaku temple. Using all of these methods, Obaku expanded to include 1,043 temples spread out through fifty-one of the sixty-six provinces in Japan by the time they submitted their first comprehensive list of main and branch temples in 1745.[36]

An important factor to bear in mind is that Obaku monks of the early generations faced a shortage of temples unknown in other sects. As the sect attracted Japanese converts, the number of Obaku monks far outweighed the number of Obaku temples that they could expect to inherit from their master. More and more Obaku monks found themselves without temples they could call their permanent homes. Tetsugen was in just this situation when he acquired his primary temple of residence, Zuiryū-ji in Osaka, though he later founded other temples in much the same way. In the case of Zuiryū-ji, Tetsugen and his disciples had moved to Osaka to begin work on the Obaku edition of the Chinese Buddhist Scriptures. As there were no Obaku temples in the immediate vicinity, they lived temporarily with a family of Obaku lay believers. Some time later, a community group in the Tamba district offered to restore a ruined temple and invited Tetsugen to become the resident monk. He renamed the temple Zuiryū-ji, and he is listed on the official records as its founder-restorer.

As the above example also illustrates, Obaku masters sometimes borrowed or even rented houses or land for temporary quarters. The bakufu actually granted the sect official permission to do so in 1673. The practice was obviously not standard at the time and elicited some scornful remarks from other Buddhists. This is almost certainly the import of one short passage from the Obaku geki. "Today in the Obaku line there are some who claim to transmit the Dharma but have no temple in which to reside. They are all over the city, in front of shops and behind them. They are the so-called Senior Guardian [who protects] the heavens and the Minister of Works [who protects] all the earth." [37] Given the conditions facing a new Buddhist sect at the time, few other options existed for those monks who had not yet made a name for themselves but had received an invitation to establish a temple from a prominent government official or a local group of believers.

Obaku's Change of Perspective

Buddhism has traditionally relied upon the secular authorities for a measure of support and in turn has had to accept varying degrees of secular control and limitation. Chinese Buddhism certainly fit this pattern in the late Ming period, and the Chinese monks would have taken it for granted that the same would hold true in Japan. Indeed, in Japan, both the imperial court and the military governments have acted the part of benefactor to Buddhism and, depending on the period, exerted some control over its growth and internal affairs. There is nothing unusual, then, in Obaku Zen enjoying the degree of secular patronage described above. Although relations between the bakufu and the court were still strained in the mid-seventeenth century, this did not prevent them from sharing a common cause, such as the anti-Christian movement, nor from sponsoring the same Buddhist groups. For its part, Obaku benefited from both its relationship with the imperial family, especially Emperor Gomizunoo, and its relationship with bakufu and *han* officials. Needless to say, the benefits differed in accordance with the spheres of power proper to each. While the bakufu and *han* officials could provide financial support, permission to build new temples, assistance in sponsoring the emigration of Chinese monks, and so on, close relations with the emperor brought Obaku prestige in the social realm.

The emperor's actual authority was effectively limited by the Tokugawa bakufu to the cultural and artistic spheres. Even at a time when the emperor had no political or military power, however, imperial support still lent Obaku prestige in Japanese society. When the emperor conferred purple robes and honorific titles on various Obaku masters (with bakufu permission, of course), he gave them status in the hierarchical world of Japanese Buddhism. Likewise, the shogun's personal support for Obaku raised the new sect's standing with the military houses. Since the bakufu held the monopoly on political power, Obaku had to abide by the bakufu's system of government and answer to its authority whenever disputes arose. On a very practical level, like all Buddhist groups at the time, Obaku fell under bakufu control in a wide variety of monastic concerns, including building and restoring temples, publishing texts, and appointing a new abbot for the main monastery. From time to time, the bakufu did exercise its authority to ban certain Buddhist practices, and even outlawed entire Buddhist movements and organizations. Therefore it would be a mistake to underestimate the actual coercive power that the bakufu possessed to control Buddhist sects or the level of voluntary cooperation this potential use of power engendered among Buddhist groups. There was no comparable type of imperial control operative over Buddhist sects until after the Meiji Restoration. Therefore, during the Tokugawa period, though imperial support was an asset for Obaku, bakufu support was a necessity for its very existence.

Following the Meiji Restoration, the situation changed significantly for Obaku Zen and the whole of the Buddhist world in Japan. Buddhism in general fell on hard times. The Meiji government preferred the native Shinto as a state religion, placing Buddhism, which had cooperated so thoroughly with the bakufu, in an inferior position. Existing tendencies that viewed Buddhism as a foreign religion detrimental to Japanese ways of thinking became dominant in intellectual and political circles. While Buddhism had been on the defensive on the intellectual front during much of the Tokugawa period, it had still enjoyed extensive government protection from any serious attacks on its personnel, property, and economic base. Now, in the new environment of Meiji Japan, Buddhism came under fire from government policies as well as popular outcry. The Meiji government actively pursued a policy of separating Shinto from long-standing elements of Buddhist influence (*shinbutsu bunri*). This led to the closing of numerous temples, particularly those built within shrine grounds, and to the laicization of shrine priests (*shasō*) who had served at those temples, as well as many other Buddhist monks and nuns. Buddhist temples on all levels of the Buddhist hierarchy lost the financial security they had previously enjoyed under the Tokugawa system, first in 1871, when temple lands granted by bakufu or *han* certificates were reclaimed. A second blow came in 1872, when the *danka seido* system was abolished. A popular backlash against Buddhism, known as *haibutsu kishaku*, called for its eradication. The popular movement lead to the destruction of temples and looting of monastic treasure houses in some parts of the country.[38]

Obaku found itself in an especially precarious position during the

Meiji era because of its previous ties to the bakufu. As a consequence, Obaku leaders would have to shift their perspective on the sect's history and teachings in an attempt to stabilize the situation. First, in the matter of monetary support, Mampuku-ji lost several sources of income, including resources not directly associated with the *danka seido*. Obviously, once the bakufu fell, the yearly government stipend of 400 *koku* ceased to exist. In addition, the Meiji government repossessed the bulk of Mampuku-ji's land grant under the land reclamation act of 1871. Loss of land would have entailed a further drop in actual and potential revenues. Other, private sources of income also dried up during the financial crises that occurred toward the end of the Tokugawa period and continued into early Meiji.

Throughout most of the Tokugawa period, Mampuku-ji received a regular yearly donation from a medical academy in Edo, established by one of its early Japanese converts Ryōō Dōkaku (1630–1707). Ryōō founded the academy and its affiliated pharmacy, known respectively as Kintaien and Kangakuya, in 1665. During his lifetime, Ryōō used the money that he raised to support various Buddhist institutions and projects, including Mampuku-ji. He later established a trust in his will so that the academy and pharmacy would continue as a philanthropic agency. Surplus profits from the academy and pharmacy accumulated in the trust and were donated on a yearly basis to various Buddhist groups including Tendai, Jōdo Shinshū, and Zen. Over the years 1701 through 1844, Obaku received approximately 7,800 *ryō* of gold and 1,500 *ryō* of silver for routine upkeep at Mampuku-ji. Toward the end of the period, the institute ceased to thrive in the face of incoming Western medicine; as a result, the stipend distributed to Mampuku-ji gradually decreased, and then stopped altogether.[39] With the loss of government support and other private resources, Obaku found itself in financial straits like many other Buddhist organizations. It desperately needed to cultivate other sources of income, especially on a popular level.

With the possible exception of the Sōtō sect, Zen had never really enjoyed the broad spectrum of popularity among the common people that other sects such as the Pure Land and Nichiren groups had. Although lay believers relied upon Zen temples for funeral and memorial services, the practice of Zen meditation remained a somewhat elite practice that did not draw large numbers of laypersons. This meant that during the Meiji era, when membership became voluntary, Zen

temples had smaller bases of lay believers to depend upon for donations. Obaku was no exception. Although early generations of Japanese Obaku monks had worked extensively with the common people,
this work had gradually declined as the sect became more firmly established. Once mandatory Buddhist affiliation was abolished by the
Meiji authorities, Obaku once again made an effort to popularize its
teachings in order to build up voluntary membership. This process included a renewed stress on the Pure Land elements that had always existed in their Zen style but had gradually faded under the influence of
Hakuin's koan Zen. In the modern period before and during the
Pacific War years, elements within Obaku presented the sect as the
one Zen lineage with teachings designed to reach people of all ranges
of ability; for those of high capacity they continued to stress meditation and koan practice, and for those of medium and low capacity
they renewed their stress on the practice of chanting the *nembutsu*.

At the same time that Obaku faced crises in its financial stability
and popular acceptance, it also found itself in a new and uncomfortable position within the new political order. Because of its close
ties with the bakufu, Obaku was discredited when the bakufu lost
power. The close association, which had originally been necessary for
Obaku's establishment and growth, now became a hindrance to its
continuing existence. Obaku therefore reinterpreted its history to
magnify the role of the emperor and attenuate its ties to the bakufu.
As the emperor system gained dominance in the world of Meiji
thought, Obaku became more and more an imperial sect in its own
version of its history. The old story, found in sectarian writings during
the Tokugawa period, that the shogun had invited Yin-yüan to Japan
was dropped. New versions seem to have emerged sometime during
Meiji suggesting that Yin-yüan came to Kyoto (or to Japan, depending on the source) at the emperor's invitation. Moreover, it was said
that Yin-yüan chose land in Uji for Mampuku-ji in order to be near
the retired emperor. Prewar works such as Furuichi's *Gomizunoo
tennō to Obaku*, published in 1929, and many wartime Obaku histories and articles, including those by Akamatsu Shinmyō and Washio
Junkei, exhibit the same pattern. These modern efforts to recast
Obaku history were so successful that the new versions were widely
accepted as factual. They appeared in numerous nonsectarian scholarly encyclopedias, historical surveys, and the like. Remnants of this
can still be found in many postwar writings, such as *Zen Dust*, which

reports that "Eventually the reigning emperor granted [Yin-yüan] land at Uji, near Kyoto, where . . . he built an imposing monastery and temple in the late Ming style, which he named Mampuku-ji. . . ." [40]

The trend to reinterpret Obaku's history extended into early Shōwa and characterizes much of the scholarship written by Obaku scholars before and during the Second World War. These works tend to distort the facts, not by denying the bakufu's participation in the process of establishing Obaku Zen, but by a careful shifting of emphasis away from the bakufu whenever possible. Much of the recent scholarship on Obaku history, especially the work of Takenuki, has tried to restore a more realistic portrait of Obaku's relations with the secular authorities by refocusing back on Obaku's reliance on bakufu patronage. This approach is more accurate for evaluating Obaku during the Tokugawa period itself, when bakufu patronage was of preeminent importance. In light of the practical concerns that shaped Obaku's view of itself from the Meiji through the Shōwa periods, however, scholars should not underestimate the importance in the modern period of Obaku's strong ties with the emperor Gomizunoo.

ELEVEN
Conclusion

This study has traced the development of the Obaku sect of Japanese Zen Buddhism from its origins as a new religious movement in the mid-seventeenth century to its successful establishment as an independent sect. During the first decades of its existence, the movement initially achieved independent institutional status with the founding of its main monastery Obaku-san Mampuku-ji. Within the first century, a wide network of over a thousand temples grew under the administrative guidance of the main monastery. Monks and nuns practicing at Obaku temples and monasteries were governed by a distinctive sectarian monastic code, known as the *Obaku shingi*. While its teachings and practices had much in common with those of other Zen groups, especially the closely related Rinzai lineages, some aspects of the Obaku style distinguished it as a unique form of Zen Buddhism in the Japanese context.

Discussions of the early leadership have shown that the cooperative efforts of the Chinese founders and the first generation of Japanese converts provided Obaku with complementary skills. The Chinese founders established the foundations of the order, both in terms of the physical plant at Mampuku-ji and the teachings that governed the beliefs and practices of the sect. The three Chinese founders have been characterized as exemplifying a movement from a charismatic leader to an institution builder, a pattern familiar from other NRMs. Yin-yüan possessed not only the personal charisma of an effective and popular Zen teacher but that of a prominent and high-ranking Chinese master. While Yin-yüan's appeal drew in Japanese patronage and large numbers of potential converts, his successor Mu-an undertook the mundane process of administrating the physical growth of the sect and the long-term commitment to training Japanese disciples.

Early generations of Japanese converts built upon the foundation laid by the Chinese founders and actively spread the new movement throughout the country. As seen in the portrait of the first generation of Japanese Dharma heirs, most of the Japanese Obaku monks were converts from other Zen institutions, a large percentage coming from the Myōshin-ji lineage of Rinzai Zen. While a significant number were senior monks with the necessary prestige and monastic resources to serve the new movement immediately, the majority were younger men seeking the opportunity to practice under the Chinese masters.

Obaku enjoyed a productive working relationship with the secular authorities throughout the Tokugawa period. Cooperation from the government allowed the sect to take root in the first place and then promoted its overall growth. Indeed, as was demonstrated in the historical sketch of the early years, there is some reason to regard Obaku as a special favorite of the Tokugawa bakufu. Its main monastery was established with the special permission of the shogun and the governing council. It received deeded lands and an accompanying annual stipend from government coffers. In addition, the sect acquired other land and monetary donations from the Tokugawa shogun and various high-ranking bakufu and *han* officials, all of which helped to extend the sect's temple network and financial base.

Of particular interest regarding Obaku–bakufu relations was the role the government played in maintaining Obaku's connection with the Chinese home monastery and the appointment of abbots at Mampuku-ji. For over a century the government cooperated with the sect in allowing a small influx of Chinese monks from Wan-fu-ssu. These individuals were then trained to serve at Obaku temples, the more talented being chosen to hold the abbot's post at Mampuku-ji. Successive generations of abbots provided bakufu officials with a list of qualified candidates from among the Chinese emigré monks. From this list the government reserved the right to make the final, official selection of Mampuku-ji's abbot. While the government no doubt followed sectarian preferences in most cases, its direct involvement in the process symbolized its role as sponsor and patron for the sect. In the case of other major Zen monasteries, this role was more often fulfilled by the emperor.

Obaku masters also established cordial relations with the retired emperor Gomizunoo and other members of the imperial family. Although the emperor had little official authority during the Tokugawa period, his favor brought with it social prestige for individual monks and for the sect as a whole. Gomizunoo and later emperors bestowed imperial honors, including purple robes and honorific titles, on Obaku monks. Eventually, according to sectarian accounts, the emperor took the tonsure as an Obaku monk himself and became a Dharma heir within the Obaku lineage. Although at the time the claim to an imperial Dharma lineage caused some tension, the close association with Gomizunoo later served Obaku well, especially during the early decades of the modern period.

Revolutions in the Historical Perspective of Obaku

This study has attempted to introduce varying perspectives of Obaku Zen that developed throughout its history in Japan. Without attempting to adjudicate religious claims made by internal and external sectarian proponents, it has illustrated the ways in which portraits of Obaku have shifted to accommodate ever-changing social and historical circumstances. Beginning with the earliest period of the movement's history, one can distinguish differences between the insider Chinese perspectives of the Obaku style of practice from that of the initial Japanese respondents. The Chinese monks, as members of the Chinese tradition of Ch'an Buddhism, regarded Obaku as a valid transmission of the Dharma and viewed themselves as embodiments of a "true lineage of Lin-chi Ch'an." In this regard, the internal Obaku perspective has remained constant down to the present. Insiders continue to present Obaku as an alternative but valid Rinzai lineage transmitted to Japan centuries later than the previously established lines. Despite the official designation of the sect as Obaku-shū, they readily acknowledge the common historical and philosophical roots they shared with their Rinzai cousins. Even today, Obaku monks continue to identify themselves in certain sectarian contexts as members of Rinzai *shōshū*. It should be noted that modern and contemporary members of the Obaku sect speak of it in far more defensive tones that their early forebears, perhaps in response to external criticism.

The initial Japanese perspectives of Obaku encompassed a broad spectrum of attitudes toward the Chinese founders and their foreign style of practice. Supporters within the established Zen monasteries welcomed Obaku masters as a source of inspiration and renewal for the Japanese Zen community as a whole. For these individuals, Obaku represented a vital connection to China, the original source of Zen thought and practice. On the other hand, early opponents faced with the very real possibility of Obaku leadership at established Rinzai monasteries vehemently rejected the notion that the Japanese Zen community could or should reform its practice according to the Ming Chinese pattern. A generation later, the authors of the *Obaku geki* and the *Zenrin shūhei shū* would articulate some of the same negative views of Obaku still current in the early eighteenth century. Though early opponents objected to the Obaku style of practice on various grounds, they did not yet challenge its validity as a form of Rinzai Zen.

It took several generations for the anti-Obaku perspective to take on the definite shape it has assumed in the modern period. Although Obaku was sometimes regarded as an inferior style of Rinzai practice that could not benefit Japanese Zen, it was not generally characterized as Nembutsu Zen in the first century of its history. Hakuin's writings may have served to focus the external criticism in that direction. Without mentioning Obaku by name, Hakuin expressed grave misgivings about the impact the combined practice of Zen and Pure Land teachings would have on the future of Zen in Japan. After Hakuin's time, the issue of combined practice would become the standard explanation for divisions between Obaku and Rinzai Zen. By the modern period, Obaku was regularly dismissed as Nembutsu Zen, an impure form not truly compatible with true Rinzai practice. This attitude has influenced not only sectarian accounts of Japanese Zen but has shaped perceptions of Obaku in scholarly studies as well.

In the modern period, Obaku insiders reworked the sect's understanding of its own history to redefine it as a loyalist religious organization having extensive connections with the imperial family. Indeed, Obaku accounts dating from the prewar and Pacific War period sometimes present the sect as an imperial favorite from its founding, substituting imperial for bakufu sponsorship as the key to Obaku's success. At the same time, some Obaku leaders saw practical advantages in stressing the Pure Land aspects of Obaku belief and practice as a means of reaching out to a broader popular audience. They suggested that Obaku represented the ideal bridge between the high tradition of meditation Zen designed for advanced practitioners and the accessible tradition of reliance on Amida appropriate for ordinary believers.

One final alteration in Obaku's self-definition that occurred during the early decades of the twentieth century was the subtle shift of focus away from the founding Chinese masters to a renewed interest in the first generation of Japanese converts in popular sectarian literature and hagiography. Obaku's Japanese rather than its Chinese roots were gleaned for inspiration and legitimization in the modern climate of patriotic and nationalistic awareness. While Yin-yüan, Mu-an, and Chi-fei did not disappear from sectarian literature, early Japanese Obaku monks such as Tetsugen and Tetsugyū became the preferred subjects for Obaku stories about famous monks. Tetsugen and his Japanese Dharma brothers were held up as exemplary Zen monks who resisted the decadent monastic behavior rampant at the time, sullying the reputation of all Buddhist clerics, and praised as loyal Japanese citizens who aided society through their selfless social welfare efforts.

Scholarly perspectives of Obaku have similarly undergone a series of revolutions in the modern period. I have sought to broaden and, in some instances, correct modern and contemporary images of Obaku Zen as they appear in scholarly accounts. For example, I have challenged the common assumption that Obaku parted company from Japanese Rinzai to become an independent sect of Zen in Japan due largely to its incorporation of Pure Land teaching and practice. The goal of this study was not to arrive at a simple rendering of Obaku Zen but to explore the many facets of its identity as viewed from various perspectives. Rather than attempting to evaluate, for example, whether Obaku was actually an imperial favorite or a bakufu favorite, positions previously taken by scholars, I have preferred to hold the two perspectives in tension, acknowledging that each reveals something significant about Obaku's history and its place in Japanese Buddhism. Indeed, I have offered my own interpretation of Obaku as a new religious movement, not as a definitive viewpoint superior to all other perspectives, but as a window through which to view previously unexplored facets of its history.

Domestic and Imported NRMs

New religious movements can be distinguished according to their place of origin and the relation they thus bear to their host culture. Domestic NRMs, those which arise within a given culture, have organic ties to the culture, even when the movement takes a highly negative attitude toward the religious beliefs and ethical values of the society's majority. Imported NRMs take shape in one environment and then enter into a foreign culture; they therefore may not share a common heritage with the host culture. This lack of cultural familiarity may place an imported NRM at odds with its host society and seriously limit its growth potential.

The opposition and support engendered by NRMs depend to some degree on the locus of the group's origin. Domestic NRMs may be able to utilize to their advantage an extensive familiarity with the host culture and its existing religious traditions, resources that imported movements typically lack. A new domestic group may be able to make use of the established networks of existing religious institutions, as was the case, for example, with the Branch Davidians, who proselytized primarily among Seventh Day Adventist congregations. On the other hand, the leadership of a domestic NRM may face serious challenges in establishing their credentials as legitimate religious figures. Again, David Koresh of the Branch Davidians may be seen as a case in point. His authority as a church leader and biblical interpreter was not widely recognized beyond the confines of the Davidian community. An imported NRM, which may lack the advantages of preexisting networks, may yet have well-established leaders who have gained recognition in their home culture. The Dalai Lama, for example, who has transmitted Tibetan Buddhism to several areas of the world that lacked a previously existing Buddhist community, nevertheless has the advantage of being widely acknowledged as a legitimate religious leader.

The Obaku sect cannot be easily categorized as either an imported or a domestic tradition. Instead, it possessed the qualities of both types of NRMs in the context of seventeenth-century Japan. Whereas its close association with Rinzai Zen made the movement familiar to the Japanese so that it could function as a domestic tradition, the group nevertheless manifested a distinctly foreign aspect in many respects. Obaku represented an alternative option for Japanese practitioners of Zen and successfully drew membership from the existing Zen community. As demonstrated in the portrait of the first generation of converts, a large majority of the Obaku converts had previous affiliations with Zen, especially with various Rinzai temples. The Chinese founders provided the group with the prestige and legitimization associated with prominent dignitaries from China, the land of Zen's origin. The first generation of Japanese converts gave the group access to many indigenous resources that newcomers would generally lack, including connections with the military government and imperial family and support from the existing Zen community. Indeed, it may be best to regard Obaku as a rare hybrid form of a new religious movement, one produced by the reacquainting of two strands of a divided tradition.

Reacquainted Traditions

Imagine a river that splits into two distinct streams. The two streams travel along their respective courses for many miles, traversing different regions. Eventually, in a rare twist of the natural terrain, they reunite, once again becoming a single river. The reunification of two religious groups nurtured over time in different cultural environments, whose practice originally emerged from a single root tradition, would be an equally rare occurrence. Obaku and Rinzai in seventeenth-century Japan are one such case. Observing their interaction, one may begin to discern possible patterns when traditions become reacquainted.

First, traditions that share a common origin will typically also share some basic level of belief and practice. This commonality can provide a foundation for later interaction. In order for the groups to follow completely distinct trajectories during their period of isolated development, some form of geographical separation without the benefit of significant contact would be necessary. Both groups would thereby be free to develop and change according to the specific stresses and demands of their respective environments, without mutual influence. Each group would retain certain aspects of the source tradition, although not necessarily the same things. At the same time, the two groups would eventually develop new beliefs and practices and adapt others. After a period of several generations, the exact configurations of new and old, retained and adapted, would no doubt vary. The degree of difference would be related to a number of factors, such as time elapsed between periods of contact and the relative similarity of the cultures involved.

The religious groups separated in this manner may be reunited when one group emigrates and resettles within the confines of the other's territory. The reunited tradition would then encompass an emigré community within a host community. How would two groups thus reunited interact? When the waters of the two forks of a river intersect, they rejoin smoothly to flow once again as a single river. It is theoretically possible that two religious communities might find some mutually beneficial balance and be able to function as a single community. The emigré community would need to adjust in order to blend in with the host community; the host community, more often the larger and therefore more dominant one, would in turn absorb some influence from the newcomers. Compromise, adaptation, and flexibility would be required on both sides for a successful reunification to take place.

Any number of possible variations in historical circumstances would influence the eventual outcome of two streams of a religious tradition attempting to merge into a single community. Factors such as the primary reasons for emigration, the level of religious leadership within the emigré community, and the power base of the immigrants in their home culture would have significant impact on the course of events. An influx of relatively untrained lay believers would fare quite differently than would an immigrant community accompanied by professional clergy. Newcomers arriving eager to proselytize or convinced of their authority to "purify" the host community might well encounter more resistance than powerless refugees merely seeking a safe haven.

When Roman Catholic missionaries returned to Japan during the Meiji period, they discovered the existence of an indigenous Japanese Catholic community, the Kakure Kirishitan. After more than two centuries without contact, the religious beliefs and practices of the "hidden Christians" did not match the expectations of the French missionaries, who believed the Japanese Catholics had fallen into heresy. Assuming the superior position as instructors in the true faith, the missionaries worked to reclaim the Japanese believers. Some members of the Kakure Kirishitan community wished to reestablish contact with the church in Rome; they demonstrated a willingness to submit themselves to the authority of the missionaries and to alter the traditions preserved by generations of "hidden Christians." Others adamantly resisted efforts made by the Catholic church to claim their loyalty. They rejected missionary demands that they conform to orthodox belief and practice as defined by Rome. The resistance party preferred to practice their faith as it had been transmitted to them; they retained their identity as a separate Catholic community in Japan, not in communion with Rome.[1]

The separation and eventual reacquainting of Roman Catholic missionaries and the Kakure Kirishitan community bear some general resemblance to the relationship between Obaku and the Rinzai sect. In both cases, the original parting of ways did not occur as the result of a sectarian dispute. Although the communities were separated geographically for an extended period of time, they had no reason to assume at their initial reunification that serious issues of belief and practice would divide them. Both Catholic and Obaku clergy undertook the journey to Japan to serve an expatriate community living on Japanese soil. Only later did the newcomers turn their attention to proselytizing native Japanese. In fact, in both cases Japanese members of the indigenous religious community sought out the emigré clergy and requested their instruction. When the Catholic and Obaku missionaries began to reach out to a Japanese audience, they encountered both support and resistance from the indigenous population.

As seen in these two cases, reunited religious traditions may follow a different course from the unimpeded merging of reunited streams of a river. Rather than blending harmoniously, they may repel one another and split once more into two independent religious entities. In the case of Obaku and Rinzai, it may be possible to generalize the process of the reacquainting of traditions and identify common patterns in the emigré and host communities.

Whenever an emigré community wishes to establish a permanent presence in the host community it will face serious challenges to preserving its own cultural norms within the confines of a foreign culture. Some degree of acculturation is inevitable to enable a cultural minority to survive in a new environment, let alone to expand their presence effectively. A religious group needs to make decisions concerning which religious and cultural traditions are essential to their practice and which may be altered to suit the host culture. Maintaining contact with a power base in the home culture can greatly improve the chances of retaining aspects of the cultural identity. Nevertheless, gradual acculturation is to be expected.

Within the host community one may expect to find two distinct elements, the supporters who function as bridges between the two groups and the resisters who reject the possibility of reunification. In the case of Obaku, individuals such as Ryōkei, Jikuin, Tokuō, and Kyorei represent the supporters who sought to bridge the gap between the two communities and effectively to reunite them, while Gudō and his party represent the resistance movement. Supporters must discern some advantage to their own position to motivate them to undertake the process of integrating the emigré community. In contrast, those who resist perceive an inherent threat or danger to themselves or the tradition as a whole; they therefore reject the integration of the emigré community on some grounds. They may voice their objections in terms of the newcomers' unorthodox beliefs or improper practices. The rivalry between supporters and resisters may follow the pattern of an existing division within the community, although the emigré community may refocus the tension.

Although the arrival of the emigré community may cause divisions within the host community or heighten existing rifts, the overall effect of the process may nevertheless result in a revitalization of the tradition. Whether the newcomers are successfully integrated into the community or a permanent schism occurs, the host community will have the opportunity to redefine itself and to undertake a process of self-clarification. In the case of Rinzai Zen, the encounter with Obaku provided an opportunity for leaders to reassess their understanding of Zen. They gained access to aspects of the tradition they had not previously pursued while reaffirming their commitment to developments that arose in the Japanese context.

The Success and Failure of Obaku Zen

In evaluating the success and failure of new religious movements, scholars do not agree on the criteria to be applied. Bryan Wilson observes that, for most social scientists, "numbers, endurance, maintenance of commitment, persistence or attainment of goals become necessary indicators of relative success or failure."[2] In these terms, the ability to attract members in large numbers and to maintain an ongoing presence in society would be marks of relative success, while the ultimate failure would be a decline in membership and the eventual disappearance of the group altogether. In terms of this rather modest interpretation of success, Obaku presents one of the more successful movements of the Tokugawa period. Unlike other religious movements, such as Shingaku, which did not survive long in the modern period, Obaku remains a viable sect today. One may observe that it established a sufficient institutional base in its first century of growth to sustain an enduring presence of modest size.

Other scholars understand success in somewhat grander terms, suggesting that success should be the measure of a religious tradition's ability to dominate a society—that is, its power to influence behavior, culture, and public policy.[3] It has been observed in Chapter 6 that Obaku enjoyed only very limited success in directly influencing Japanese Buddhism, let alone Japanese society as a whole. The initial potential that opponents and proponents alike perceived for the new movement to act as a blueprint for Rinzai reform had faded by the end of the first century. While Obaku did serve as a catalyst for reform within the world of Zen, it did not succeed in dominating the direction of that reform. In applying this alternative standard, then, Obaku would appear to be a relative failure in the face of the successes of Hakuin Zen and Dōgen Zen.

In the context of Japanese religion, it has generally been assumed that new movements introduced from outside Japan succeed only when they effectively integrate themselves into the Japanese milieu by becoming Japanese in style. In the case of Obaku Zen, I have argued that the success it enjoyed in establishing itself as a third sect of Zen Buddhism rested largely on its identity as a distinctly Chinese form of Zen Buddhism. Throughout the first century of Obaku's history, the distinctive monastic code and style of practice established by the Chinese founders, as well as the regular contact with their home monasteries in China, fostered an ongoing maintenance of the Chinese flavor of the Obaku movement. During this century, Obaku enjoyed a period of steady institutional growth; the numbers of monks recognized as Dharma heirs grew rapidly with each successive generation, and the numbers of temples grew to keep pace with the increases in personnel.

After the first century of its history, Obaku was not successful in maintaining the early level of excitement and growth. It is not coincidental that just at the juncture when meaningful contact with the Chinese resources stagnated that Obaku's institutional growth peaked and then began to recede. After the middle of the eighteenth century the small but constant influx of Chinese monks came to an end. Obaku, by necessity, ceased the practice of appointing Chinese masters to serve as head abbot at Mampuku-ji. At the same time, other forms of Japanese Zen, especially Hakuin Zen, gained increasing influence over Obaku practice. As Obaku became more and more similar to Rinzai Zen, indeed, as it became more Japanese in style, it no longer represented a truly distinctive religious option. Ironically, in the case of Obaku, the process of Japanization marked the end rather than the beginning of its success.

Appendix: The *Obaku Geki* of Mujaku Dōchū

Perhaps a year after Yin-yüan came to Japan [in the seventh month of 1654], Lord Omura, the daimyo of the Nagasaki area,[1] gave him one hundred pieces of silver, sent by messenger. Yin-yüan used this money to buy live fish and released them into the Chinju Suwanomyōjin lake in Nagasaki. Somehow all the fish died and floated up to the surface. His interpreter, Nihei, scoffed and said: "The Japanese will never believe in you if you do this sort of thing. Isn't there some other way to spread the Dharma?" Yin-yüan was ashamed and said: "I have no connections with Japan. I should return to China." All the same, it has been a long time and he is still here.

On the ninth day of the ninth month, when Master Jikuin was living at his retreat at Zenrin-ji, Yin-yüan came there one morning, accompanied by seven or eight disciples, arriving while [Jikuin] was still asleep. He pushed open the door, entered, and stroked Jikuin's head to awaken him. When Jikuin started to get up, to his surprise, Yin-yüan patted the mattress with his hand, meaning "You are fine just as you are," and so restrained him. Jikuin sat up in bed and said, "Why have you come so early in the morning?" Yin-yüan replied: "Although I thought I should return to China, the Ch'ing Dynasty has not yet sufficiently quelled the disorders.[2] Since Japan is a country where the Buddhist Dharma flourishes, I think that I should stay here if I can. Since you know many of the daimyo, perhaps you would act as my intermediary and I could build a two-mat hut and raise my Dharma banner."[3]

Jikuin said: "I understand. While I am still alive, there will be no need for you to go back to China. If I were to die, then you would have to return to China." The following day, [Jikuin] wrapped things up in Nagasaki in a single day and then set out for Kamigata [the Kyoto area] the day after that. Master Jikuin was a native of Nagato, and he stopped there [on his way]. While he was there, Yin-yüan sent ahead a letter of about twenty pages, written on what is called *hanshi*, which was to reach him in Nagato.

A person named Takaya Shintarō of Katawara village in Hagi in Nagato province was a lay disciple of Master Jikuin. When I went there, he told me about this letter. Master Jikuin had left it there in his home, and he had it

205

in his care. In it, [Yin-yüan] said, "I would like to publish the *Gotō gentō*[4] soon. I intended to present the scroll to you, but although I have searched for the scroll box, I have not found it."[5]

Master Jikuin went up to Kyoto and consulted with Master Senzan of Taizō-in,[6] seeking for like-minded people. There were none, so he went down to Osaka and sought out Master Tangetsu.[7] Later, he withdrew. He also sought out Ryōkei and Tokuō.

Since Master Jikuin was a personal friend of Itakura Minamoto Shidemune Lord of Suo,[8] the *Shoshidai* of Kyoto at that time, he consulted with him. Jikuin said: "The thirty-second generation descendent of Lin-chi [Master Yin-yüan], a worthy teacher, has come to Nagasaki from China and says that he must soon return to China. He is an honored guest of the Rinzai sect in Japan, so I would like to show him some hospitality. By this, I don't just mean offer him food. I would like to show him the Kyoto area. I would like to go to the Edo bakufu with this petition. How should I go about submitting it? I would appreciate your suggestions."

Lord Suo was grinding the tea himself. At first he tried to put Jikuin off by saying that there was nothing he could do. Jikuin said, "Even were I banished [for trying to arrange this], I would regret nothing."

During these frequent visits for consultation, Lord Suo would sometimes invite Jikuin into his private quarters and grind tea. After they had conversed, Lord Suo was favorably impressed and said: "My advice is that you should do such and such in Edo. When you do go to Edo, stop by here the day before you leave." When Jikuin did so, Lord Suo gave him [the equivalent of] ten pieces of silver in small coins wrapped up in two packets. One packet was for his carriage expenses and the other for his lodging. (Master Jikuin said that this was because small coins are easier to use on the road. They weigh less than one *momme*.)[9]

In perhaps the tenth month [of 1654], Jikuin went to Edo and made his application at the *Hyōjōsho*,[10] entering it into register number eighteen. The counselors summoned him to their chambers. Matsudaira Lord of Izu[11] was particularly impressed. He said: "Although I have been in public office for many years, this is the first reasonable petition I have heard. I don't know Yin-yüan, but for a start this Jikuin is commendable."

Although the counselors conferred intently, they didn't make any headway. They knew Lord Izu's opinion because of his opening remark. Lord Izu said, "Since no one among the counselors will act as a leader and take some initiative, we are getting nowhere. Be that as it may, Sakai Lord of Sanuki[12] seems to have faith in Yin-yüan. It would be best to consult with him." Saying this, he withdrew and consulted with him in private. After that, the petition was settled in the fifth month of the following year [1655], as requested.

> [*Based on a letter of Makino Lord of Oribe,*[13] *it seems that Jikuin went to Edo alone to make the petition. It says that Ryōkei and Tokuō sent Jikuin to invite (Yin-yüan) to Fumon-ji.*]

At that time, Ryōge-in[14] was built at a single word from Lord Izu. On one occasion, someone at the *Hyōjōsho* said: "Let us consider Yin-yüan second. First, let us consider whether this person Jikuin is from a good family." Matsudaira Lord of Izu, said: "Certainly he is! Jikuin is said to have a large temple at Myōshin-ji, so doubtless he is." After Lord Izu returned home, he summoned Jikuin and said: "I said such and such at the *Hyōjōsho* today. I must build a temple at Myōshin-ji immediately. I will send a letter to Kyoto. Tsuda Michishige will buy a piece of land and donate it. He will buy Sōchi's[15] former residence to be used as the temple." The present *hōjō* (abbot's hall) at Ryōge-in was a hall built long ago by Sōchi. The kitchen,[16] *shoin* (study hall), gate, library, retreat hut, and toilet were all renovated by myself.

Afterward, Jikuin returned to Nagasaki and visited Yin-yüan. Yin-yüan then went to stay at Fumon-ji for a time. In the eleventh month of that year, Master Jikuin petitioned Lord Suo, saying: "It is a shame that Yin-yüan is confined in that way.[17] There are people who would like to pay him their respects briefly. Wouldn't it be acceptable to allow them to do so?" Lord Suo replied, "So long as it does not become too obvious, it would be fine for those who wish to pay their respects to do so surreptitiously." Thus official permission was granted verbally. Although [Lord Suo] expected [people to come] one by one, a crowd of thousands gathered and it became widely known from Takatsuki [in Settsu province] to Edo.

Lord Suo summoned Jikuin and severely reprimanded him. When he had finished reprimanding him, Jikuin replied: "Although it may appear that way from your vantage print, there is an explanation. There is a main temple of the Ikkō sect in that area, and the visitors who had come for the anniversary of Shinran's death in the eleventh month heard that there was a Chinese person at [Fumon-ji] temple. Although we asked them to enter one at a time, we could not control them and they became disorderly." Lord Suo said, "In that case, I understand."

From time to time, Jikuin had disagreements with Ryōkei. Yin-yüan was a monk [who sought after] fame and wealth, and so he leaned toward Ryōkei's side.

In those days, there was a well-known tailor named Nihei (later called Sōkyū) of Yamagataya, a tailor shop on Sanjō Street [in Kyoto]. Other tailors couldn't make Chinese caps and robes, but this [tailor from] Yamagataya was skilled at making them after taking a single look at them. Therefore, he hung out a signboard saying "Chinese Caps and Robes" and made them exclusively. On one occasion, Jikuin walked into his shop and saw him sewing a Chinese robe out of purple. Jikuin was shocked and asked, "Who is that for?" Nihei answered, "For the Zen master Yin-yüan."

Then Jikuin went to [Fumon-ji in] Tonda to ask Ryōkei [about this]. Ryōkei said, "The Lady Enkōin in Hataeda (Emperor Gosai's foster mother)[18] made a request to the Retired Emperor Gomizunoo and then gave it to Yin-yüan." Jikuin said: "In Zen monasteries in Japan, one only wears a purple robe if one has received an imperial order from the court. One cannot be allowed to wear a purple robe without both the knowledge of the military government and permission from the imperial court."[19]

The monks on Ryōkei's side cried, "He will wear it!" Monks on Jikuin's side answered: "Just try it! We'll tear it off!"

In his heart, Yin-yüan did not approve of Jikuin at all. Some time later, someone gave Yin-yüan a Sendai paper garment that looked purple in color. Yin-yüan called Jikuin and showed him this paper garment and asked, "Would it be all right if I wore this?"

It says in the *Daizuiroku*,[20] "He would not accept the purple robe that the Szechuan king offered him. He refused all three times."[21]

On the evening of the fifteenth day of the eighth month, an evening when they were moon viewing at Fumon-ji, Yin-yüan asked Jikuin, "Would it be better if I relied upon Ryōkei?" In his own mind, Jikuin was thinking that he should resign, so he answered, "You should do as you see fit."

In the end, when Ryōkei and Tokuō went to Edo to petition the bakufu for an audience, Jikuin said: "The illustrious monks of antiquity were sometimes summoned by the king or a minister, but they would not go. Still less would they themselves have desired an audience. It is entirely wrong for this bearded Chinese to act as if he wants an audience. Yin-yüan has lost his morals." Although he tried to restrain [Ryōkei and Tokuō] with this remark, they did not agree with him. That evening, Jikuin went alone to consult with the Edo bakufu and told the counselors that he absolutely had to resign.

His official statement for that occasion said, "Since my superior Ryōkei will relieve me as mediator in Yin-yüan's case, hereafter, please consult with Ryōkei about Yin-yüan." Sakai Lord of Sanuki said: "Yin-yüan will soon be in attendance in Edo. Please wait until then and then it will be fine." Jikuin resigned without acknowledging him.

At the time, the counselors criticized Jikuin for not being a good and trustworthy person. Later on, when they criticized Yin-yüan for not being good, Lord Abe of Bungo said, "Jikuin is a man of deep understanding."

Nanzan[22] said that when Jikuin was returning to Kyoto, he encountered Yin-yüan, then on his way to Edo, at Mount Hakone. At the time, Nanzan was going to Edo as Yin-yüan's attendant. He said that they passed one another without either saying a single word to the other.

Someone said to me, "When you called Master Yin-yüan a monk [who seeks] fame and wealth, that was a slip of the tongue." I replied, "It's not as if I were speaking carelessly and without evidence, trying to manipulate someone. I knew from his first words that he was that kind of monk. When Yin-yüan first turned to my teacher Jikuin, he said, "Since you know many of the daimyo, if you were to act as intermediary in building me a two-mat grass hut, I could set up my Dharma banner." When he said that, I knew for certain that he was a monk [seeking] fame and fortune. In ancient times, truly worthy teachers would never have said such a thing even by mistake, because it wouldn't have entered their minds in the first place. As you might expect, his followers are fools taken in by his deceiving spirit. They fan the fire of decadence all the more. The nation is full of lawless and debauched men who add and subtract from the teachings and do not preserve the precepts at all. Although people say that he will rekindle Japanese Zen, one would better say that he will corrupt it."

The *Jikusen oshō jōchiroku*,[23] the Tsai-sung commentary,[24] says:

"Shen-hsiu[25] told [the emperor], 'You should speak with the Sixth Patriarch and ask him about the Way.' The Sixth Patriarch firmly [refused] to go. . . . If something like this were to happen to someone today, they would shout for joy in their heart. If I were virtuous in the Way and the emperor summoned me, then I would visit and be made a National Teacher. If necessary, I would make some connections and go to the imperial audience myself. Why would such a summons come? There are those who pile up empty reputation. Ridiculous! Let the person go and ask an acquaintance to visit the teacher. . . ."[26]

I (Ho̅u) say that Yin-yüan's seeking out an official audience would be hateful to Jikusen. How shameful! How shameful!

Sometime later, when Egoku[27] . . . was at Kenju-ji in Kaga province, he asked the daimyo to admit him to the hall to preach the Dharma. The governor was well versed in matters past and present. He said: "Illustrious monks of the ancient past refused to go even when they had been invited by officials. Egoku seeking an audience now without my even inviting him is at odds with the illustrious monks of the past." At these words, the group of officials grew jocular. Egoku became ill-at-ease and eventually left the province. This is also evidence of the lingering style of Yin-yüan.

When I asked him, Tōshuku[28] said: "Jikuin took charge of Yin-yüan's [case] and went up to Kyoto from Nagasaki. He asked Senzan about bringing Yin-yüan's case before the bakufu and allowing him to take up [teaching] the Way. Senzan gave his permission. Jikuin consulted with Lord Suo and then went on to Edo. However, I don't know when Ryōkei and Tokuō joined him. I never had the chance to ask Jikuin."

Tōshuku said that, in the beginning, a book dealer in Kyoto had twenty to thirty volumes tied together. He came to Senju-in[29] and said: "You can buy all of these together. If you buy them all, I can give you a good price. I won't sell them if you want to sort through them and take [just the ones you want]." Tokuō bought them all, and among them were two volumes of Yin-yüan's writings. He read them and found them wonderful.

At that time, [Ryōkei] generously allowed [Tokuō, who was living at] Senju-in, to bathe in the bathhouse at Ryōan-ji.[30] One time Tokuō met Ryōkei in the bathhouse and talked about Yin-yüan's recorded sayings. Ryōkei borrowed them, read them, and also found them marvelous.

Three years later, when Yin-yüan was coming to Japan, Ryōkei and Tokuō awaited this with great pleasure. They wondered whom they could send to

Nagasaki to invite him [to visit Myōshin-ji] and decided that there was no one better than Jikuin. The two of them encouraged him [to go], so he went down to Nagasaki. Soon many people, such as Kyorei[31] from Hiroshima, Teishū[32] from Inaba, and Bansetsu[33] from Daiyū-in at Myōshin-ji, gathered in Nagasaki.

> I have reasoned it out based on this, that since this was the situation origi-
> nally, Master Jikuin went up to Kyoto, reported directly to Ryōkei and
> Tokuō, and then the three of them seem to have gone to Edo.

Tōshuku said that, according to the records of the monks from Konchi-in in Edo,[34] there was no need for Yin-yüan to remain in secret. Therefore, one time when Tokuō met with Lord Kuze, the daimyo of Yamato,[35] Lord Kuze was also entertaining the magistrate of Christian affairs. Lord Kuze said: "It is most uncouth of you [to ask that] Yin-yüan be allowed to stay. I say this because even if you associate with a person for three to five years, it is still difficult to fathom what is in their hearts. The idea that I could just hear about Yin-yüan and then mediate for him is most uncouth." Tokuō replied: "Although that may be, you can understand and believe in someone like Yüan-wu[36] or Ta-hui[37] of the distant past based on just three to five lines of their writings. Certainly in this case, when you have writings such as these of Yin-yüan's, you can believe in him. What is more, Yin-yüan's writings came three years before he arrived. He definitely possesses the rightful transmission from Wu-chun,[38] so there is no reason not to trust him." Lord Kuze turned to the magistrate of Christian affairs and said, "What he says is reasonable."

> This is a false story. It says in the *Ingen fusōroku* that Jikuin took the let-
> ter from Ryōkei and Tokuō and brought it [to Edo].

Tokuō also said that when Yin-yüan went to Tonda, his petition to the Edo [bakufu] had not yet been decided. At that time, the government generously [allowed] him to go and stay in Tonda while his petition was being decided in Edo.

> I say that this is conjecture and not the case.
> I say that there is a letter at this temple [Ryōge-in] addressed to the coun-
> selors with the three seals of Ryōkei, Tokuō, and Jikuin. Under the cir-
> cumstances, it seems that they never sent it. In the letter, they explain that
> Yin-yüan wanted to return to China. How can that be?

According to Tōshuku, Yin-yüan thought that he should return to China because he had been told that it would be difficult for them to decide on his petition to the Edo government while he was staying in Tonda. It was prob-ably a note from that period. (This is false.) However, he was granted thirty thousand *tsubo* in Owada for temple lands and built a temple there.

> It seems that this petition was written in the first month. After spending the
> winter retreat [at Fumon-ji] in Tonda, Yin-yüan asked to return to China.
> It was written by Tokuō and Ryōkei.

At that time, Tokuō [sent] his apologies to Lord Sado,[39] the *Shoshidai* of Kyoto at the time. He said: "I was originally a monk from the Myōshin-ji line. The three-hundred-year anniversary of [Kanzan Egen,] the founder of Myōshin-ji, is coming up soon. Since there are many things going on at the temple, I will no longer be mediating for Yin-yüan." With this notification, he resigned. His notice never reached Edo; it was stopped by the *Shoshidai*.

When Yin-yüan went to Edo to request an audience with the shogun, Jikuin gave his notice to the counselors. He resigned, saying, "Hereafter, please consult with Ryōkei about Yin-yüan." For that reason, Ryōkei and Tokuō accompanied Yin-yüan to Edo. Lord Matsudaira of Izu summoned Ryōkei and Tokuō and ordered that at the time of Yin-yüan's audience, he should bow three times. Tokuō told him that, generally speaking, monks do not bow to kings and high-ranking officials according to the rules of Buddhist etiquette, and so they begged his leniency. Lord Izu said that since this was Buddhist etiquette, he would exempt [Yin-yüan] from bowing.

> I say that this is quite strange. Lord Izu could not change a decision of the counselors so easily.

> I heard from my Dharma brother Sekkan[40] that at that time the counselors said in council that when the Zen master Ming-chi[41] . . . came to Japan, he was made to bow three times to Emperor Godaigo. This was to show the dignity of Japan. This time as well, Yin-yüan should bow three times in like manner.

Ryōkei and Tokuō were troubled. Although they made various apologies, none were accepted. They asked if Yin-yüan could bow once and each of them perform one of the other two bows. Finally that was accepted.

Yin-yüan appeared extremely angry with the lords and went on and on about it. (The *Gyōzan*,[42] section 99/2, says that he clucked his tongue constantly.) They say that this is generally kept secret by the Obaku line.

Tōshuku's story is that this matter of not bowing to the shogun was at first kept a deep secret by Tokuō and that his followers still don't know about it.

Tōshuku said that when Yin-yüan went for his audience with the shogun [Tokugawa Iemitsu at his residence] Ganyū-in, Ryōkei was a former abbot [of Myōshin-ji], so Tokuō went as his attendant. At that time, Tokuō only had the rank of *zendō*, so he could not go before the shogun, and waited outside in another room.

It is said that Yin-yüan sat down in front of the shogun without hesitation. Then he stood up and boldly headed directly toward him. Ryōkei said [in Chinese], "Master, come back!"[43] Yin-yüan withdrew.

Tōshuku said that when Yin-yüan returned to Kyoto, he first came to Senju-in. He came unattended from the center of the city through the *torii* and across the field in front of Tōji-in. He drew a crowd of spectators as if he were leading them with a hand chime. He stayed two nights at Senju-in and then entered Myōshin-ji. He stopped in at Taizō-in and composed a verse when he viewed the founder's pagoda. (There is a specimen of his handwriting in the storehouse.) Then he came to Ryōge-in and stayed three nights before returning to Tonda.

The twelfth day of the eighth month of Kyōhō 5 (1720).
Written by Dōchū of Ryōge-in.

Gudō Criticizes Yin-yüan

While Daien Hōkan Kokushi[44] [Gudō Tōshoku] was at Kazan,[45] Gentei (Daishun)[46] returned home. It was cold, and Gudō faced the fire and asked him, "Where have you come from?" Gentei replied, "Recently I have been staying at Fumon-ji in Tonda and passed the summer there." Gudō said, "Ever since the Chinese monk Yin-yüan came to Japan, the whole country has been in an uproar. I have not crossed the threshold of his gate. How do the monks at Tonda feel about him?" Gentei said, "Some slander him, and others think that he is wonderful."

Gudō drew in the ashes with the fire tongs and said: "To begin with, Yin-yüan does not understand courtesy. I am the highest-ranking monk in the Zen monasteries of Japan. If he wants to spread his Dharma in Japan, then he should first come and consult with me. After that, it would be time enough to save sentient beings according to their ability. If I went to Ch'ing China, then I would do as much. And as for that Ryōkei, he's bald and wrinkled. He's old enough to know better. But when he encounters something new he gets himself turned upside down and loses his head. He really should be pitied."

I say that during the Yüan dynasty, monks from India and other central Asian nations were revered and were quite successful as a group. They came and went on horseback like lords and princes. They received the red fur headdresses and were solemn and proud. Famous and virtuous monks throughout the country would always tuck up their robes and rush to meet them to ask them for their blessing. Hsing Hung-chiao made a small bow, turned around, and said: "I myself follow the Way. Why would I seek for it from them?" (from the *Daimin kōsō den*).[47] Oh! Yin-yüan came to Japan and received respect no less than that of the great Yüan. The words of Gudō surpass those of Lord Hsing. How noble!

Did the Bottom of the Bucket Drop Out?

Master Daishun Gentei [said] that some days when Master Yin-yüan was at Fumon-ji in Tonda, he hung up his staff and mingled with the monks. At lunchtime one day, Gentei was serving the others. He lost his grip and dropped the rice bucket. The rice scattered all over the floor. Yin-yüan saw this from a distance, laughed, and said: "Did the bottom drop out of the bucket? Did the bottom drop out of the bucket?"[48]

I say that frivolity of this sort shows the vacuity of Yin-yüan's Zen style.

Yin-yüan Speaks Japanese Well

My master Jikuin told Fukuma Takayasa that after Yin-yüan had been in Japan for a long time, he could speak Japanese well. His servants were mostly Japanese, and he managed to answer them in Japanese. However, he acted as if he didn't know Japanese with all his important guests. Our monks saw this and despised it. Would a truly great teacher be like this? In the long run, his intention was to belittle others.

I say that in his dying instructions, Yin-yüan said that, from age to age, Obaku-san [Mampuku-ji] should invite Chinese monks to become abbot. As a result of acting as if he didn't know Japanese in dealing with honored guests, his intentions created a single rut [in which his line is trapped]. His group deceives the people, and all of this comes from their founder.

Ryōkei Offers His Whisk

The retired emperor Gomizunoo first asked Daien Hōkan Kokushi [Gudō] about the essentials of Zen. After Gudō had passed away, the emperor summoned Ryōkei. After a time, Ryōkei offered the retired emperor one of his whisks. This meant that he wanted to place the emperor's name exclusively on his list of Dharma heirs. The emperor looked upon [the whisk] as a worldly implement. Later, Ryōkei drowned to death in a high flood tide in Naniwa. When the emperor himself was facing death, he sent the whisk, along with a message, to Akenomiya[49] (the emperor's daughter who later became a nun and resided at Rinkyū-ji).[50] [The message] said: "This is something for a monk to use; it is useless at the palace. It was originally Ryōkei's religious implement. Please have Kao-ch'üan return it to one of Ryōkei's disciples."

After the emperor passed away, his daughter did exactly what he had requested. Kao-ch'üan accepted the whisk but told a lie. He said that the emperor wanted to be Ryōkei's Dharma heir. (The emperor merely wanted to return the whisk to Ryōkei's disciples.) Kao-ch'üan did not complete the task of returning it for a long time, so someone slandered him. That person said: "Kao-ch'üan wanted to sever Ryōkei's line. Probably Ryōkei died suddenly in the flood tide without having any Dharma heirs in the capital." Kao-ch'üan said: "That is not the case. Ryōkei had two high-ranking disciples. I wanted to see which of them was more advanced and give [the whisk] to him." It happened that one [of Ryōkei's two disciples] died, so Kao-ch'üan planned to give the whisk to the other man. Kao-ch'üan gave him the name Kaiō.[51] Tu-chan, then the abbot of Obaku-san [Mampuku-ji], said: "Our patriarch Fei-yin sternly expelled someone who had received something in another's stead. His descendent [Kao-ch'üan] has dared to violate this [rule], has he not?" (Fei-yin debated with Yung-chüeh[52] before the Ming court. Fei-yin was defeated, and so the court destroyed the woodblocks for his [book], the *Gotō gentō*.)[53] Kao-ch'üan replied: "I only know that I received a dying wish of the emperor. I don't know anything else."

The internal squabbling did not cease, and Master Dokushō of Jikishi-in lamented this.[54] As a peace settlement, he suggested, "Someone from either Kao-ch'üan's or Tu-chan's disciples should be selected and then [the whisk] should be given to him."

Kao-ch'üan wrongly said: "It was the emperor's intention to be Ryōkei's Dharma heir. If he were not recognized as Ryōkei's Dharma heir, that would be wrong." This is Kao-ch'üan's lie. The emperor merely wanted to return the whisk to Ryōkei's disciples. It had nothing to do with Dharma transmission. Ultimately there was a petition [to the government]. The superintendent of temples and shrines[55] in Edo made the determination. He said: "As a rule, Chinese monks living in Japan must honor the commands of the Japanese emperor. Kao-ch'üan has single-mindedly honored the retired emperor's dying wish. He should receive it."

Tu-chan was defeated, and all those who had supported him, such as Kōkoku[56] and Enzū,[57] were driven out. Finally, Kao-ch'üan received the whisk and gave it to Kaiō, making him Ryōkei's Dharma heir. Kaiō was abbot of Shōmyō-ji in Hino, in Omi province.

Someone said that a person named Sekisō,[58] who was abbot at Shosan [Hōrin-ji] (founded by Tu-chan) in Totomi province,[59] visited Master Daishun at Jikei-ji in Mino province. Daishun said: "I saw in a letter that Kao-ch'üan sent to Tu-chan, in which he quoted the emperor as saying, 'We take Yin-yüan to be Bodhidharma, Ryōkei to be the second Patriarch, and ourself to be the third Patriarch.' Within which imperial letter does one find such words as these?" Sekisō said that Kao-ch'üan had only heard the emperor's words secondhand. There was absolutely no proof. Daishun said that in Empō 3 (1675) the emperor conferred an honorary title on Master Isshi. In his letter, the emperor said, "Our debt of gratitude toward this teacher is very deep." It is as clear as that! How can it be that the emperor said, "Ryōkei is the second Patriarch and we are the third?" It makes me think that Kao-ch'üan's lie brings slander on the emperor and makes a mockery of the Japanese people. Kao-ch'üan hopes to take in later generations with all of his writings. A poem by Po-tzu T'ing says, "What in this world is more hateful than fleas, lice, mosquitoes, flies, rats, thieves and monks?"[60] [The answer] is Kao-ch'üan.

Yin-yüan Gave a Verse to Jikuin

(This piece of calligraphy is at Ryōge-in.)

> The space is narrow, but the heart is large.
> It encompasses all the ten directions.
> It feels sincere compassion for the impoverished
> And skillfully protects the king of the Dharma.
> I heard that the Way flourishes in the East.
> First I came and faced the jeweled vessel.
> The correct mind is always devoid of darkness.

It purifies the self whiter than the frost.
The original thought fulfills beginning and end.
Why should it be forgotten even in one thousand years.
[In China] the Way has dwindled to a single petal,
but the Great Way comes to full bloom in Japan.

Written by the Obaku monk Yin-yüan Lung-ch'i and given to Master Jikuin.

The [Obaku] Assembly Supports Insincere People

Jikuin said to Yin-yüan: "It is said that if [a monk] wishes to reside at a temple, then he must have someone pay for all his food and expenses. This is the rule of Zen temples in Japan. If this were not the case, then evil monks wanting to sponge off [the temple] would be numerous, and the assembly would not comprise true practitioners. One who truly wishes to follow a virtuous teacher would sell his belongings to pay for his food and would not shun hardship."

Yin-yüan said: "It's no good! If that's the way it's done, then cart drivers and ship hands will join the order. Yesterday [a cart driver or a ship hand] and today a monk! Hundreds will flock to join the group."

I say that (in the fifty-fourth section of the *San'an*),[61] Jochū said: "The master's own eyes are not yet open. He strives to seize the joy from others using sugar and honey. . . . Master Chōro Fuku's Dharma eye was not open. He always used the alms he received on the Upper Yangtze to feed himself as if he were a monk."[62] This is the intention of the Obaku sect.

I say that the Zen Master Daie[63] said, "Everyone has food in the back of their mind."[64]

The commentary says (thirty-fourth section, fourth page, on the right), "The true teacher is the model of the true teaching."[65]

Those without the Way and without Learning Transmit the Dharma

Today in the Obaku line there are some who claim to transmit the Dharma but have no temple in which to reside. They are all over the city, in front of shops and behind them. They are the so-called Senior Guardian, [who protects] the heavens, and the Minister of Works, [who protects] all the earth.[66]

In a swampy arbor of weeping willows . . .
Examining the water and the land, I encountered mist. Inside appears
    the spirit of the dead.
To a whetstone of saltpeter and sulfur add herbs. (*I-chiang* 4/10)[67]

Ingen Fusōroku

In the third fascicle, the *Settsu Jiun-san Fumon Fukugen-ji roku* says: During the first four days of the eleventh month of Meireki 1 (1655), the great lay patron Minamoto Shigemune, the Second in Command of Hamura,[68] the abbot of this temple [Ryōkei] Shōsen, Kaishū, [Jikuin] Somon, Chōso, Danhō, and a host of other Zen worthies invited the master to settle at Jiun-san Fumon Fukugen-ji and hold the opening ceremony [as the new abbot].[69]

In the eighth fascicle (section 34): "Lord Itakura, Daimyo of Suō, asked me [Yin-yüan] the reason. . . . I do not think that Jikuin criticizes the two masters Ryōkei and Tokuō for writing extensively to invite me to be abbot at Fumon-ji. His intentions for resigning were sincere. . . . Jikuin also agreed to it [the invitation]." [70]

In the sixteenth fascicle (verses):

> Given to Jikuin when passing by Ryōge-an
> Behind the single hut, there waits
> A phoenix singing to [greet] the dawn.
> Everyone dances and sings, wanting to perfect the woods.
> Going and coming on strange paths,
> They beckon to the wind, the rain and the snow.
> Afterwards they will know the season (learn true morality)
> and control their minds.

Next a verse [titled] "Passing by Myōshin-ji . . ." and another, "In response to Masters Senzan, Saie, and all the other worthies. . . ." [71]

Kao-ch'üan Returns to the Pure Land

Master Tenryō (n.d.) was in Owada studying, [he observed that] Kao-ch'üan commonly used Japanese characters with facility in all five fascicles [of his work]. [Tenryō] arranged them on his desk and read them. (*En'nan kidan kōshū, first section*).[72]

Many of the [Obaku] Sect's Monks Are Thieves and Have Been Expelled

In Fushimi, a monk from the Obaku line lived in a small retreat with his younger sister, a nun. Once when the monk went up to Kyoto, a thief came in and stole all the household wares. The nun raised [her fist] to strike the thief. The thief killed her and left. When the monk returned, he said: "I have always said that if a thief comes, then it would be best to let him do as he pleases with our things. One must never fight. She did not follow my advice, and so suffered this fate."

The magistrate of Fushimi looked for the thief and conducted a long investigation. In order to fathom the monk's thoughts, the magistrate grilled him. As a result, he submitted and confessed.

Someone said that the signboard read, "This monk from Yin-yüan's line killed a person and stole everything from her." [The monks at] Obaku-san often complained to the authorities that they wanted Yin-yüan's name removed, but that was not possible.

In 1739, in the Kitano pleasure quarters, there was an Obaku monk who was in love with a prostitute. For a long time he harbored a grudge against her and finally came at the woman with a knife. She screamed aloud, went down the stairs, and ran away. The monk turned the knife on himself and died.

The authorities purified the monk's corpse with salt and buried him. The woman suffered from her wounds and after a month or two finally died.

The authorities exhumed the monk's body and crucified it at Awataguchi.

Notes

Chapter One: Introduction

1. There are two recent exceptions to this generalization, both historical surveys of Zen in Japan: Heinrich Dumoulin, *Zen Buddhism: A History,* vol. 2, *Japan;* and Takenuki Genshō, *Nihon zenshūshi.*

2. The extent to which Japanese Zen masters faithfully preserved the Sung style of practice transmitted from China is itself an interesting topic, but one outside the range of this discussion. There is ample evidence to suggest that Japanese masters were creative in fashioning Zen to suit the differing context of Japan. See, for example, Bielefeldt, *Dōgen's Manuals of Zen Meditation,* pp. 26–28.

3. Yanagida Seizan has championed this view, see his *Rinzai nōto* and *Rinzai no kafū.*

4. Although Washio Junkei was actually a member of the True Pure Land sect, I have included him here among the Obaku scholars because of the deep sympathy for the Obaku position displayed in his writings. Hayashi Bunshō and Nakao Fumio are both Obaku monk-scholars.

5. I shall have more to say on this issue later. For the present, I shall mention the major example of this trend. Obaku scholars, especially Akamatsu Shinmyō, writing before and during the Pacific War, were at some pains to paint a picture of Obaku as especially close to the imperial family and to downplay its relations with the Tokugawa bakufu. In the postwar period this trend has abated, and in recent works Obaku scholars have described relations with the bakufu in more complete and accurate terms.

6. I would include in this category Dieter Schwaller, Minamoto Ryōen, and Takenuki Genshō.

7. See, for example, Minamoto, *Tetsugen,* pp. 85–86, 98–99, 100–103, and 106–107.

8. See Hirakubo, *Ingen,* pp. 225–226; Hayashi, "Obaku o kataru," p. 16; and Ōtsuki, "Obakushū," p. 40.

9. Bielefeldt, *Dōgen's Manuals of Zen Meditation,* pp. 10–11.

10. Akamatsu argues strenuously that Obaku expresses the true meaning of Rinzai Zen. He defends the use of Pure Land practices with a detailed explanation of the proper Obaku belief in Amida Buddha and the Pure Land within the self and the use of the *nembutsu* as a koan. He suggests that to teach Zen without the balancing influence of Pure Land is to one-sidedly exclude the practice of compassion. Such an exclusion necessarily entails forsaking the needs of people of moderate and low capacity. Because of its balance between high-level practice and the moderating influence of more accessible practices, then, Obaku rather than Japanese Rinzai fulfills the true meaning of Rinzai Zen. "Obaku kōyō," pp. 17–34.

11. A prime example of a scholar taking the more neutral position is Takenuki Genshō. While recognizing that philosophical differences existed between Obaku masters and Japanese Rinzai masters, Takenuki does not discuss them. Instead, he stresses the role that competition played in the schism. He maintains that the Rinzai sect, the Myōshin-ji line in particular, felt the need to defend its human and material resources from the encroachment made by Obaku. Takenuki, *Nihon zenshūshi,* pp. 231–233.

12. Ibid., p. 2.

13. Regulations limiting foreign trade were issued gradually, but the basic structure of the so-called closed-country policy was in place by the year 1641, when Dutch traders were transferred to Deshima Island in Nagasaki Bay and foreign trade with China was restricted to the city of Nagasaki under direct bakufu control. Scholars have recently made it clear that Japan was not actually closed off from foreign contact as the expressions "closed country" and "national isolation" (*sakoku*) suggest. See Toby, *State and Diplomacy in Early Modern Japan,* and Jansen, *China in the Tokugawa World.*

Chapter Two: School, Sect, or Lineage

1. Foulk, "The Ch'an Tsung in Medieval China: School, Lineage or What?" *The Pacific World,* no. 8 (Fall 1992): 18–31; Mano Shōjun, *Bukkyō ni okeru shū kannen no seiritsu;* Weinstein, "The Schools of Chinese Buddhism," in *Buddhism and Asian History,* ed. Kitagawa and Cummings, pp. 257–265.

2. Foulk, "The 'Chan School' and Its Place in the Buddhist Monastic Tradition," pp. 30–34; Weinstein, pp. 257–262; Foulk, "The Ch'an Tsung in Medieval China," pp. 18–31.

3. Foulk, "The Ch'an Tsung in Medieval China," p. 20.

4. For purposes of internal consistency and clarity, I have chosen not to adopt Foulk's terminology in this discussion. He employs the terms "school" and "denomination" in a manner analogous to my own stated preference for school and sect.

5. For a copy of the text of the decree, see Date Mitsuyoshi, *Nihon shūkyō seido shiryō ruishūkō,* no. 212, p. 627.

6. Takenuki, Genshō, *Nihon zenshūshi*, p. 283.

7. *Japanese Religion: A Survey by the Agency for Cultural Affairs*, pp. 161–170.

8. Ibid., pp. 253–254.

9. See Stark and Bainbridge, "Of Churches, Sects, and Cults: Preliminary Concepts for a Theory of Religious Movements," *Journal for the Scientific Study of Religion* 18, no. 2 (1979): 117–133.

10. Robert S. Ellwood, "New Religions: New Religions in Japan," in *Encyclopedia of Religion*, 10:410.

11. Stark, "How New Religions Succeed: A Theoretical Model," in *The Future of New Religious Movements*, ed. Bromeley and Hammond, pp. 11–29.

12. Marc Galanter, *Cults, Faith, Healing, and Coercion*. Oxford: Oxford University Press, 1989.

Chapter Three: Beginnings

1. Ooms, *Tokugawa Ideology*, pp. 4–5. Ooms' discussion of beginnings is dependent on Said's work, *Beginnings* (1975).

2. Miura and Sasaki, *Zen Dust*, pp. 209–210.

3. See, for instance, the short sections on Obaku Zen in Daigan and Alicia Matsunaga's *Foundation of Japanese Buddhism*, 2:262–264; Dale E. Saunders' *Buddhism in Japan*, pp. 252–253; and Dumoulin's 1963 volume, *A History of Zen Buddhism*, pp. 228–231.

4. The style of Ch'an that Mi-yun, Fei-yin, and Yin-yüan promoted incorporated elements of Pure Land teaching, as did those of all Ch'an masters in China at the time. Some contemporary scholars therefore question, on historical and theological grounds, whether or not this represents an "authentic" revival of Lin-ch'i's Ch'an style. This notion of authenticity is based on the unproven and almost certainly faulty assumption that Ch'an existed originally in a pristine state and was only later corrupted by Pure Land influences.

5. Washio Junkei, "Obaku kairitsu no jidai," in *Nihon zenshūshi no kenkyū*, p. 98.

6. Also read Sūfuku-ji. Here and elsewhere I have followed the preferences of Obaku sources in the reading of Obaku names.

7. See, for example, Dumoulin, *Zen Buddhism: A History*, 2:303; Takenuki Genshō, *Nihon zenshūshi*, p. 218; and Minamoto Ryōen, *Tetsugen*, p. 74. Takenuki actually uses the date of the opening ceremonies in 1663, when Yin-yüan and his disciples took up residence at the temple, but this does not significantly alter the argument.

8. For intrasectarian purposes, Obaku masters tended to prefer the term Rinzai shōshū (True Heirs of Lin-chi sect), the designation chosen by Mi-yun and Fei-yin to symbolize their dedication to restoring Lin-chi's Ch'an style. The term "Rinzai shōshū" was not originally selected to reflect any polemi-

cal evaluations in regard to the Rinzai lineage in Japan, but rather toward other Chinese lineages. According to Hayashi Bunshō, Obaku monks continued to use the name Rinzai shōshū until 1874, when Obaku was officially placed under the Rinzai sect by the Meiji government. See Hayashi, "Obaku o kataru," pp. 8–9. One can still find examples of its use for internal sectarian purposes on memorial stones made since World War II and on current personal monastic seals.

9. Ibid., p. 9.

10. Primary source material on the history of Huang-po Wan-fu-ssu can be found in the *Huang-po shan ssu chih,* originally edited by Yin-yüan, reprinted in the *Chung-kuo fo ssu chih* series, volume 4. Secondary accounts of the temple's history include Fan Hui, "Ingen zenji to chūnichi ryō Obakusan no yurai," pp. 118–123.

11. Miura and Sasaki, *Zen Dust,* pp. 209–210.

12. Most of what is known about the practices at Huang-po Wan-fu-ssu is actually drawn from information about Obaku-san Mampuku-ji in Japan, which was modeled on the Chinese temple. Some information can also be drawn from Yin-yüan's recorded sayings from before his emigration to Japan. For a detailed discussion of that material, see Chapter 7.

13. The full lineage chart is traced in several secondary sources. See Ōtsuki, Katō, and Hayashi, *Obaku bunka jinmei jiten,* p. 406, and Dieter Schwaller, *Der japanische Obaku-Mönch Tetsugen Dōkō,* p. 211.

14. See Torigoe Fumikuni, *Hiin zenji to sono cho, Gotō gentō,* pp. 17–28; Nagai Masano, "Minmatsu ni ikita zenshatachi—Hiin Tsūyō ni yoru *Gotō gentō* no seiritsu," pp. 327–343; and Miura and Sasaki, *Zen Dust,* pp. 430–432.

15. *The Cambridge History of China,* vol. 7, *The Ming Dynasty, 1368–1644, Part 1,* ed. Frederick W. Mote and Denis Twitchett, gives a detailed account of the disintegration of the Ming dynasty, including the years known as the Southern Ming, 1644–1662, when Ming loyalists continued to oppose the Ch'ing forces. See especially pp. 585–725.

16. Cheng Ch'eng-kung is commonly known in the West as Coxinga, the Europeanized version of his name. Coxinga has been the subject of numerous historical and literary works. For further information, see Keene, *The Battles of Coxinga,* and Foccardi, *The Last Warrior.*

17. For details about Ming requests for Japanese military assistance from the Chinese perspective, see *The Cambridge History of China,* 7:699–700. For the Japanese perspective, see Takenuki, *Nihon zenshūshi,* pp. 212–213.

18. For more explanation and a review of the historical documents related to the founding of each temple, see Ri Kenshō, "Nagasaki santōji no seiritsu," pp. 73–90.

19. Ri Kenshō, "Nagasaki santōji no seiritsu."

20. Obaku-san Mampuku-ji has an image of Kuan-ti enshrined as the

main image in the Garan-dō. See Takahashi Ryōwa, *Obakusan Mampukuji*, pp. 128–132, for a description of the hall's history.

21. See Ri Kenshō, "Nagasaki santōji no seiritsu," p. 74.

22. Most sources follow the *Zengaku daijiten* and list Tao-che's year of death as 1660 and date of birth as unknown. I have given here the dates provided by the entry in Ōtsuki, Katō, and Hayashi, *Obaku bunka jinmei jiten*, p. 263. Almost nothing is known about Tao-che except for his years in Japan. There are two short volumes of his recorded sayings from that period, the *Nanzan Dōsha zenji goroku* and the *Dōsha zenji goroku*, each one fascicle. Tao-che is also mentioned by several monks who practiced under him in their recorded sayings and sermons. For a complete summary of these materials, see Furuta Shōkin, "Dōsha Chōgen no raichō to sono eikyō," pp. 343–365. See also Tsuji Zennosuke, *Nihon bukkyōshi*, pp. 296–300. For brief accounts in English, see Heinrich Dumoulin, *Zen Buddhism: A History*, 2:300 and 313, and Peter Haskel, *Bankei Zen*, pp. xxv–xxvi.

23. Furuta Shōkin maintains that Tao-che was influential in the nascent movement to reform Sōtō through his contact with Sōtō monks who later became leaders of the revival. Furuta, "Dōsha Chōgen," p. 350.

24. Bankei said as much in one of his sermons: "Among the Zen masters of that time, only Dōsha was able, to this modest extent, to confirm for me my experience of enlightenment; but, even so, I wasn't fully satisfied. Now looking back, today I wouldn't even find Dōsha acceptable. If only Dōsha had gone on living till now, I might have made a better man of him." Translation by Haskel, *Bankei Zen*, p. 9. For the original, see Akao Ryūji, ed., *Bankei zenji zenshū*, pp. 11–12.

25. Furuta Shōkin suggests that the problem was probably related to his position as abbot at Sōfuku-ji. Yin-yüan's disciple Yeh-lan had been invited to serve there as abbot in 1651, but died on the way from China. Yin-yüan's disciples may have felt that Sōfuku-ji was therefore Yin-yüan's by right and bullied Tao-che into leaving. Furuta notes that there is no evidence to suggest that the friction marred the relationship between Yin-yüan and Tao-che themselves. (See Furuta, "Dōsha Chōgen," pp. 361–363.) Tsuji presents an alternative story in which the source of tension revolved around a letter sent to Tao-che by his master in China. According to this account, Mu-an, Yin-yüan's leading disciple, intercepted the letter and Tao-che later learned of this. (See Tsuji, *Nihon bukkyōshi*, pp. 298–299.) Norman Waddell provides a translation of a document supporting Tsuji's account. According to it, Mu-an intercepted and destroyed a letter certifying Tao-che's Dharma transmission; he then accused Tao-che of teaching without credentials. See Waddell, *The Unborn: The Life and Teaching of Zen Master Bankei*, pp. 30–31, n. 26. Tao-che left Sōfuku-ji in 1655 and spent his last three or four years in Japan on Hirado at the invitation of Lord Matsuura Shigenobu.

26. According to Dumoulin, Yeh-lan was invited by the abbot at

Kōfuku-ji (*Zen Buddhism: A History,* 2:300–301). The abbot there at the time was I-jan Hsing-jung, another of Yin-yüan's disciples. I-jan was instrumental in bringing Yin-yüan to Nagasaki, and it is possible that he was involved in Yeh-lan's invitation as well. However, all other sources indicate that the invitation came from the Sōfuku-ji community. According to Hirakubo Akira, the lay believers at Sōfuku-ji invited Yeh-lan at the suggestion of Wu-hsin Hsing-chien, a friend of Yeh-lan who was already in Nagasaki. See Hirakubo, *Ingen* (1962), pp. 78–79.

27. According to Hirakubo Akira, it was Wu-hsin who actually suggested the idea to I-jan after he heard about Yeh-lan's death; ibid., p. 79.

28. These letters were dated 4/6/1652, 8/27/1652, 3/1653, and 11/3/1653. The second never arrived, so some sources refer to only three invitations. For details, see ibid., pp. 79–82.

29. The letter is given in full in the *Ingen zenshū,* 5:2196–2200. A partial translation is given below.

30. Hui-men remained at Wan-fu-ssu until his death, but his line became one of the most important in the Obaku sect. One of his eleven Dharma heirs was Kao-ch'üan Hsing-tun (1633–1695; J. Kōsen Shōton), the fifth abbot of Obaku-san Mampuku-ji.

31. I have found no complete list of this group and doubt that any exists. The most complete list of twenty names can be found in Akamatsu, "Obakushū kōyō," p. 59, but he indicates that there were others in the group. Partial lists can be found in Hirakubo, *Ingen,* p. 89, and Tsuji, *Nihon bukkyōshi,* p. 320.

32. Hirakubo's treatment of the issue can be found in his biography of Yin-yüan, *Ingen,* pp. 68–85. I have drawn heavily from his work, but have added materials that he did not discuss, especially Mujaku's *Obaku geki.*

33. Tsuji acknowledges that, on the face of it, Yin-yüan was responding to invitations from the community in Nagasaki, but that the underlying reason was to flee China's unrest. See Tsuji, pp. 319–321. Other scholars who follow Tsuji's lead include Takenuki Genshō, *Nihon zenshūshi,* pp. 214–215, and Dumoulin, *Zen Buddhism: A History,* 2:300 and 355, n. 7.

34. Tsuji, pp. 286–290.

35. See ibid., p. 321. Unfortunately, he does not document this claim with examples.

36. See Hirakubo, *Ingen,* pp. 84–85.

37. Minamoto Ryōen gives some examples to this effect from Yin-yüan's writings, *Tetsugen,* pp. 57–58. For the originals, see Hirakubo, *Ingen zenshū,* 3:1192–1193 and 1537.

38. For a complete translation, see Appendix.

39. *Obaku geki,* pp. 1b–2a. This translation is my own, based on the original document written in Mujaku's own hand. See Chapter 9 for more information about versions of the *Obaku geki.*

40. Tsuji maintains that, in several cases, when Yin-yüan spoke of going home he was speaking rhetorically or as a ploy to coerce the authorities to expedite his case. He concedes that in some instances Yin-yüan's desire to return to China was probably quite genuine, especially when he was living under house arrest at Fumon-ji and was therefore uncomfortable (Tsuji, *Nihon bukkyōshi*, pp. 334–336). Tsuji follows Mujaku's lead here. When sorting out the actual order of events, based on the written sources at his disposal, Mujaku comments on a letter of petition to the authorities indicating that Yin-yüan wanted to leave Japan. Mujaku indicates that he doubts the sincerity of that emotion except when life at Fumon-ji proved unacceptable. The relevant passage, written with Mujaku as first person, reads: "I say that there is a letter at this temple [Ryōge-in], addressed to the counselors, with the three seals of Ryōkei, Tokuō, and Jikuin. Under the circumstances, it seems that they never sent it. In the letter, they explain that Yin-yüan wanted to return to China. How can that be? According to Tōshuku, Yin-yüan thought that he should return to China because he had been told that it would be difficult for them to decide on his petition to the Edo government while he was staying in Tonda. It was probably a note from that period. It seems that this petition was written in the first month. After staying the winter retreat [at Fumon-ji] in Tonda, Yin-yüan asked to return to China. It was written by Tokuō and Ryōkei" (*Obaku geki*, 9b). It is, of course, possible to interpret Yin-yüan's statements in a more sympathetic light. Yin-yüan became quite serious about returning home to China after 1657, when he had been in Japan for nearly three years. He had promised his disciples in China that he would return home to Wan-fu-ssu after a period of three years and received several letters from them encouraging him to return and reminding him of his promise. By that time he was living under much less constrained circumstances and had made some powerful allies in the Edo bakufu but may have preferred to return home despite his improved circumstances.

41. The *Zenrin shūhei shū* was first published in 1700 in two fascicles. Its preface identifies the author as "an anonymous Hanazono monk," but it is generally believed that the author was actually Keirin Sūshin (1652–1728). The first fascicle contains twenty-two sections, each describing some persistent evil that characterized the Zen sect of that time. The second fascicle bears the title *Zoku zenrin shūhei shū*, with an additional fifteen cases, believed to be by the same author. Scholars generally refer to the two volumes as a single work. Several of the sections are critical of Obaku practice. The section at issue here is the fourteenth in the second volume, pp. 14b–15b. For a detailed discussion of the work, see Chapter 9. Hirakubo also makes reference to this passage (Hirakubo, *Ingen*, p. 70).

42. See Hirakubo, *Ingen*, p. 69.

43. See ibid., pp. 71–76. Hirakubo theorizes that the source of this claim is the wording in Yin-yüan's *nempu* (biography), where reference is made to

I-jan receiving an official order. Most likely this was based on an interpretation of I-jan's fourth letter that mentions the shogunate's official in Nagasaki (Kurokawa Masanao). Hirakubo believes that Kurokawa gave I-jan his permission to extend the invitation and himself notified Edo later. However, the term used in the *nempu, ōmei,* could be interpreted to mean that I-jan received a direct command from either the emperor or the shogun.

44. Washio Junkei mentions a similar story, circulating in the modern period, that Emperor Gomizunoo had been responsible for Yin-yüan's invitation; Washio dismisses it as mistaken. See Washio, *Nihon zenshūshi no kenkyū,* p. 98.

45. For the complete text in the original Chinese, see *Ingen zenshū,* 5:2198–2200.

Chapter Four: Laying the Foundation

1. Hirakubo gives a quotation from Yin-yüan's *nempū* which I have been unable to find in the original. Hirakubo, *Ingen,* p. 92.

2. The relevant portions of Yin-yüan's biography provide names for prominent visitors. See *Ingen zenshū,* 11:5198–5219.

3. Numbers are based on an account given by Kyorei Ryōkaku; see Chapter 9 for a translation of Kyorei's letter.

4. Collcutt, *Five Mountains,* pp. 123–129.

5. The standard history of Myōshin-ji, *Myōshinjishi* by Kawakami Kozan, explains the positions taken by the participants in this dispute and suggests that Yin-yüan became a party to it because of his strong emphasis on Jikai Zen (Maintain the Precepts Zen); see pp. 453–454. See also Ogisu Jundō, "Ingen zenji to Obakusan," pp. 17–18, and Hirakubo, *Ingen,* op.cit., p. 104.

6. The great eighteenth-century reformer Hakuin came from Gudō's line. More will be said of Gudō and his faction in Chapter 9.

7. Isshi Monju (also read Bunshu) originally studied under Takuan Sōhō (1573–1646), but later went to Myōshin-ji, where he practiced under Gudō Tōshoku (1577–1661) and Ungo Kiyō (1583–1659). He became Gudō's Dharma heir, but the two disagreed on a number of issues, notably the proper interpretation of the precepts. His early death was a loss in many respects but may have been a relief to his master, who was disappointed in the direction Isshi had taken. Ungo Kiyō studied at Myōshin-ji and received *inka* from his master Itchū Tōmoku (n.d.). He is best known as the restorer of Zuigan-ji in Matsushima and as an advocate of Nembutsu Zen.

8. *Obaku geki,* p. 8b.

9. Tsuji Zennosuke provides the text of Kyorei's letter in *Nihon bukkyōshi,* pp. 322–325. Yin-yüan's own letters to Fei-yin from this period confirm the makeup of the group. See Hirakubo, *Ingen,* pp. 99–100.

10. Kawakami Kozan, *Myōshinjishi,* pp. 453–454; Tamamura Takeji,

Rinzaishūshi, p. 251; Itō Kokan, "*Gudō* Kokushi no zen," pp. 120–121; Ogisu Jundō, *Myōshinji*, p. 96.

11. Fumon-ji is in Tonda, a small town between Kyoto and Osaka in the province of Settsu. The temple was founded in 1390. According to Mujaku Dōchū's *Myōshin-ji shi*, it was a branch temple of Tōfuku-ji for about three hundred years. Other sources indicate that it was actually affiliated with Ken-chō-ji in Kamakura (see Takenuki, *Nihon zenshūshi*, pp. 215–216). At the time of the eighth abbot, Chūshitsu Genshō (n.d.), it became a branch temple of Ryōan-ji and so came under the Myōshin-ji line. Ryōkei entered the temple when he was sixteen, in 1617 and became the ninth resident monk just three years later, at the age of nineteen, when Chūshitsu died.

12. Itakura Shigemune was the oldest son of Katsushige; both men fought for Tokugawa Ieyasu at Sekigahara. Afterward, Katsushige was appointed to the position of *shoshidai* of Kyoto in 1601. Shigemune succeeded his father to the office in 1620 and served until 1654. Even after retiring from that post, he continued to use his influence to assist Jikuin and Yin-yüan. He visited Yin-yüan at Fumon-ji twice in late 1655 and became his lay disciple, receiv-ing the Dharma name Dokushin Shōkū. In 1656 he became daimyo and was given the domain of Sekiyado (in present-day Chiba prefecture), where he died that same year. Ōtsuki, Katō, and Hayashi, pp. 13–14.

13. *Obaku geki,* p. 3b.

14. The council sent out letters of instruction to the shogunate's officials in Nagasaki, Osaka, Settsu, and Kyoto regarding this decision, all dated 6/1/1655. For the full texts, see Tsuji, *Nihon bukkyōshi*, pp. 329–331.

15. Hirakubo suggests that the invitation to visit Fumon-ji came as a complete surprise to Yin-yüan. Relevant passages from Yin-yüan's recorded sayings, translated into Japanese, can be found in Hirakubo, *Ingen,* pp. 105–106. I have been unable to identify the passage in the original texts.

16. Shigemune and the new governor of Kyoto, Makino Chikashige, re-ceived a letter from the bakufu confirming this provision. The letter was dated 11/8/1655, and signed by Sakai Tadakatsu and Matsudaira Nobutsuna, among others. For the text, see Hirakubo, *Ingen,* p. 110.

17. *Obaku geki,* pp. 4a–5a.

18. The text of the letter can be found in Tsuji, *Nihon bukkyōshi,* pp. 338–339.

19. A Buddhist monastic robe was bestowed on high-ranking monks in China and Japan as an imperial honor in recognition of service to the court or the nation. The color purple was not traditionally used in other parts of Asia for Buddhist monastic robes. The practice began in China, where the im-perial court established a hierarchy of honorific robes classified by color for individuals, monastic and secular, who had performed meritorious service. Among the various colors, purple robes ranked as the highest honor. The Jap-anese imperial court later adopted the practice. Unlike honorific titles, which

are commonly granted posthumously, the purple robe is often given to a living master.

20. *Obaku geki,* pp. 4b–5b. The dispute probably occurred in 1656, because Ryōkei began making trips to Edo himself in 1657. He definitely petitioned the bakufu to grant Yin-yüan a purple robe in 1657, perhaps in response to Jikuin's criticism. The petition was rejected.

21. Ogisu Jundō, "Ingen to Obaku-san," pp. 16–17.

22. Tsuji gives the text in Chinese, *Nihon bukkyōshi,* p. 351. Hirakubo includes a photo of the original document, the Chinese text, and a Japanese paraphrase (*Ingen,* pp. 124–125.

23. Hirakubo, *Ingen,* p. 125.

24. Dokushō later attained enlightenment while practicing under Yin-yüan's guidance. He received Yin-yüan's *inka* in 1670.

25. Takenuki, *Nihon zenshūshi,* pp. 217–218.

26. Sasaki Gōzō provides a chart of the original buildings and dates of completion and, where available, provides the names of the donors (*Mampukuji,* pp. 16–17).

27. Aoki Shigekane was at this time the daimyo of Kai province, but had previously been assigned to the Settsu region. He met Yin-yüan while he was living at Fumon-ji and had already had a long-standing relationship with Yin-yüan and other Obaku monks before he received this assignment.

28. Takenuki gives a more complete listing of the donations (*Nihon zenshūshi,* pp. 218–220).

29. Since the characters are identical in Chinese and Japanese, it became customary to add the characters "old" and "new" to the names to distinguish the two temples. This rubric is unnecessary in translation and has been replaced by transliterating the Chinese and Japanese pronunciations respectively.

30. There are a number of descriptive books about Mampuku-ji that give some historical information about the buildings and art. See, for example, Sasaki Gōzo, *Mampukuji;* Takahashi Ryōwa, *Obakusan Mampukuji;* and Fuji Masaharu and Abe Zenryō, *Mampukuji.*

31. Figures are based on the *Enkyō matsujichō,* produced in the second year of the Enkyō period. See Takenuki, *Nihon zenshūshi,* p. 25.

Chapter Five: The Chinese Founders

1. Dates for formal recognition are based upon dates provided in the Obaku lineage chart in *Obaku bunka jinmei jiten,* pp. 405ff.

2. The *Kinsei Obakushū matsujichō shūsei* (A compilation of Early Modern Obaku sect registries of branch temples) is a modern publication of the official registries prepared by the Obaku sect during the Tokugawa period for submission to the bakufu officials.

3. The issue of how to measure prominence will be taken up in the next chapter. It includes factors such as positions the individual previously held

within the Zen monastic hierarchy, attainment of *inka,* and whether or not the individual could bring existing temples into the Obaku sect.

4. The ritual is described in Chapter 7.

5. *Obaku Mokuan Oshō nempu,* fascicle 2, p. 21b.

6. Takahashi, *Obakusan Mampukuji,* p. 126.

7. At least two of Mu-an's heirs, Ichimyō Dōgen (1635–1685) and Tesshin Dōhan (1641–1710), were born in Japan, the offspring of Chinese expatriates. See Chap. 6, n. 4 below.

8. The major lines and sublines of Dharma transmission do not represent schismatic breaks or distinctions in style of practice within the Obaku sect. They represent the various branches of descent emerging from the most prominent of the early masters. In many cases, the lines are (or were) associated with a specific subtemple at Mampuku-ji that was founded by the line's founding figure.

9. See *Obaku bunka jinmei jiten,* pp. 404ff.

10. See Nakamura Shūsei, "Mokuan zenji to sono wasō shihōsha," pp. 11–13.

11. Takahashi, *Obakusan Mampukuji,* pp. 197–198.

12. Ibid., p. 198.

13. Washio, *Nihon zenshūshi no kenkyū,* p. 102.

14. The dispute centered on naming one of Ryōkei's disciples as his designated Dharma heir after Ryōkei died in a flood tide in 1670. The situation was complicated by the involvement of Emperor Gomizunoo. For a detailed discussion, see Chapter 10.

15. *Obaku bunka jinmei jiten* gives a complete listing of his writings at the end of his biography, Ōtsuki, "Obakushū," p. 117.

Chapter Six: Japanese Converts

1. At least one Dharma heir of Mu-an mentioned elsewhere is not recorded in the *Obaku kanroku.* According to Mu-an's biography (*Obaku Mokuan Oshō nempu,* fascicle 2, p. 25a), Tanzan Shōshō received *inka* from Mu-an in the spring of 1679. Tanzan Dōshō is the Dharma name for Aoki Shigekane (1606–1682), the daimyo of Settsu province. Aoki Shigekane was at one time a lay disciple of Gudō Tōshoku at Myōshin-ji. He first met Yin-yüan at Fumon-ji in 1656 and became a strong patron of the Obaku movement. He retired in 1672, taking the name Tanzan. He took the tonsure in 1682 and became Mu-an's Dharma heir soon after. The reason for the omission of Tanzan's name in the *Obaku kanroku* is unclear. Ōtsuki, Katō, and Hayashi, pp. 3–4.

2. Three of the first-generation converts practiced first under the guidance of Tao-che and later made contact with Yin-yüan.

3. The two former members of Jōdo Shinshū were Jitsuden Dōkin (1627–1704) and Tetsugen Dōkō (1630–1682), the twelfth and fifteenth Dharma heirs of Mu-an, respectively. Jitsuden was born at a Jōdo Shinshū temple in

Himeji. He eventually developed an interest in Zen and took the precepts from a Rinzai monk named Shūdō from Unshō-ji. He inherited Shūdō's temple in 1655. In 1666 he traveled to Mampuku-ji to practice Obaku Zen under Mu-an, remaining at the main monastery until 1674, when he received *inka*. Jitsuden later became the fourth abbot at Zuishō-ji, the Obaku headquarters in Edo. A brief biography of Tetsugen is provided below.

4. Ichimyō Dōgen (1635–1685) and Tesshin Dōhan (1641–1710) were both born in Nagasaki of Chinese parentage; they are Mu-an's twenty-first and twenty-second Dharma heirs. Nothing is known about Ichimyō's family except that they were Chinese. He entered Buddhist orders at a young age, originally taking the tonsure at a Sōtō temple. He later became a disciple of Mu-an at Fukusai-ji sometime between 1655 and 1661. He accompanied Mu-an to Mampuku-ji and lived out his life there. He became Mu-an's Dharma heir in 1679. Tesshin presents a more special case, being the son of a Japanese mother from the Nishimura family and a Chinese merchant father from Fukien. His mother came from an upper-class family. After his father died when he was eight, she saw to it that her son received a formal education in the Chinese classics. At the age of thirteen or fourteen, Tesshin decided to become a monk after meeting Yin-yüan in 1654 and Mu-an in 1655. At first his mother refused to grant her permission. One night Tesshin shaved his own head and made his way to Mu-an's quarters. Finally gaining his mother's approval, he took the tonsure and practiced under Mu-an's direction. Tesshin later served as Mu-an's translator at Fumon-ji and at Mampuku-ji and received *inka* from Mu-an in 1677. Tesshin had many lay patrons among the upper ranks of the samurai class. On a number of occasions he was summoned to audiences with the shogun or to give lectures at the castle. He served twice as abbot at Zuishō-ji in Edo. Tesshin is also known for the relief work he conducted in Nagasaki during the famine of 1703. He is said to have saved some sixty thousand lives through his food distribution project.

5. Baikoku Dōyō (1640–1701) was born in Nagasaki to a family named Nakamura. Nothing else is known about the family. The Nakamura family may have been low-ranking samurai, although the name is not distinctive. Alternatively, they may have been rural elites or wealthy merchants granted special permission by the authorities to use a surname. Baikoku was orphaned at a young age and raised by an elder brother. At age twelve he took the tonsure at Kōfuku-ji under the Chinese monk I-jan. It is somewhat unusual for a young Japanese to have entered a Chinese temple without previous contact with the Chinese expatriate community or the attraction of a prominent master such as Yin-yüan.

6. Only three of the thirty-four available biographies list the individuals' birth position. In several other cases, the biographies indicate that the parents or other guardians entrusted the child to a temple for education or ordination. It is likely that many of these individuals were second or third sons.

7. Shōmyō-ji is in Hino in Shiga prefecture. It was originally built by Shōtoku Taishi and burned to the ground in the late sixteenth century. Gomizunoo had originally intended Isshi Monju to serve as founder/restorer, but Isshi died before the work had progressed significantly. Other monks served as abbot in the interim between Isshi's death in 1646 and Ryōkei's assuming that office in 1664. See Nakao, *Gomizunoo hōō to Ōbakushū,* p. 13.

8. The term saidō, also pronounced seidō, is an honorific title used for senior monks who have previously served as abbot or head monk at another Zen temple. In this case, it indicates that Chōon served as the most senior monk under Mu-an during the seasonal retreat.

9. *Zenrin shūheishū,* 1:17b–18a. The text criticizes Chōon's activity as inappropriate because he charged fees to those who received the precepts, like a traveling minstrel. The *Zenrin shūhei shū* as a whole is harshly critical of the Obaku sect and may be categorized as an anti-Obaku text.

10. Tetsugen's edition is known alternatively as *Obaku Tetsugen Issaikyō* and the *Obakuban Daizōkyō.* It consists of 6,956 volumes, based primarily on the Wan-li edition from Ming China, which were supplemented by additional materials, including Obaku sectarian texts. See Baroni, "Buddhism in Early Tokugawa Japan," especially pp. 209–252.

11. Tetsugen's extensive public lectures on the topic brought him into direct conflict with members of the Jōdo Shinshū sect. See Helen J. Baroni, "Bottled Anger: Episodes in Obaku Conflict in the Tokugawa Period," *Japanese Journal of Religious Studies* 21, nos. 2–3 (June–September): 191–210.

12. Ōtsuki, "Obakushū," p. 12.

Chapter Seven: Obaku's Monastic Style

1. Obaku materials maintain this position despite the fact that, as with the other sects of Japanese Zen, most Obaku monks today do not meditate regularly. In fact, most modern Zen monks do not continue to practice meditation after completing their years of training at a sectarian monastery.

2. Woodblock editions of the recorded sayings of most of the prominent Obaku masters were published at Mampuku-ji, and copies are preserved in the library there, where they are readily available to sectarian scholars. In addition, modern editions of the complete works of the three founding Chinese masters, Yin-yüan, Mu-an, and Chi-fei, have all been published in recent years; the *Ingen zenshū, Mokuan zenshū,* and *Sokuhi zenshū,* all edited by Hirakubo Akira, are published by Kaimyō shoin.

3. Hayashi, "Obaku wo kataru," pp. 5 and 8.

4. The *Obaku shingi* is included in the Taishō edition of the Tripitaka, vol. 82, no. 2606, pp. 766–785. Original copies of the first woodblock editions, as well as the woodblocks themselves, are still preserved at Mampuku-ji. I have preferred to use the woodblock edition because it is much easier to read than the Taishō. It includes *kambun* markings, indicating the sect's own

manner for reading the text. I have followed these in all translations included here. The Taishō version does not include all of these *kambun* markings, but otherwise the texts appear identical.

5. According to Hirakubo, even the preface was ghost-written by Kao-ch'üan under Yin-yüan's direct supervision (*Ingen*, p. 167).

6. Theodore Griffith Foulk, "The Ch'an School and Its Place in the Buddhist Monastic Tradition," pp. 1–25.

7. For a discussion of Pai-chang's code, see Collcutt, *Five Mountains,* pp. 136–138.

8. The entire text is translated in Yifa, "The Rules of Purity for the Chan Monastery: An Annotated Translation and Study of the Chanyuan qinggui," (Ph.D. diss., Yale University, 1996).

9. T. 48, no. 2025.

10. For a detailed description of the daily routine for the monks in training at Mampuku-ji in the modern period, see Akamatsu Shinmyō, "Obakushū kōyō," pp. 40–46.

11. Oishi Morio, "*Obaku shingi* no kenkyū," p. 146.

12. Normally *segaki* is associated with Urabon-e festivities, and Obaku temples are famous even today for their Chinese version of this service held at several of their larger temples. However, Yin-yüan made provision for a shorter version of the service, to be held at the abbot's discretion.

13. T. 82, pp. 780–781.

14. Yin-yüan wrote a more detailed description of the *Sandan Kaie,* the *Gukai hōgi,* published in a woodblock edition by Tetsugen Dōkō in 1658. Yin-yüan based his work on the *Hung-chieh-fa* (J. *Gukai hōgi*), a text written by San-feng Fa-ts'ang in 1623. Fa-ts'ang had himself drawn upon earlier work by Yun-ch'i Chu-hung. Yin-yüan's *Gukai hōgi* can be found in the *Zengaku taikei,* vol. 7 (the *kaiho* section), pp. 1–68. Yin-yüan's edition of Fa-ts'ang's text appears in the ZZ, 2.11.5. A Ch'ing dynasty edition of Fa-ts'ang's text, called the *Ch'uan-shou san-tan hung-chieh fa* (J. *Denju san-dan gukai hōgi*), appeared in 1688. That edition is also found in the ZZ, 2.12.1.

15. Ritsu movements have occurred in several different sects in Japan and are not limited to the Ritsu school transmitted to Japan in the Nara period. The primary example of these movements was the Shingon Ritsu sect, which was very strong during the Kamakura period and revived in the Tokugawa period. Other Ritsu movements include Tendai's Anrakuritsu, Nichiren's Hokkeritsu, and Pure Land's Jōdoritsu, all active in the early Tokugawa period. See Paul B. Watt, "Jiun Sonja (1718–1804): A Response to Confucianism within the Context of Buddhist Reform," p. 213. In a sense, Obaku represents a Ritsu movement within Rinzai Zen, although it never used that term to describe itself.

16. *Zenrin shūheishū,* pp. 17b–18a.

17. See note 14 above.

18. Historians at Mampuku-ji whom I consulted could not account for this. Nor did they know when the ceremony had last been held.

19. T. 82, p. 769c–770a.

20. The precepts are based on the Ssu-fen lu (Vinaya in Four Parts; J. Shibun ritsu).

21. See Paul Groner, *Saichō: The Establishment of the Japanese Tendai School,* especially pp. 49–50 and 213–246. Chinese Ch'an masters conferred these on both clergy and lay people alike as symbols of their connection to the Ch'an school. For a historical account of their use in Ch'an monasteries in China, see Foulk, "The 'Ch'an School,'" pp. 78–87.

22. According to Washio Junkei, this caused antagonism between the monks at Mampuku-ji and those at Zuishō-ji, *Nihon zenshūshi no kenkyū,* p. 102.

23. Foulk, "The 'Ch'an School,'" pp. 85–87.

24. For a description of the Sōtō school's use of mass ordinations as a means to strengthen the sect on the popular level, see William M. Bodiford, "The Growth of the Sōtō Zen Tradition in Medieval Japan," pp. 397–424.

25. Hirakubo, *Ingen,* p. 160.

26. Takenuki Genshō, *Nihon zenshūshi,* p. 227.

27. The term *mokugyo* may be used in reference to two distinct ritual implements, the instrument described above and another known alternatively as *hō.* The *hō* is a large wooden gong carved in the shape of a fish with a pearl in its mouth. It usually hangs outside of the dining hall or the monks' hall and is struck to signal mealtimes. The *hō* has a much longer history in Japan.

28. Hayashi Bunshō, "Obaku o kataru," p. 23.

29. Kyorei commented that the music was interesting but inappropriate in Japan and grating on his ears day after day. See Chapter 9.

30. See the seventh item in Yin-yüan's final instructions, the *Yoshokugo,* in the *Obaku shingi,* T. 82, p. 781a.

31. See Kyorei's commentary in his letter describing life at Kōfuku-ji, translated below in Chapter 9.

32. *Obaku geki,* p. 4b.

33. *Zenrin shūhei shū,* pp. 6a–6b.

34. *Ingen zenshū,* 11:5115.

35. Ibid., 11:5147–5149.

36. Baroni, "Buddhism in Early Tokugawa Japan," pp. 209ff.

37. T. 82, p. 769a–b.

38. The dates are listed in section 7 of the *Obaku shingi* under the month-by-month calendar of events: under the fourth month, on the fifteenth day, we find *ketsuge jōdō,* the opening lecture for the summer retreat; the fifteenth day of the seventh month lists the *gege jōdō,* the closing lecture. Similarly, for the winter retreat, we find *kessei,* the opening ceremony for the winter retreat

under the fifteenth day of the tenth month, and *kaisei,* the closing ceremony on the fifteenth day of the first month. T. 82, p. 772c–773b.

39. We know this from Tetsugen's case. Mu-an made a special exception in allowing Tetsugen to carry on with his scripture project throughout the year.

40. Hakuin reinstituted the practice of keeping the yearly retreats in the mid-eighteenth century; Miura and Sasaki, *Zen Dust,* p. 27.

Chapter Eight: Pure Land Outside, Zen Inside

1. See Tsuji Zennosuke, *Nihon bukkyōshi,* p. 325, for the original Japanese of Kyorei's letter written from Kōfuku-ji in 1655. See Chapter 9, "Initial Responses to Obaku Zen," for an English translation.

2. Articles and books related to the subject are too numerous to allow for a complete listing here. The most prolific writer on the subject is Fujiyoshi Jikai. In addition to numerous articles, his work includes two books, *Zen to Jōdokyō,* which includes a sampling of his writings found elsewhere, and *Zen to nembutsu, Sono gendaiteki igi,* a compendium of scholarly articles he edited. The following are examples of other scholars' works representing a variety of approaches to the issue. Historical reviews include: David W. Chappell, "From Dispute to Dual Cultivation: Pure Land Responses to Ch'an Critics"; Kōchi Eigaku, "Chūgoku ni okeru zenjō kankei"; Hirada Hiromichi, "Chūsei zenshū to nembutsu zen"; Chun-fang Yu, *The Renewal of Buddhism in China: Chu-hung and the Late Ming Synthesis,* especially pp. 29–63. Theoretical articles include Hattori Eijun, "Zenjō yūgō shisō ni okeru jōdo no kaimei"; Daisetz Teitaro Suzuki, "Zen and Jōdo, Two Types of Buddhist Experience"; Heng-ching Shih, "The Syncretism of Chinese Ch'an and Pure Land Buddhism." For a more psychological approach, see D. T. Suzuki, "The Koan Exercise, Part II," in *Essays in Zen Buddhism (Second Series),* pp. 146–199; and Onda Akira, "Zen to nembutsu no shinrigakuteki hikaku kōsatsu," pp. 1–7.

3. For example, see Kōchi, "Chūgoku," p. 2.

4. Translation taken from Philip Yampolsky, *The Platform Sutra of the Sixth Patriarch,* pp. 156–157.

5. See Kōchi, "Chūgoku," p. 2, for an explanation of Tao-hsin's position.

6. Wusang's method is described by Kōchi, p. 3, and Chun-fang Yu, *The Renewal of Buddhism,* p. 51.

7. Hirano Sōjō suggests the theory that even the early Zen masters may have practiced *nembutsu* of a more traditional type, but that the evidence for this was removed by later generations of disciples. Hirano bases his theory on the third episode in the *Hekigan roku,* in which a visitor asks the ailing Ma-tsu Tao-i (709–788; J. Baso Dōitsu) how he is feeling and receives the cryptic reply, "Sun-faced Buddha, Moon-faced Buddha" *(nichimen butsu gatsumen butsu).* Hirano notes that in the source for this quotation, the *Butsumyōkyō,* the word *namu* was originally attached to each name. He thus

theorizes that in a time of serious illness Ma-tsu practiced recitation of Buddha names much as Pure Land believers would, but that later generations found this shameful and removed the word *namu* to mask it. "Rinzai zen to nembutsu," p. 84.

8. For studies of Yung-ming Yen-shou, see Mochizuki Shinkō, *Chūgoku jōdo kyōrishi*, pp. 329–341, Heng-ching Shih, "Yung-ming's Syncretism of Pure Land and Ch'an" and "The Syncretism of Chinese Ch'an and Pure Land Buddhism," and Chun-fang Yu, *The Renewal of Buddhism in China*, p. 52.

9. See Chappell, "From Dispute to Dual Cultivation," for a discussion of the early disputes between the Pure Land and Ch'an schools in China.

10. It is not completely clear from the secondary sources the relative value that Yen-shou placed on Pure Land and Zen practices. In Chun-fang Yu's presentation, Yen-shou's teachings gave Pure Land practice an equal or even superior position compared to Zen meditation (Yu, *The Renewal of Buddhism*, p. 52). However, as Heng-ching Shih explains it, Yen-shou used the familiar Zen interpretation of Pure Land belief, including the *nembutsu*, to overcome contradictions between the schools; this approach suggests that Yen-shou gave Zen the primary position ("The Syncretism of Chinese Ch'an and Pure Land Buddhism," pp. 74–78).

11. Heng-ching Shih, "The Syncretism of Chinese Ch'an and Pure Land Buddhism," pp. 76–78.

12. Translated from a quotation from Yen-shou's *Sanzen nembutsu shiryōken ge*, in Fujiyoshi's *Zen to Jōdokyō*, p. 104. The passage can also be found in Mochizuki Shinkō, *Chūgoku Jōdo kyōrishi*, p. 341. Original not located.

13. See, for example, Dumoulin, *Zen Buddhism: A History*, 1:284–287, and Ch'en, *Buddhism in China*, pp. 445–446.

14. Cheng, pp. 52–54, and 61–64; Nagai, "Minmatsu ni ikita zenshatachi," p. 326.

15. ZZ, 1/7/5, pp. 457–458.

16. T. 13, no. 418.

17. These sutras are *Muryōjukyō* (T. 12, no. 360), *Kanmuryōjukyō* (T. 12, no. 365), and *Amidakyō* (T. 12, no. 366).

18. Chun-fang Yu, *The Renewal of Buddhism*, p. 38.

19. Daniel B. Stevenson, "The Four Kinds of Samadhi in Early T'ien-t'ai Buddhism," pp. 59–60.

20. Bielefeldt, "Ch'ang-lu Tsung-tse's *Tso-ch'an I* and the Secret of Zen Meditation," p. 150.

21. When the Pure Land master Chu-hung concurred with this observation found in the writings of Zen masters he studied, he took their ideas one step further. He concluded that *nembutsu* is actually superior to Zen meditation because it is accessible to more people. Chun-fang Yu, *The Renewal of Buddhism*, pp. 47 and 62.

22. In its instructions for services during the illness of a monk found in

section 7, the *Ch'ih-hsiu pai-chang ch'ing-kuei* suggests chanting the names of the ten Buddhas for ordinary situations. However, when the illness is serious, it calls for reciting "Namu Amida Butsu" one hundred times. This is repeated for the funeral service on the day of cremation (T. 48, p. 1147b and 1148c).

23. Chun-fang Yu reviews the writing of several Ming period Zen masters who used the *nembutsu* koan (*The Renewal of Buddhism*, pp. 53–57).

24. See Hirada Hiromichi, "Chūsei zenshū to nembutsu zen," pp. 61–65.

25. Sung-peng Hsu, *A Buddhist Leader in Ming China*, p. 47.

26. Matsunaga, "*Obakuban* daizōkyō no saihyōka," 2:7.

27. Suzuki Shōsan has received extensive attention in Western literature. See, for example, Winston L. King, *Death Was His Koan: The Samurai Zen of Suzuki Shōsan;* Royall Tyler, trans., *Selected Writings of Suzuki Shōsan;* Herman Ooms, *Tokugawa Ideology: Early Constructs, 1570–1680,* pp. 122–143.

28. Ogisu Jundō, *Myōshinji,* pp. 71–84.

29. For example, in his discussion of Yin-yüan's Zen style, Dieter Schwaller explains the history of the *nembutsu* koan and gives examples from Yin-yüan's recorded sayings to illustrate its use in Obaku Zen, but offers no explanation for Obaku's use of Pure Land elements in its monastic ritual (*Der japanische Obaku-Mönch Tetsugen Dōkō,* pp. 43–45).

30. Such examples can be found in the *Ingen zenshū,* vol. 3, p. 1089; vol. 6, p. 2843; vol. 9, p. 4291; and vol. 10, p. 5030.

31. Translation from Philip Yampolsky, *The Zen Master Hakuin: Selected Writings,* p. 130.

32. See, for example, his biography, in Ōtsuki, Katō, and Hayashi, *Obaku bunka jinmei jiten,* pp. 278–279, and Akamatsu Shinmyō, "Obakushū kōzō," p. 21.

33. Akamatsu Shinmyō, "Obakushū kōyō," pp. 12–13. Akamatsu explains and defends the *nembutsu* koan at some length and highly recommends it to lay people as an appropriate form of *zazen* for them to practice (ibid., pp. 23–32). He is the best example in the modern period of a scholar-monk promoting Obaku Zen as Nembutsu Zen. However, he never loses his Zen orientation and is quite explicit that there is no Buddha or Pure Land outside the self.

34. Rinzai funeral services for lay believers include references to Amida even today. However, that portion of the service is read in the Chinese fashion, and most laypersons would probably not recognize it for what it is. Hirano Sōjō, "Rinzai zen to nembutsu," pp. 89–90.

35. T. 82, p. 771b–c.

36. T. 19, no. 945.

37. T. 12, no. 368.

38. "Obaku o kataru," p. 15.

39. See Hayashi Bunshō, "Obaku o kataru," p. 9.

40. In Japan, the same expression, *sankyō itchi,* usually referred to Buddhism, Confucianism, and the native Shinto. Until the Meiji period, the harmony between Buddhism and Shinto was graphically illustrated by the incorporation of small Shinto shrines into the compounds of most Buddhist temples. Many of the older examples of these Shinto shrines were removed during the Meiji period, when efforts were made forcibly to separate the two traditions. Obaku temples have some Shinto shrines dating back to the Tokugawa period.

41. See, for example, Sung-peng Hsu, *A Buddhist Leader in Ming China,* pp. 150–163; Chun-fang Yu, *"The Renewal of Buddhism,"* pp. 7, 64–66; Chang Sheng-yen, *Minmatsu Chūgoku bukkyō no kenkyū,* pp. 30–34.

42. *Ingen zenshū,* 5:2477–2479.

43. Yin-yüan wrote several verses in praise of filial piety; see *Ingen zenshū,* 9:4218, for one example.

44. T. 82, p. 769b.

45. A copy of this catalogue was published under the title "Ingen zenji no yuisho mokuroku," in *Zenshū* 264 (1917): 21–25.

46. Yoshikawa Kōjirō comments on Sorai's friendship with Yüeh-fêng Tao-chuang (1655–1734; J. Eppō Dōshō) in his biography of Sorai, in *Jinsai, Sorai, Norinaga,* pp. 121–122, 126–127, 201, and 206. Yüeh-fêng was a native of Chekiang who came to Japan in 1868 at the invitation of Kōfuku-ji, where he served as abbot and did much restoration work. Tu-chan Hsing-jung made him a Dharma heir in 1691. He became the eighth abbot of Mampuku-ji in 1707 and was honored with a purple robe in the same year.

Chapter Nine: Obaku in the World of Japanese Zen Buddhism

1. *Shuso* is a title used for the head monk, who ranks just below the abbot. It may also refer to the monk who serves as supervisor of the summer or winter retreat. The identity of the monk designated only by Shin, the second character of his name, is unknown. None of the Chinese monks listed in the Obaku lineage have the character in their names.

2. *Seidō* is the title given to a monk who has previously served as head monk at another temple. I have rendered the names in Japanese as Kyorei would have read them, since he does not seem to have been certain of the exact characters used by the Chinese monks. The identity of Dokuō is uncertain. He is probably the monk Tu-wang Hsing-yu (n.d.; J. Dokuō Shōyū) who became Yin-yüan's disciple in 1651 and accompanied him to Nagasaki in 1654.

3. Identity uncertain. Probably the monk also known as Tu-chi (n.d.; J. Dokuchi) who accompanied Yin-yüan to Nagasaki in 1654 and returned to China the following year.

4. Identity unknown.

5. Tu-chan Hsing-jung (1628–1706; J. Dokutan Shōkei), who would later become the fourth abbot at Mampuku-ji. See Chapter 5 for more information.

6. Tsuji, *Nihon bukkyōshi*, pp. 322–325.

7. See *Zenrin shūhei shū*, 1:5b.

8. See Kawakami, *Myōshinjishi*, pp. 453–454; Tamamura Takeji, *Rinzai-shūshi*, p. 251; Itō Kokan, *Gudō*, pp. 120–121; Ogisu Jundō, *Myōshinji*, p. 96.

9. For a discussion of *musō kai* in the *Platform sutra*, see Yanagida Seizan, *Shoki zenshū shishō no kenkyū*, pp. 153ff.

10. Yampolsky, *Zen Master Hakuin*, p. 145.

11. According to Ogisu Jundō, even Ungo's own disciples were scandalized by their master's popular teaching style and sought his help in understanding his position. It eventually became clear that Ungo was advocating a form of *koshin no mida* (Amida within the self) and *yuishin jōdo* (Pure Land only in the mind), which was closer to the Obaku understanding than to a strict Pure Land interpretation (Ogisu, *Myōshinji*, pp. 71–84). See also Hirano Sōjō, *Ungo oshō nempū*, especially pp. 18 and 23.

12. Kawakami, *Myōshinjishi* pp. 453–454.

13. Itō *Gudō* pp. 228–231.

14. See Ogisu, *Myōshinji*, p. 96, and Itō, *Gudō*, p. 121, for quotations from Gudō's original argument.

15. *Obaku geki*, p. 12b.

16. See, for instance, Kawakami, *Myōshinjishi*, pp. 462–463, and Itō's version, *Gudō*, p. 121.

17. The passage in the original Chinese can be found in Itō Kokan's article "Gudō kokushi no zen," p. 13. For a Japanese translation, see Itō, *Gudō*, p. 123.

18. According to the *Zengaku daijiten*, rev. ed. (Tokyo: Komazawa University, 1985; p. 1099), Fumon-ji reverted to its former status as a Myōshin-ji line temple after Ryōkei's death. Nonetheless, Obaku sources continued to include it in their official listings of branch temples as late as the Meiji period. See Takenuku Genshō, *Kinsei Obakushū matsuji chōshūsei*, p. 301.

19. According to the listings of Obaku temples in Takenuki, *Kinsei Obakushū matsuji chōshūsei*, Chōon founded twenty-two temples and Tetsugyū founded twenty.

20. Cited in Tsuji, *Nihon bukkyōshi*, p. 359. Hirakubo also relates a similar account in *Ingen*, pp. 225–226, indicating that his source was Kawakami Kozan's *Myōshinjishi*. He does not give a full citation and I have been unable to locate the passage.

21. *Obaku geki*, p. 9b.

22. Kawakami, *Myōshinjishi*, p. 463. Although Kawakami gives Tangetsu's as Hōzan, the *Obaku bunka jinmei jiten* lists his name as Tangetsu

Shōen. Based on the contents of the biography, it is clearly the same person. See Ōtsuki, Katō, and Hayashi, *Obaku bunka jinmei jiten,* pp. 221–222.

23. Ryōkei had originally received *inka* under Master Hakubu Eryo and became his Dharma heir. Hakubu died in 1629, and Ryōkei succeeded him as abbot at Ryōan-ji. Little else is known about Hakubu except that he was one of the monks who took a moderate position toward the bakufu in the Purple Robe Affair. See the discussion of the Purple Robe Affair in Chapter 9, "Obaku and Sōtō Zen."

24. According to Tamamura, fourteen or fifteen other monks were also expelled at the same time (*Rinzaishūshi,* pp. 251–252). I have found no other reference to these numbers. It is possible that most of these monks are not mentioned elsewhere because they were of low rank.

25. Translation is based on the full text found in Minamoto Ryōen, *Tetsugen,* pp. 88–89. Tsuji provides a portion of the text, *Nihon bukkyōshi,* p. 359.

26. Minamoto provides a lengthy summary of the original text, *Tetsugen,* pp. 90–94. Tsuji gives a much shorter summary, *Nihon bukkyōshi,* p. 360.

27. I have been unable to locate the original document. Minamoto and Tsuji provide only very brief descriptions of it, so it is difficult to evaluate the nature of the argument. See Minamoto, pp. 94–95 and Tsuji, pp. 360–361.

28. *Zenrin shūhei shū,* woodblock edition, two fascicles (Kyoto, 1700).

29. Hsin-yueh Hsing-ch'ou (1639–1696; J. Kōchū Shin'etsu) was a Chinese monk of the Ts'ao-tung sect who came to Japan in 1677. Although he received *inka* from a Ts'ao-tung master in China long before he came to Japan, he visited and practiced under a number of Obaku and Rinzai masters while traveling through Japan.

30. Tsuji includes these two sections in his listing of sections from the *Zenrin shūhei shū* related to Obaku, with the observation that they apply to Ryōkei in particular (Tsuji, *Nihon bukkyōshi,* pp. 362–363). Unfortunately, Tsuji provides no other analysis of the material. In most cases he merely lists the title of the section without further comment.

31. Bodiford, "Dharma Transmission in Sōtō Zen: Manzan Dōhaku's Reform Movement," p. 443.

32. Ibid., p. 434.

33. Ranking based on personal advancement refers to the practice of seating retired superiors, monks who had served as abbots, either in their current temple of residence (*tōdō*) or in another temple (*seidō*), ahead of the other monks regardless of actual years of practice. It is not clear that Gozan temples used only personal advancement and years of practice since ordination as criteria for ranking their monks. In the *Rinsen kakun,* a monastic code written for the *jissetsu* ranked temple Rinsen-ji, the Zen Master Musō Soseki [1275–1351] argued for a combination of years since ordination and the age of the monks involved. See Collcutt, *Five Mountains,* pp. 157–158.

34. *Zenrin shūhei shū,* 1:5a.

35. Ibid., 1:7a–b.

36. Ibid., 1:6a.

37. The mention of worldly appearance refers to the Chinese monastic custom of allowing the hair to grow for a longer period of time before shaving, as discussed in Chapter 7, "Maintenance of Chinese Cultural Identity."

38. Dōgen taught that to maintain the concentration of seated meditation during the breaks for *kinhin*, monks should walk at a slow, measured pace. See Bielefeldt, *Dōgen's Manuals of Zen Meditation*, p. 116 n.

39. *Zenrin shūhei shū*, 1:5b–6a.

40. *Rinzai nōto*, pp. 203–204.

41. The author has been unable to examine these texts and is thus unable to verify the passages cited in the *Zenrin shūhei shū*.

42. Yampolsky provides some background information on this system in his introduction to *The Zen Master Hakuin*, p. 14.

43. *Zenrin shūhei shū*, 1:18b.

44. See "Chōon Dōkai no Rinzai/Sōtō hihan," pp. 420–422.

45. For a brief description of the contents of the *Bukai nanshin*, see Ogisu Jundō, "Chōon Dōkai ni tsuite," in *Zenshūshi no sansaku*, pp. 219–233.

46. *Zenrin shūhei shū*, 1:16b–17a.

47. According to Furuta, Chōon not only objected to koan practice as it was known in his time, but to koan practice in general; he says that Chōon felt that all koan practice led almost inevitably to the danger of "counting Zen," in which the student tries to master the language of one koan after another rather than seeking enlightenment. See "Chōon Dōkai no Rinzai/Sōtō hihan," pp. 418–420.

48. For a description of some of Hakuin's reforms, including his koan system, see Miura and Sasaki, *Zen Dust*, pp. 25–30.

49. Ta-hui Tsung-kao (1089–1163; J. Daie Sōkō) destroyed the original woodblocks for the text soon after its first publication in 1128. The text was later reconstructed and published again in 1300 by the lay believer Chang Ming-yüan (n.d.; J. Chō Myōen). See Dumoulin, *Zen Buddhism: A History*, 1:248. It was the second edition, transmitted in the early fourteenth century, that was commonly used in Japan. Dōgen had earlier brought a handwritten copy to Japan in 1228, but his copy was preserved as a secret document at Daijō-ji and only made widely available in the modern period. See Miura and Sasaki, *Zen Dust*, pp. 357–358.

50. *Zenrin shūhei shū*, 1:2a.

51. A variety of schools arose during the Tokugawa period, not all related to Buddhist temples and Neo-Confucian academies. See R. P. Dore, *Education in Tokugawa Japan*.

52. *Zenrin shūhei shū*, 1:13a.

53. Ibid., 1:14b.

54. Detailed information on Fei-yin's claims and the resulting debates can

be found in Torigoe Fumikuni, *Hiin zenji to sono cho, Gotō gentō;* and Nagai Masano, "Minmatsu ni ikita zenshatachi—Hiin Tsūyō ni yoru *Gotō gentō* no seiritsu," pp. 327–343.

55. *Zenrin shūhei shū,* 2:15b.

56. Ibid., 2:15a.

57. Ibid., 1:19a–b.

58. Ibid., 2:3b.

59. Hirakubo, *Ingen,* p. 226.

60. *Zenrin shūhei shū,* 1:17b–18a.

61. To my knowledge, the text has been published twice in recent years, but neither edition is readily available even in Japan. There is a printed copy in the Obaku journal, the *Obaku bunka,* nos. 41–43 (Sept. 1978–Jan. 1979). The other edition is a modern handwritten copy prepared by the Sōtō scholar Kagamishima Genryū, which appeared along with Mujaku's *Shōbō genzō senpyō* in a folio published by Komazawa University in 1960.

62. *Gakushō Mujaku Dōchū,* p. 298.

63. *Obaku geki,* p. 11b. All references are to my own numbering of the leaves of the original Shunkō-in copy.

64. *Obaku geki,* p. 20b.

65. Minamoto's discussion of the *Obaku geki* can be found in *Tetsugen,* pp. 99–107. He deals with the issue of authorship on pp. 99–100.

66. *Obaku geki,* p. 7a.

67. Yanagida examined the entire text at my request and aided me with some of the more difficult passages. Yanagida's work related to Mujaku includes editing the photo reproduction of Mujaku's original copy of the *Zenrin shokisen* (first published by Baiyō shoin in 1909, reissued by Seishin shōbō in 1963, and by Chubun shuppansha in 1979) and his earlier article, "Mujaku Dōchū no gakumon," describing Mujaku's scholarly methods.

68. Minamoto describes an episode involving a misunderstanding that occurred while Yin-yüan was building the Monks' hall (*Sōdō*) at Fumon-ji (*Tetsugen,* p. 101). There is no corresponding passage in the Shunkō-in copy.

69. *Obaku geki,* p. 6b.

70. Ibid., pp. 4b–5b.

71. Ibid., p. 5b.

72. Ibid. pp. 12b–13a.

73. This episode will be examined in more detail in Chapter 10.

74. *Obaku geki,* pp. 9a–9b.

75. Ibid., p. 7b. Egoku is discussed in Chapter 5 as one of the first-generation Japanese converts. For a full biography of Egoku, see Rinoie Masafumi, *Obaku sanketsu Egoku Dōmyō zenji den.*

76. *Obaku geki,* pp. 20b–21a.

77. Ibid., p. 7b.

78. Mujaku authored a twenty-fascicle commentary on the *Ch'ih-hsiu*

Pai-chang ch'ing-kuei titled *Chokushu Hyakujo shingi sae*. A modern facsimile edition in two volumes was edited by Yanagida Seizan and published by Chubun shuppansha in 1977. Iida Rigyō lists the titles of a number of *shingi* Mujaku composed for individual temples among his other writings (*Gakusei Mujaku Dōchū*, pp. 297–331).

79. *Obaku geki*, p. 1b.

80. Ibid., p. 13b.

81. *Hsüeh-feng I-ts'un ch'an-shih yu-lu* (J. *Seppō Gison Zenji goroku*), in ZZ, 2.25.5, p. 473a.

82. *Obaku geki*, p. 13b.

83. Ibid., p. 17b.

84. Ibid., p. 12b.

85. Ibid., pp. 10a–11a.

86. Ibid., pp.13b–14a.

87. Yampolsky, *The Zen Master Hakuin*, p. 130.

88. Ibid., p. 145.

89. Ibid., p. 146.

90. Hakuin criticized Chu-hung throughout his writings, including the *Orategama zokushū*. From that text and others, it appears that Hakuin regarded Chu-hung as the first cause, as it were, of the combined practice of Ch'an and Pure Land becoming acceptable in Ch'an monasteries; see Yampolsky, *The Zen Master Hakuin*, pp. 147–148. Hakuin appears to have been unaware or to have ignored the fact that earlier Zen masters, notably the late Sung/early Yüan dynasty Lin-chi master Chung-feng Ming-pen (1263–1323; J. Chūhō Myōhon), had advocated forms of combined practice.

91. Ibid., p. 148.

92. Ibid., p. 149.

93. Ibid., p. 171.

94. Ibid.

95. Ibid.

96. Ibid., p. 176.

97. Yuie Dojo was commonly called Tokugan Yuie after the Tokugan-ji temple where he was abbot.

98. The Sōtō scholar Kagamishima Genryū makes this point in various books and articles. See, for example, his volume in the Zen no goroku series, *Manzan/Menzan*, p. 47.

99. Bodiford, "Dharma Transmission in Sōtō Zen: Manzan Dōhaku's Reform Movement," p. 434.

100. Bodiford explains that the historical and textual material is highly ambiguous on these issues and that Manzan interpreted them to suit his purposes. He provides some historical examples to illustrate this point; ibid., pp. 425–431. He also notes that the key passages that Manzan attributes to Dōgen cannot be found in Dōgen's known writings; ibid., pp. 438–439.

101. There are no modern editions of the *Shōjurin shingi*. Information on the contents and Obaku influences is based on the explanatory notes (*kaisetsu*) from the *Sōtōshū zensho, Kaidai sakuin,* 6:152–154.

Chapter Ten: Obaku and the Secular Authorities

1. See, for example, Akamatsu, "Obakushū kōyō," pp. 7–9, and idem, "Obaku no shinpū," pp. 76–78.

2. Takenuki discusses Obaku's development and the Edo bakufu's role in its spread in very similar terms in two works: *Nihon zenshūshi*, pp. 210–240; and *Kinsei Obakushū matsuji chōshūsei*, pp. 17–42.

3. See Neil McMullin, *Buddhism and the State in Sixteenth-Century Japan*.

4. The *"Chokkyo shie no hatto"* specifically named Daitoku-ji, Myōshin-ji, Chion-in, Jōke-in, Sennyū-ji, and Awaokōmyō-ji; Funaoka Makoto, *Takuan*, p. 42.

5. Funaoka provides the text of the "Daitokuji shohatto," dated the seventh month of that year; Funaoka, *Takuan*, pp. 51–52.

6. Miura and Sasaki, *Zen Dust*, p. 352.

7. See Ooms, *Tokugawa Ideology*, pp. 169–170.

8. The most lucid account of the *hatto* affecting Zen temples, and especially the Purple Robe Affair, is found in Takenuki, *Nihon zenshūshi*, pp. 187–197. Funaoka gives a detailed account, including excerpts from many of the primary sources; Funaoka, *Takuan*, pp. 41–81. Murai Sanae provides a brief summary of the three primary Buddhist figures involved, Takuan, Gyokushitsu, and Kōgetsu, in "Shie jikengo no chōbaku kankei," pp. 1–11.

9. Murai provides details about Takuan, Gyokushitsu, and Kōgetsu, and their later relations with the bakufu, including the favors received and services rendered in the anti-Christian movement (ibid., p. 7).

10. According to Obaku genealogical charts, the emperor's Dharma line includes two abbots of Mampuku-ji and continues down to the present.

11. Nakao Fumio, *Gomizunoo hōō to Obakushū*, pp. 4–6.

12. Ibid., p. 6. See also Gomizunoo's biography in Ōtsuki, Katō, and Hayashi, *Obaku bunka jinmei jiten*, pp. 127–129.

13. The essay "Gomizunoo Tennō to Obaku," published at Mampuku-ji to commemorate the 250th anniversary of Gomizunoo's death, indicates that Ryōkei first introduced the Obaku style of Zen to Gomizunoo in the summer of 1657. Furuichi Katsuzen, ed., *Gomizunoo tenno to Obaku*, p. 2.

14. Mujaku identifies Gosai (r. 1656–1663) by his reign name, Kambun-tei. Gosai was Gomizunoo's son. He ascended the throne after his brother Gokōmyō (r. 1643–1654) abdicated in his favor.

15. *Obaku geki*, pp. 4b–5a.

16. Tsuji, *Nihon bukkyōshi*, pp. 272–273.

17. The text of the *hōgo* is quite short and can be found (repeated twice from different sources) in the *Ingen zenshū,* 7:3233–3238.

18. Nakao, *Gomizunoo hōō to Obakushū,* pp. 61–65.

19. See ibid., p. 13.

20. The Oak Tree koan appears as the thirty-seventh case in the *Mumonkan.*

21. Nakao provides the text of the emperor's letter; *Gomizunoo hōō to Obakushū,* pp. 36–37.

22. Ibid., p. 39.

23. If the emperor's letter has been preserved, I have found no evidence of it. Secondary sources do not even provide direct quotations from the text. All information in the secondary literature seems to come from Kao-ch'üan's writings. Perhaps a copy of the letter will be found in Kao-ch'üan's complete works, when the project to publish them comes to fruition.

24. *Obaku geki,* p. 14b. This passage is one of the Chinese vignettes in the second portion of the *Obaku geki.* Mujaku includes all of the pertinent information concerning the various negative reactions, internal and external alike, as well as a less coherent explanation of the petition to the bakufu and the *Jisha bugyō's* response.

25. Ibid., p. 15a.

26. Ibid., p. 15b.

27. Ibid., pp. 15b–16a.

28. See Takenuki, *Nihon zenshūshi,* p. 220.

29. The entire plot of land that the bakufu acquired from the Konoe family in 1659 was assessed at 1,400 *koku.* The bakufu retained the larger portion of the land, granting Obaku-san the smaller parcel.

30. Aoki Shigekane was already a lay patron of Yin-yüan, whom he had met at Fumon-ji when he was serving in Settsu in the mid-1650s. It is said that he received Mu-an's Dharma in 1679 and was given the name Tanzan Shōshō. This was not recorded in any official sectarian records, but an episode is recorded in Mu-an's *nempū.* See Chap. 6, n. 1.

31. A listing of the smaller donations made by the other military houses is too lengthy to include here. Takenuki details the names and contributions in a number of places: *Nihon zenshūshi,* pp. 218–220 and 235–236; and *Kinsei Obakushū matsuji chōshusei,* pp. 21–22.

32. Collcutt, *Five Mountains,* p. 61.

33. See Hashimoto Hiroshi, *Kaitei zōho Daibukan,* 2:1054–1091.

34. See Collcutt, *Five Mountains,* pp. 100–101.

35. See McMullin, *Buddhism and the State,* p. 21. For a detailed description of *honmatsu seido,* from its origins in the medieval period through its full development in the Tokugawa period, see Toyoda Takeshi, *Nihon shūkyō seido shi no kenkyū,* pp. 30–72.

36. These numbers are based on the *Enkyō matsujichō* published in Enkyō 2 (1745). See *Kinsei Obakushu matsuji chōshūsei,* pp. 25–28.

37. *Obaku geki,* p. 17b. The final line, *manten taiho manchi shikū,* translated here as "Senior Guardian [who protects] the heavens and the Minister of Works [who protects] the earth," is obscure. The terms *taiho* and *shikū* refer to government posts during the Chou dynasty. The former was the senior guardian of the heir apparent and the latter the minister of works, responsible for overseeing the land and the people.

38. For descriptions of the conditions facing Buddhism during the Meiji period, see James Edward Ketelaar, *Of Heretics and Martyrs in Meiji Japan: Buddhism and Its Persecution,* and Martin Colcutt, "Buddhism: The Threat of Eradication."

39. See Hirakubo Akira, "Edo jidai ni okeru Mampukuji no shūrishi ni tsuite," *Kinsei bukkyō: shiryō to Kenkyū* 3, no. 1 (November 1963): 13, no. 1 (November 1963): 1–11.

40. Miura and Sasaki, *Zen Dust,* p. 22.

Chapter Eleven: Conclusion

1. Ann M. Harrington, *Japan's Hidden Christians,* especially pp. 99–123.

2. Bryan R. Wilson, "Factors in the Failure of the New Religious Movements," in *The Future of New Religious Movements,* ed. Bromley and Hammond, p. 31.

3. Rodney Stark, "How New Religions Succeed: A Theoretical Model," in *The Future of New Religious Movements,* ed. Bromley and Hammond, p. 12.

Appendix: The *Obaku geki*

This translation is based on a photostat copy of the original handwritten copy preserved at Shunkō-in at Myōshin-ji. The handwriting on the original has been identified by Yanagida Seizan, the leading expert on Mujaku's writings, as Mujaku's own.

1. Omura Suminaga (1636–1706) was daimyo from 1651 until his death in 1706, a period that encompasses Yin-yüan's entire stay in Nagasaki.

2. This remark refers to the military resistance waged by Ming loyalists against Ch'ing forces, which continued for nearly twenty years after the suicide of the Ch'ung-chen emperor in 1644. At the time of Yin-yüan's emigration to Japan, Cheng Ch'eng-kung, better known to the West as Coxinga, was successfully extending his military authority over southeastern China. See *The Cambridge History of China:* vol. 7, *The Ming Dynasty, 1368–1644, Part 1,* ed. Frederick W. Mote and Denis Twitchett, pp. 710–721.

3. *Hōdō,* a banner used to announce a sermon or, in the Sōtō sect, to announce a summer or winter retreat. The practice of raising a Dharma banner to announce the location of a sermon is said to have originated in India.

4. The *Gotō gentō,* or *Wu-téng yen-t'ung,* was a compilation of Zen lineages written by Yin-yüan's master, Fei-yin Tung-yung, and Pai-chi Yüan-

kung (n.d.), first published in China in 1653. The original woodblocks were destroyed by government order in 1654. The text was later published in Japan by Yin-yüan in 1657.

5. Mujaku used indentations to indicate his own insertions into the narrative. Here and elsewhere I have followed the same convention.

6. Senzan Genshō (n.d.) was the fifth head monk of Taizō-in, one of the subtemples at Myōshin-ji. He was Jikuin's Dharma master. See Kawakami, *Myōshinjishi*, p. 481.

7. Tangetsu Shōen (1607–1672) was a Myōshin-ji line monk, born into the Nakagawa family in Nara. His home temple was Daisen-ji in Osaka, but he served in various capacities at subtemples at Myōshin-ji and twice became abbot, first in 1654 and then again in 1661. He corresponded with Yin-yüan while he was in Nagasaki and sent at least one disciple to participate in Yin-yüan's first winter retreat in Nagasaki.

8. Itakura Shigemune (1586–1656) retired from his post as Shoshidai of Kyoto in the final months of 1654 but remained in the immediate Kyoto area and continued to have influence until his death.

9. The units of measure used during the Tokugawa period were not fixed throughout the country. In the modern period, one *momme* weighs 3.75 grams, or 0.1325 ounces.

10. The Hyōjōsho was the highest judicial office of the Tokugawa bakufu. It was established in the 1630s to handle problems that involved more than one jurisdiction or were too complicated for one office alone to determine. For a description of its development, see Kate Wildman Nakai, *Shogunal Politics: Arai Hakuseki and the Premises of Tokugawa Rule*, pp. 152–153.

11. Matsudaira Nobutsuna (1596–1662) was a prominent and powerful member of the bakufu. He became Tokugawa Iemitsu's page at a very young age, in 1604. When Iemitsu became the third shogun, Nobutsuna rose in power. He advanced to the position of Senior Counselor in 1635.

12. Sakai Tadakatsu (1587–1662) became Iemitsu's attendant in 1620. After Iemitsu became shogun, Tadakatsu advanced rapidly and became deeply involved in bakufu affairs. He retired from public office in 1660, and took the tonsure. His religious name was Kūin.

13. Makino Chikashige (also read Chikanari) (1607–1677) began service as page to the Shogun Iemitsu. He was daimyo of various areas, including Sekiyado and Settsu provinces, and succeeded Itakura Shigemune as Shoshidai of Kyoto in 1655.

14. Ryōge-in is one of the subtemples at Myōshin-ji. Jikuin was the first head monk. Mujaku inherited that position from his master and greatly expanded the temple.

15. Unidentified.

16. Mujaku has used the term *kusu,* the title used for the six monks charged with administration of the temple, which makes no sense in this con-

text. The sound and characters suggest that he may have meant *kujū*, the kitchen, and I have tentatively translated the term as such.

17. For a description of limitations placed on Yin-yüan during his time at Fumon-ji, see Chapter 3.

18. Mujaku identifies Gosai (r. 1656–1663) by his reign name, Kambun-tei. Gosai was Gomizunoo's son. He ascended the throne after his brother Gokōmyō (r. 1643–1654) abdicated in his favor.

19. The Rinzai sect had been involved in a scandal about unauthorized imperial distinctions, including purple robes, before Yin-yüan's arrival in Japan. See the discussion in Chapter 10, "Tokugawa Hatto and the Purple Robe Affair."

20. *Ta-sui Fa-ch'en ch'an-shih yü-lu* (J. *Daizui Hosshin zenji goroku*), one fascicle, included in the *Kosonshuku goroku*, fascicle 35, ZZ, 2:23.4.

21. ZZ, 2:23.4, p. 310a. The quotation appears in the biography of Ta-sui, the *Daizui kaizan shinshō zenji*, which is appended to the *goroku*.

22. Another name for Tao-che Ch'ao-yüan (1602–1662).

23. *The Jikusen oshō goroku*, the recorded sayings of Chu-hsien Fan-hsien (1292–1348; J. Jikusen Bonsen), seven fascicles, first published in 1702, contains a section called *Jōchiji goroku*. T. 80, no. 2554.

24. The *Jikusen oshō goroku* contains references to the teachings of the master Tsai-sung. Tsai-sung is an alternate name used for the Fifth Patriarch Hung-jen (601–674; J. Gunin). It is unclear what relation he bears to the passage quoted here by Mujaku.

25. Shen-hsiu (605?–706), a Dharma heir of the Fifth Patriarch Hung-jen, was the founder of the Northern School of Zen. His Zen style came to be known as the gradual teaching, in contrast to the sudden teaching of Hui-neng's Southern School.

26. Unidentified.

27. Egoku Dōmyō (1632–1721) had been a Myōshin-ji line monk in his youth, and had practiced for a time with Tao-che before becoming Mu-an's disciple. He received *inka* from Mu-an in 1671. See Rinoie, *Obaku sanketsu Egoku Dōmyō zenji den*.

28. Tōshuku Shōha (n.d.), a Myōshin-ji line monk from the lineage of Gyokuho. Little is known of him. He inherited the Dharma from Master Dairin Shōi (n.d.), and himself had no Dharma heirs. He attained the monastic rank of *Zendō shuso* in 1722.

29. Senju-in is one of the subtemples at Myōshin-ji.

30. Ryōkei became head monk at Ryōan-ji in 1629, inheriting that position from his Dharma master Hakubo, who died that year.

31. Kyorei Ryōkaku (1600–1691) visited Yin-yüan at Kōfuku-ji and wrote a long report of conditions there. See Chapter 9 for a full translation of that letter.

32. Unidentified.

33. Bansetsu Chizen (d. 1697) was the third-generation head monk at Daiyū-in, a subtemple at Myōshin-ji, at the time of Yin-yüan's arrival in Nagasaki. At Tangetsu's urging, he went to Nagasaki and joined Yin-yüan's assembly. His initial enthusiasm for Obaku waned, and he returned to Myōshin-ji in 1659.

34. Konchi-in, located in Musashi province, was one of the temples designated by the Tokugawa bakufu to keep an official registry of Japanese monks, in this case, monks from the Gozan temples.

35. Kuze Hiroyuki (1609–1679) became daimyo after his father in 1632 and served until his death.

36. Yüan-wu K'o-ch'in (1063–1135; J. Engo Kokugon) was the fourth generation of the Yang-ch'i line of the Lin-ch'i school. He compiled the *Hekigan roku.*

37. Ta-hui Tsung-kao (1089–1163; J. Daie Sōkō) was one of Yüan-wu's Dharma heirs. He is best known for his harsh criticism of "silent illumination Zen," the style preferred by the Ts'ao-tung (Sōtō) school.

38. Wu-chun Shih-fan (1177–1249; J. Bujun or Mujun Shihan) was a descendent of the Yang-ch'i line. His line was transmitted to Japan in the thirteenth century by Enni Ben'en (1201–1280).

39. Makino Chikashige. See note 11 above.

40. Unidentified.

41. Ming-chi Ch'u-chün (1261–1336; J. Minki Soshun), a Chinese master from the Lin-chi school, who came to Japan in 1300 and became abbot at Nanzen-ji under the patronage of Emperor Godaigo.

42. *Gyōzandō geki,* a Ming period text of a hundred fascicles, composed by Chin-lung and Chiang I-k'ui and edited by Chung Shu-fu.

43. The text indicates that Ryōkei spoke in Chinese by giving the pronunciation *"hojan poiki"* with the characters.

44. The honorific title Daien Hōkan Kokushi was bestowed on Gudō in 1662, one year after his death.

45. Kazan, often referred to as Kazan-ji, is a hill near the city of Uji, southeast from Kyoto. The reference here is to Gudō's temple, Jitoku-ji, which he built in 1658. The hill was originally the site of Gankei-ji, a Heian period temple of the Tendai sect, founded by the Fujiwara family.

46. Daishun Gentei (n.d.) was from the Daiga line at Myōshin-ji. He attained the rank of *zendō* in 1669.

47. *Ta-ming kao-seng ch'uan* (J. *Daimin kōsōden*), eight fascicles, a compendium of biographies of Buddhist masters from the Ming period in China. Compiled by Ju-hsing, published in 1617 (T. 50, no. 2062). The name Hung-chiao appears twice, on pages 906b and 907b. The passage is unidentified.

48. The expression *tōtei datsu* alludes to a passage from the recorded sayings of Hsüeh-feng I-ts'un's (822–908; J. Seppō Gison), in which the experience of enlightenment is compared to the bottom falling out of a bucket.

Hsüeh-feng I-ts'un ch'an-shih yu-lu (J. *Seppō Gison Zenji goroku*), in the ZZ, 2.25.5, p. 473a.

49. Akenomiya is another name for Mitsuko Naishinnō (1624–1727), fifth child of Emperor Gomizunoo. Her Dharma name was Shōzan Genyō. She received the precepts from Ryōkei at the same time as her father, in 1665. Kao-ch'üan gave her the name Shōzan in 1681.

50. Rinkyū-ji was originally built for Emperor Gomizunoo by the Tokugawa bakufu. He then willed it to his daughter, and she resided there after his death. It is now a Rinzai Daitoku-ji line temple.

51. Kaiō Hōkō (1635–1712), was officially named as Gomizunoo's successor in 1685. Kaiō received Ryōkei's whisk and the emperor's monastic robe and was appointed abbot at Shōmyō-ji.

52. Yung-chüeh Yüan-hsien (1578–1657; J. Eigaku Genken).

53. See Chapter 3, "The Restoration of Huango-po Wan-fu-ssu."

54. Dokushō Shōen (1617–1694) was a disciple, first of Takuan and later of Isshi Monju. He inherited the temple Jikishi-an upon Isshi's death in 1646. Dokushō went to Nagasaki while Yin-yüan was still at Kōfuku-ji and became one of his attendants. He later attained enlightenment and received Yin-yüan's *inka* in 1670.

55. *Senseiin* was the name for the Yüan dynasty office governing Buddhist monks. Mujaku uses it as an alternate term for *jisha bugyō*.

56. Unidentified.

57. Enzū Dōjō (1643–1726), born in Kumano in Kii province, met Tu-chan and became his disciple sometime around 1667. He became Tu-chan's Dharma heir in 1675, at the age of thirty-three. He had seventeen Dharma heirs and was regarded as one of the leading Japanese disciples responsible for spreading the Obaku sect.

58. Sekisō Dōkō (1638–1704) became Tu-chan's Dharma heir in 1676. He practiced under Tu-chan at Hōrin-ji and later became abbot there. He followed Tu-chan to Mampuku-ji when Tu-chan served as abbot and held various high offices at the temple.

59. Shosan Hōrin-ji was founded by Tu-chan in 1664 at the order of the bakufu and with its funding.

60. Unidentified.

61. *Shan-an tsa-lu* (J. *San'an zatsuroku*), composed by the Rinzai monk Shu-chung Wu-yün (1309–1386), first appeared in 1390. Isshi Monju published an edition in 1643. ZZ, 2B:21.2.

62. ZZ, 2B:21.2, p. 170b.

63. Probably Ta-hui Tsung-kao (1089–1163; J. Daie Sōkō), the Sung monk who destroyed the woodblocks of the *Hekigan roku*, known for his strong emphasis on koan practice.

64. Unidentified.

65. Unidentified.

66. The reference is obscure. I have been unable to identify the expression *manten taiho manchi shikū*. The terms *taiho* and *shikū* refer to government posts during the Chou dynasty. The former was the senior guardian of the heir apparent and the latter the minister of works, responsible for overseeing the land and the people.

67. The *I-chiang chih* was a Sung dynasty novel about spirits and other mysterious matters, in fifty fascicles, written by Hung-mai. This fragment, which appears to be verse, is nearly illegible, and the terms used obscure. The translation is tentative at best.

68. Unidentified.

69. *Ingen zenshū*, 4:1749. The monks Kaishū, Chōso, and Danhō are unidentified.

70. Ibid., 5:2421 and 2422–2423.

71. Ibid., 6:2894–2895. Mujaku gives only the title for the latter two verses.

72. *En'nan kidan*, six fascicles, written by Tenryō Shōkū, published in 1725.

Glossary

Akishino　秋篠
Amidakyō　阿弥陀経
ango　安居
Aoki Shigekane　青木重兼
Awaokōmyō-ji　粟生光明寺

Baikoku Dōyō　梅谷道用
Bankei Yōtaku　盤珪永琢
Bansetsu Chizen　万拙知善
Batsu issaigosshō kompon tokushō
　jōdojinshu　拔一切業障根本得生
　淨土神呪
Benmeiron　辨明論
bongyō　梵行
bosatsukai　菩薩戒
Bukai nanshin　霧海南針
bukan　武鑑
Bukkoku-ha　仏国派
Butsumyōkyō　仏名経

Ch'ang-lu Tsung-tse　長蘆宗頤
Chang Ming-yüan　張明遠
Ch'an-yüan ch'ing-kuei　禅苑清規
Chao-chou　趙州
Cheng-kan　正幹
Cheng Ch'eng-kung　鄭成功

Cheng Chih-lung　鄭芝龍
Cheng-yüan Chung-t'ien　正圓中天
Chiang I-k'ui　蔣一葵
Chien-fu-ssu　建福寺
Chi-fei Ju-i　即非如一
Chih-hsien　智詵
Ch'ih-hsiu Pai-chang ch'ing-kuei
　敕修百丈清規
Chih-i　智顗
Chih-wei　智威
ch'ing-kuei　清規
Ching-té ch'uan-téng lu　景德傳燈録
Chin-lung　晉陵
Chion-in　智恩院
Chokushū Hyakujō shingi　敕修百
　丈清規
Chokushū Hyakujō shingi sae
　敕修百丈清規佐觡
Chōon Dōkai　潮音道海
Chōro Fuku　長蘆福
Chōshōge　長松下
Chōso　澄祖
Ch'uan-shou san-tan hung-chieh
　fa-i　伝授三檀弘戒法儀
Ch'u-chi　処寂
chūdō　厨堂

251

Chu-hsien Fan-hsien　竺仙梵僊

Chung-feng Ming-pen　中峰明本

Chung Shu-fu　仲舒甫

Chūshitsu Genshō　籌室玄勝

Daien Hōkan Kokushi　大円宝鑑
国師

daifu jiken　代付事件

daifu ronsō　代付論爭

daiga　大雅

Daigu Sōchiku　大愚宗築

Daihō-san Hōun-ji　大宝山法雲寺

Dajōdaijin　大政大臣

Daijō-ji　大乘寺

Daikō fushō kokushi　大光普照
国師

daimin kōsō den　大明高僧傳

daimyo　大名

Daisen-ji　大仙寺

Daishun Gentei　大春元貞

Daishūshōtō Zenji　大宗正統禪師

Daitoku-ji　大德寺

Daiyūhōden　大雄宝殿

Daiyū-in　大雄院

Daizuiroku　大隨録

Daizui kaizan shinshō zenji gyōjō
大隨開山神照禪師行状

Danhō　団法

danka seido　檀家制度

Denju sandan gukai hōgi　伝授三檀
弘戒法儀

Dōchū　道忠

dōjō　道場

Dokuan Genkō　独庵玄光

Dokuchi　独知

Dokuhon Shōgen　独本性源

Dokushin Shōkū　独真性空

Dokushō Shōen　独照性圓

Dokutan Shōkei　独湛性瑩

Dōsha Chōgen　道者超元

Egoku Dōmyō　慧極道明

Eigaku Genken　永覚元賢

Eihei shingi　永平清規

Eisai　榮西

Emon Nyohai　慧門如沛

Enjō Dōkaku Hōō　円淨道覚法皇

Enkōin　圓光院殿

Enkyō matsujichō　延享末寺帳

En'nan kidan kōshū　燕南紀談后集

Enni Ben'en　圓爾辯圓

Enzū Dōjō　円通道成

Eppō Dōshō　悦峰道章

Erin Shōki　慧林性機

Etsuden Dōfu　越伝道付

Fa-chih　法持

Fei-yin T'ung-jung　費隱通容

fucha ryōri　布茶料理

fuju　諷誦

Fukuju-ji　福聚寺

Fukuma Takayasa　福間隆廉

Fukusai-ji　福濟寺

Fumon-ji　普門寺

furigana　振り仮名

fushin　普請

Gankei-ji　元慶寺

garan-dō　伽藍堂

ge　下

gege jōdō　解夏上堂

Gentei Daishun　元貞大春

Gesshū Sōko　月舟宗胡

Godaigo　後醍醐

gokai 五戒

Gokōmyō 後光明

Gomizunoo 御水尾

goroku 語録

Gosai 後西

Goyōzei 御陽成

gozan 五山

Gudō Tōshoku 愚堂東寔

Gukai hōgi 弘戒法儀

Gukai no nittan 弘戒日單

gyōdō 行道

Gyokuho 玉浦

Gyokushitsu Sōhaku 玉室宗珀

Gyōzandō geki 堯山堂外紀

haibutsu kishaku 廃仏毀釈

hakkai 八戒

Hakubu Eryō 伯蒲慧稜 or 伯蒲
慧陵

Hanazono no matsuyō mumyōshi
花園末葉無名子

Hanju zammaikyō 般舟三昧教

Han-shan Te-ch'ing 寒山德清

hatto 法度

Hekigan roku 碧巖録

hekigo 碧後

hekiso 壁書

hekizen 碧前

Hiin Tsūyō 費隱通容

hikken sammai 筆硯三昧

hō 梛

hōdō 法堂

hōdō 法幢

hōgo 法語

hōhon 報本

Hojan poiki 和尚迴去

hōjō 方丈

Hōjōchi 放生池

hōjō gishiki 放生儀式

hōki 法諱

hōkō 法香

Hōnen 法然

honmatsu seido 本末制度

Hōrin-san Shōmyō-ji 法輪山正
明寺

hossu 拂子

Hōu 葆雨

Hsing-shou Chien-yüan 興寿鑑源

Hsing-tz'u Ching-yüan 興慈鏡源

Hsin-yueh Hsing-ch'ou 興儔心越

Hsüeh-feng I-ts'un 雪峰義存

Hsüeh-feng I-ts'un ch'an-shih yu-lu
雪峰義存禅師語録

Huang-po Hsi-yün 黄檗希運

Huang-po-shan 黄檗山

*Hua-yen ching hsing-yüan p'in shu-
ch'ao* 華嚴經行願品疏鈔

Hui-lin Hsing-chi 慧林性機

Hui-men Ju-p'ei 慧門如沛

Hui-neng 慧能

Hung-chieh-fa-i 弘戒法儀

Hung-jen 弘忍

Hung-mai 洪邁

Hyakujō Ekai 百丈懷海

Hyakujō shingi 百丈清規

Hyakujō shingi sakei 百丈清規
佐觽

Hyōjōsho 評定所

Ichimyō Dōgen 一明道源

I-jan Hsing-jung 逸然性融

Ingen fusōroku 隱元扶桑録

Ingen Ryūki 隱元隆

in'inekishi 因院易嗣

inka 印可

ishin denshin 以心傳心

isshi inshō 一師印證

Isshi Monju 一絲文守

Itakura Katsushige 板倉勝重

Itakura Shigemune 板倉重宗

Itchū Tōmoku 一宙東默

Itō Jinsai 伊藤仁斎

Itsunen Shōyū 逸然性融

jiin hatto 寺院法度

jikai Zen 持戒禅

Jikei-ji 慈溪寺

Jikishi-an 直指庵

Jikuin Somon 竺印祖門

Jikusen oshō goroku 竺仙和尚
語録

Jikusen oshō jōchiroku 竺仙和尚
淨智録

jiriki 自力

jisha 侍者

Jitoku-ji 慈德寺

Jitsuden Dōkin 実伝道鈞

Jiun-san 慈雲山

Jōchiji goroku 淨智寺語録

Jōke-in 淨花院

Ju-chung jih-yung ch'ing-kuei
入衆日用清規

Ju-hsing 如惺

jūji 住持

jūjūkai shijūhachikyōkai 十重戒四
十八軽戒

kaidan 戒壇

kaigen 開眼

kaihō 戒法

Kaiō Hōkō 晦翁宝曇

kaisei 解制

kaisetsu 解説

Kaishū 戒周

kaizan 開山

Kambun-tei 寛文帝

kana hōgo 假名法語

kanchō 管長

Kan'ei no shoshū honjichō 寛永
の諸宗本寺帳

Kangakuya 勧学屋

Kanmuryōjukyō 観無量寿経

kanrinbō 寒林榜

Kanzan Egen 關山慧玄

Kanzan Tokusei 寒山德清

Kao-ch'üan Hsing-tung 高泉性潡

Kazan 花山

Keirin Sūshin 桂林崇琛

Keitoku dentōroku 景德傳燈録

Keizan Jōkin 瑩山紹瑾

Keizan shingi 瑩山清規

Keizui-ji 慶瑞寺

Kengan Zen'etsu 賢巖禪悦

Keng-hsin Hsing-mi 亘信行弥

Kenju-ji 獻珠寺

Kenpō hongi 憲法本紀

kenshō jōbutsu 見性成佛

kessei 結制

ketsuge jōdō 結夏上堂

kinhin 經行

Kinsei Obakushū matsujichō shūsei
近世黄檗宗末寺帳集成

Kintaien 錦袋園

koan 公案

Kōdō Genchō 杲堂元昶

Kōfuku-ji 廣福寺

Kōgetsu Sōgan 江月宗玩

korō 鼓楼

Kōsen Shōton 高泉性潡

koshin no mida 己心弥陀

Kosonshuku goroku 古尊宿語録

Kuan-ti 関帝

Kuan-yü 関羽

kūin 空印

kun 訓

Kurokawa Masanao 黒川正直

Kuze Hiroyuki 久世廣之

kusu 庫司

Kyōge betsuden 教外別伝

Kyorei Ryōkaku 虚櫺了廓

li 理

Lin-chi I-hsuan 臨済義玄

Lin-chi cheng-ch'uan 臨済正伝

Lin-chi chēng-tsung 臨済正宗

Makino Chikashige 牧野親成

Mampuku-ji 萬福寺

Manjuha 萬寿派

manten taiho manchi shikū 満天太保満地司空

Manzan Dōhaku 卍山道白

mappō 末法

Maso 媽祖

Ma-tsu 媽祖

Matsudaira Nobutsuna 老中松平信綱

Ma-tsu Tao-i 馬祖道一

meishō 明正

Menzan Zuihō 面山瑞方

Ming-chi Ch'u-chün 明極楚俊

Mitsuko Naishinnō 光子内親王

Mitsuun Engo 密雲圓悟

Mi-yun Yüan-wu 密雲圓悟

Mokuan Shōtō 木庵性瑫

mokugyo 木魚

mokushōzen 默照禪

mondō 問答

mōsu 帽予

Mu-an Hsing-t'ao 木庵性瑫

Mujaku Dōchū 無著道忠

Mumon Genshin 無門原真

Mumonkan 無門関

Muryōjukyō 無量寿経

Musang 無相

musōkai 無相戒

musō shinchi kai 無相心地戒

Musō Soseki 夢窓疎石

Mutoku Ryōgo 無得良悟

Myōshin-ji 妙心寺

namu 南無

Nan-yüan Hsing-p'ai 南源性派

Nanzan 南山

nembutsu 念仏

nempu 年譜

Nichimen butsu gatsumen butsu 日面佛月面佛

Nihei 仁兵衛

Nyusshu nichiyō shingi 入衆日用清規

Obakuban Daizōkyō 黄檗版大藏經

Obaku bonbai 黄檗梵唄

Obaku geki 黄檗外記

Obaku-ha 黄檗派

Obaku-san 黄檗山

Obaku shingi 黄檗清規

Obaku shōmyō 黄檗声明

Obaku-shū 黄檗宗

Obakushū kanroku 黄檗宗鑑録

Obaku Tetsugen Issaikyō　黃檗鐵眼
　一切經

Ogyū Sorai　荻生徂徠

Ojōju　往生咒

Okamura Seiichirō　奥村清一郎

Omura Suminaga　大村純長

on　音

on　恩

Ou-i Chih-hsu　蕅益智旭

Orategama zokushū　遠羅天釜
　續集

Pai-chang ch'ing-kuei　百丈清規

Pai-chang Huai-hai　百丈懷海

Pai-chi Yüan-kung　百癡願公

Po-jo-t'ang　般若堂

Po-tzu T'ing　柏子底

raihō　禮法

Ran'ō　懶翁

Reiki-san Kyūshin-in　靈亀山九
　島院

Rinkyū-ji　林丘寺

Rinsen kakun　臨川家訓

Rinzai Gigen　臨済義玄

Rinzai roku　臨済録

Rinzai shōden　臨済正伝

Rinzai-shōshū　臨済正宗

rissō hinpotsu　立僧秉拂

ritsu　律

rōjū　老中

Ryōan-ji　龍安寺

Ryōen　良演

Ryōga-kyō　楞伽經

Ryōge-in　龍華院

Ryōkei Shōsen　龍溪性潜

Ryōō Dōkaku　了翁道覚

Ryūge-in　龍華院

Ryūhō-ji　龍峰寺

Ryūkōge　龍興下

Saeki　佐伯

saidō　齋堂

Saigin　西吟

Sakai Tadakatsu　酒井忠勝

sakoku　鎖国

sandan kaie　三壇戒会

San-feng Fa-ts'ang　三峰法藏

sankyō itchi　三教一致

Sanzen nembutsu shiryōken ge
　参禅念仏四料揀偈

segaki　施餓鬼

seidō　西堂

Sekisō Dōkō　石窓道鏗

Sekkan　雪関

Sendai kuji daiseikyō　先代旧事大
　成経

Senge　遷化

Senju-in　仙寿院

Sennyū-ji　泉涌寺

Senseiin　宣政院

Senzan　千山

Setsujo　節序

*Settsu Jiun-san Fumon Fukugen-ji
　roku*　摂州慈雲山普門福元寺録

shami jikkai　沙弥十戒

Shan-an tsa-lu　山奄雑録

Shan-tao　善導

shariden　舍利殿

shasō　社僧

Shen-hsiu　神秀

shibun ritsu　四分律

shichirei hachiraku　七零八落

shie jiken　紫衣事件

shih 事

shihōkō 嗣法香

shinbutsu bunri 神仏分離

shingi 清規

Shinran 親鸞

Shishirinha 獅子林派

Shiun-ha 紫雲派

Shōbō genzō shōtenroku 正法眼藏
渉典録

Shōbō Tekiden Shishi Ikkushū
正法嫡伝獅子一吼集

Shōfuku-ji 聖福寺

shōgyōdō 省行堂

shoin 書院

Shōin-dō 松隠堂

Shōjurin shingi 椙樹林清規

shoki 書記

Shōmyō-ji 正明寺

Shōringe 聖林下

shōrō 鐘楼

Shōsan Hōrin-ji 初山宝林寺

shōsejiki 小施食

shoshidai 所司代

Shōtoku Taishi 聖德太子

Shōzan Genyō 照山元瑶

shū 宗

Shu-chung Wu-yün 恕中無愠

Shūhō Myōchō 宗峰妙超

Shukuri 祝釐

shukutetsu 叔姪

Shūmon shōtōroku 宗門正燈禄

Shunkō-in 春光院

shuso 首座

Shūtō fukko shi 宗統復古志

Shūtōroku 宗統録

Sōchi 宗知

sōdō 僧堂

Sōdō shingi gyōhōshō 僧堂清規行
法鈔

Sōdō shingi kōtei betsuroku 僧堂
清規考訂別録

Sōfuku-ji 崇福寺

Sōkyū 宗休

Sokuhi Nyoitsu 即非如一

sonso 尊祖

Sōtō 曹洞

Ssu-fen lu 四分律

Suzuki Shōsan 鈴木正三

Tai-hsiu 大休

Ta-hui Tsung-kao 大慧宗杲

Taishi kuji hongi 太子旧事本紀

Taizō-in 退藏院

Takaya Shintarō 鷹屋新太郎

Takkyakumon 答客問

Takuan Sōhō 澤庵宗彭

Tangetsu Shōen 湛月紹円

Tannen Dōjaku 湛然道寂

Tanzan Shōshō 端山性正

Tao-che Ch'ao-yüan 道者超元

Tao-hsin 道信

tariki 他力

Ta-sui Fa-ch'en ch'an-shih yü-lu
大隨法真禅師語録

Teijū Ezen 提宗慧全

Tei Seikō 鄭成功

teisetsu 定説

Teishū 鼎宗

teizen hakuju 底前柏樹

Tennōden 天王殿

Tenryō Shōkū 天嶺性空

Tesshin Dōin 鉄心道印

Tetsugen-ban 鉄眼版

Tetsugen Dōkō 鉄眼道光

Tetsugyū Dōki 鉄牛道機   Wu-hsin Hsing-chien 無心性覚
tōdō 東堂   Wu-teng yen-t'ung 五燈嚴統
Tōji-in 等持院

Tokugan Yuie 得巖惟慧   *Yabukōji* 薮柑子
Tokugawa Hidetada 德川秀忠   *yakuseki* 藥石
Tokugawa Iemitsu 德川家光   Yang-ch'i 楊岐
Tokugawa Ieyasu 德川家康   Yaran Shōkei 也嬾性圭
Tokuō Myōkō 禿翁妙宏   Yeh-lan Hsing-kue 也嬾性圭
Tokuō Ryōkō 德翁良高   Yin-yüan Lung-ch'i 隱元隆琦
Tōshuku Shōha 東叔紹坡   *yokudō* 浴堂
tōtei datsu 桶底脱   *Yoshokugo* 予嘱語
Tōyō Eichō 東陽英朝   Yüan-wu K'o-ch'in 圜悟克勤
tōzai no hōjō 東西の方丈   Yüeh-feng Tao-chang 悦峰道章
Tsai-sung 栽松   Yuie Dōjō 惟慧道定
Ts'ao-tung 曹洞   *yuishin jōdo* 唯心淨土
Tsuda Michishige 津田道茂   Yun-ch'i Chu-hung 雲棲袾宏
tsung 宗   Yung-chüeh Yüan-hsien 永覚元賢
Tsung-mi 宗密   Yung-ming Yen-shou 永明延寿
Tu-chan Hsing-jung 獨湛性瑩
Tu-chi 独痴   *zendō* 前堂
Tu-wang Hsing-yu 独往性幽   *zendō* 禅堂
Tzu-po Chen-k'o 達観真可   *zenkyō itchi* 禪教一致
                             Zennen shingi 禅苑清規
Undō jōki 雲堂常規   *Zen'on shingi* 禅苑清規
Ungo Kiyō 雲居希膺   Zenrin-ji 禅林寺
Unsei Shukō 雲棲袾宏   *Zenrin shūhei shū* 禪林執弊集
Unzan Guhaku 雲山愚白   *Zenshū* 禅宗
                             Zoku zenrin shūhei shū 續禪林執
Wan-fu-ssu 万福寺   弊集
Wu-chun Shih-fan 無準師範   Zuiryū-ji 瑞龍寺

Bibliography

Addiss, Stephen. *Obaku: Zen Painting and Calligraphy.* Lawrence, Kans.: Helen Foresman Spencer Museum of Art, 1978.

Akamatsu Shinmyō. "Obakushū kōyō." In *Bukkyō daigaku kōza*, vol. 5. Tokyo: Bukkyō nenkansha, 1934.

———. *Tetsugen zenji.* Tokyo: Kōbundō shobō, 1942.

———. *Tetsugen.* Tokyo: Yūzankaku, 1943.

———. "Obaku no shinpū." *Daihōrin* 24, no. 5 (1957): 76–78.

———. "Tetsugen to Issaikyōhan." In *Zen bunka*, no. 18 (March 1960), pp. 56–64.

———, ed. *Tetsugen zenji kana hōgo.* Tokyo: Iwanami shoten, 1989. Reprint of 1941 edition.

Akao Ryūji, ed. *Bankei zenji zenshū.* Tokyo: Daizō shuppan, 1970.

Ashikaga Zuigi. *Ryūkoku daigaku sanbyakunen shi.* Kyoto: Ryūkoku daigaku shuppanbu, 1939.

Ban Kōkei. *Kinsei kijinden.* Vol. 2. Kyoto: Hishiya Magobe, 1790.

———. *Sentetsu zō den, Kinsei kijin den, Hyakka kikō den.* Tokyo: Yūhōdō bunko, 1927.

———. *Kinsei kijin den.* Tokyo: Iwanami shoten, 1940.

Baroni, Helen J. "Buddhism in Early Tokugawa Japan: The Case of Obaku Zen and the Monk Tetsugen Dōkō." Ph.D. diss., Columbia University, 1993.

———. "Bottled Anger: Episodes in Obaku Conflict in the Tokugawa Period." *Japanese Journal of Religious Studies* 21, nos. 2–3 (June–September 1994): 191–210.

Beckford, James A. *Cult Controversies: The Societal Response to New Religious Movements.* London: Tavistock Publications, 1985.

Bellah, Robert. *Tokugawa Religion: The Cultural Roots of Modern Japan.* New York: The Free Press, 1985.

Berling, Judith A. *The Syncretic Religion of Lin Chao-en.* New York: Columbia University Press, 1980.

Bielefeldt, Carl. *Dōgen's Manuals of Zen Meditation*. Berkeley: University of California Press, 1988.

———. "Ch'ang-lu Tsung-tse's *Tso-ch'an I* and the Secret of Zen Meditation." In *Traditions of Meditation in Chinese Buddhism*, ed. Peter N. Gregory, pp. 129–161. Honolulu: University of Hawai'i Press, 1986.

Blacker, Carmen. *The Catalpa Bow: A Study of Shamanistic Practices in Japan*. London: George Allen & Unwin, 1982.

Bloom, Alfred. *Shinran's Gospel of Pure Grace*. Tucson: The University of Arizona Press, 1985.

Bodiford, William M. *"The Growth of the Sōtō Zen Tradition in Medieval Japan."* 2 vols. Ph.D. diss., Yale University, 1989.

———. "Dharma Transmission in Sōtō Zen: Manzan Dōhaku's Reform Movement." *Monumenta Nipponica* 46, no. 4 (Winter 1991): 423–451.

———. *Sōtō Zen in Medieval Japan*. Studies in East Asian Buddhism 8. Honolulu: University of Hawai'i Press, 1993.

Bromeley, David G., and Phillip E. Hammond, eds. *The Future of New Religious Movements*. Macon, Ga.: Mercer University Press, 1987.

Chan, Wing-tsit, trans. *Reflections on Things at Hand: The Neo-Confucian Anthology*. New York: Columbia University Press, 1967.

Chang, Garma C. C. *The Buddhist Teaching of Totality*. University Park: Pennsylvania State University Press, 1971.

Chang Sheng-yen. *Minmatsu Chūgoku bukkyō no kenkyū—toku ni Chigyoku o chūshin to shite*. Tokyo: Sankibō busshorin, 1975.

Chappell, David W. "From Dispute to Dual Cultivation: Pure Land Responses to Ch'an Critics." In *Traditions of Meditation in Chinese Buddhism*, ed., Peter N. Gregory. pp. 163–197. Honolulu: University of Hawai'i Press, 1986.

Ch'en, Kenneth. *Buddhism in China: A Historical Survey*. Princeton, N.J.: Princeton University Press, 1964.

Collcutt, Martin. *Five Mountains: The Rinzai Zen Monastic Institution in Medieval Japan*. Cambidge, Mass.: Council on East Asian Studies, Harvard University, 1981.

———. "Buddhism: The Threat of Eradication." In *Japan in Transition from Tokugawa to Meiji*, ed. Marius B. Jansen and Gilbert Rozman, pp. 143–167. Princeton, N.J.: Princeton University Press, 1986.

Conze, Edward. *Buddhist Scriptures*. Middlesex, Eng.: Penguin Books, 1959.

———. *Buddhist Wisdom Books: The Diamond and the Heart Sutra*. London: Unwin Hyman, 1988.

Dai nihon bukkyō zensho. Ed. Suzuki Gakujutsu. 100 vols. Tokyo: Kodansha, 1970–1974.

Date Mitsuyoshi. *Nihon shūkyō seido shiryō ruishūkō*. Tokyo: Ganshōdō shoten, 1930.

David L. Davis. "*Ikki* in Late Medieval Japan." In *Medieval Japan: Essays in Institutional History,* ed. John W. Hall and Jeffrey P. Mass. Stanford, Calif.: Stanford University Press, 1974.

Dōkei and Ouchi Seiran. *Zoku nihon kōsō den. Dai nihon bukkyō zensho* 64, no. 473 (1970–1973): 1–98.

Dore, R. P. *Education in Tokugawa Japan.* London: The Athlone Press, 1984.

Dumoulin, Heinrich. *A History of Zen Buddhism.* Trans. Paul Peachey. New York: Pantheon Books, 1963.

———. *Zen Buddhism: A History.* Vol. 1, *India and China.* New York: Macmillan Publishing Company, 1988.

———. *Zen Buddhism: A History.* Vol. 2, *Japan.* New York: Macmillan Publishing Company, 1990.

Fan Hui. "Ingen zenji to chūnichi ryō Obakusan no yurai," trans. Nishio Kenryū. *Zengaku kenkyū* 61 (1982): 118–123.

Foccardi, Gabriele. *The Last Warrior: The Life of Cheng Ch'eng-kung The Lord of the "Terrace Bay," a Study on the T'ai-wan wai chih by Chiang Jih-sheng (1704).* Wiesbaden: Otto Harrassowitz, 1986.

Foulk, Theodore Griffith. "The 'Chan School' and Its Place in the Buddhist Monastic Tradition." Ph.D. diss., University of Michigan, 1987.

———. "The Ch'an Tsung in Medieval China: School, Lineage or What?" *The Pacific World,* no. 8 (Fall 1992): 18–31.

Fuji Masaharu and Abe Zenryō. *Koji junrei Kyōto,* vol. 9: *Mampukuji.* Kyoto: Tankōsha, 1977.

Fujiyoshi Jikai, ed. *Zen to nembutsu: Sono gendaiteki igi.* Tokyo: Daizō shuppan, 1983.

———. *Zen to Jōdokyō.* Tokyo: Kodansha, 1989.

Funaoka Makoto. *Takuan.* Tokyo: Chūō kōronsha, 1988.

Furuichi Katsuzen, ed. *Gomizunoo tenno to Obaku.* Uji, Japan: Tōrin-in, 1929.

Furuta Shōkin. *Zenshū kana hōgo.* Tokyo: Daizō shuppan, 1980.

———. "Dōsha Chōgen no raichō to sono eikyō." In *Furuta Shōkin chosakushū,* 2:343–365. Tokyo: Kodansha, 1981.

———. "Chōon Dōkai no Rinzai/Sōtō zen hihan." In *Furuta Shōkin chosakushū,* 2:412–424. Tokyo: Kodansha, 1981.

———. *Furuta Shōkin chosakushū.* 14 vols. Tokyo: Kodansha, 1981.

———. *Kinsei no zensha-tachi.* Tokyo: Kodansha, 1981.

———. "Tetsugen Dōkō o shinobu." *Daihōrin* 53, no. 5 (May 1986): 62–67.

Galanter, Marc. *Cults, Faith, Healing, and Coercion.* Oxford: Oxford University Press, 1989.

Gregory, Peter N., ed. *Traditions of Meditation in Chinese Buddhism.* Honolulu: University of Hawai'i Press, 1986.

Groner, Paul. "Saichō and the Bodhisattva Precepts." 2 vols. Ph.D. diss., Yale University, 1979.

————. *Saichō: The Establishment of the Japanese Tendai School.* Berkeley, Calif.: Institute of Buddhist Studies, 1984.

Harrington, Ann M. *Japan's Hidden Christians.* Chicago: Loyola University Press, 1993.

Hasabe Yūkei. "Min Shin jidai ni okeru zenritsu ryōshū kōka no dōkō." *Zen kenkyūsho kiyō* 20 (1991): 83–203.

Hashimoto Hiroshi. *Kaitei zōho Daibukan.* 3 vols. Tokyo: Meicho Kankokai, 1965. (Reprint of 1940 edition.)

Haskel, Peter. *Bankei Zen: Translations from the Record of Bankei.* Ed. Yoshita Hakeda. New York: Grove Press, 1984.

Hattori Eijun. "Zenjō yūgō shisō ni okeru jōdo no kaimei." *Bukkyō daigaku* 50 (September 1966): 83–91.

Hattori Fumio. "Ingen to Obaku jiin." *Gekkan bunka zai* 163 (1977): 4–13.

Hayashi Bunshō. "Obaku o kataru." In *Obaku kenkyū shiryō,* no. 2, pp. 1–23. Kyoto: Obakushū shūmu hōin, n.d.

Heng-ching Shih. "The Syncretism of Chinese Ch'an and Pure Land Buddhism." In *Buddhist Thought and Ritual,* ed. David Kalupahana, pp. 69–84. New York: Paragon House Publishers, 1991.

Hirada Hiromichi. "Chūsei zenshū to nembutsu zen." *Indogaku bukkyōgaku kenkyū* 31, no. 2 (1983): 61–65.

Hirakubo Akira. *Ingen.* Tokyo: Yoshikawa kōbunkan, 1962.

————. "Edo jidai ni okeru Mampukuji no shūrishi ni tsuite." *Kinsei bukkyō: shiryō to kenkyū* 3, no. 1 (November 1963): 1–11.

————. *Ingen zenshū.* 12 vols. Tokyo: Kaimyō shoin, 1979.

————. "Mokuan zenshū no henshū ni tsuite." *Obaku bunka,* no. 67 (January 1983): 1–2.

Hirano Sōjō. *Ungo oshō nempu.* Kinsei zensōden, no. 3. Kyoto: Shibunkaku shuppan, 1983.

————. "Rinzai zen to nembutsu." In *Zen to nembutsu: Sono gendaiteki igi,* pp. 77–94. Tokyo: Daizō shuppan, 1983.

————. *Mokuan zenshū.* 8 vols. Tokyo: Kaimyō shoin, 1992.

————. *Sokuhi zenshū.* 4 vols. Tokyo: Kaimyō shoin, 1993.

Hsu, Sung-peng. *A Buddhist Leader in Ming China: The Life and Thought of Han-shan Te-ch'ing.* University Park: The Pennsylvania State University Press, 1979.

Iida Rigyō. *Gakusei Mujaku Dōchū.* Kyoto: Zen bunka kenkyūsho, 1986.

"Ingen zenji no yuisho mokuroku." *Zenshū* 264 (1917): 21–25.

Ishida Seisai. *Tetsugen to Hōshū.* Osaka: Ishida bunkō, 1922.

Itō Kokan. "Gudō kokushi no zen." *Zengaku kenkyū* 49 (Feb. 20, 1959): 1–22.

————. *Nihon zen no shōtō Gudō.* Tokyo: Shunjūsha, 1969.

Jansen, Marius B. *China in the Tokugawa World.* Cambridge, Mass.: Harvard University Press, 1992.

Jansen, Marius B., and Gilbert Rozman, eds. *Japan in Transition from Tokugawa to Meiji.* Princeton, N.J.: Princeton University Press, 1986.

Japanese Religion: A Survey by the Agency for Cultural Affairs. Tokyo: Kodansha, 1972.

Jōetsu Kyōiku Daigaku shozō Obaku Tetsugenban Issaikyō Mokuroku. Jōetsu-shi, Japan: Jōetsu kyōiku daigaku fuzoku toshokan, 1988.

Jorgensen, John. "The 'Imperial' Lineage of Ch'an Buddhism: The Role of Confucian Ritual and Ancestor Worship in Ch'an's Search for Legitimation in the Mid-T'ang Dynasty." *Papers in Far Eastern History* 35 (1987): 89–133.

Kagamishima Genryū. *Manzan/Menzan.* Nihon no zen goroku, 18. Tokyo: Kodansha, 1978.

Kagamishima Genryū, Satō Tatsugen, and Kosaka Kiyū. *Yakuchū Zen'en shingi.* Tokyo: Sōtōshū shūmuchō, 1972.

Kalupahana, David, ed. *Buddhist Thought and Ritual.* New York: Paragon House Publishers, 1991.

Kasahara Kazuo. *Ikkō ikki no kenkyū.* Tokyo: Yamakawa shuppan, 1962.

———. *Ikkō ikki—sono kōdō to shisō.* Tokyo: Hyōronsha, 1970.

Kawakami Kozan. *Myōshinjishi.* Kyoto: Shinbunkaku, 1984.

Keene, Donald. *The Battles of Coxinga.* London: Taylor's Foreign Press, 1951.

Ketelaar, James Edward. *Of Heretics and Martyrs in Meiji Japan: Buddhism and Its Persecution.* Princeton, N.J.: Princeton University Press, 1990.

King, Winston L. *Death Was His Koan: The Samurai Zen of Suzuki Shōsan.* Berkeley, Calif.: Asian Humanities Press, 1986.

Kishimoto Hideo. *Japanese Religion in the Meiji Era.* Trans. and ed. John F. Howes. Tokyo: Ōbunsha, 1956.

Kitagawa, Joseph M. *Religion in Japanese History.* New York: Columbia University Press, 1966.

Kitagawa, Joseph M., and Mark D. Cummings, eds. *Buddhism and Asian History.* New York: Macmillan Publishing Company, 1989.

Kōchi Eigaku. "Chūgoku ni okeru zenjō kankei." *Komazawa daigaku bukkyō gakubu kenkyū kiyō* 30 (March 1972): 1–6.

Kumakura Isao. *Gomizunooin.* Tokyo: Asahi Shinbunsha, 1982.

Kurabayashi Kando. "Gesshu no Undō jōki to *Obaku shingi.*" *Indogaku bukkyōgaku kenkyū* 5, no. 1 (1957): 108–109.

Mano Shōjun. *Bukkyō ni okeru shū kannen no seiritsu.* Tokyo: Risōsha, 1964.

Maruyama Masao. *Studies in the Intellectual History of Tokugawa Japan.* Trans. Mikiso Hane. Tokyo: University of Tokyo Press and Princeton University Press, 1974.

Matsui Shōten. "Sōtōshū to shoki Obaku to no kōshō." *Indogaku bukkyōgaku kenkyū* 15, no. 1 (1966): 324–326.

Matsunaga Chikai. "*Obakuban* daizōkyō no saihyōka." *Bukkyō shigaku kenkyū* 4, no. 2 (October 1991): 132–162.

Matsunaga, Daigan, and Alicia Matsunaga. *Foundation of Japanese Buddhism.* Vols. 1 and 2. Los Angeles: Buddhist Books International, 1974 and 1976.

McMullin, Neil. *Buddhism and the State in Sixteenth-Century Japan.* Princeton, N.J.: Princeton University Press, 1984.

McRae, John R. *The Northern School and the Formation of Early Ch'an Buddhism.* Honolulu: University of Hawai'i Press, 1986.

Miura, Isshu, and Ruth Fuller Sasaki. *Zen Dust.* New York: Harcourt, Brace & World, 1966.

Minamoto Ryōen. *Tetsugen.* Nihon no zen goroku, vol. 17. Tokyo: Kodansha, 1979.

———. *Tetsugen kanaji hōgo.* Zen no koten, vol. 9. Tokyo: Kodansha, 1982.

Mochizuki Shinkō. *Chūgoku jōdo kyōrishi.* Kyoto: Hōzōkan, 1964.

Morimoto Sangai. "Ryōō." *Zen bunka,* no. 18 (March 1960): 45–50.

———. "Obaku no nembutsu zen." *Zen bunka,* no. 18 (March 1960): 76–78.

Moriya Katsuhisa. "Urban Networks and Information Networks." In Chie Nakane and Shinzaburō Oishi, *Tokugawa Japan: The Social and Economic Antecedents of Modern Japan,* ed. Conrad Totman, pp. 97–123. Tokyo: University of Tokyo Press, 1990.

Mote, Frederick W., and Denis Twitchett, eds. *The Cambridge History of China.* Vol. 7, *The Ming Dynasty, 1368–1644, Part I.* Cambridge: Cambridge University Press, 1988.

Mujaku Dōchū. "Obaku geki." Manuscript. N.d.

Murai Sanae. "Shie jikengo no chōbaku kankei." *Kinsei bukkyō: shiryō to kenkyū* 6, no. 1 (March 1983): 1–11.

Nagai Masano. "Minmatsu ni ikita zenshatachi—Hiin Tsūyō ni yoru Gotō gentō no seiritsu." *Shūkyōgaku ronshū* 9 (1978–1979): 329–343.

Nakai, Kate Wildman. *Shogunal Politics: Arai Hakuseki and the Premises of Tokugawa Rule.* Cambridge, Mass.: Council on East Asian Studies, Harvard University, 1988.

Nakamura Shū sei. "Mokuan zenji to sono wasō shihōsha." *Obaku bunka,* no. 67 (January 1983): 11–13.

Nakane, Chie, and Shinzaburō Oishi. *Tokugawa Japan: The Social and Economic Antecedents of Modern Japan.* Ed. Conrad Totman. Tokyo: University of Tokyo Press, 1990.

Nakao Fumio. *Gomizunoo hōō to Obakushū.* Uji, Japan: Obaku-san Mampuku-ji, 1979.

———. "Obakushū to wa." In *Obaku kenkyū shiryō,* no. 2, pp. 30–33. Kyoto: Obakushū shūmu hōin, n.d.

Nihon kyōkasho taikei, kindaihen, vols. 7 and 8 *(kokugo).* Ed. Kaigo Tokiomi. Tokyo: Kodansha, 1963.

Nishio Kenryū. "Obaku kankei zasshi ronbun mokuroku." *Zengaku kenkyū* 61 (1982): 10–12.

Nosco, Peter, ed. *Confucianism and Tokugawa Culture.* Princeton, N.J.: Princeton University Press, 1984.

Obakushū kanroku. Woodblock edition. 2 fascicles. 1693.

Obaku Mokuan oshō nempu. Woodblock edition. 2 fascicles. Kyoto: Inbōsho, 1695.

Ogisu Jundō. "Ingen zenji to Obakusan." *Zen bunka,* no. 18 (March 1960): 9–21.

———. "Meiji jidai no zenshū." *Zen bunka,* no. 47 (January 1968): 30–39.

———. *Myōshinji.* Jisha shirizu, 2. Kyoto: Tōyōbunkasha, 1977.

———. *Zenshūshi no sansaku.* Kyoto: Shibunkaku shuppan, 1981.

Oishi Morio. "*Obaku shingi* no kenkyū." *Zengaku kenkyū* 41 (1959): 142–149.

Onda Akira. "Zen to nembutsu no shinrigakuteki hikaku kōsatsu." *Indogaku bukkyōgaku kenkyū* 23, no. 1 (1974): 1–7.

Ooms, Herman. *Tokugawa Ideology: Early Constructs, 1570–1680.* Princeton, N.J.: Princeton University Press, 1985.

Ōtsuki Mikio. "Obakushū." *Obaku kenkyū shiryō,* no. 2, pp. 34–41. Kyoto: Obakushu shūmu hōin, n.d.

Ōtsuki Mikio, Katō Shōshun, and Hayashi Yukimitsu. *Obaku bunka jinmei jiten.* Kyoto: Shinbunkaku Shuppan, 1988.

Ri Kenshō. "Nagasaki santōji no seiritsu." *Kinsei bukkyō: shiryō to kenkyū* 3, no. 1 (October 1963): 73–90.

Rinoie Masafumi. *Obaku sanketsu Egoku Dōmyō zenji den.* Tokyo: Daizō shuppan, 1981.

Robinson, Richard H., and Willard L. Johnson. *The Buddhist Religion: A Historical Introduction.* 3d ed. Belmont, Calif.: Wadsworth Publishing Company, 1982.

Said, Edward W. *Beginnings: Intention and Method.* New York: Basic Books, 1975.

Sasaki Gōzo. *Mampukuji.* Tokyo: Chūō koron bijutsu shuppan, 1964.

Satō Tatsugen. "Obakushū." In *Nihon no shūkyō,* vol. 3, ed. Takachiho Tetsujō, pp. 121–162. Tokyo: Hōbunkan shuppan, 1962.

Saunders, Dale E. *Buddhism in Japan.* Westport, Conn.: Greenwood Press, 1964.

Schwaller, Dieter. *Der japanische Obaku-Mönch Tetsugen Dōkō: Leben, Denken, Schriften.* Bern: Peter Lang, 1989.

Sekida, Katsuki. *Two Zen Classics: Mumonkan and Hekiganroku.* Ed. A. V. Grimstone. New York: Weatherhill, 1977.

Shibata Masumi. "Tetsugen zenji kana hōgo no furansugoyaku ni tsuite." *Zen bunka*, no. 18 (March 1960): 78–80.

Shih, Heng-ching. "Yung-ming's Syncretism of Pure Land and Ch'an." *The Journal of the International Association of Buddhist Studies* 10, no. 1 (1987): 117–135.

———. "The Syncretism of Chinese Ch'an and Pure Land Buddhism." In *Buddhist Thought and Ritual*, ed. David Kalupahana, pp. 69–84. New York: Paragon House Publishers, 1991.

Shimoda Kyokusui, ed. *Kokutei kyōkasho ni arawaretaru meisō Tetsugen.* Kumamoto: Kumamoto-ken kyōikukai, 1928.

Sōtōshū zensho, vol. 5: *Kaidai sakuin.* Tokyo: Sōtōshū Zensho Kankokai, 1978.

Stark, Rodney. "How New Religions Succeed: A Theoretical Model." In *The Future of New Religious Movements*, ed. David G. Bromeley and Phillip E. Hammond, pp. 11–29. Macon, Ga.: Mercer University Press, 1987.

———. "Why Religious Movements Succeed or Fail: A Revised General Model." *Journal of Contemporary Religion* 11, no. 2 (May 1996): 133–146.

Stark, Rodney, and William Sims Bainbridge. "Of Churches, Sects, and Cults: Preliminary Concepts for a Theory of Religious Movements." *Journal for the Scientific Study of Religion* 18, no. 2 (1979): 117–133.

Stevenson, Daniel B. "The Four Kinds of Samadhi in Early T'ien-t'ai Buddhism." In *Buddhist Thought and Ritual*, ed. Peter N. Gregory, pp. 45–97. Honolulu: University of Hawai'i Press, 1986.

Suzuki Daisetz Teitaro. "Zen and Jōdo, Two Types of Buddhist Experience." *The Eastern Buddhist* 4 , no. 2 (July–September, 1927): 89–121.

———. *Essays in Zen Buddhism (Second Series).* Ed. Christopher Humphreys. New York: Samuel Weiser, 1970.

Suzuki Ryūshu, ed. *Tetsugen zenji kana hōgo.* Uji-shi, Japan: Obaku-san Hōzō-in, 1981.

Takahashi Chikumei. *Ingen, Mokuan, Sokuhi.* Tokyo: Kokushori kōkai, 1978. Reprint of 1916 edition.

Takahashi Ryōwa. *Obakusan Mampukuji.* Kyoto: Tankyūsha, 1976.

Takemura Shin'ichi. *Minchōtai no genryū.* Kyoto: Shibunkaku shuppan, 1986.

Takenuki Genshō. *Nihon zenshūshi.* Tokyo: Daizō shuppan, 1989.

———. *Kinsei Obakushū matsuji chōshūsei.* Tokyo: Yuzankan, 1990.

———. "Obakushū no kenkyū—matsujichō to sore ni miru kyōdan." *Hanazono daigaku kenkyū kiyō*, no. 21 (March 1990): 34–52.

———. *Nihon zenshūshi kenkyū.* Tokyo: Yuzankan, 1993.

Tamamura Takeji. *Rinzaishūshi.* Tokyo: Shunjūsha, 1991.

Tetsugen Dōkō. *Tetsugen zenji yuiroku*. Woodblock edition. 2 fascicles. Published 1691.

Toby, Ronald P. *State and Diplomacy in Early Modern Japan: Asia in the Development of the Tokugawa Bakufu*. Princeton, N.J.: Princeton University Press, 1984.

Torigoe Fumikuni. *Hiin zenji to sono cho, Gotō gentō*. Ōmuta-shi, Japan: Daijisan Enichizenji, 1986.

Toyama Mikio. *Nagasaki rekishi no tabi*. Tokyo: Asahi shimbunsha, 1990.

Toyoda Takeshi. *Nihon shūkyō seido shi no kenkyū*. Tokyo: Daiichi shobō, 1973.

Tsuji Zennosuke. *Nihon bukkyōshi: Kinseihen*, vol. 3. Tokyo: Iwanami shoten, 1970.

Tyler, Royall, trans. *Selected Writings of Suzuki Shōsan*. Ithaca, N.Y.: Cornell University Press, 1977.

Ueda, Yoshifumi, and Dennis Hirota. *Shinran: An Introduction to His Thought*. Kyoto: Hongwanji International Center, 1989.

Waddell, Norman. *The Unborn: The Life and Teaching of Zen Master Bankei*. San Francisco: North Point Press, 1984.

Washio Junkei. *Nihon zenshūshi no kenkyū*. Tokyo: Kyoden shuppan kabushiki kaisha, 1945.

Watt, Paul B. "Jiun Sonja (1718–1804): A Response to Confucianism within the Context of Buddhist Reform." In *Confucianism and Tokugawa Culture*, ed. Peter Nosco, pp. 188–214. Princeton, N.J.: Princeton University Press, 1984.

Webb, Herschel. *The Japanese Imperial Institution in the Tokugawa Period*. New York: Columbia University Press, 1968.

Weinstein, Stanley. "The Schools of Chinese Buddhism," in *Buddhism and Asian History*, ed. Joseph M. Kitagawa and Mark D. Cummings, pp. 257–265. New York: Macmillan Publishing Company, 1989.

Wijayaratna, Mohan. *Buddhist Monastic Life: According to the Texts of the Theravada Tradition*. Trans. Claude Grangier and Steven Collins. Cambridge: Cambridge University Press, 1990.

Wilson, Bryan R. "Factors in the Failure of the New Religious Movements." In *The Future of New Religious Movements*, ed. David G. Bromeley and Phillip E. Hammond, pp. 30–45. Macon, Ga.: Mercer University Press, 1987.

Yampolsky, Philip. *The Platform Sutra of the Sixth Patriarch*. New York: Columbia University Press, 1967.

———. *The Zen Master Hakuin: Selected Writings*. New York: Columbia University Press, 1971.

Yanagida Seizan. "Mujaku Dōchū no gakumon." *Zengaku kenkyū* 55 (February 1966): 14–55.

————. *Rinzai no kafū.* Nihon no bukkyō, vol. 9. Tokyo: Chikuma shobō, 1967.

————. *Shoki zenshū shisho no kenkyū.* Kyoto: Hōzōkan, 1967.

————. *Rinzai nōto.* Tokyo: Shunjūsha, 1971.

Yifa. "The Rules of Purity for the Chan Monastery: An Annotated Translation and Study of the Chanyuan qinggui." Ph.D. diss., Yale University, 1996.

Yin-yüan Lung-ch'i. *Huang-po shan ssu chih.* Chung-kuo fo ssu chih, vol. 4. Taipei: Tan ch'ing t'u shu kung ssu, 1985. Reprint of 1922 edition.

Yokoyama Hideya. "Zenshū kenchiku zuisō (9)—Obaku no Tennōden." *Zen bunka,* no. 18 (March 1960): 51–55.

Yoshikawa Kōjirō. *Jinsai, Sorai, Norinaga: Three Classical Philologists of Mid-Tokugawa Japan.* Tokyo: The Institute of Eastern Culture, 1983.

Yu, Chun-fang. *The Renewal of Buddhism in China: Chu-hung and the Late Ming Synthesis.* New York: Columbia University Press, 1981.

Zen bunka kenkyūsho, ed. *Zenmon itsuwa sen.* 3 vols. Kyoto: Zen bunka kenkyūsho, 1987.

Zengaku taikei hensankyoku, ed. *Zengaku taikei,* Vol. 7: *Kaihōbu.* Tokyo: Kokusho kankōkai, 1977. Reprint of 1913 edition.

Zenrin shūheishū. Woodblock edition. 2 fascicles. 1700.

Index

About the Author

Helen J. Baroni received her Ph.D. from Columbia University. Her previous publications include *An Illustrated Encyclopedia of Zen Buddhism* (1999). She is currently associate professor of Japanese religion at the University of Hawai'i.